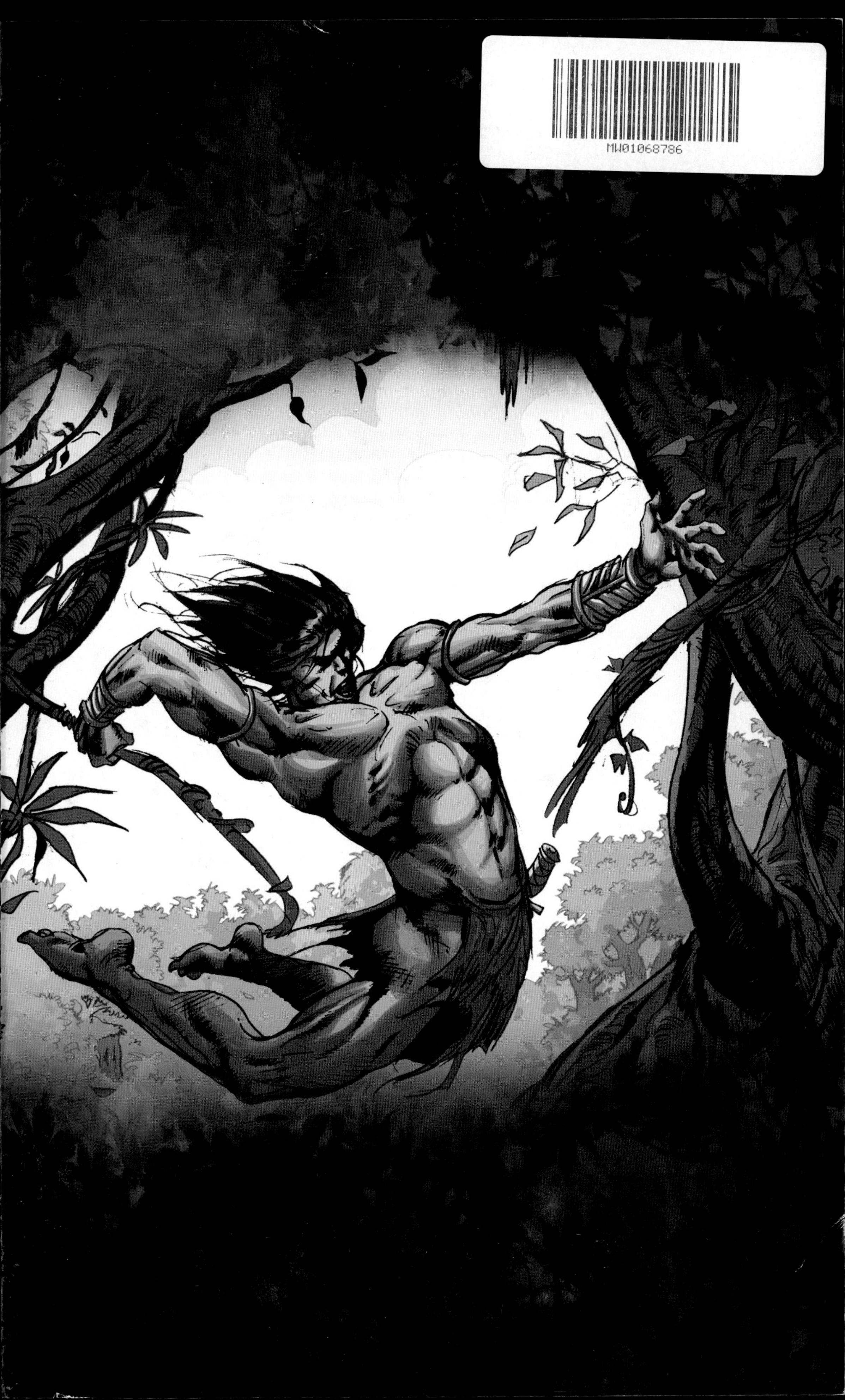

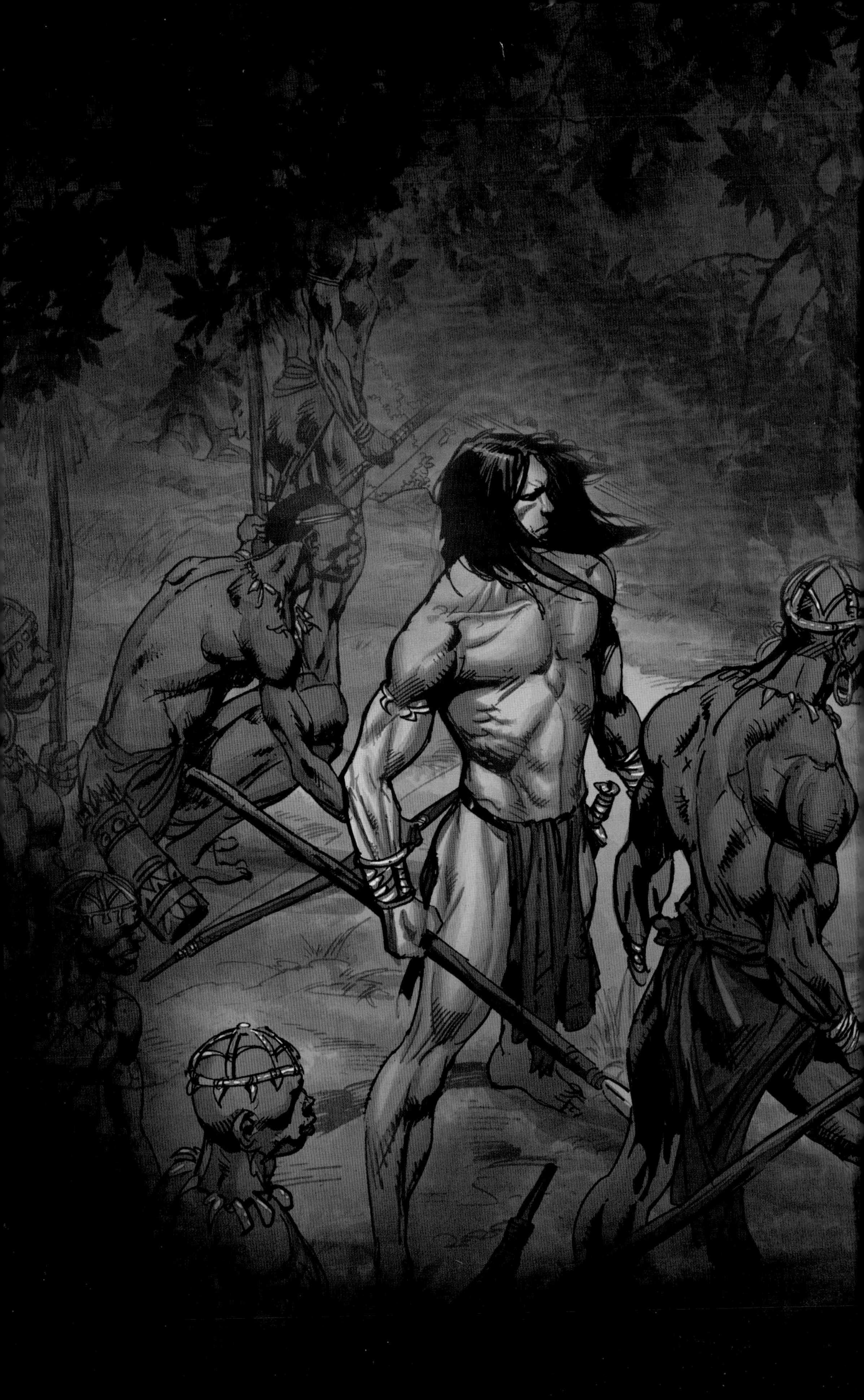

LORD OF THE JUNGLE™

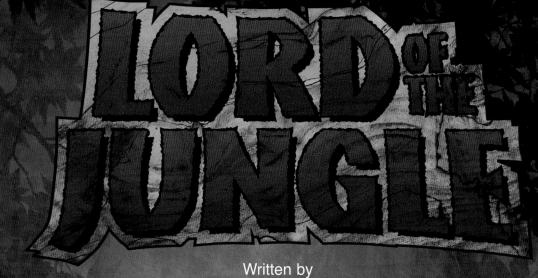

Written by
ARVID NELSON

Illustrated by
ROBERTO CASTRO (Issues 9-14)
WAGNER REIS (Issue 15)

Lettered by
SIMON BOWLAND (Issues 9,10)
MARSHALL DILLON (Issues 11-15)

Colored by
ALEX GUIMARAES (Issues 9-14)
INLIGHT STUDIO (Issue 15)

Collection cover by
LUCIO PARRILLO

Based on the stories by
EDGAR RICE BURROUGHS

Collection design by
KATIE HIDALGO

This volume collects issues 9-15 of *Lord of the Jungle* by Dynamite Entertainment

DYNAMITE®

Nick Barrucci, CEO / Publisher
Juan Collado, President / COO
Rich Young, Director Business Development
Keith Davidsen, Marketing Manager

Joe Rybandt, Senior Editor
Sarah Litt, Digital Editor
Josh Green, Traffic Coordinator

Josh Johnson, Art Director
Jason Ullmeyer, Senior Graphic Designer
Chris Caniano, Production Assistant

ISBN-10: 1-60690-391-8
ISBN-13: 978-1-60690-391-9
First Printing
10 9 8 7 6 5 4 3 2 1

Visit us online at **www.DYNAMITE.com**
Follow us on Twitter **@dynamitecomics**
Like us on Facebook **/Dynamitecomics**
Watch us on YouTube **/Dynamitecomics**

For information regarding press, media rights, foreign rights, licensing, promotions, and advertising e-mail: marketing@dynamite.com

ISSUE 9

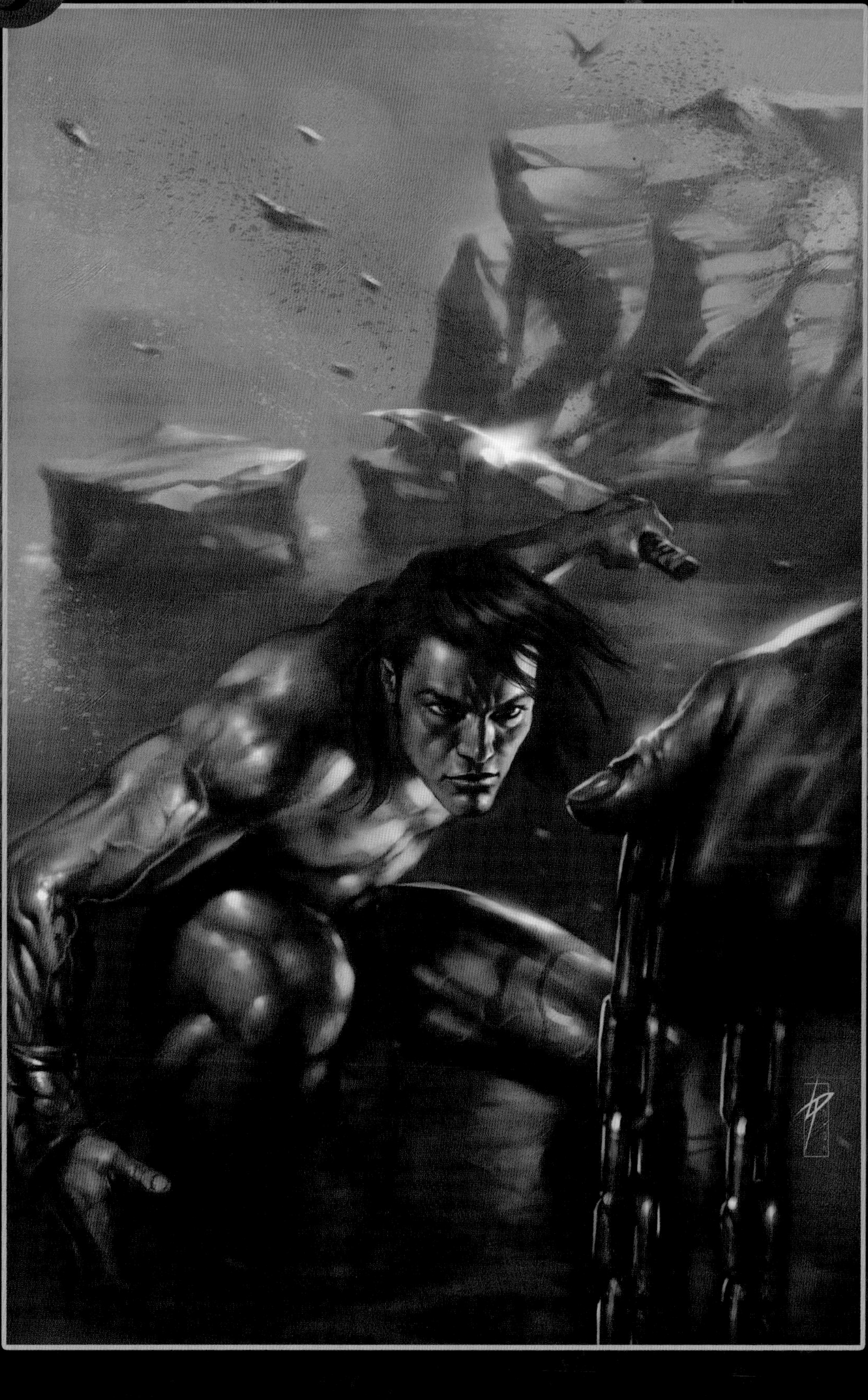

COVER BY LUCIO PARRILLO

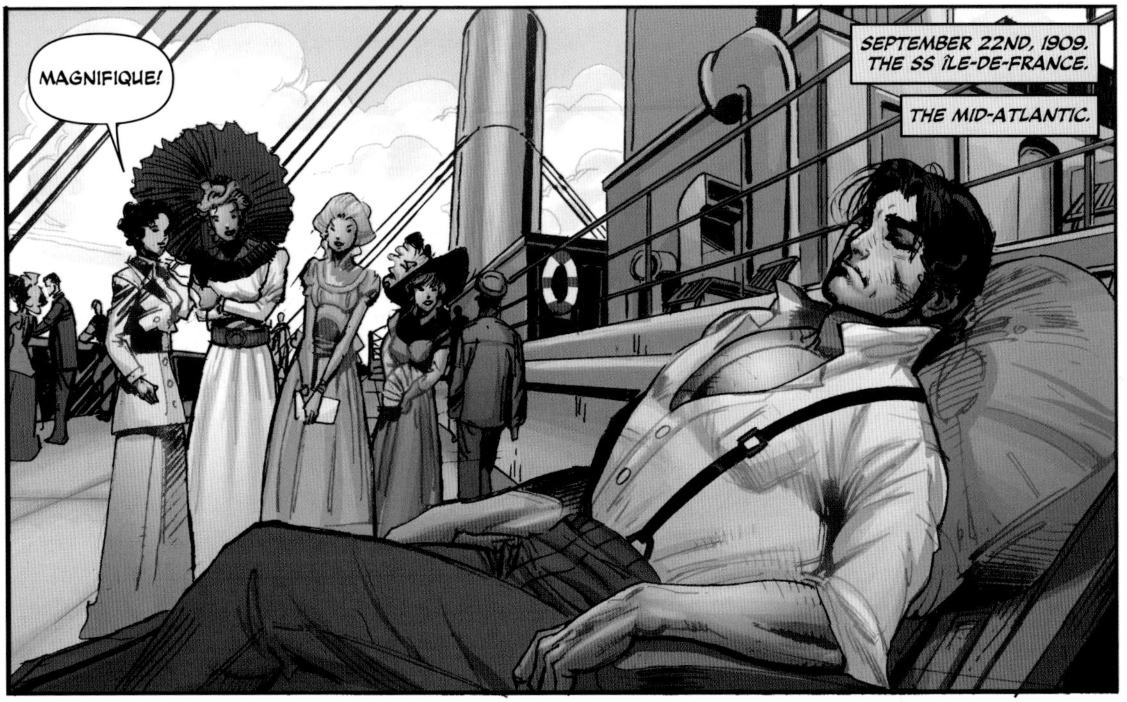
SEPTEMBER 22ND, 1909. THE SS ÎLE-DE-FRANCE.
THE MID-ATLANTIC.
MAGNIFIQUE!

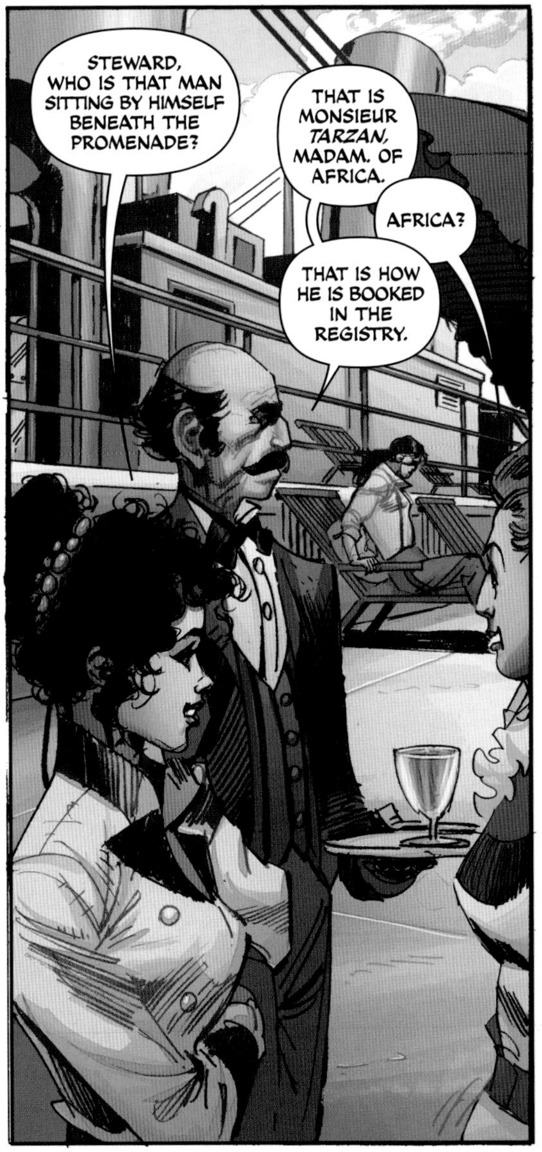
STEWARD, WHO IS THAT MAN SITTING BY HIMSELF BENEATH THE PROMENADE?
THAT IS MONSIEUR *TARZAN,* MADAM. OF AFRICA.
AFRICA?
THAT IS HOW HE IS BOOKED IN THE REGISTRY.

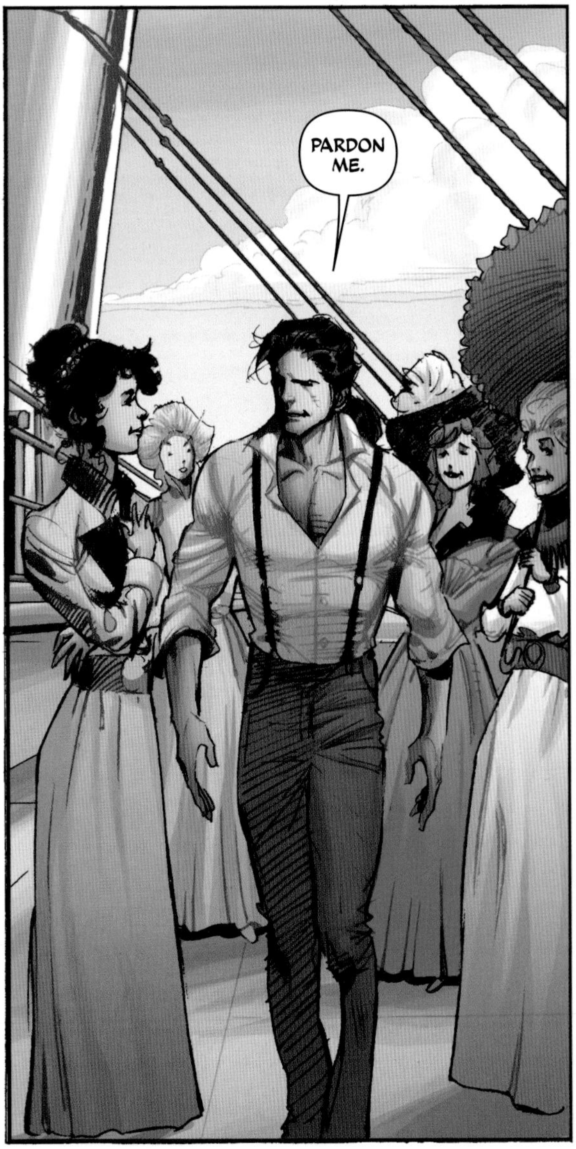
PARDON ME.

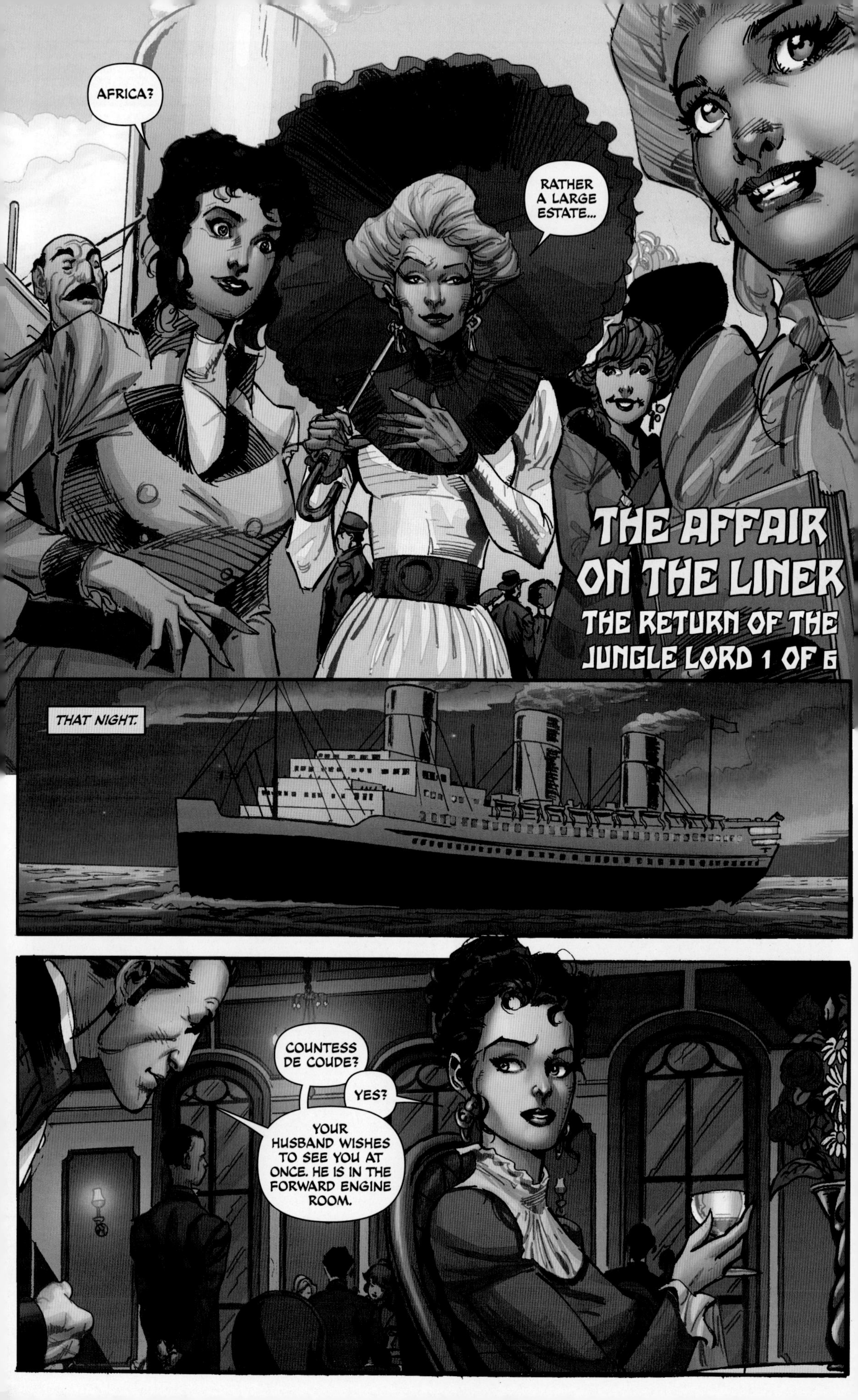
AFRICA?
RATHER A LARGE ESTATE...
THE AFFAIR ON THE LINER
THE RETURN OF THE JUNGLE LORD 1 OF 6
THAT NIGHT.
COUNTESS DE COUDE?
YES?
YOUR HUSBAND WISHES TO SEE YOU AT ONCE. HE IS IN THE FORWARD ENGINE ROOM.

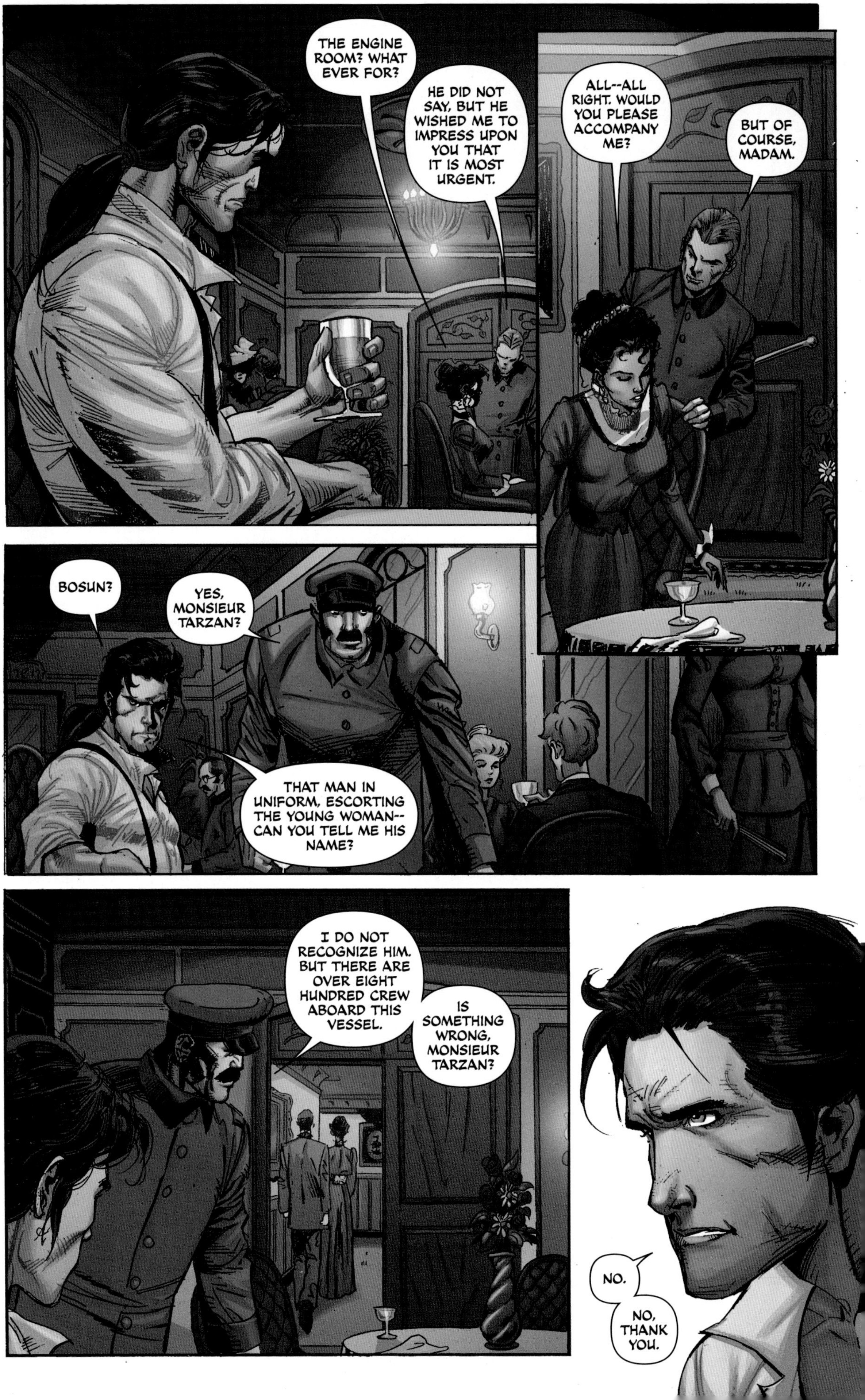
THE ENGINE ROOM? WHAT EVER FOR?
HE DID NOT SAY, BUT HE WISHED ME TO IMPRESS UPON YOU THAT IT IS MOST URGENT.
ALL--ALL RIGHT. WOULD YOU PLEASE ACCOMPANY ME?
BUT OF COURSE, MADAM.
BOSUN?
YES, MONSIEUR TARZAN?
THAT MAN IN UNIFORM, ESCORTING THE YOUNG WOMAN--CAN YOU TELL ME HIS NAME?
I DO NOT RECOGNIZE HIM. BUT THERE ARE OVER EIGHT HUNDRED CREW ABOARD THIS VESSEL.
IS SOMETHING WRONG, MONSIEUR TARZAN?
NO.
NO, THANK YOU.

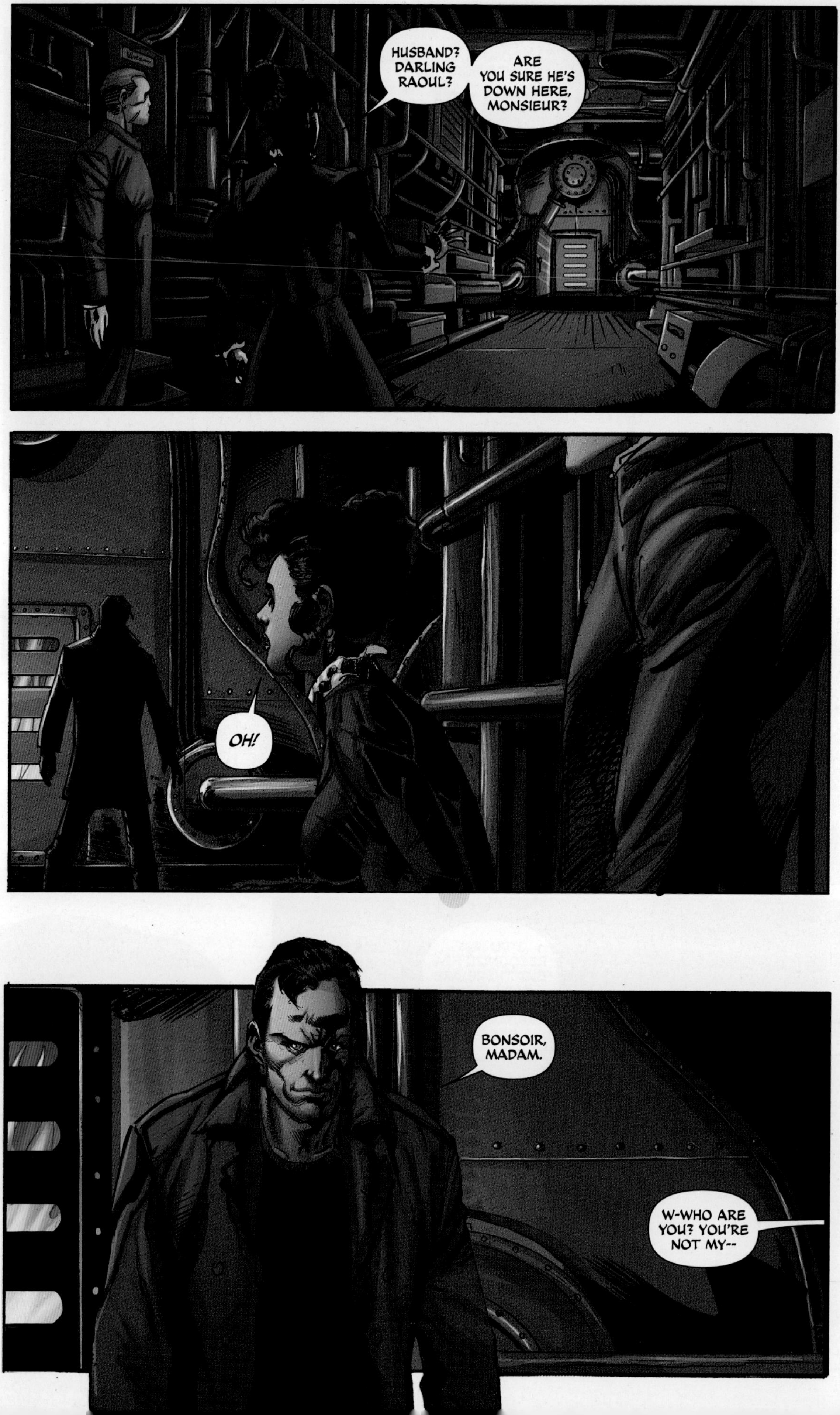
HUSBAND? DARLING RAOUL?
ARE YOU SURE HE'S DOWN HERE, MONSIEUR?
OH!
BONSOIR, MADAM.
W-WHO ARE YOU? YOU'RE NOT MY--

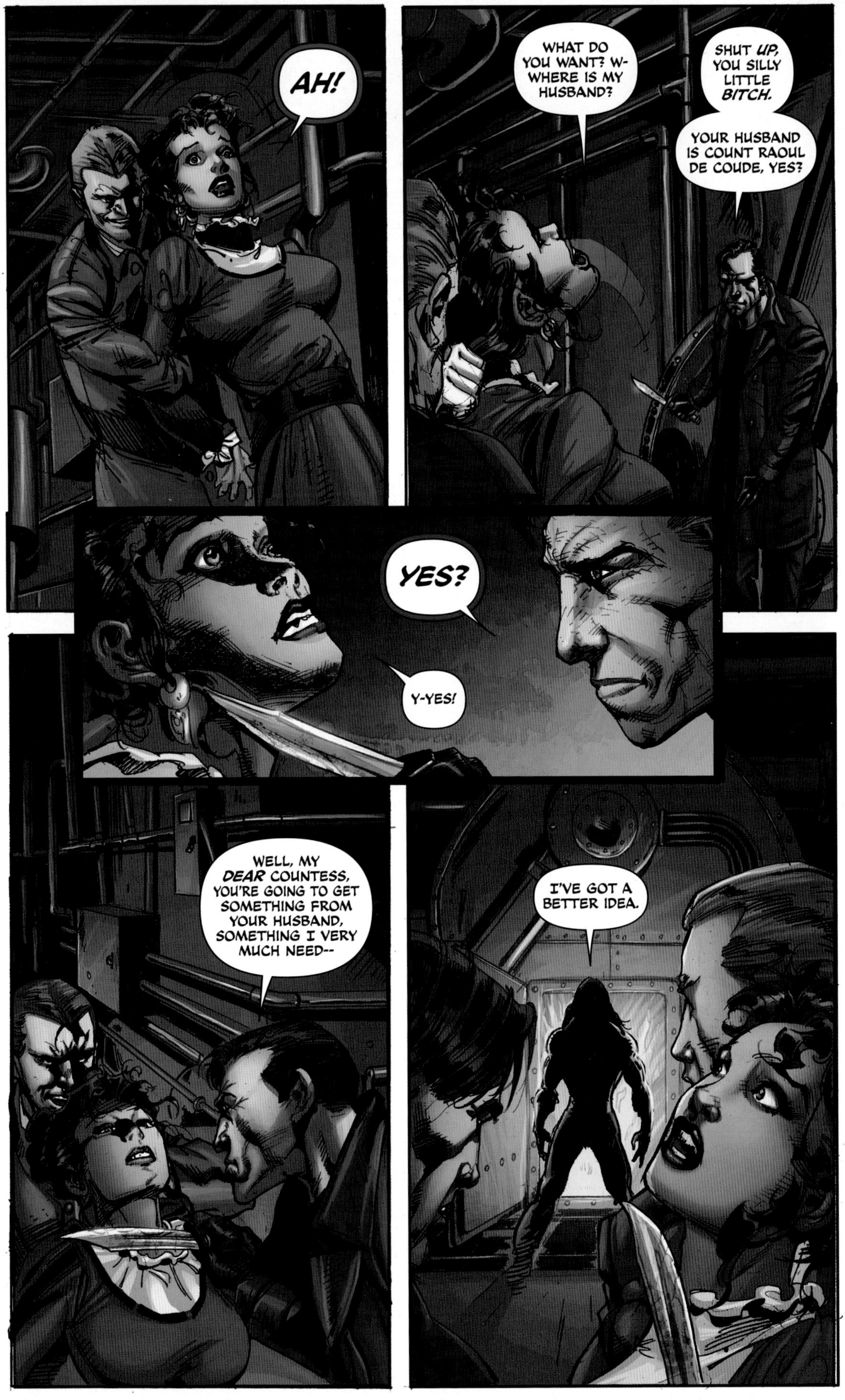
AH!
WHAT DO YOU WANT? W-WHERE IS MY HUSBAND?
SHUT *UP*, YOU SILLY LITTLE *BITCH.*
YOUR HUSBAND IS COUNT RAOUL DE COUDE, YES?
YES?
Y-YES!
WELL, MY *DEAR* COUNTESS, YOU'RE GOING TO GET SOMETHING FROM YOUR HUSBAND, SOMETHING I VERY MUCH NEED--
I'VE GOT A BETTER IDEA.

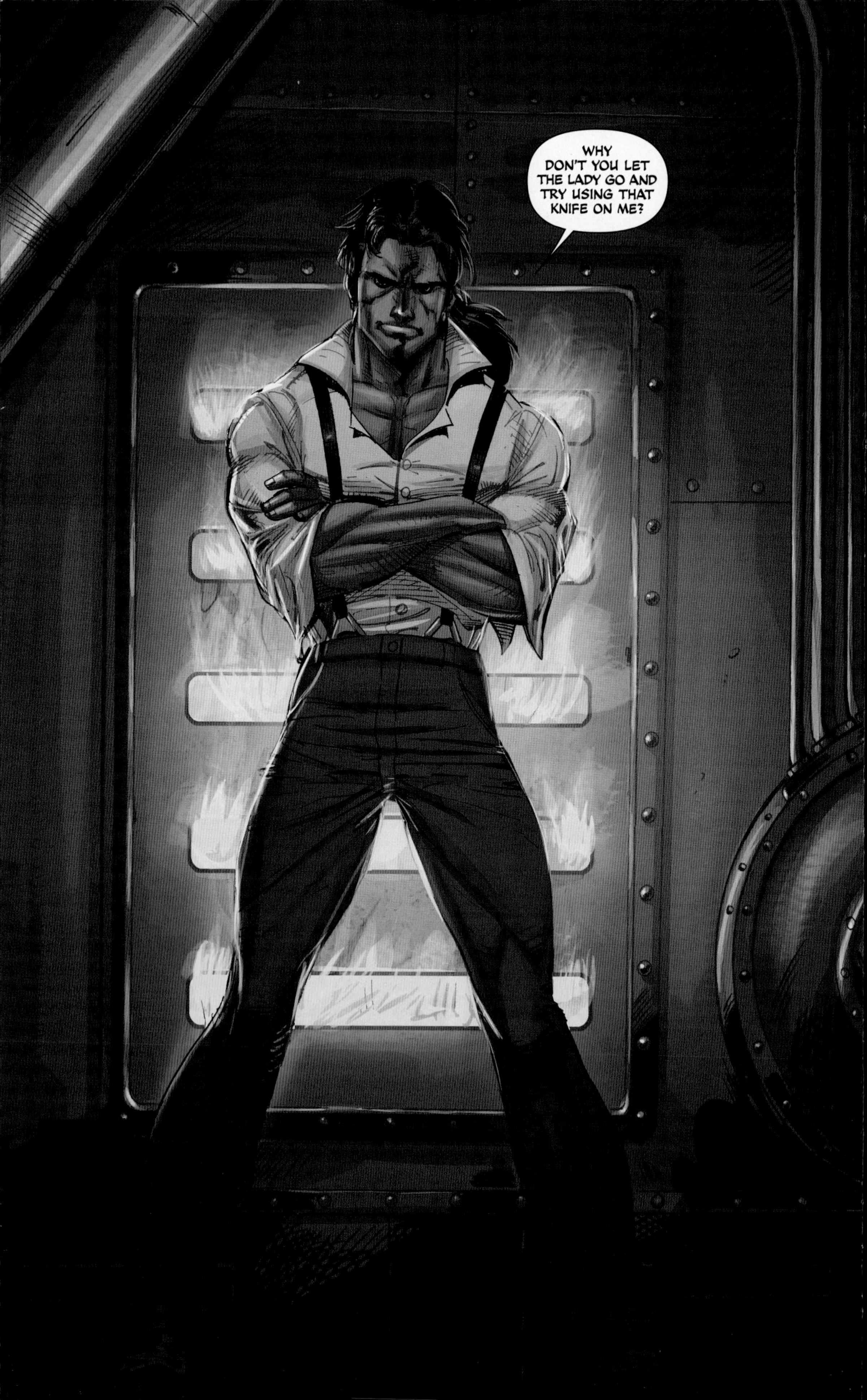
WHY DON'T YOU LET THE LADY GO AND TRY USING THAT KNIFE ON ME?

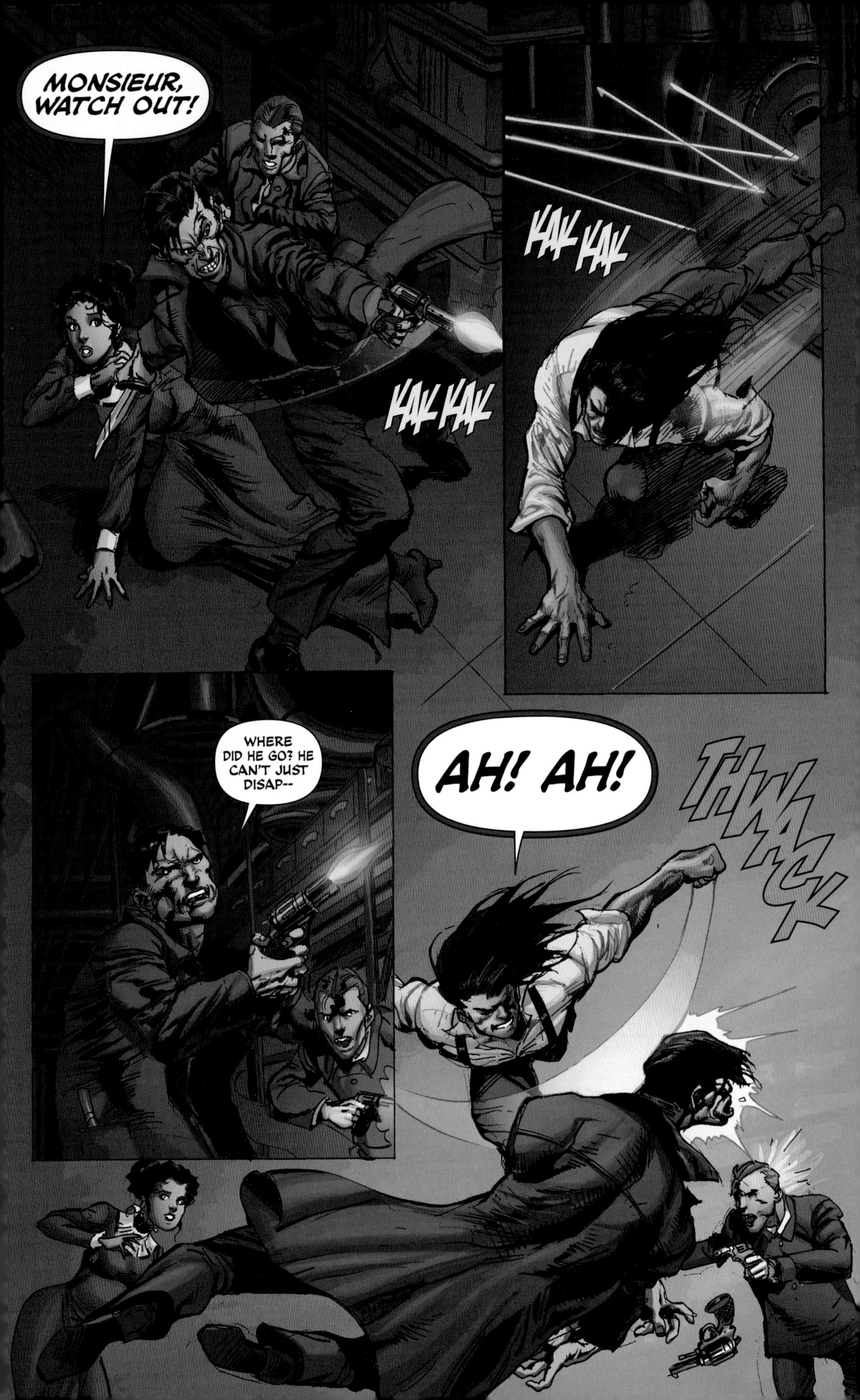
MONSIEUR, WATCH OUT!
KAK KAK
KAK KAK
WHERE DID HE GO? HE CAN'T JUST DISAP--
AH! AH!
THWACK

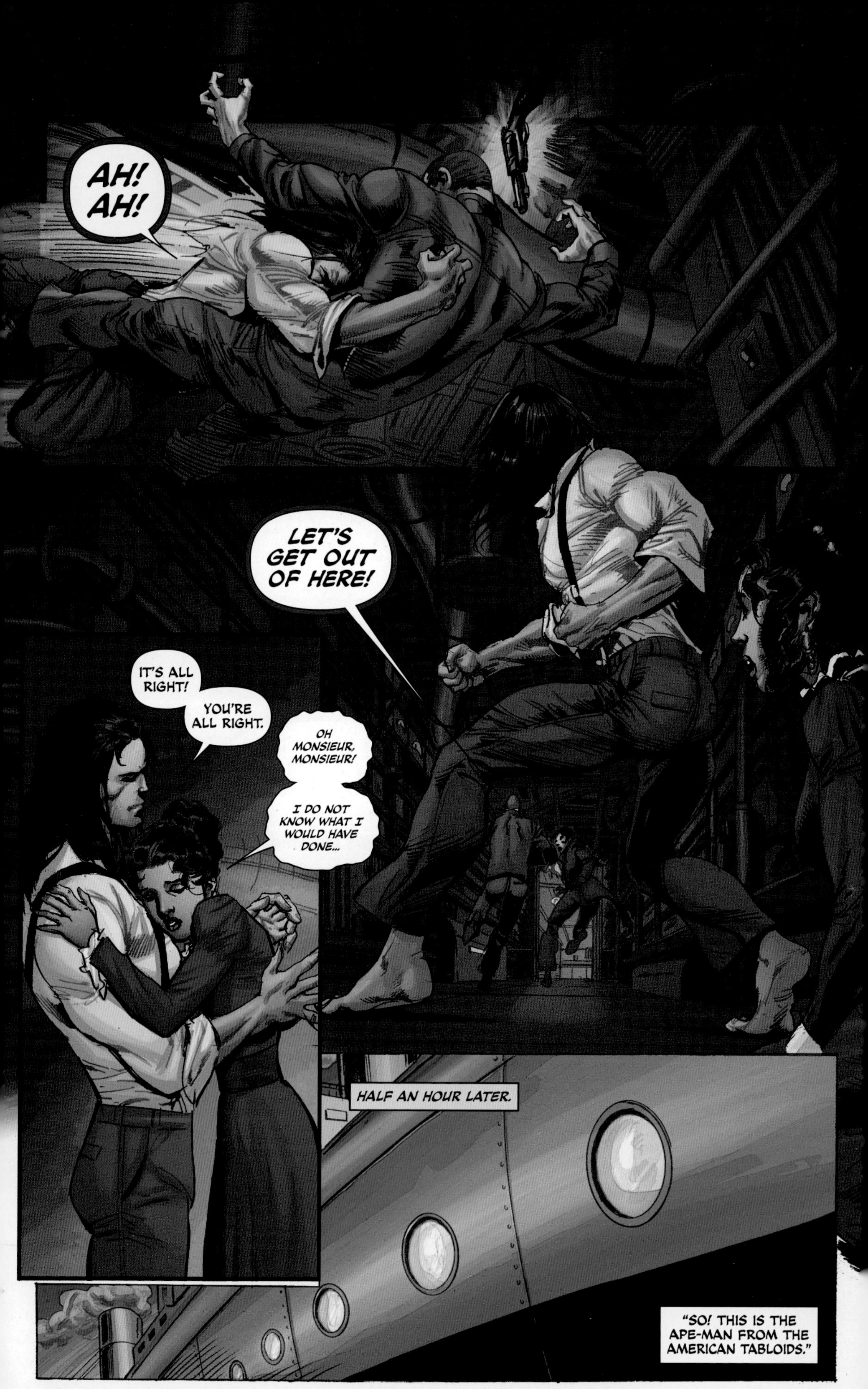
AH! AH!
LET'S GET OUT OF HERE!
IT'S ALL RIGHT!
YOU'RE ALL RIGHT.
OH MONSIEUR, MONSIEUR!
I DO NOT KNOW WHAT I WOULD HAVE DONE...
HALF AN HOUR LATER.
"SO! THIS IS THE APE-MAN FROM THE AMERICAN TABLOIDS."

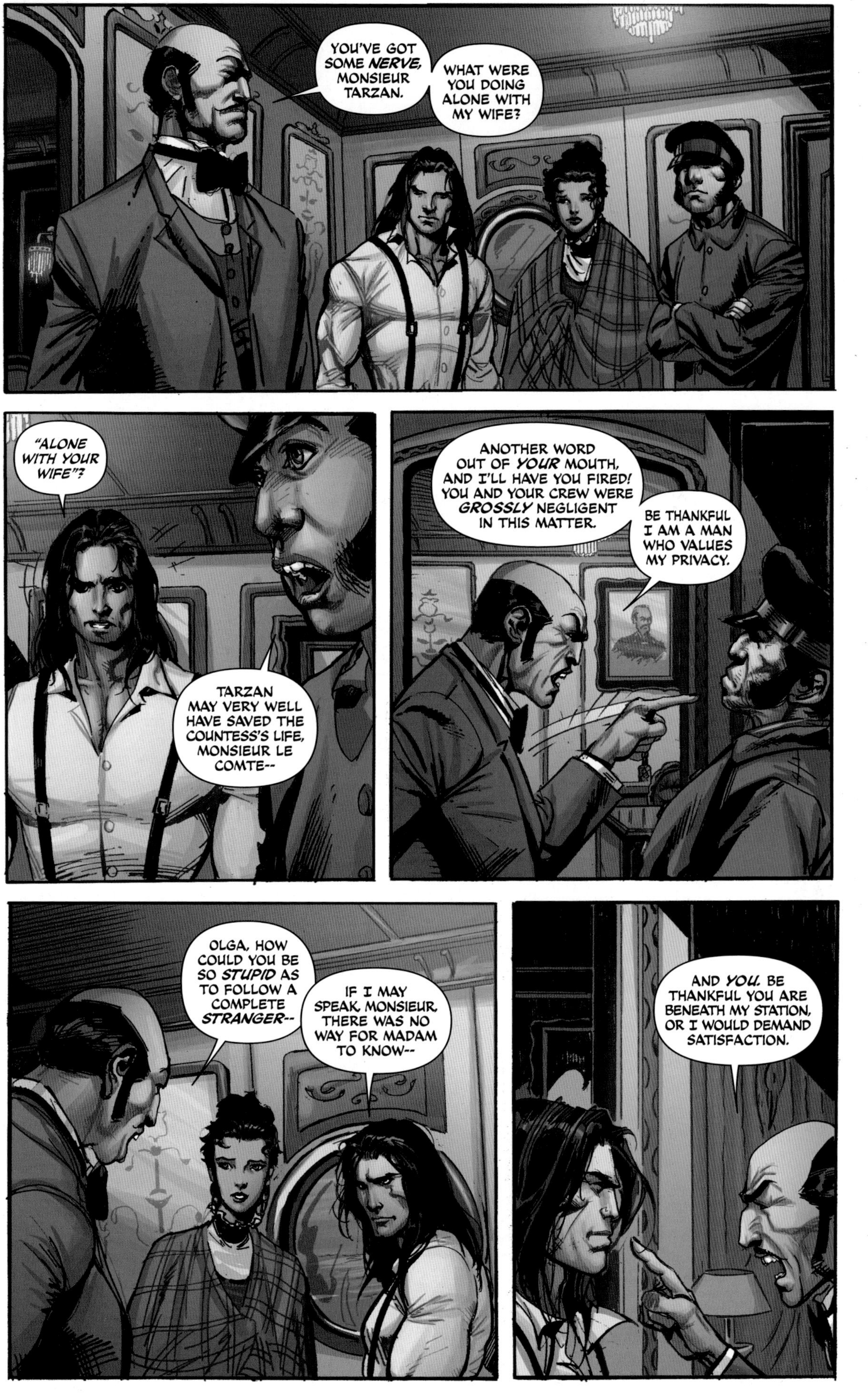
YOU'VE GOT SOME *NERVE*, MONSIEUR TARZAN.
WHAT WERE YOU DOING ALONE WITH MY WIFE?
"ALONE WITH *YOUR* WIFE"?
TARZAN MAY VERY WELL HAVE SAVED THE COUNTESS'S LIFE, MONSIEUR LE COMTE--
ANOTHER WORD OUT OF *YOUR* MOUTH, AND I'LL HAVE YOU FIRED! YOU AND YOUR CREW WERE *GROSSLY* NEGLIGENT IN THIS MATTER.
BE THANKFUL I AM A MAN WHO VALUES MY PRIVACY.
OLGA, HOW COULD YOU BE SO *STUPID* AS TO FOLLOW A COMPLETE *STRANGER*--
IF I MAY SPEAK, MONSIEUR, THERE WAS NO WAY FOR MADAM TO KNOW--
AND *YOU*. BE THANKFUL YOU ARE BENEATH MY STATION, OR I WOULD DEMAND SATISFACTION.

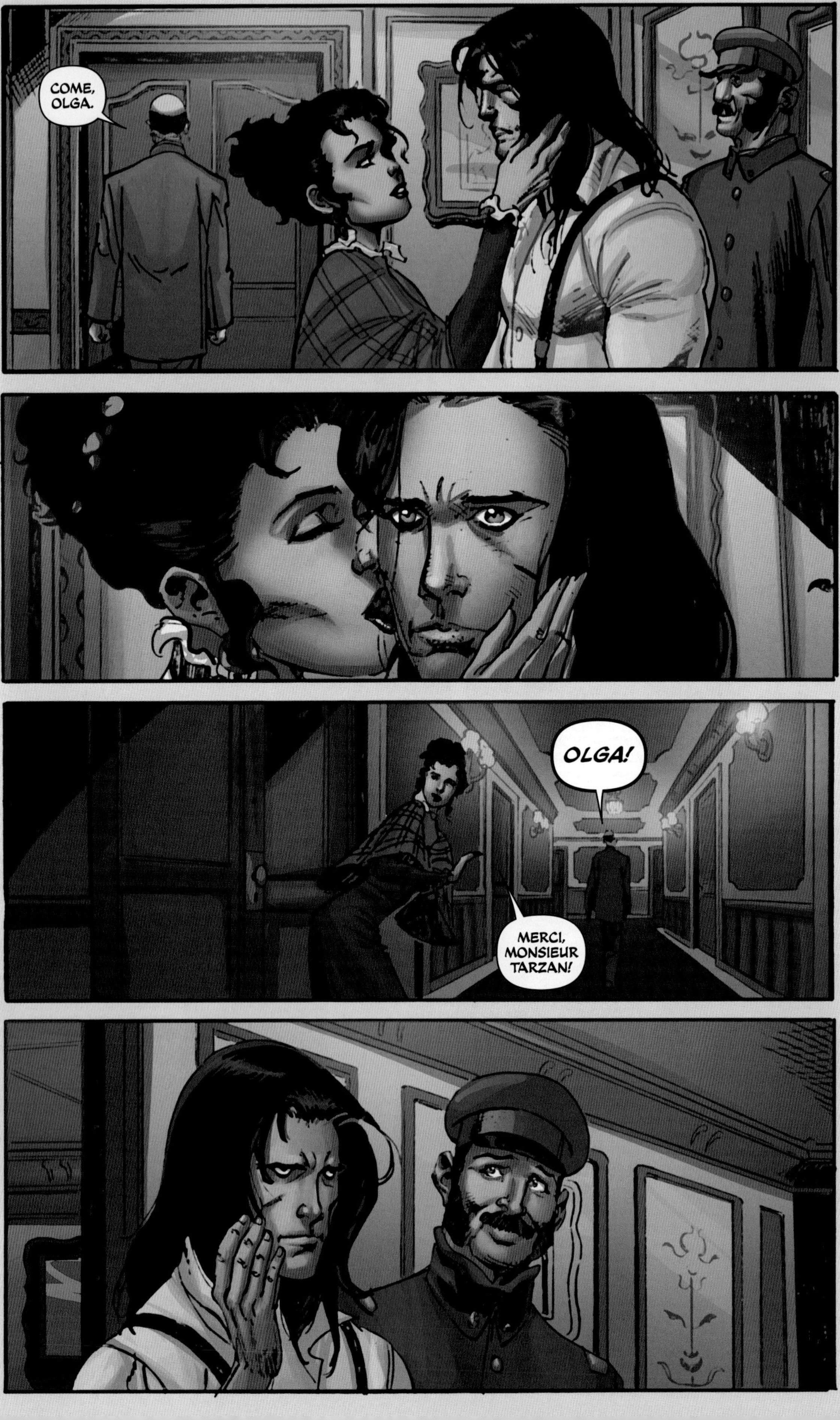

COME, OLGA.
OLGA!
MERCI, MONSIEUR TARZAN!

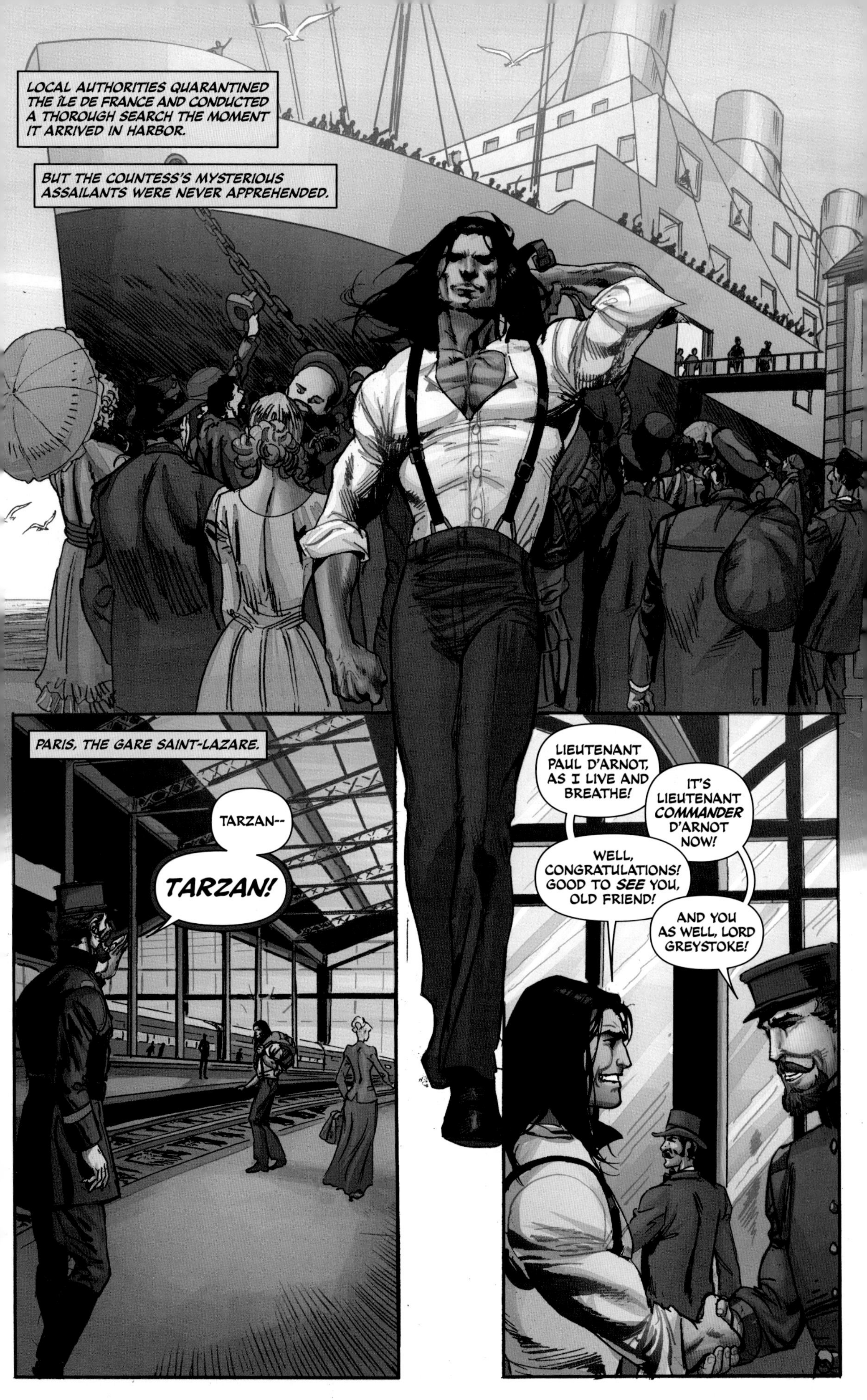
LOCAL AUTHORITIES QUARANTINED THE ÎLE DE FRANCE AND CONDUCTED A THOROUGH SEARCH THE MOMENT IT ARRIVED IN HARBOR.
BUT THE COUNTESS'S MYSTERIOUS ASSAILANTS WERE NEVER APPREHENDED.
PARIS, THE GARE SAINT-LAZARE.
TARZAN--
TARZAN!
LIEUTENANT PAUL D'ARNOT, AS I LIVE AND BREATHE!
IT'S LIEUTENANT COMMANDER D'ARNOT NOW!
WELL, CONGRATULATIONS! GOOD TO SEE YOU, OLD FRIEND!
AND YOU AS WELL, LORD GREYSTOKE!

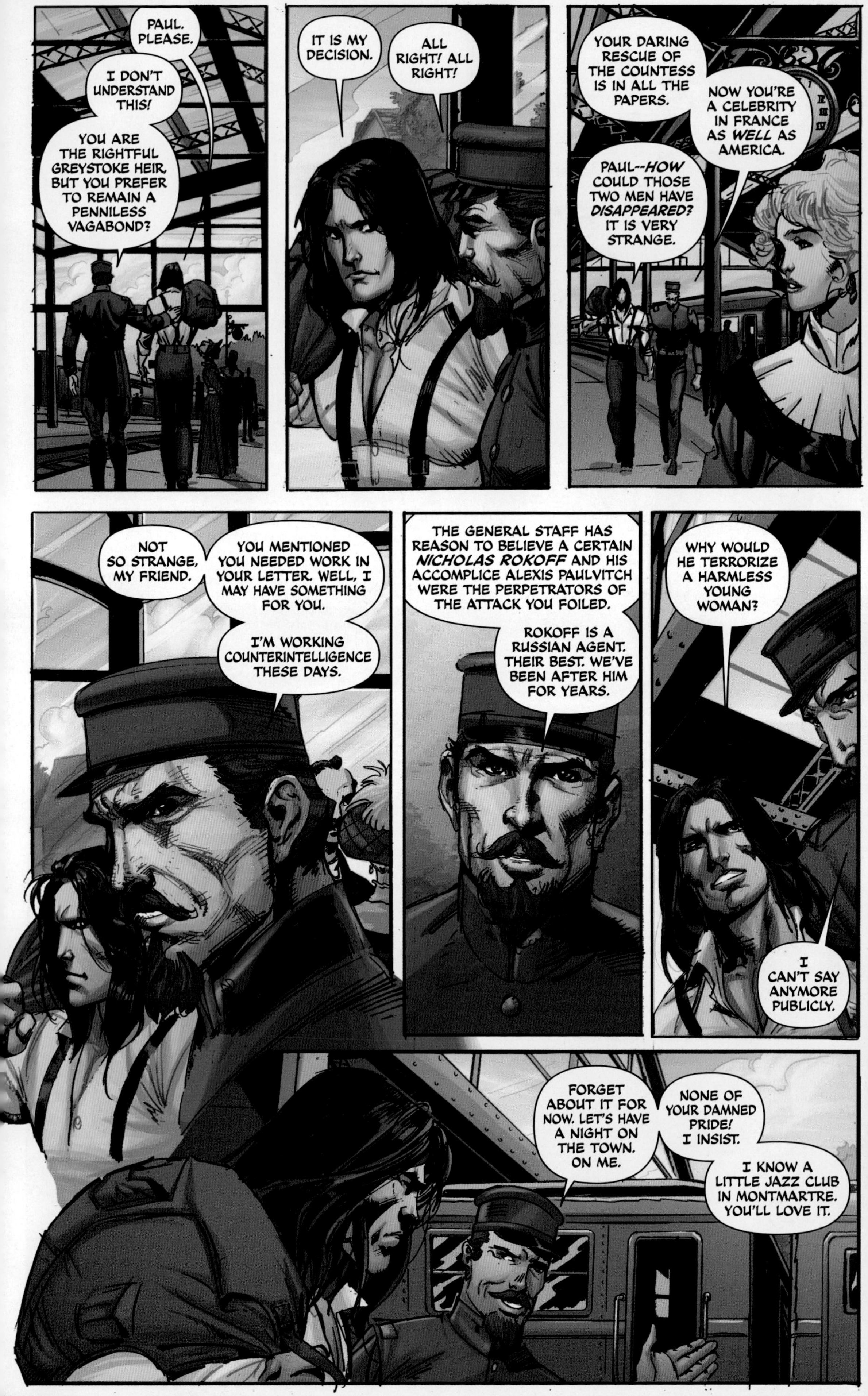
PAUL. PLEASE.
I DON'T UNDERSTAND THIS!
YOU ARE THE RIGHTFUL GREYSTOKE HEIR, BUT YOU PREFER TO REMAIN A PENNILESS VAGABOND?
IT IS MY DECISION.
ALL RIGHT! ALL RIGHT!
YOUR DARING RESCUE OF THE COUNTESS IS IN ALL THE PAPERS.
NOW YOU'RE A CELEBRITY IN FRANCE AS *WELL* AS AMERICA.
PAUL--*HOW* COULD THOSE TWO MEN HAVE *DISAPPEARED?* IT IS VERY STRANGE.
NOT SO STRANGE, MY FRIEND.
YOU MENTIONED YOU NEEDED WORK IN YOUR LETTER. WELL, I MAY HAVE SOMETHING FOR YOU.
I'M WORKING COUNTERINTELLIGENCE THESE DAYS.
THE GENERAL STAFF HAS REASON TO BELIEVE A CERTAIN *NICHOLAS ROKOFF* AND HIS ACCOMPLICE ALEXIS PAULVITCH WERE THE PERPETRATORS OF THE ATTACK YOU FOILED.
ROKOFF IS A RUSSIAN AGENT. THEIR BEST. WE'VE BEEN AFTER HIM FOR YEARS.
WHY WOULD HE TERRORIZE A HARMLESS YOUNG WOMAN?
I CAN'T SAY ANYMORE PUBLICLY.
FORGET ABOUT IT FOR NOW. LET'S HAVE A NIGHT ON THE TOWN. ON ME.
NONE OF YOUR DAMNED PRIDE! I INSIST.
I KNOW A LITTLE JAZZ CLUB IN MONTMARTRE. YOU'LL LOVE IT.

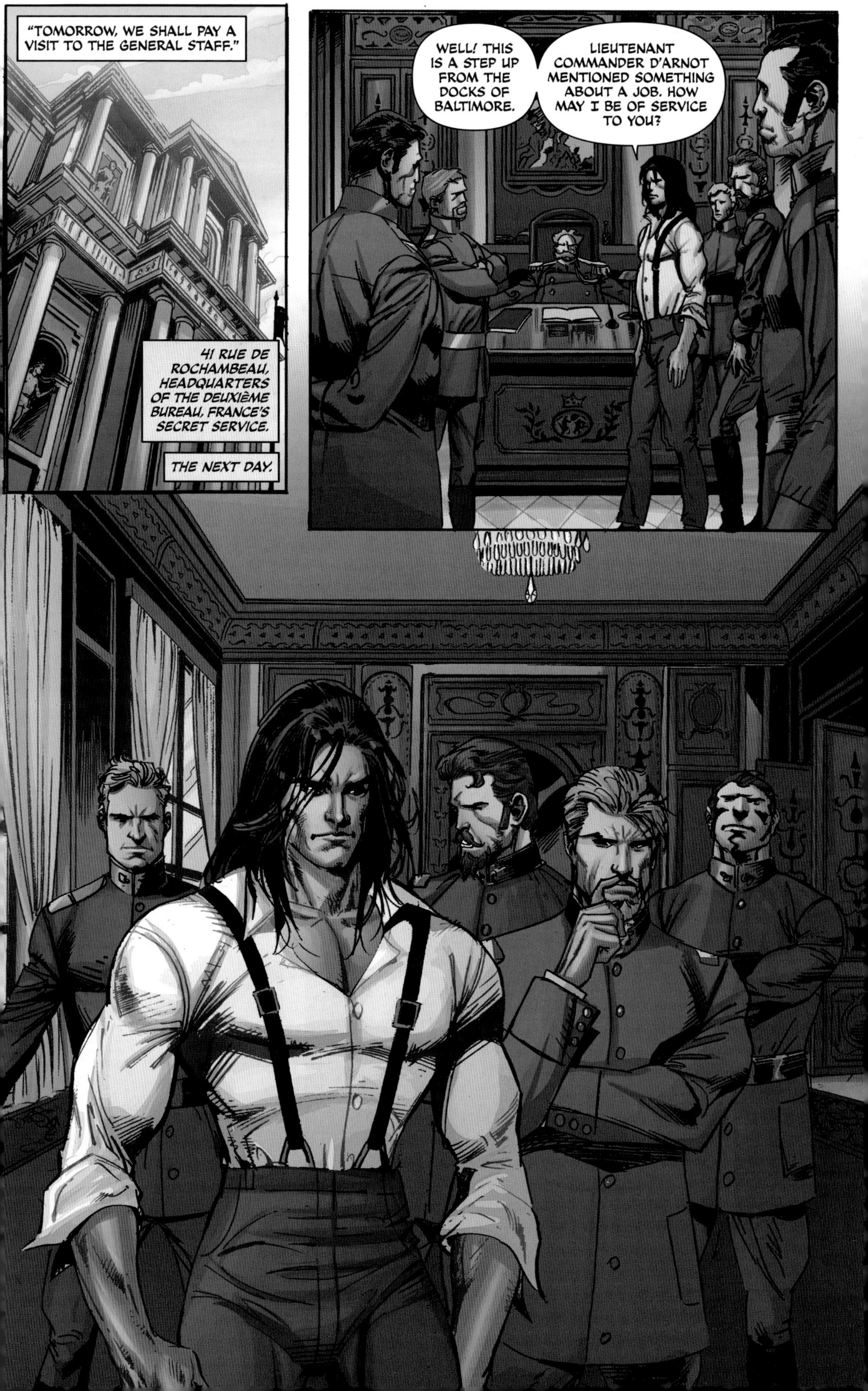
"TOMORROW, WE SHALL PAY A VISIT TO THE GENERAL STAFF."
41 RUE DE ROCHAMBEAU, HEADQUARTERS OF THE DEUXIÈME BUREAU, FRANCE'S SECRET SERVICE.
THE NEXT DAY.
WELL! THIS IS A STEP UP FROM THE DOCKS OF BALTIMORE.
LIEUTENANT COMMANDER D'ARNOT MENTIONED SOMETHING ABOUT A JOB. HOW MAY I BE OF SERVICE TO YOU?

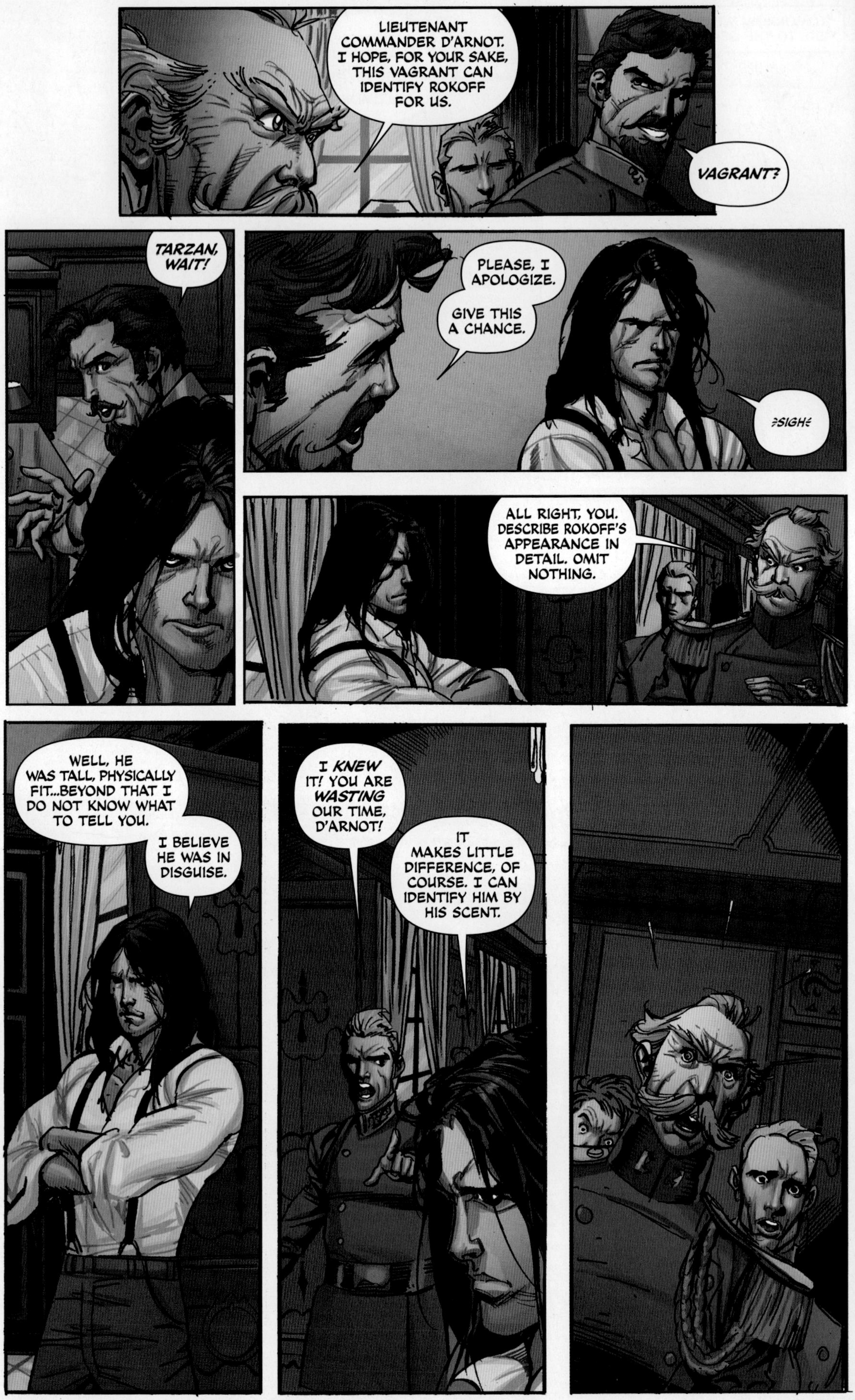
LIEUTENANT COMMANDER D'ARNOT. I HOPE, FOR YOUR SAKE, THIS VAGRANT CAN IDENTIFY ROKOFF FOR US.
VAGRANT?
TARZAN, WAIT!
PLEASE, I APOLOGIZE.
GIVE THIS A CHANCE.
SIGH
ALL RIGHT, YOU. DESCRIBE ROKOFF'S APPEARANCE IN DETAIL. OMIT NOTHING.
WELL, HE WAS TALL, PHYSICALLY FIT...BEYOND THAT I DO NOT KNOW WHAT TO TELL YOU.
I BELIEVE HE WAS IN DISGUISE.
I KNEW IT! YOU ARE WASTING OUR TIME, D'ARNOT!
IT MAKES LITTLE DIFFERENCE, OF COURSE. I CAN IDENTIFY HIM BY HIS SCENT.

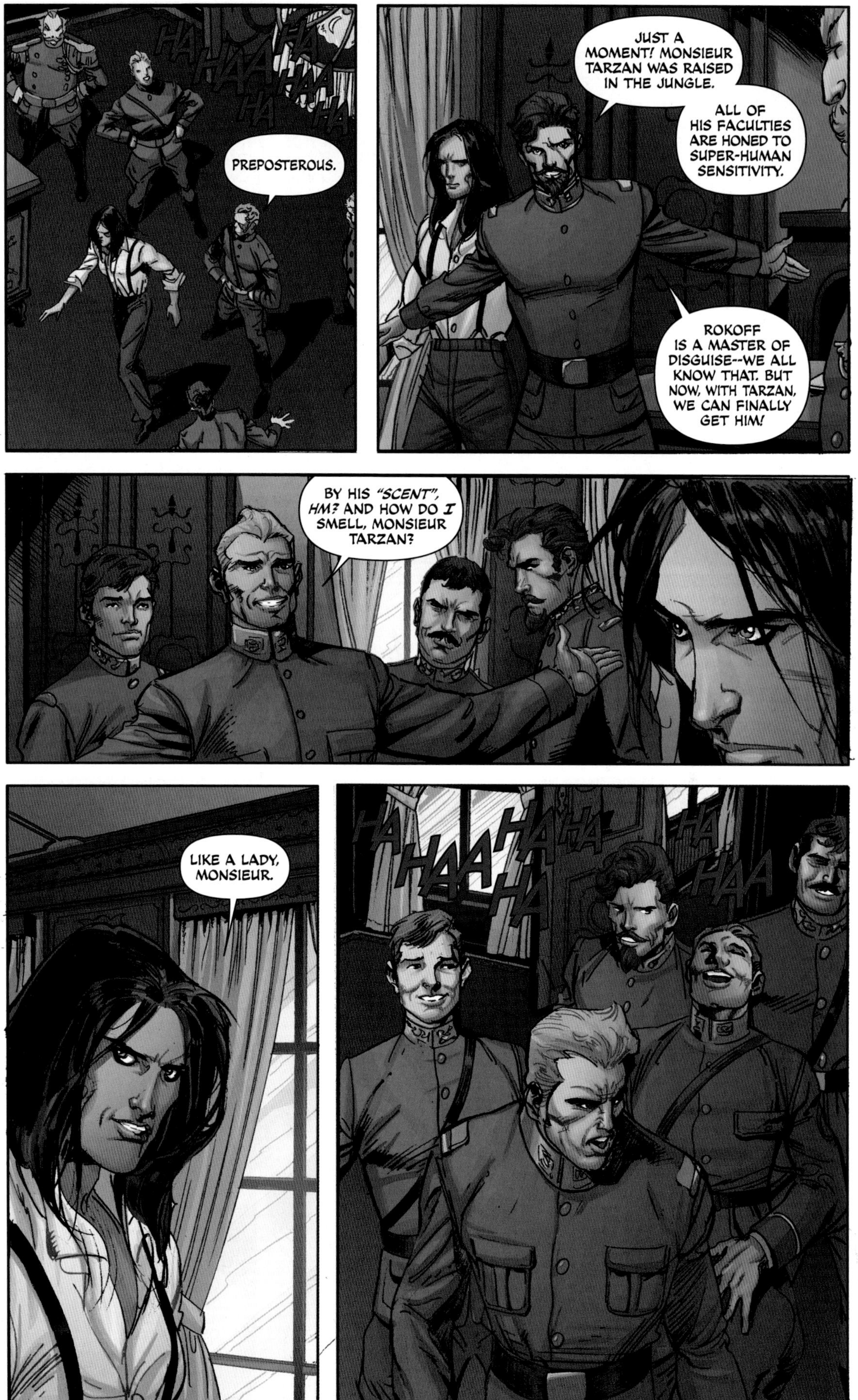
HA HA HAA HA HA HA
PREPOSTEROUS.
JUST A MOMENT! MONSIEUR TARZAN WAS RAISED IN THE JUNGLE.
ALL OF HIS FACULTIES ARE HONED TO SUPER-HUMAN SENSITIVITY.
ROKOFF IS A MASTER OF DISGUISE--WE ALL KNOW THAT. BUT NOW, WITH TARZAN, WE CAN FINALLY GET HIM!
BY HIS "SCENT", HM? AND HOW DO I SMELL, MONSIEUR TARZAN?
LIKE A LADY, MONSIEUR.
HA HAA HA HA HA HA HA HAA

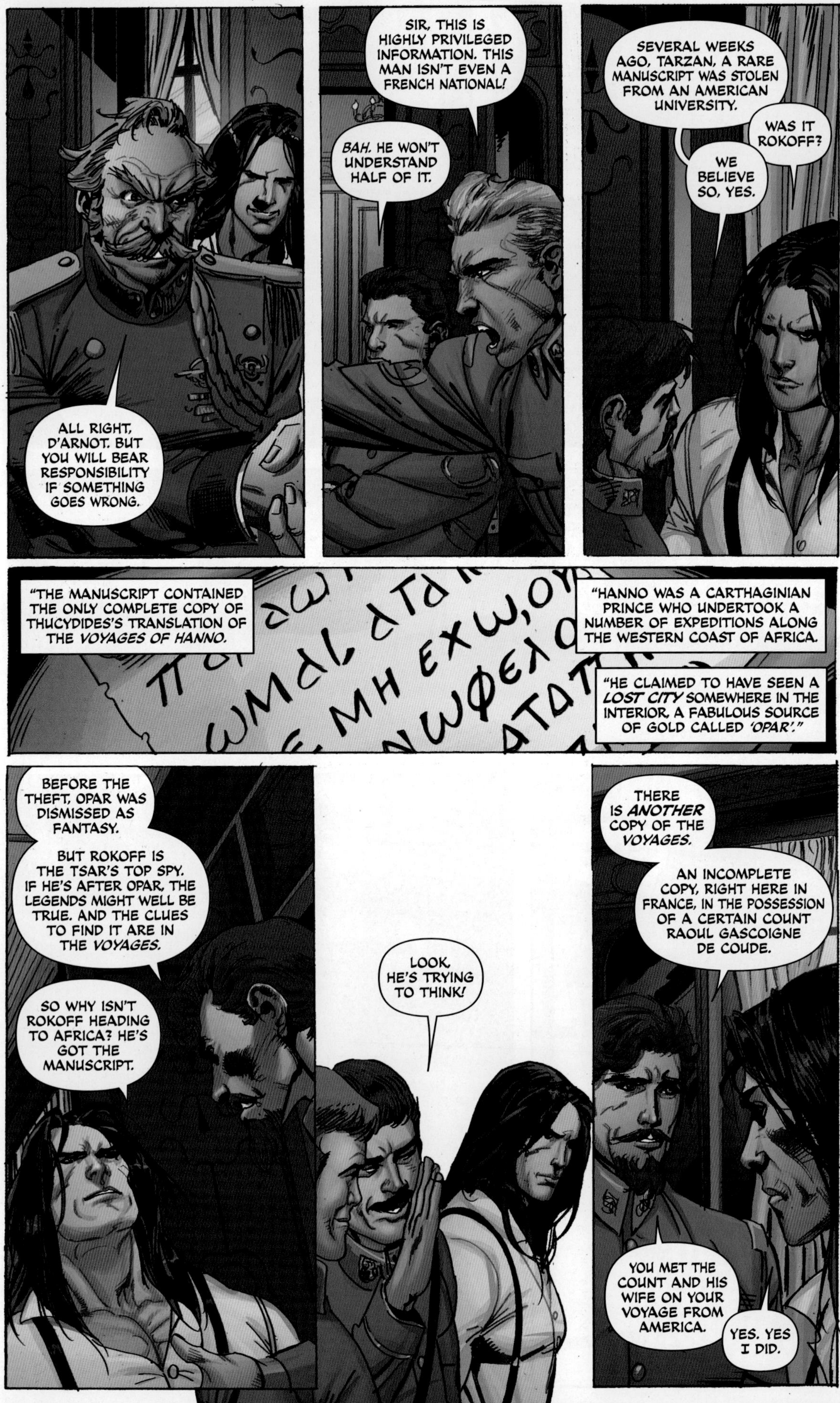
ALL RIGHT, D'ARNOT. BUT YOU WILL BEAR RESPONSIBILITY IF SOMETHING GOES WRONG.
SIR, THIS IS HIGHLY PRIVILEGED INFORMATION. THIS MAN ISN'T EVEN A FRENCH NATIONAL!
BAH. HE WON'T UNDERSTAND HALF OF IT.
SEVERAL WEEKS AGO, TARZAN, A RARE MANUSCRIPT WAS STOLEN FROM AN AMERICAN UNIVERSITY.
WAS IT ROKOFF?
WE BELIEVE SO, YES.
"THE MANUSCRIPT CONTAINED THE ONLY COMPLETE COPY OF THUCYDIDES'S TRANSLATION OF THE VOYAGES OF HANNO.
"HANNO WAS A CARTHAGINIAN PRINCE WHO UNDERTOOK A NUMBER OF EXPEDITIONS ALONG THE WESTERN COAST OF AFRICA.
"HE CLAIMED TO HAVE SEEN A LOST CITY SOMEWHERE IN THE INTERIOR, A FABULOUS SOURCE OF GOLD CALLED 'OPAR'."
BEFORE THE THEFT, OPAR WAS DISMISSED AS FANTASY.
BUT ROKOFF IS THE TSAR'S TOP SPY. IF HE'S AFTER OPAR, THE LEGENDS MIGHT WELL BE TRUE. AND THE CLUES TO FIND IT ARE IN THE VOYAGES.
SO WHY ISN'T ROKOFF HEADING TO AFRICA? HE'S GOT THE MANUSCRIPT.
LOOK, HE'S TRYING TO THINK!
THERE IS ANOTHER COPY OF THE VOYAGES.
AN INCOMPLETE COPY, RIGHT HERE IN FRANCE, IN THE POSSESSION OF A CERTAIN COUNT RAOUL GASCOIGNE DE COUDE.
YOU MET THE COUNT AND HIS WIFE ON YOUR VOYAGE FROM AMERICA.
YES. YES I DID.

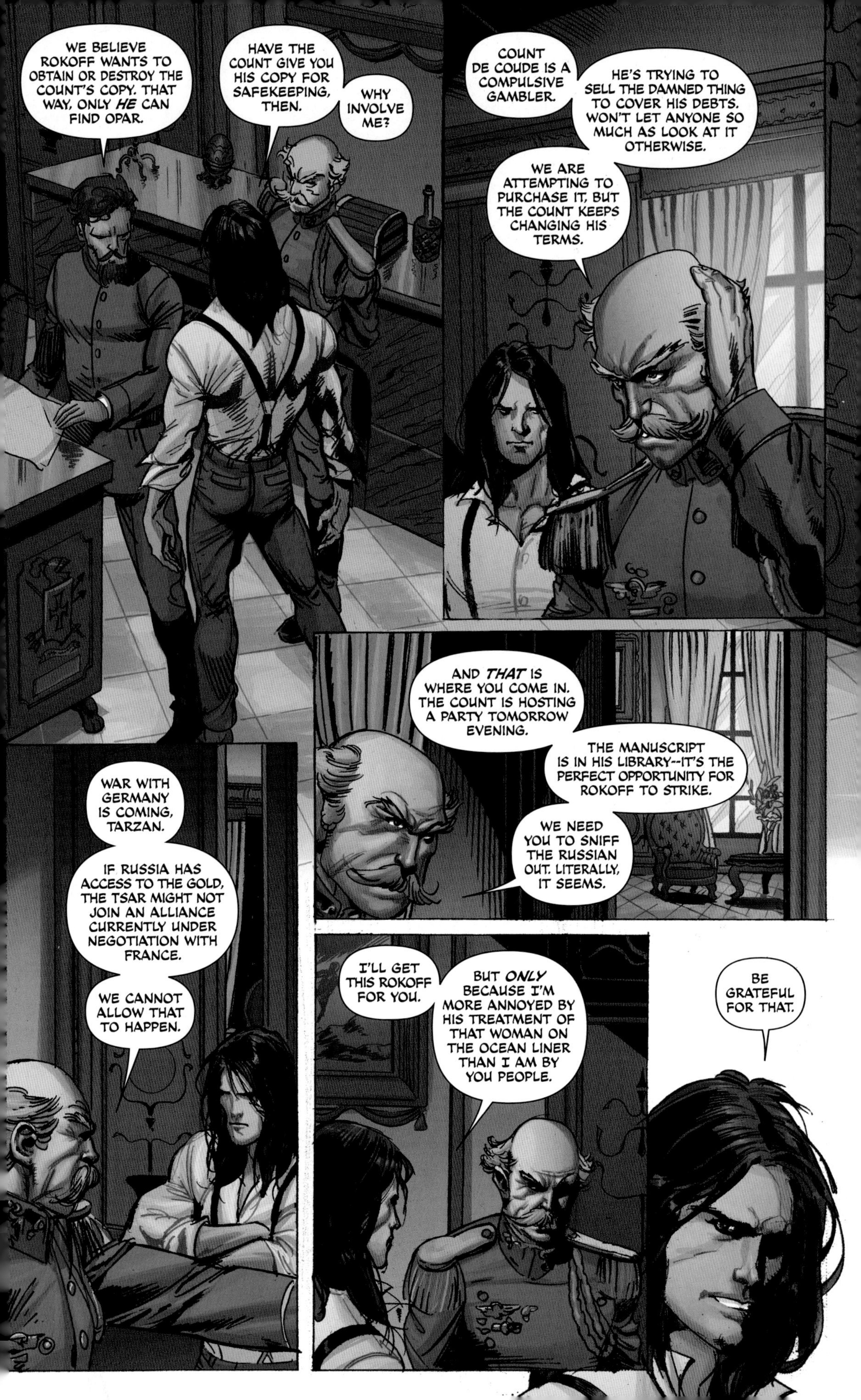
WE BELIEVE ROKOFF WANTS TO OBTAIN OR DESTROY THE COUNT'S COPY. THAT WAY, ONLY *HE* CAN FIND OPAR.
HAVE THE COUNT GIVE YOU HIS COPY FOR SAFEKEEPING, THEN.
WHY INVOLVE ME?
COUNT DE COUDE IS A COMPULSIVE GAMBLER.
HE'S TRYING TO SELL THE DAMNED THING TO COVER HIS DEBTS. WON'T LET ANYONE SO MUCH AS LOOK AT IT OTHERWISE.
WE ARE ATTEMPTING TO PURCHASE IT, BUT THE COUNT KEEPS CHANGING HIS TERMS.
AND *THAT* IS WHERE YOU COME IN. THE COUNT IS HOSTING A PARTY TOMORROW EVENING.
THE MANUSCRIPT IS IN HIS LIBRARY--IT'S THE PERFECT OPPORTUNITY FOR ROKOFF TO STRIKE.
WE NEED YOU TO SNIFF THE RUSSIAN OUT. LITERALLY, IT SEEMS.
WAR WITH GERMANY IS COMING, TARZAN.
IF RUSSIA HAS ACCESS TO THE GOLD, THE TSAR MIGHT NOT JOIN AN ALLIANCE CURRENTLY UNDER NEGOTIATION WITH FRANCE.
WE CANNOT ALLOW THAT TO HAPPEN.
I'LL GET THIS ROKOFF FOR YOU.
BUT *ONLY* BECAUSE I'M MORE ANNOYED BY HIS TREATMENT OF THAT WOMAN ON THE OCEAN LINER THAN I AM BY YOU PEOPLE.
BE GRATEFUL FOR THAT.

THE PARIS ESTATE OF COUNT RAOUL GASCOIGNE DE COUDE, THE FOLLOWING EVENING.

NO SIGN OF ROKOFF YET.

PAUL, ARE YOU SURE YOU DON'T WANT ME TO GRAB HIM WHEN HE SHOWS UP?

I SUGGESTED IT, BELIEVE ME. BUT I WAS OVERRULED.

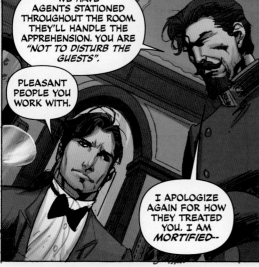

WE HAVE AGENTS STATIONED THROUGHOUT THE ROOM. THEY'LL HANDLE THE APPREHENSION. YOU ARE "NOT TO DISTURB THE GUESTS".

PLEASANT PEOPLE YOU WORK WITH.

I APOLOGIZE AGAIN FOR HOW THEY TREATED YOU. I AM *MORTIFIED*--

HOLD ON.

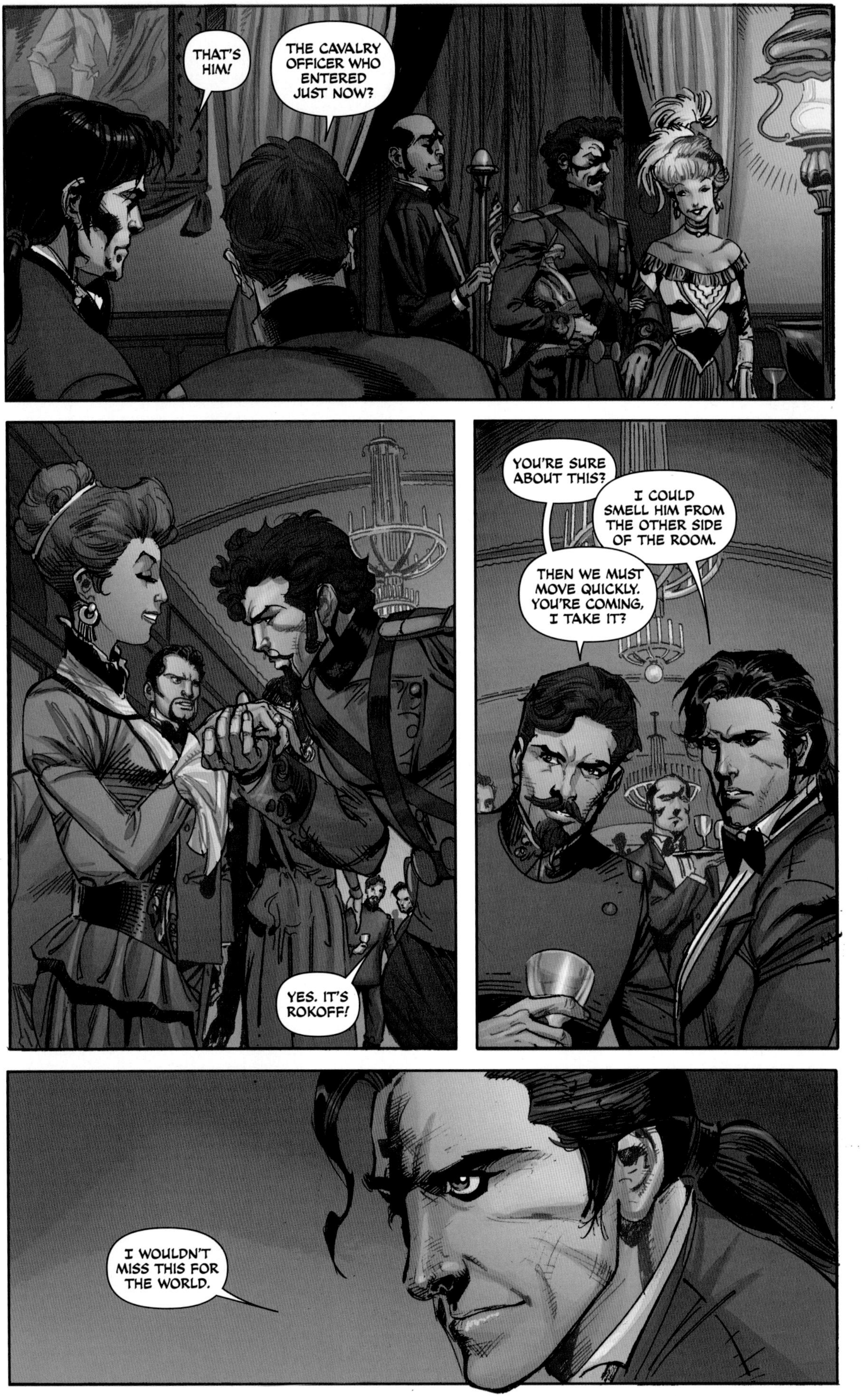
THAT'S HIM!
THE CAVALRY OFFICER WHO ENTERED JUST NOW?
YES. IT'S ROKOFF!
YOU'RE SURE ABOUT THIS?
I COULD SMELL HIM FROM THE OTHER SIDE OF THE ROOM.
THEN WE MUST MOVE QUICKLY. YOU'RE COMING, I TAKE IT?
I WOULDN'T MISS THIS FOR THE WORLD.

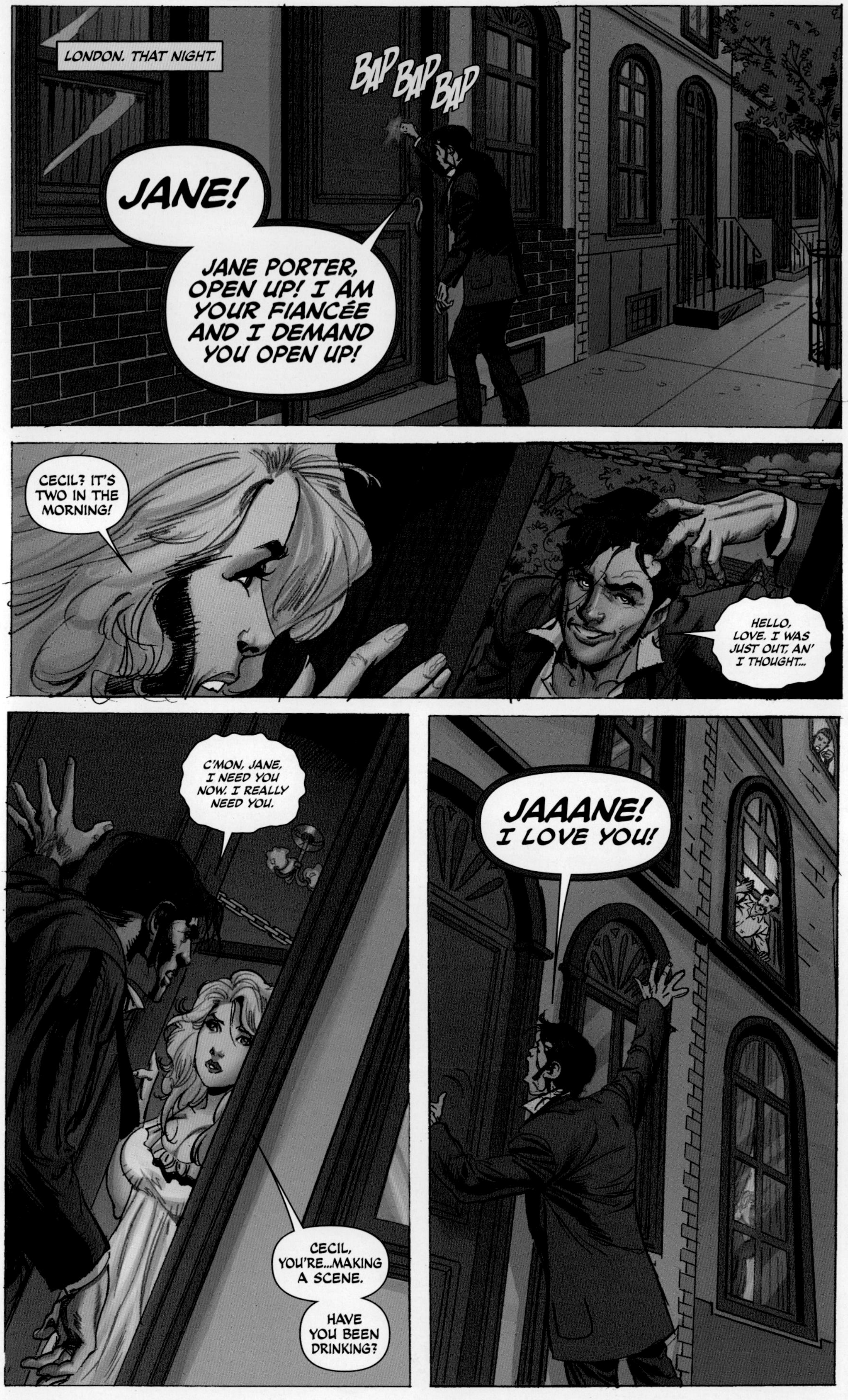
LONDON. THAT NIGHT.
BAP BAP BAP
JANE!
JANE PORTER, OPEN UP! I AM YOUR FIANCÉE AND I DEMAND YOU OPEN UP!
CECIL? IT'S TWO IN THE MORNING!
HELLO, LOVE. I WAS JUST OUT, AN' I THOUGHT...
C'MON, JANE, I NEED YOU NOW. I REALLY NEED YOU.
CECIL, YOU'RE...MAKING A SCENE.
HAVE YOU BEEN DRINKING?
JAAANE! I LOVE YOU!

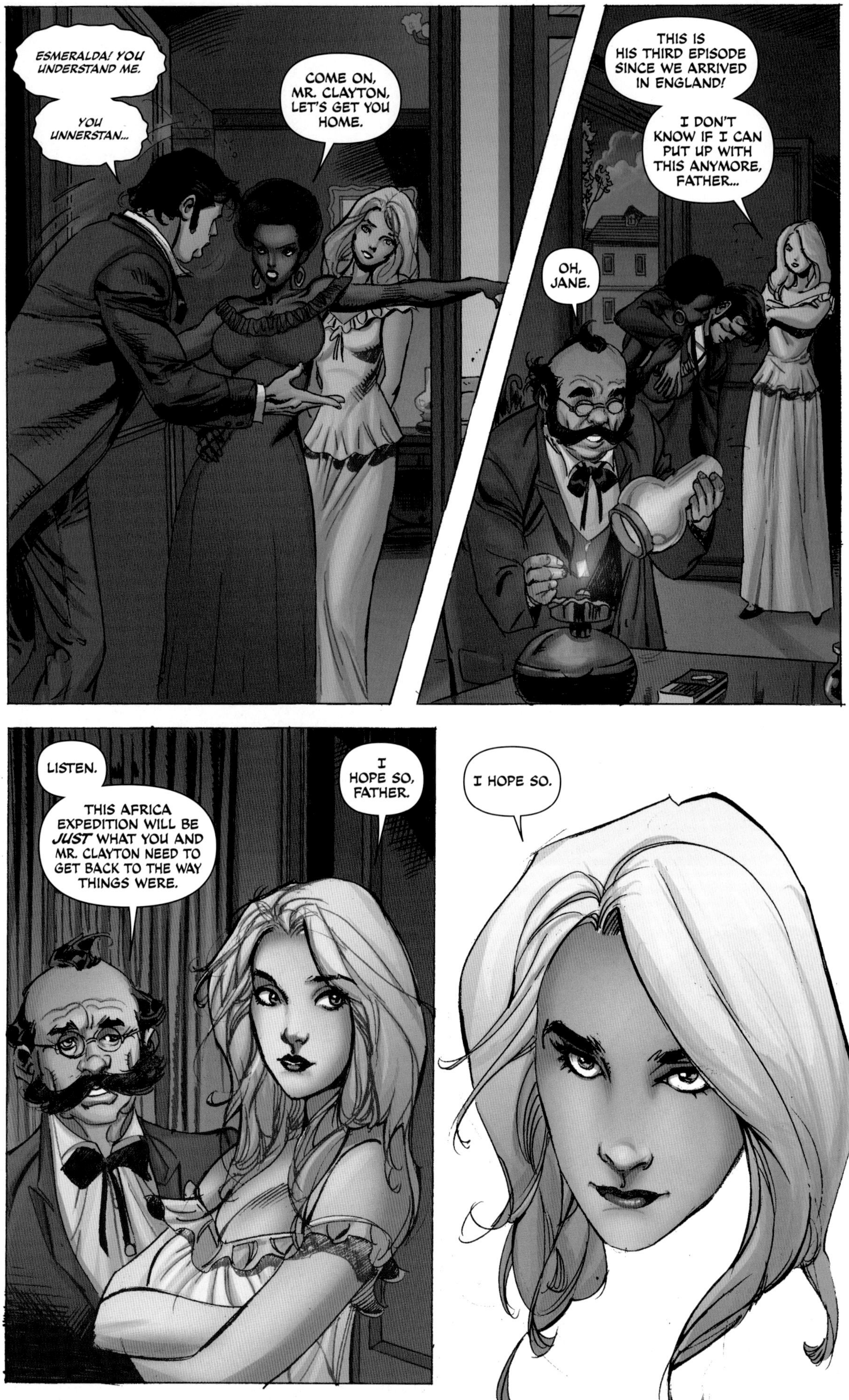
ESMERALDA! YOU UNDERSTAND ME.
YOU UNNERSTAN...
COME ON, MR. CLAYTON, LET'S GET YOU HOME.
THIS IS HIS THIRD EPISODE SINCE WE ARRIVED IN ENGLAND!
I DON'T KNOW IF I CAN PUT UP WITH THIS ANYMORE, FATHER...
OH, JANE.
LISTEN.
THIS AFRICA EXPEDITION WILL BE *JUST* WHAT YOU AND MR. CLAYTON NEED TO GET BACK TO THE WAY THINGS WERE.
I HOPE SO, FATHER.
I HOPE SO.

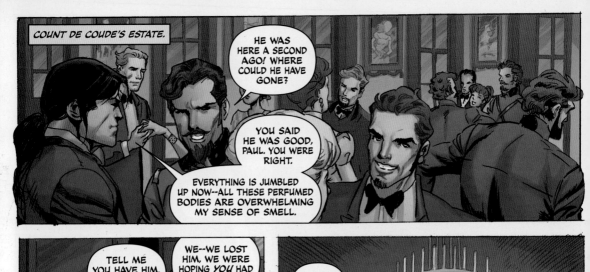

COUNT DE COUDE'S ESTATE.

HE WAS HERE A SECOND AGO! WHERE COULD HE HAVE GONE?

YOU SAID HE WAS GOOD, PAUL. YOU WERE RIGHT.

EVERYTHING IS JUMBLED UP NOW--ALL THESE PERFUMED BODIES ARE OVERWHELMING MY SENSE OF SMELL.

TELL ME YOU HAVE HIM. PLEASE TELL ME.

WE--WE LOST HIM, WE WERE HOPING *YOU* HAD SOMETHING...

WHERE ARE YOU GOING?!

WHERE DO YOU *THINK,* YOU IDIOT?

THE LIBRARY!

I JUST PRAY WE'RE NOT TOO LATE.

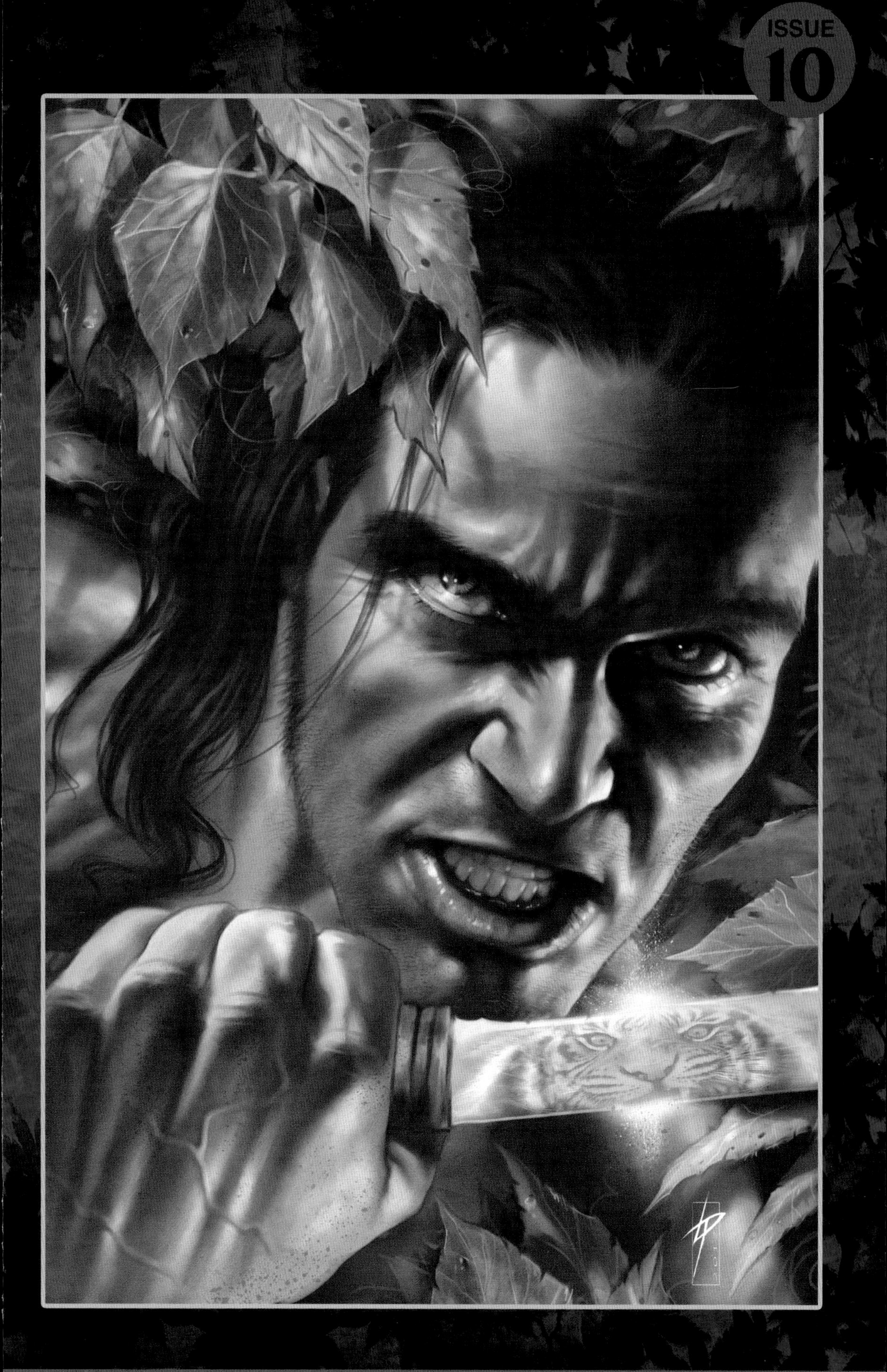
ISSUE
10

COVER BY LUCIO PARRILLO

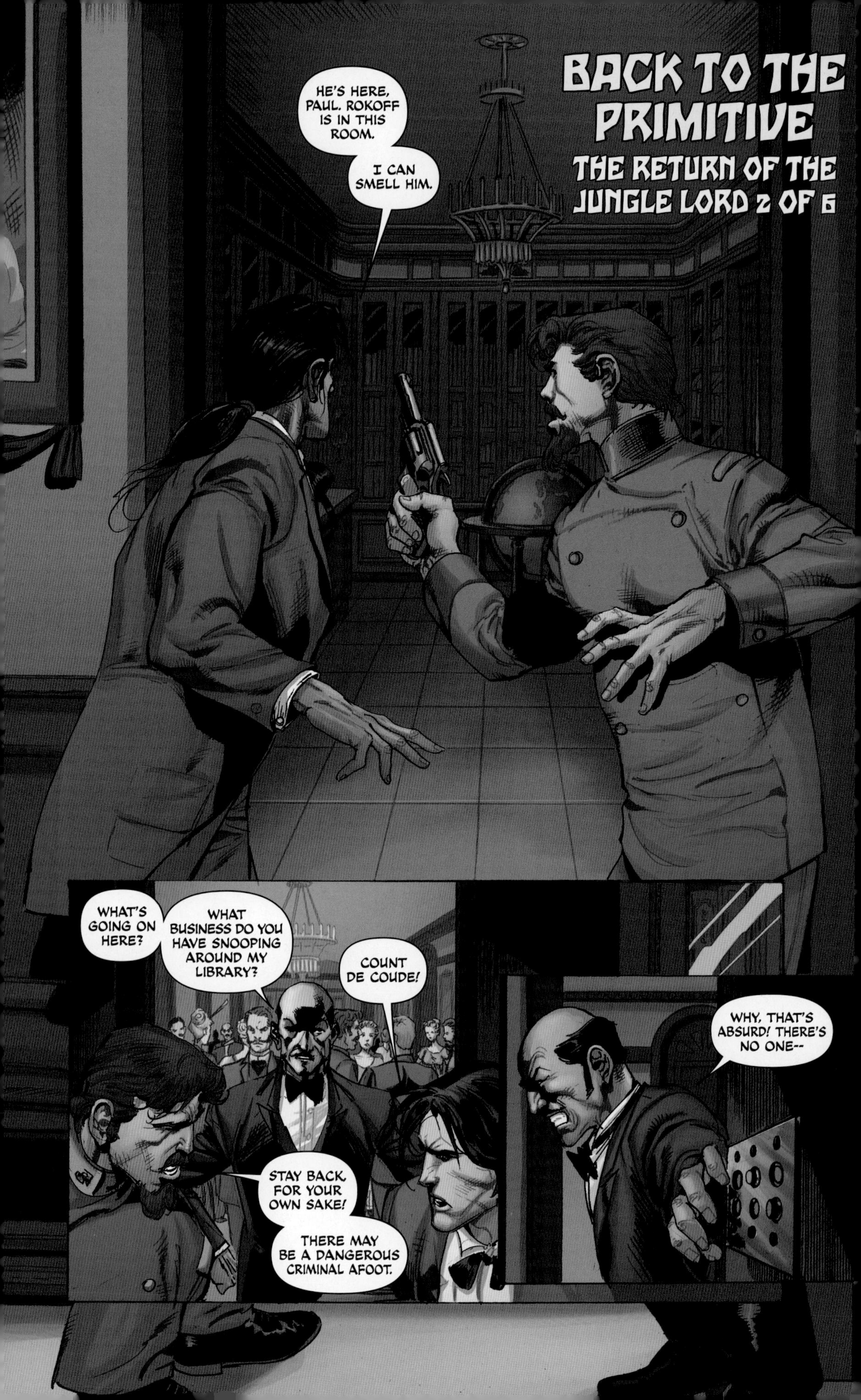
BACK TO THE PRIMITIVE
THE RETURN OF THE JUNGLE LORD 2 OF 6
HE'S HERE, PAUL. ROKOFF IS IN THIS ROOM.
I CAN SMELL HIM.
WHAT'S GOING ON HERE?
WHAT BUSINESS DO YOU HAVE SNOOPING AROUND MY LIBRARY?
COUNT DE COUDE!
STAY BACK, FOR YOUR OWN SAKE!
THERE MAY BE A DANGEROUS CRIMINAL AFOOT.
WHY, THAT'S ABSURD! THERE'S NO ONE--

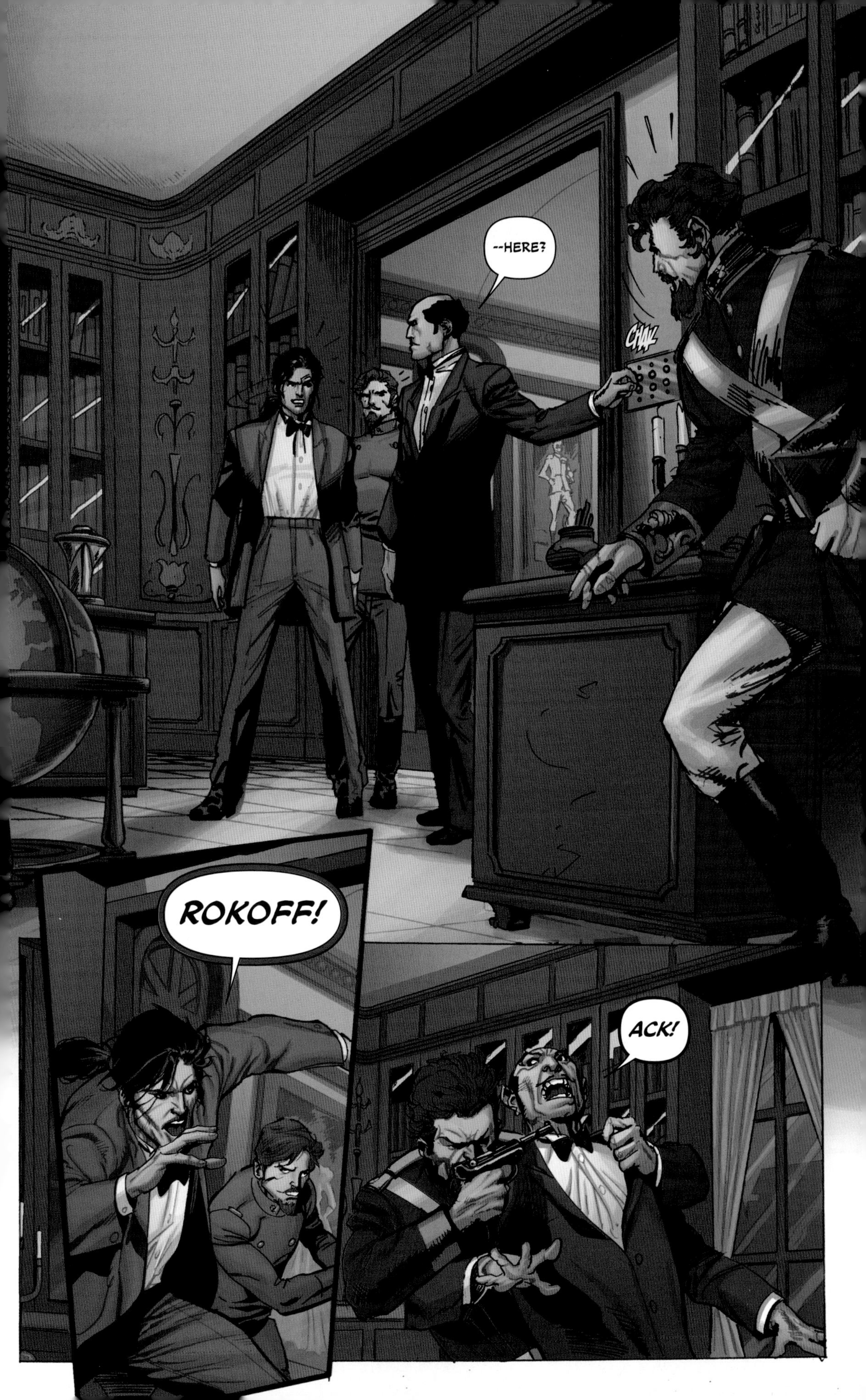
--HERE?
CHAK
ROKOFF!
ACK!

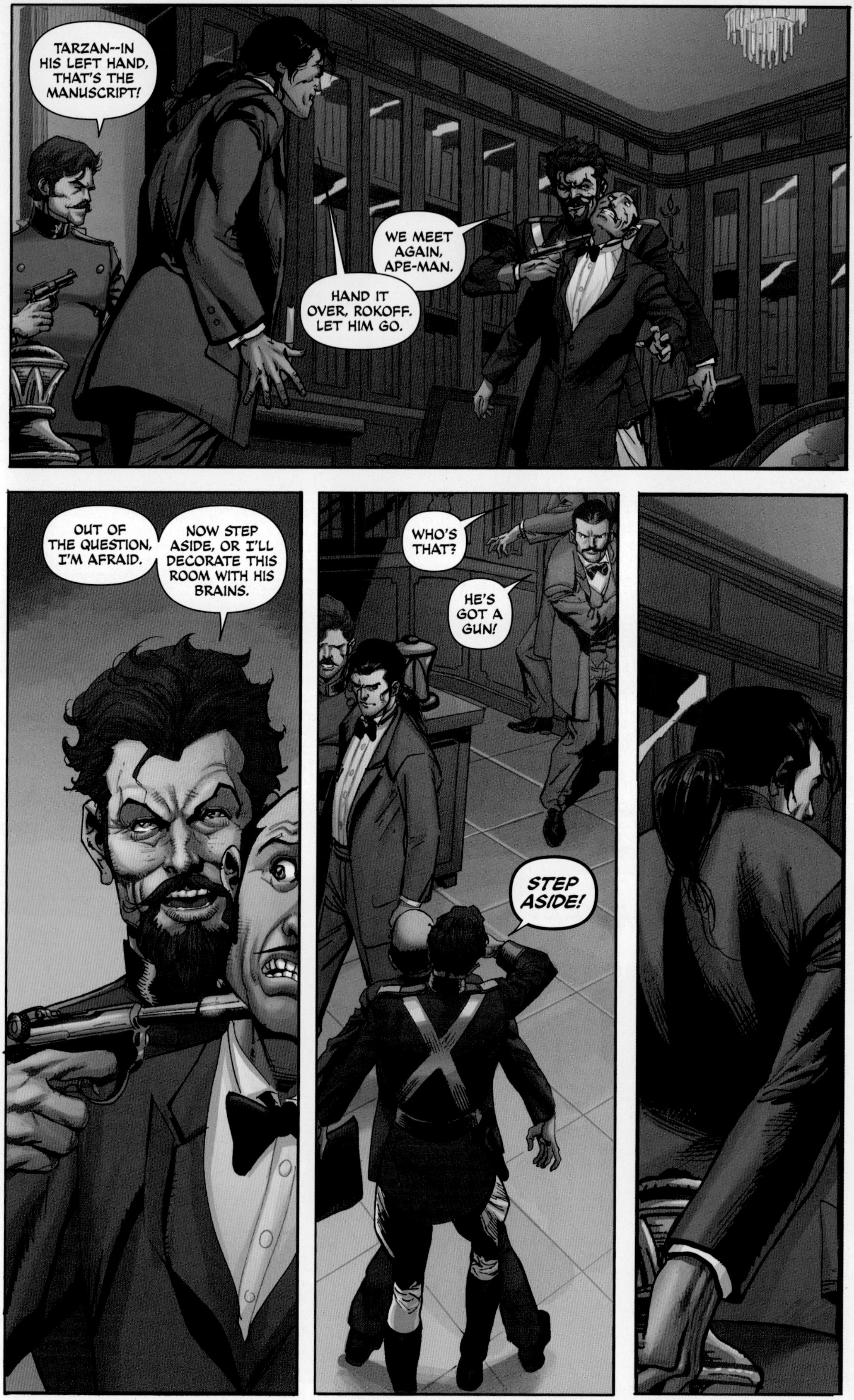
TARZAN--IN HIS LEFT HAND, THAT'S THE MANUSCRIPT!
WE MEET AGAIN, APE-MAN.
HAND IT OVER, ROKOFF. LET HIM GO.
OUT OF THE QUESTION, I'M AFRAID.
NOW STEP ASIDE, OR I'LL DECORATE THIS ROOM WITH HIS BRAINS.
WHO'S THAT?
HE'S GOT A GUN!
STEP ASIDE!

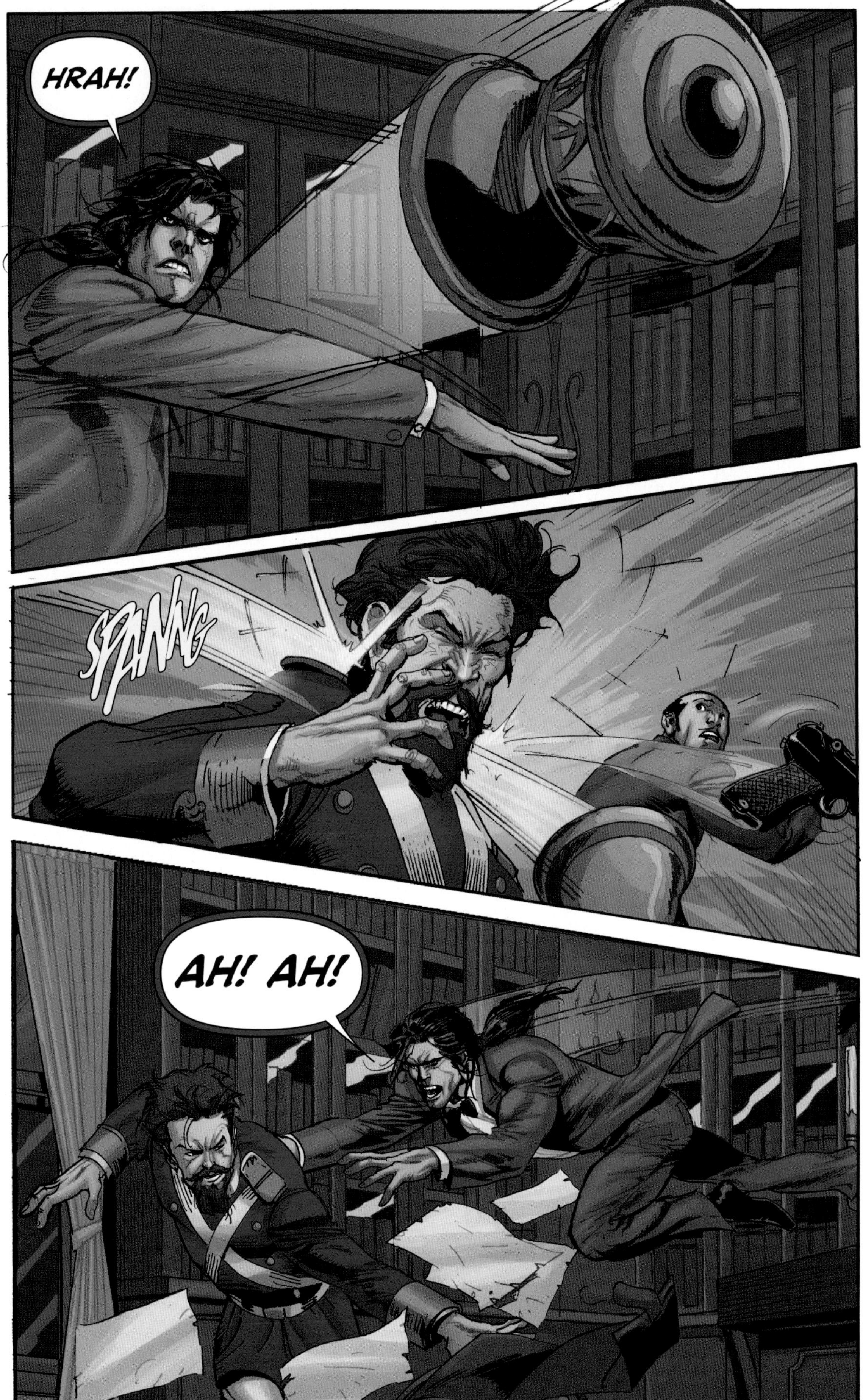
HRAH!
SPANNG
AH! AH!

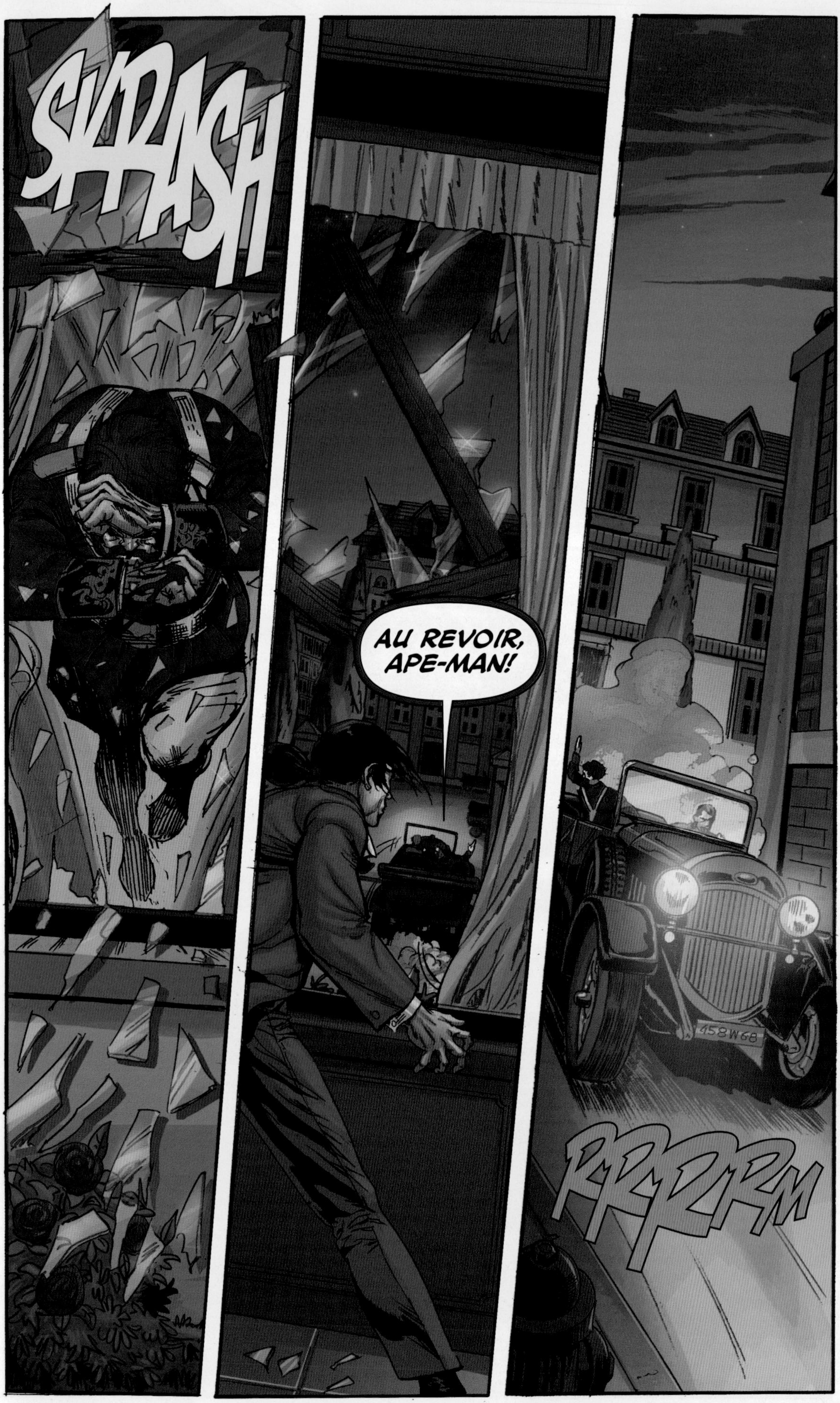
SKRASH
AU REVOIR, APE-MAN!
458 W 68
RRRRM

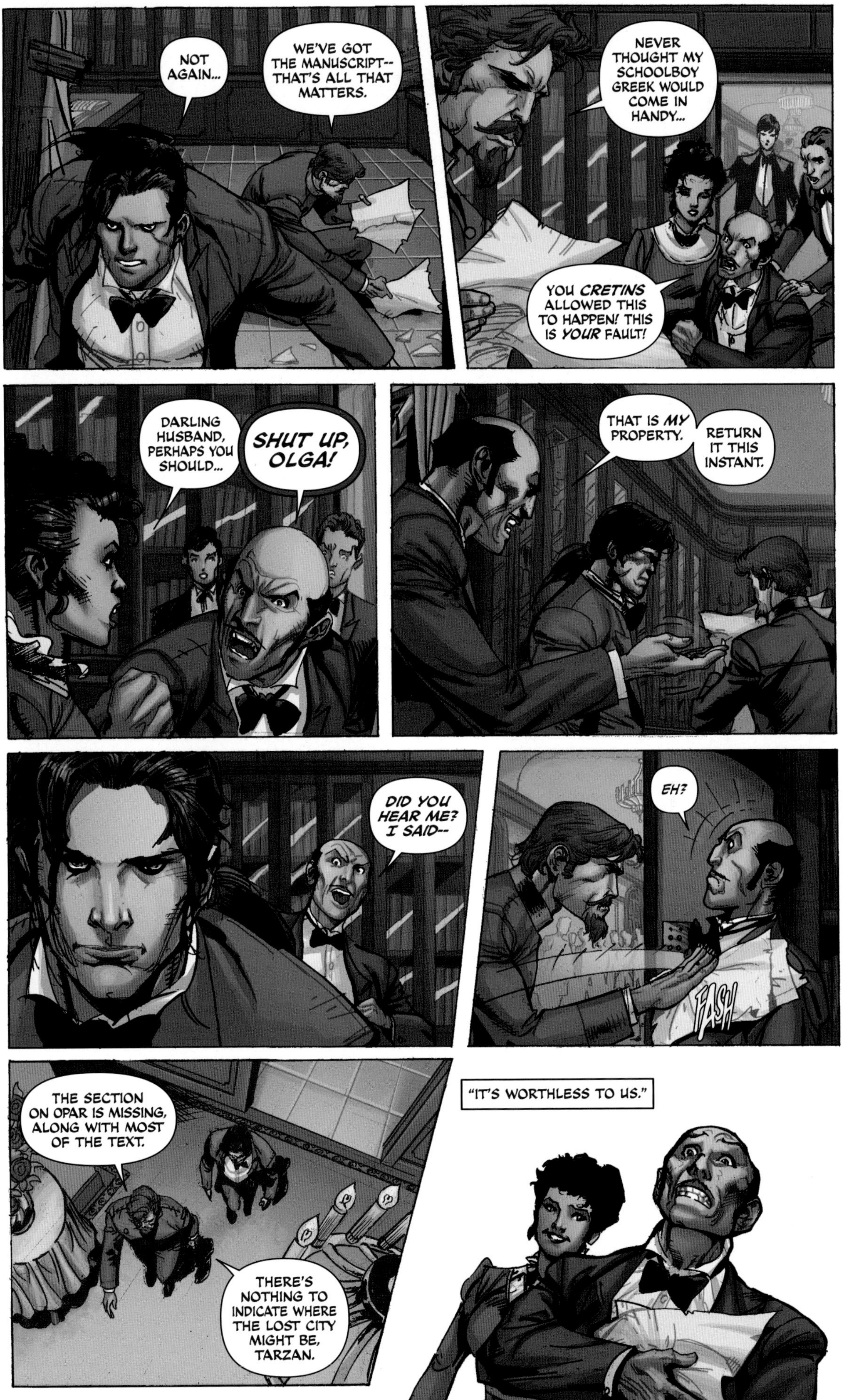
NOT AGAIN...
WE'VE GOT THE MANUSCRIPT-- THAT'S ALL THAT MATTERS.
NEVER THOUGHT MY SCHOOLBOY GREEK WOULD COME IN HANDY...
YOU *CRETINS* ALLOWED THIS TO HAPPEN! THIS IS *YOUR* FAULT!
DARLING HUSBAND, PERHAPS YOU SHOULD...
SHUT UP, OLGA!
THAT IS *MY* PROPERTY.
RETURN IT THIS INSTANT.
DID YOU HEAR ME? I SAID--
EH?
FASH
THE SECTION ON OPAR IS MISSING, ALONG WITH MOST OF THE TEXT.
THERE'S NOTHING TO INDICATE WHERE THE LOST CITY MIGHT BE, TARZAN.
"IT'S WORTHLESS TO US."

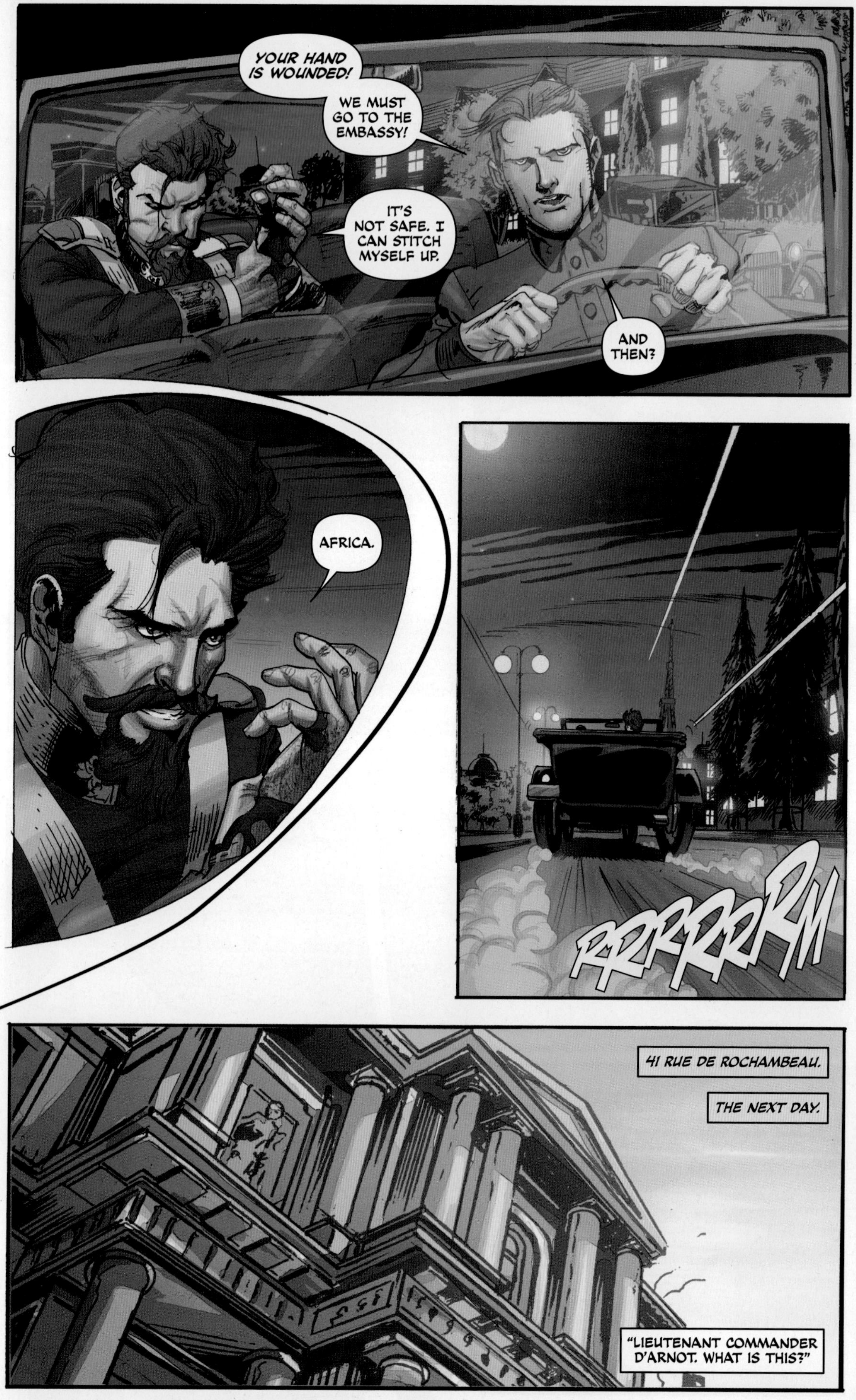
YOUR HAND IS WOUNDED!
WE MUST GO TO THE EMBASSY!
IT'S NOT SAFE. I CAN STITCH MYSELF UP.
AND THEN?
AFRICA.
RRRRRRRM
41 RUE DE ROCHAMBEAU.
THE NEXT DAY.
"LIEUTENANT COMMANDER D'ARNOT. WHAT IS THIS?"

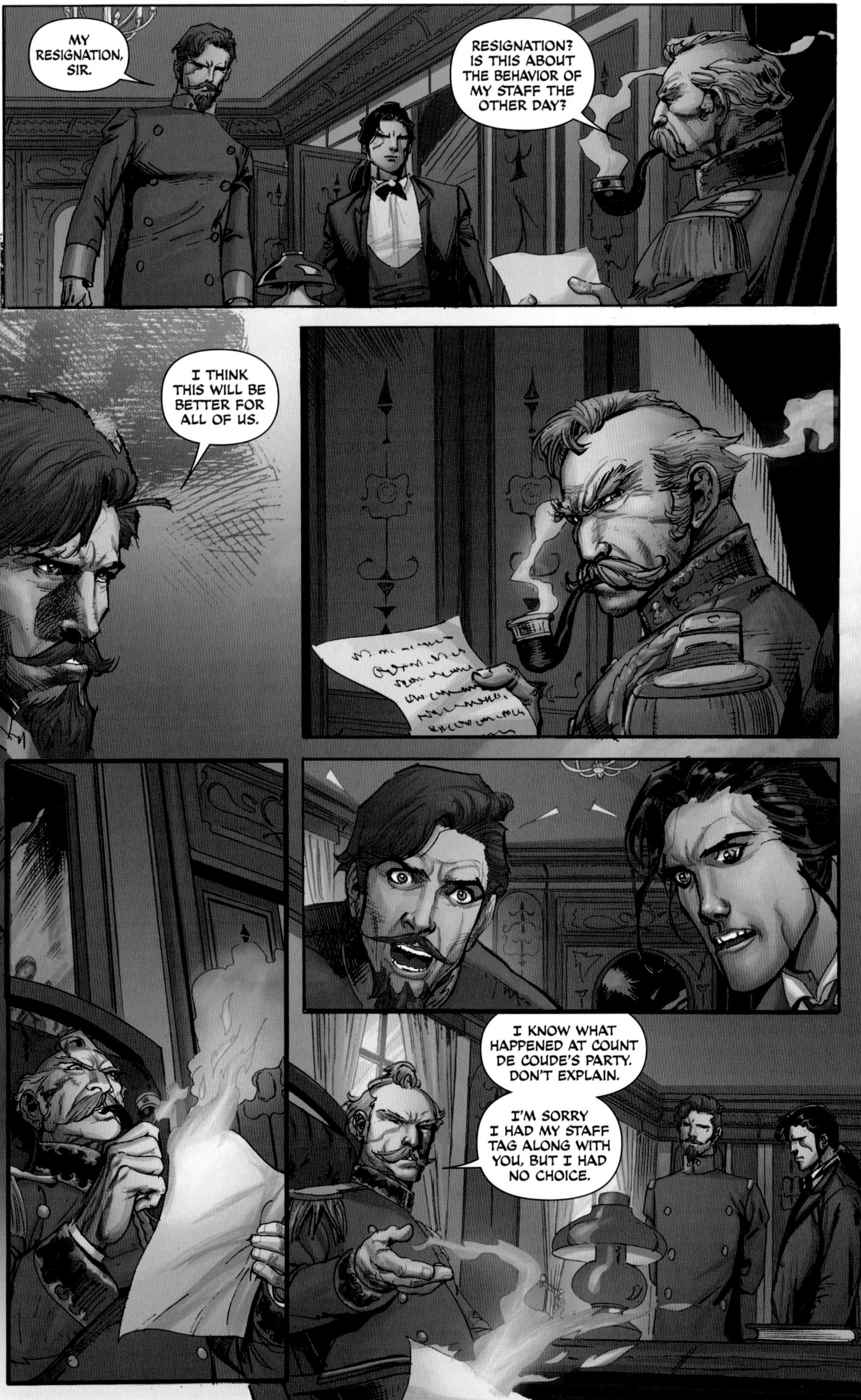
MY RESIGNATION, SIR.
RESIGNATION? IS THIS ABOUT THE BEHAVIOR OF MY STAFF THE OTHER DAY?
I THINK THIS WILL BE BETTER FOR ALL OF US.
I KNOW WHAT HAPPENED AT COUNT DE COUDE'S PARTY. DON'T EXPLAIN.
I'M SORRY I HAD MY STAFF TAG ALONG WITH YOU, BUT I HAD NO CHOICE.

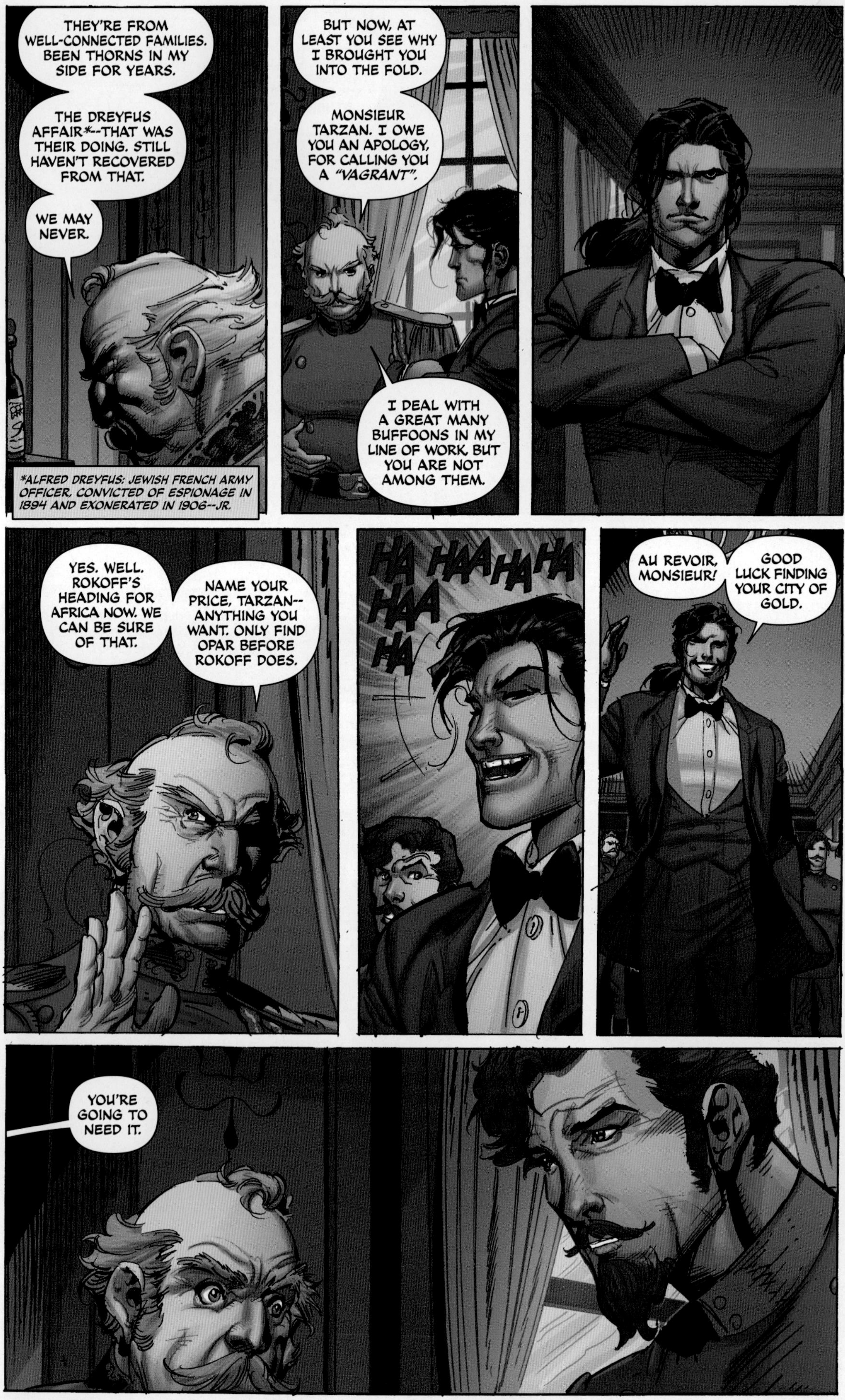
THEY'RE FROM WELL-CONNECTED FAMILIES. BEEN THORNS IN MY SIDE FOR YEARS.
THE DREYFUS AFFAIR*--THAT WAS THEIR DOING. STILL HAVEN'T RECOVERED FROM THAT.
WE MAY NEVER.
*ALFRED DREYFUS: JEWISH FRENCH ARMY OFFICER, CONVICTED OF ESPIONAGE IN 1894 AND EXONERATED IN 1906--JR.
BUT NOW, AT LEAST YOU SEE WHY I BROUGHT YOU INTO THE FOLD.
MONSIEUR TARZAN. I OWE YOU AN APOLOGY, FOR CALLING YOU A "VAGRANT".
I DEAL WITH A GREAT MANY BUFFOONS IN MY LINE OF WORK, BUT YOU ARE NOT AMONG THEM.
YES. WELL. ROKOFF'S HEADING FOR AFRICA NOW. WE CAN BE SURE OF THAT.
NAME YOUR PRICE, TARZAN--ANYTHING YOU WANT. ONLY FIND OPAR BEFORE ROKOFF DOES.
HA HAAHAHA HAA HA
AU REVOIR, MONSIEUR!
GOOD LUCK FINDING YOUR CITY OF GOLD.
YOU'RE GOING TO NEED IT.

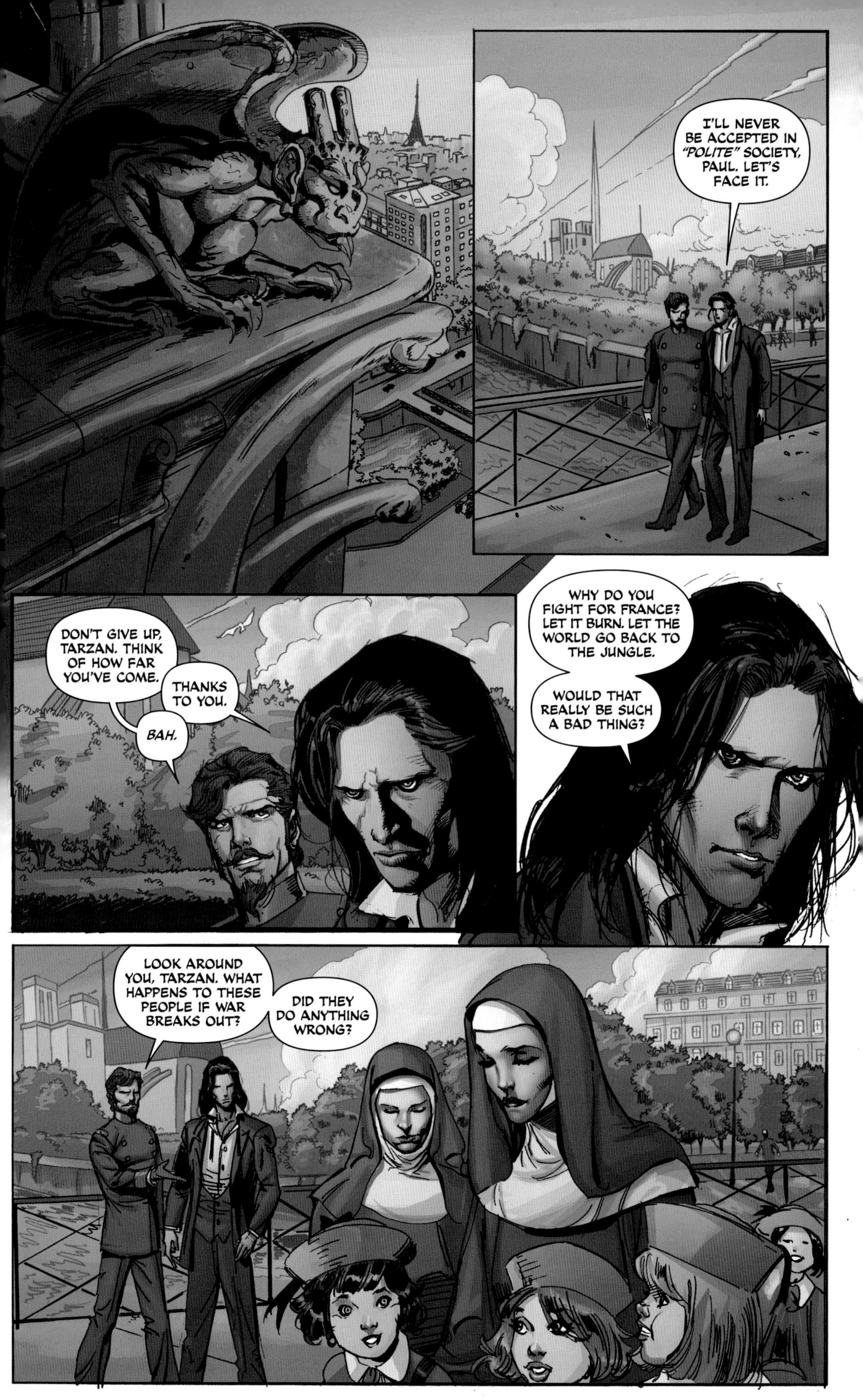
I'LL NEVER BE ACCEPTED IN "POLITE" SOCIETY, PAUL. LET'S FACE IT.
DON'T GIVE UP, TARZAN. THINK OF HOW FAR YOU'VE COME.
THANKS TO YOU.
BAH.
WHY DO YOU FIGHT FOR FRANCE? LET IT BURN. LET THE WORLD GO BACK TO THE JUNGLE.
WOULD THAT REALLY BE SUCH A BAD THING?
LOOK AROUND YOU, TARZAN. WHAT HAPPENS TO THESE PEOPLE IF WAR BREAKS OUT?
DID THEY DO ANYTHING WRONG?

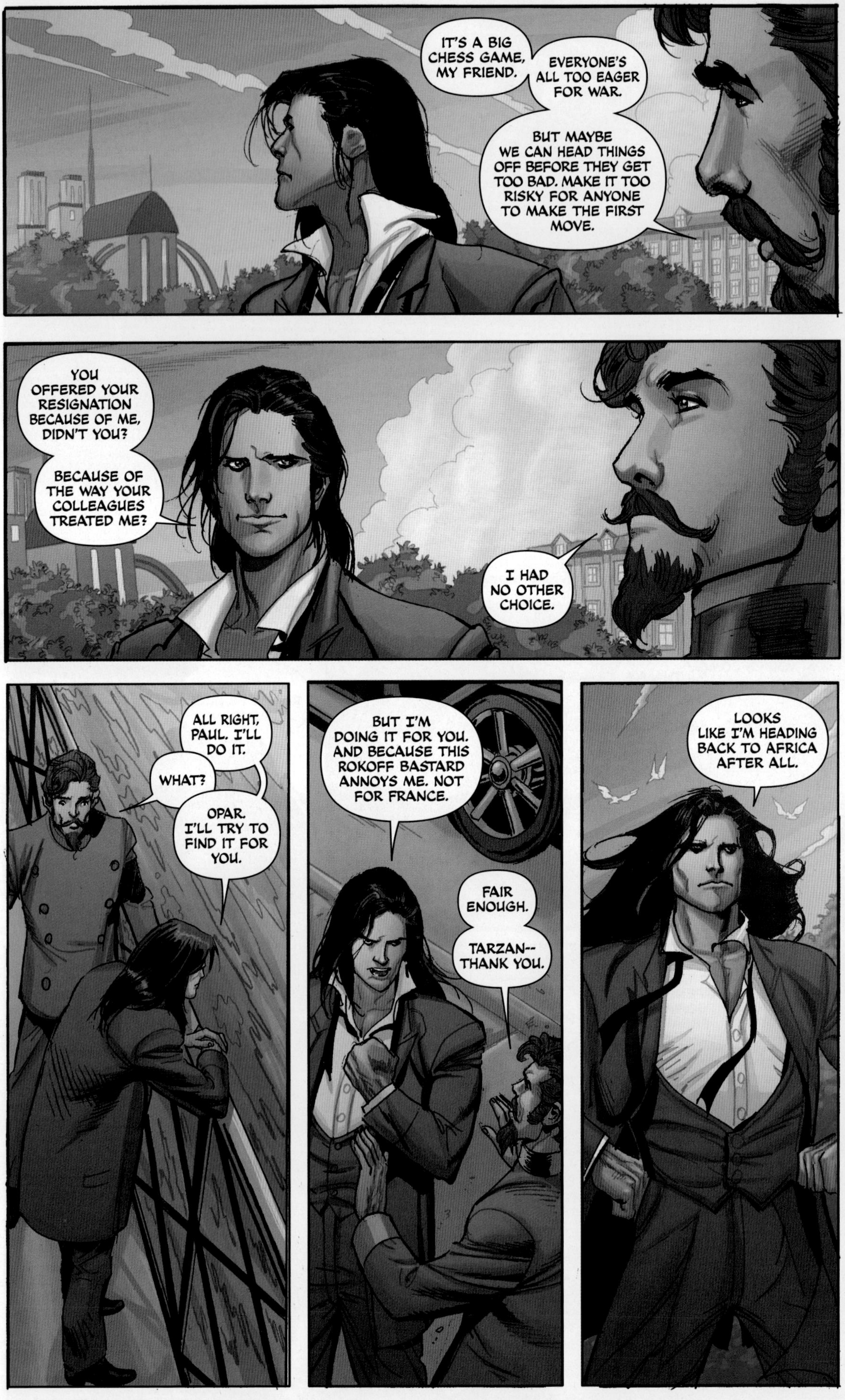
IT'S A BIG CHESS GAME, MY FRIEND.
EVERYONE'S ALL TOO EAGER FOR WAR.
BUT MAYBE WE CAN HEAD THINGS OFF BEFORE THEY GET TOO BAD. MAKE IT TOO RISKY FOR ANYONE TO MAKE THE FIRST MOVE.
YOU OFFERED YOUR RESIGNATION BECAUSE OF ME, DIDN'T YOU?
BECAUSE OF THE WAY YOUR COLLEAGUES TREATED ME?
I HAD NO OTHER CHOICE.
ALL RIGHT, PAUL. I'LL DO IT.
WHAT?
OPAR. I'LL TRY TO FIND IT FOR YOU.
BUT I'M DOING IT FOR YOU. AND BECAUSE THIS ROKOFF BASTARD ANNOYS ME. NOT FOR FRANCE.
FAIR ENOUGH.
TARZAN-- THANK YOU.
LOOKS LIKE I'M HEADING BACK TO AFRICA AFTER ALL.

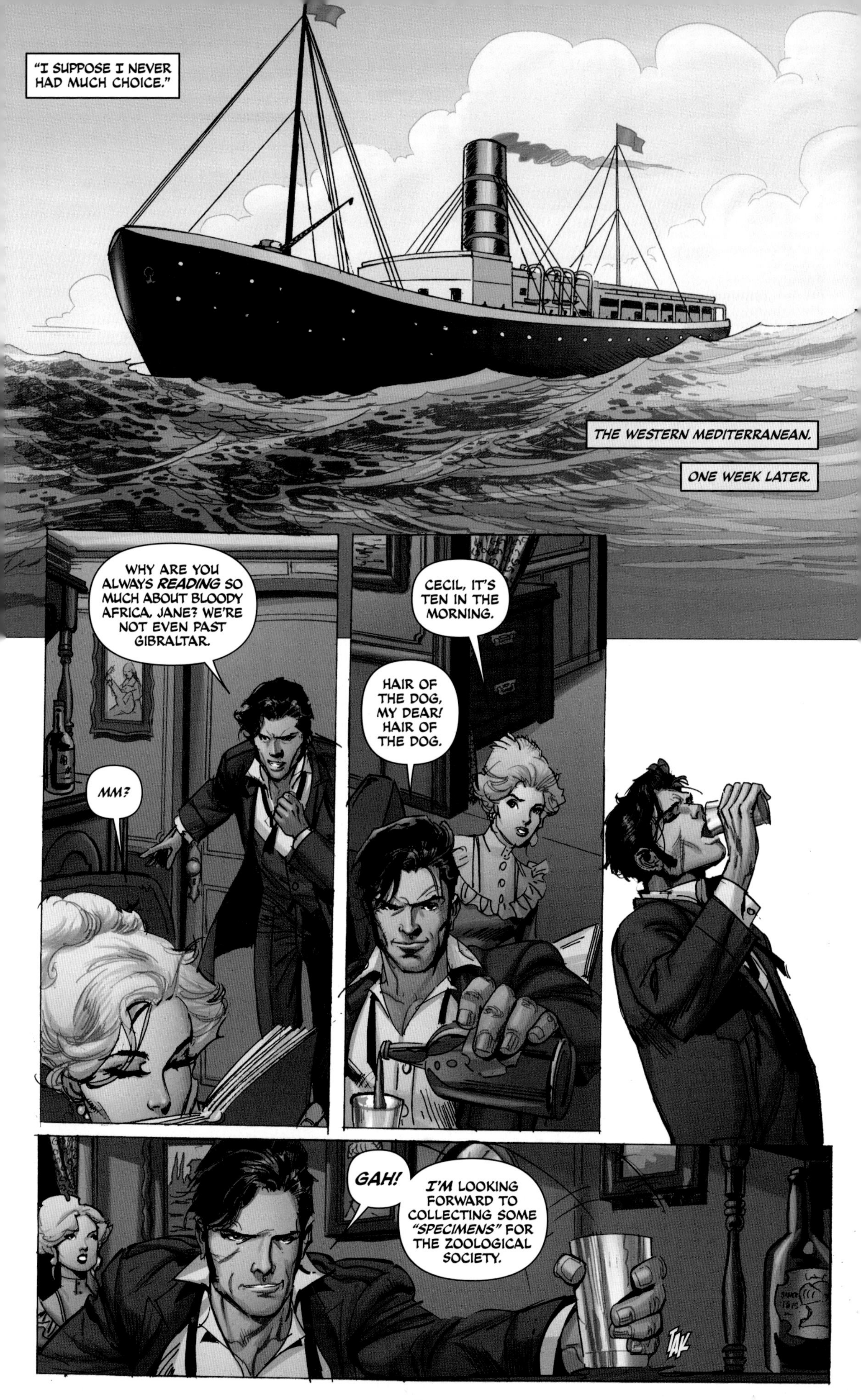
"I SUPPOSE I NEVER HAD MUCH CHOICE."
THE WESTERN MEDITERRANEAN.
ONE WEEK LATER.
WHY ARE YOU ALWAYS *READING* SO MUCH ABOUT BLOODY AFRICA, JANE? WE'RE NOT EVEN PAST GIBRALTAR.
MM?
CECIL, IT'S TEN IN THE MORNING.
HAIR OF THE DOG, MY DEAR! HAIR OF THE DOG.
GAH!
I'M LOOKING FORWARD TO COLLECTING SOME *"SPECIMENS"* FOR THE ZOOLOGICAL SOCIETY.

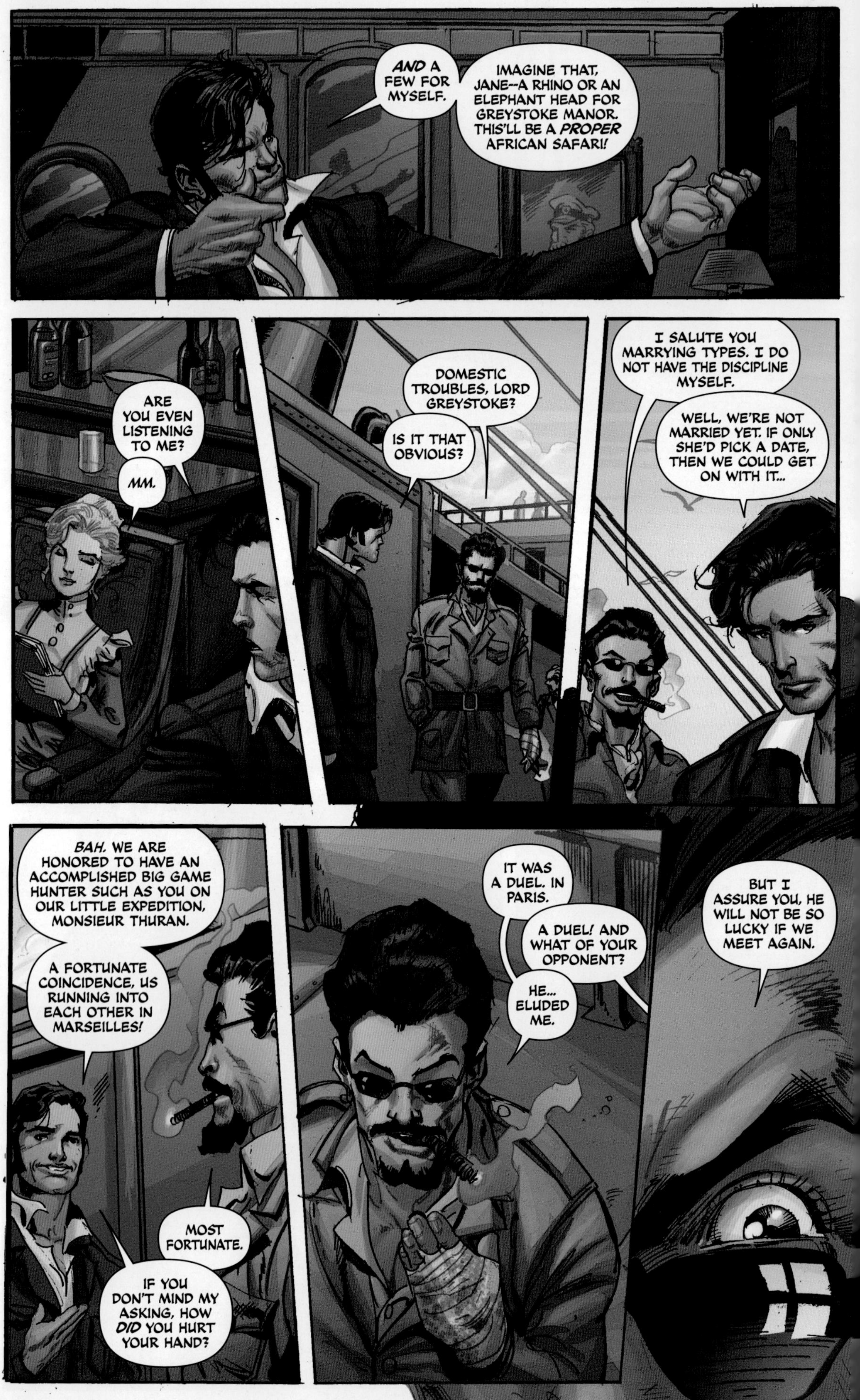
AND A FEW FOR MYSELF.
IMAGINE THAT, JANE--A RHINO OR AN ELEPHANT HEAD FOR GREYSTOKE MANOR. THIS'LL BE A PROPER AFRICAN SAFARI!
ARE YOU EVEN LISTENING TO ME?
MM.
DOMESTIC TROUBLES, LORD GREYSTOKE?
IS IT THAT OBVIOUS?
I SALUTE YOU MARRYING TYPES. I DO NOT HAVE THE DISCIPLINE MYSELF.
WELL, WE'RE NOT MARRIED YET. IF ONLY SHE'D PICK A DATE, THEN WE COULD GET ON WITH IT...
BAH. WE ARE HONORED TO HAVE AN ACCOMPLISHED BIG GAME HUNTER SUCH AS YOU ON OUR LITTLE EXPEDITION, MONSIEUR THURAN.
A FORTUNATE COINCIDENCE, US RUNNING INTO EACH OTHER IN MARSEILLES!
MOST FORTUNATE.
IF YOU DON'T MIND MY ASKING, HOW DID YOU HURT YOUR HAND?
IT WAS A DUEL. IN PARIS.
A DUEL! AND WHAT OF YOUR OPPONENT?
HE... ELUDED ME.
BUT I ASSURE YOU, HE WILL NOT BE SO LUCKY IF WE MEET AGAIN.

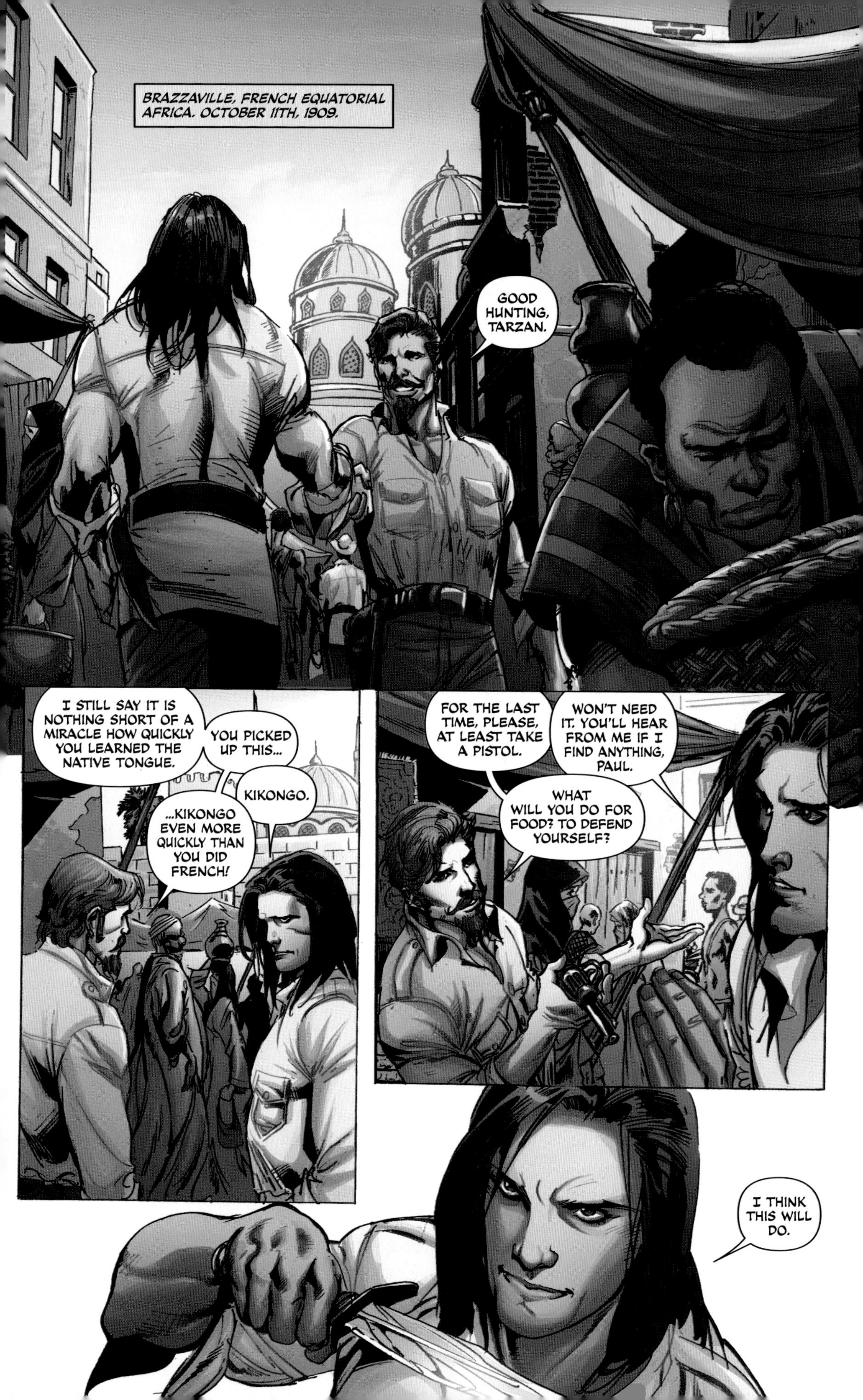
BRAZZAVILLE, FRENCH EQUATORIAL AFRICA. OCTOBER 11TH, 1909.
GOOD HUNTING, TARZAN.
I STILL SAY IT IS NOTHING SHORT OF A MIRACLE HOW QUICKLY YOU LEARNED THE NATIVE TONGUE.
YOU PICKED UP THIS...
KIKONGO.
...KIKONGO EVEN MORE QUICKLY THAN YOU DID FRENCH!
FOR THE LAST TIME, PLEASE, AT LEAST TAKE A PISTOL.
WON'T NEED IT. YOU'LL HEAR FROM ME IF I FIND ANYTHING, PAUL.
WHAT WILL YOU DO FOR FOOD? TO DEFEND YOURSELF?
I THINK THIS WILL DO.

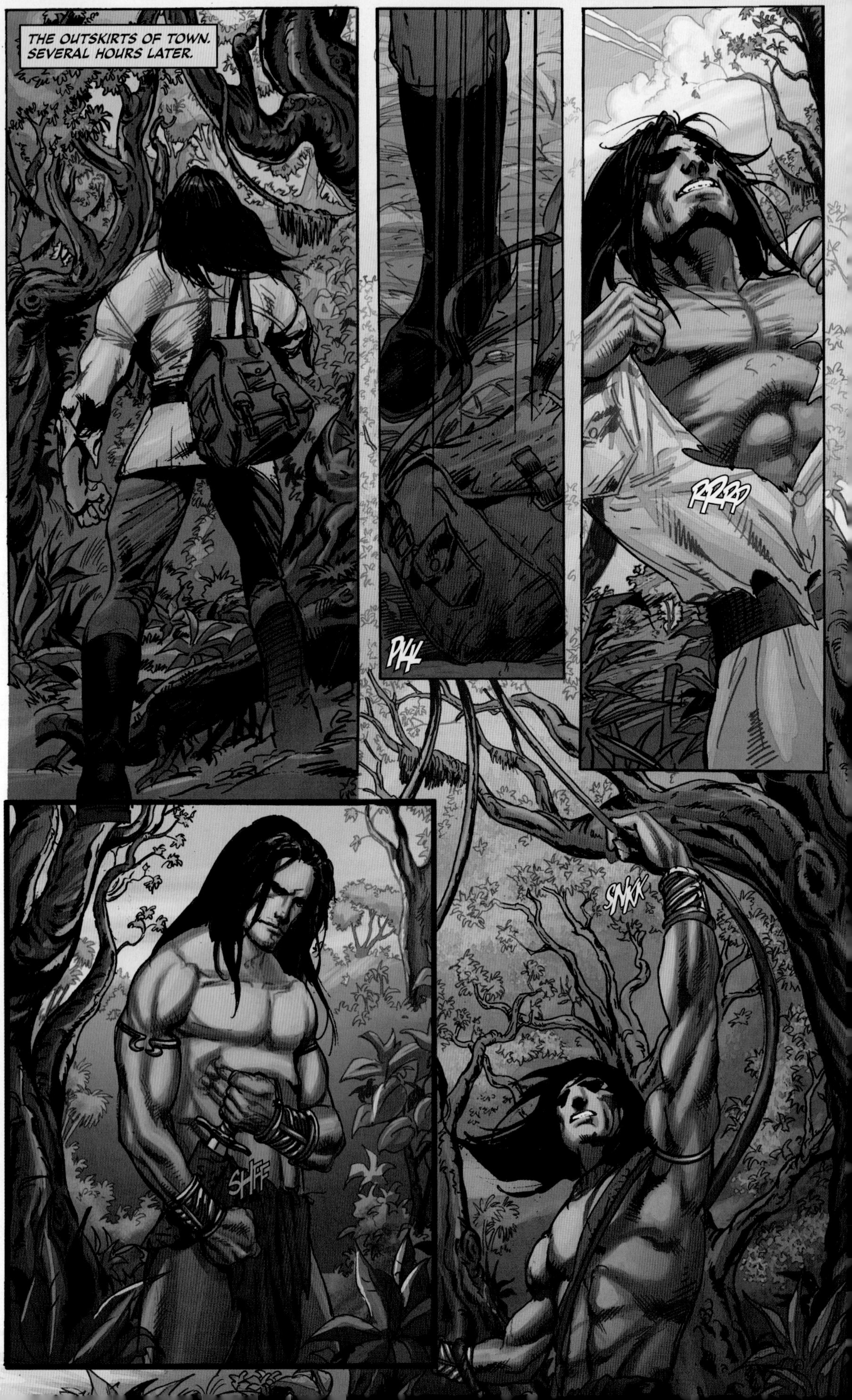
THE OUTSKIRTS OF TOWN. SEVERAL HOURS LATER.
PLUK
RRRIP
SHIFF
SNIKK

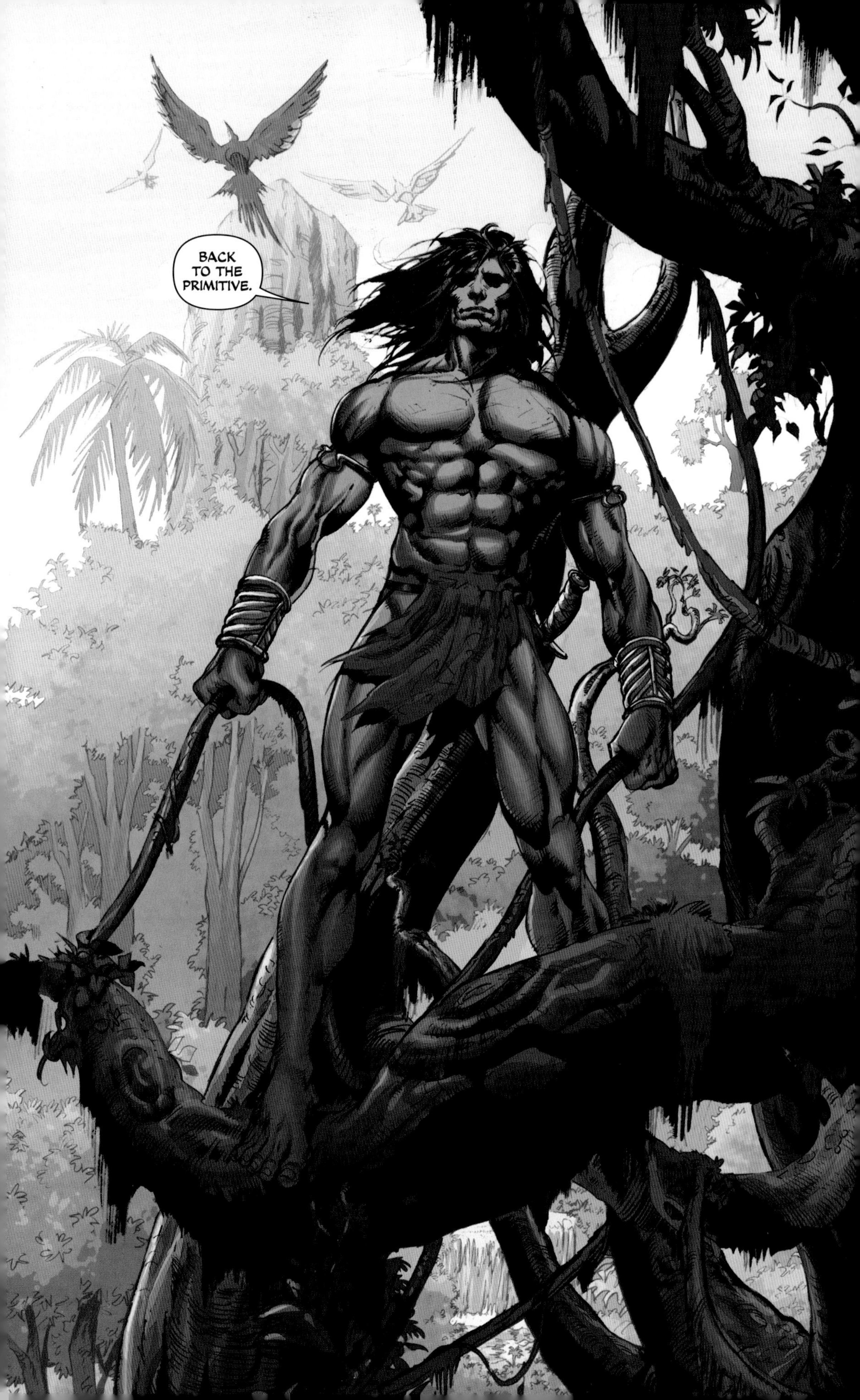
BACK TO THE PRIMITIVE.

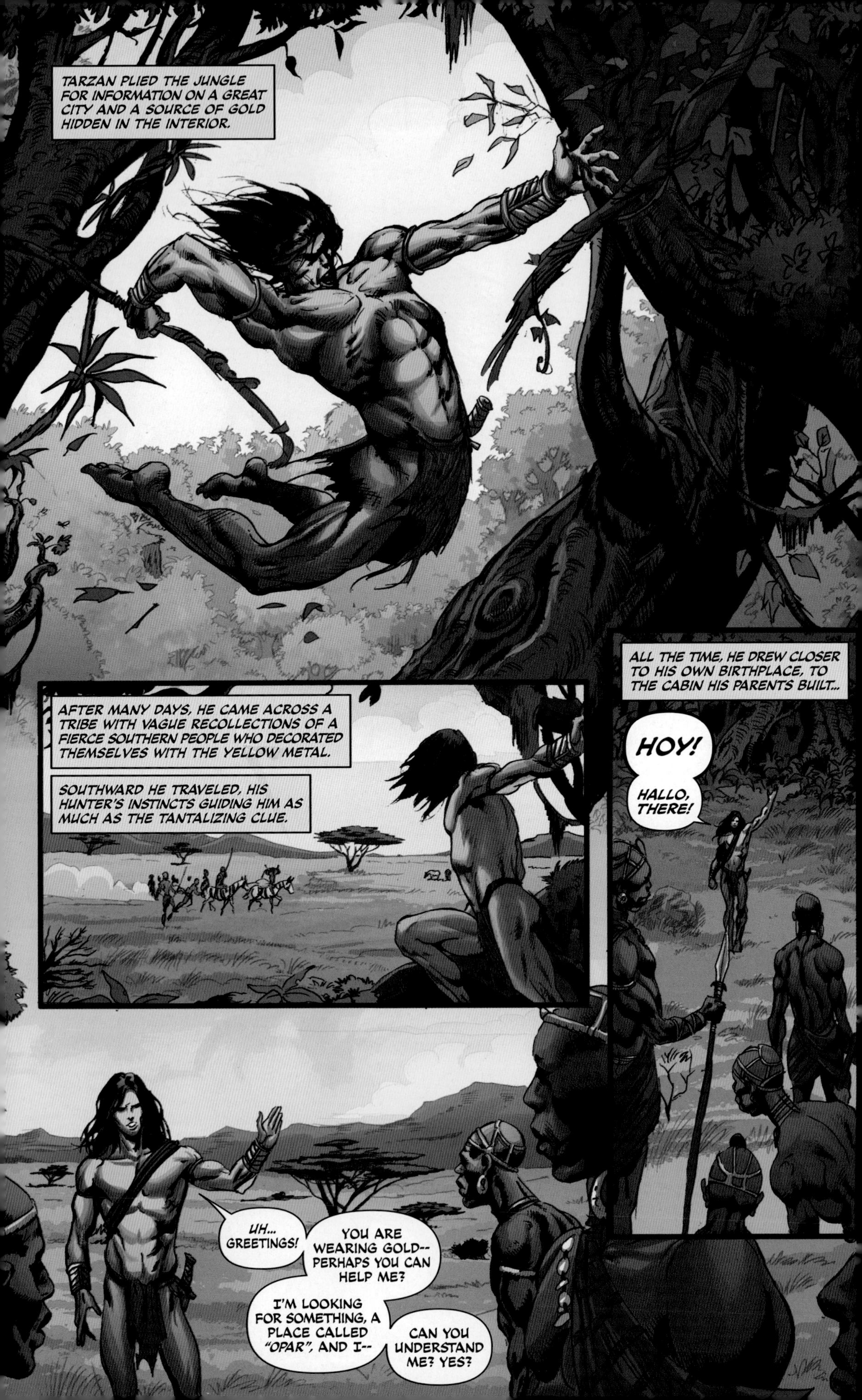
TARZAN PLIED THE JUNGLE FOR INFORMATION ON A GREAT CITY AND A SOURCE OF GOLD HIDDEN IN THE INTERIOR.
AFTER MANY DAYS, HE CAME ACROSS A TRIBE WITH VAGUE RECOLLECTIONS OF A FIERCE SOUTHERN PEOPLE WHO DECORATED THEMSELVES WITH THE YELLOW METAL.
SOUTHWARD HE TRAVELED, HIS HUNTER'S INSTINCTS GUIDING HIM AS MUCH AS THE TANTALIZING CLUE.
ALL THE TIME, HE DREW CLOSER TO HIS OWN BIRTHPLACE, TO THE CABIN HIS PARENTS BUILT...
HOY!
HALLO, THERE!
UH... GREETINGS!
YOU ARE WEARING GOLD-- PERHAPS YOU CAN HELP ME?
I'M LOOKING FOR SOMETHING, A PLACE CALLED "OPAR", AND I--
CAN YOU UNDERSTAND ME? YES?

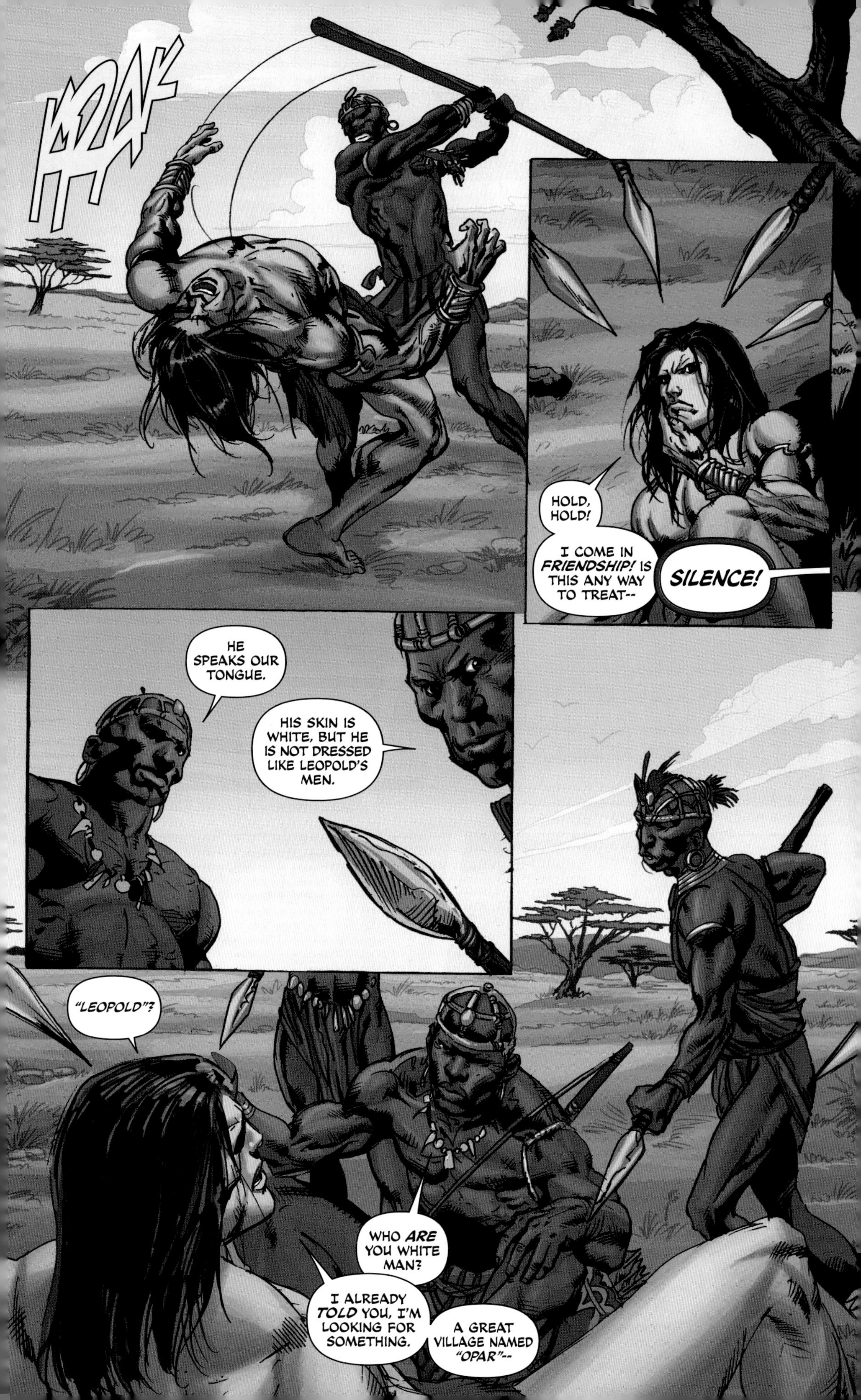
KRAK
HOLD, HOLD!
I COME IN *FRIENDSHIP!* IS THIS ANY WAY TO TREAT--
SILENCE!
HE SPEAKS OUR TONGUE.
HIS SKIN IS WHITE, BUT HE IS NOT DRESSED LIKE LEOPOLD'S MEN.
"LEOPOLD"?
WHO *ARE* YOU WHITE MAN?
I ALREADY *TOLD* YOU, I'M LOOKING FOR SOMETHING.
A GREAT VILLAGE NAMED *"OPAR"*--

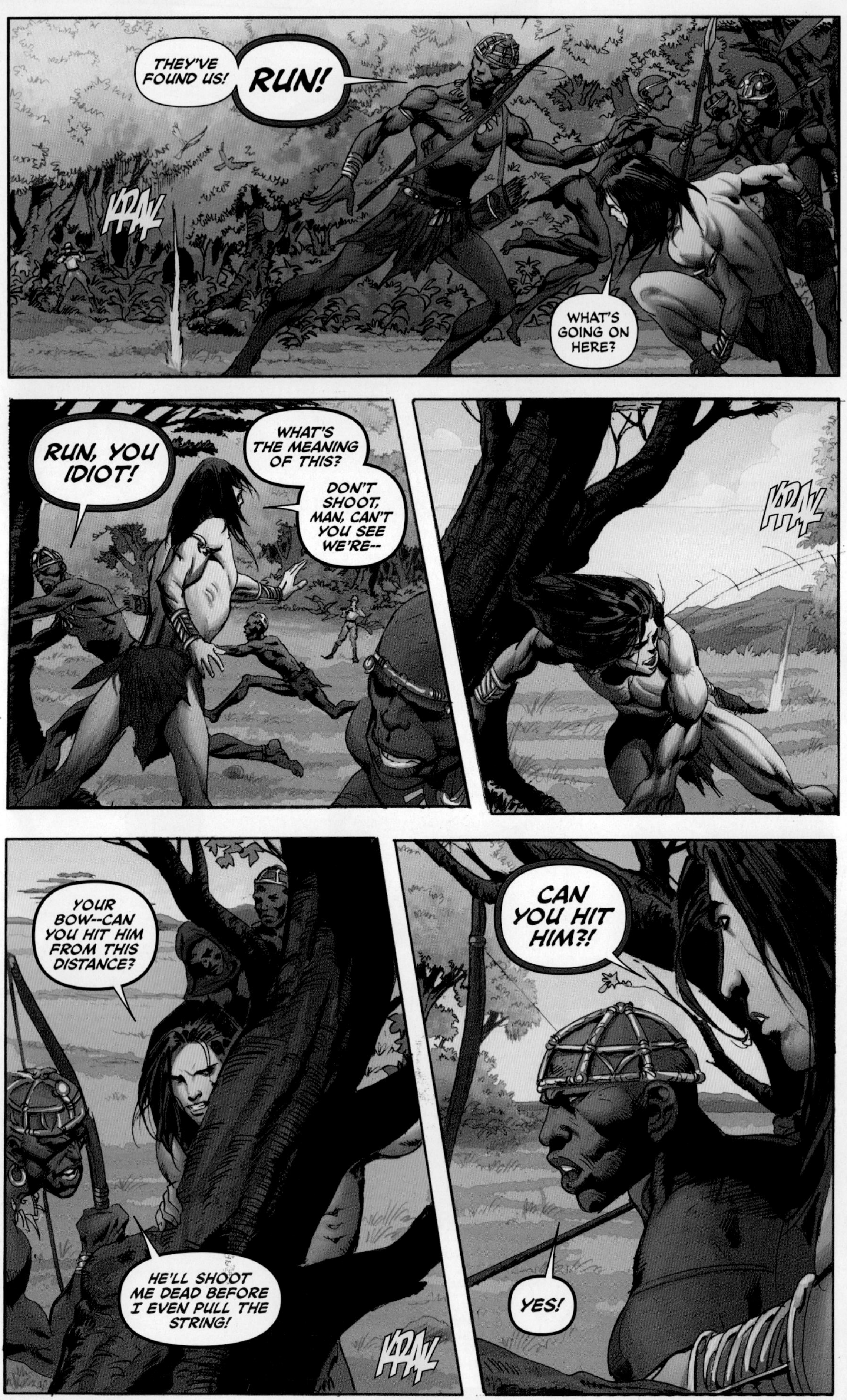
THEY'VE FOUND US!
RUN!
KRAK
WHAT'S GOING ON HERE?
RUN, YOU IDIOT!
WHAT'S THE MEANING OF THIS?
DON'T SHOOT, MAN, CAN'T YOU SEE WE'RE--
KRAK
YOUR BOW--CAN YOU HIT HIM FROM THIS DISTANCE?
HE'LL SHOOT ME DEAD BEFORE I EVEN PULL THE STRING!
KRAK
CAN YOU HIT HIM?!
YES!

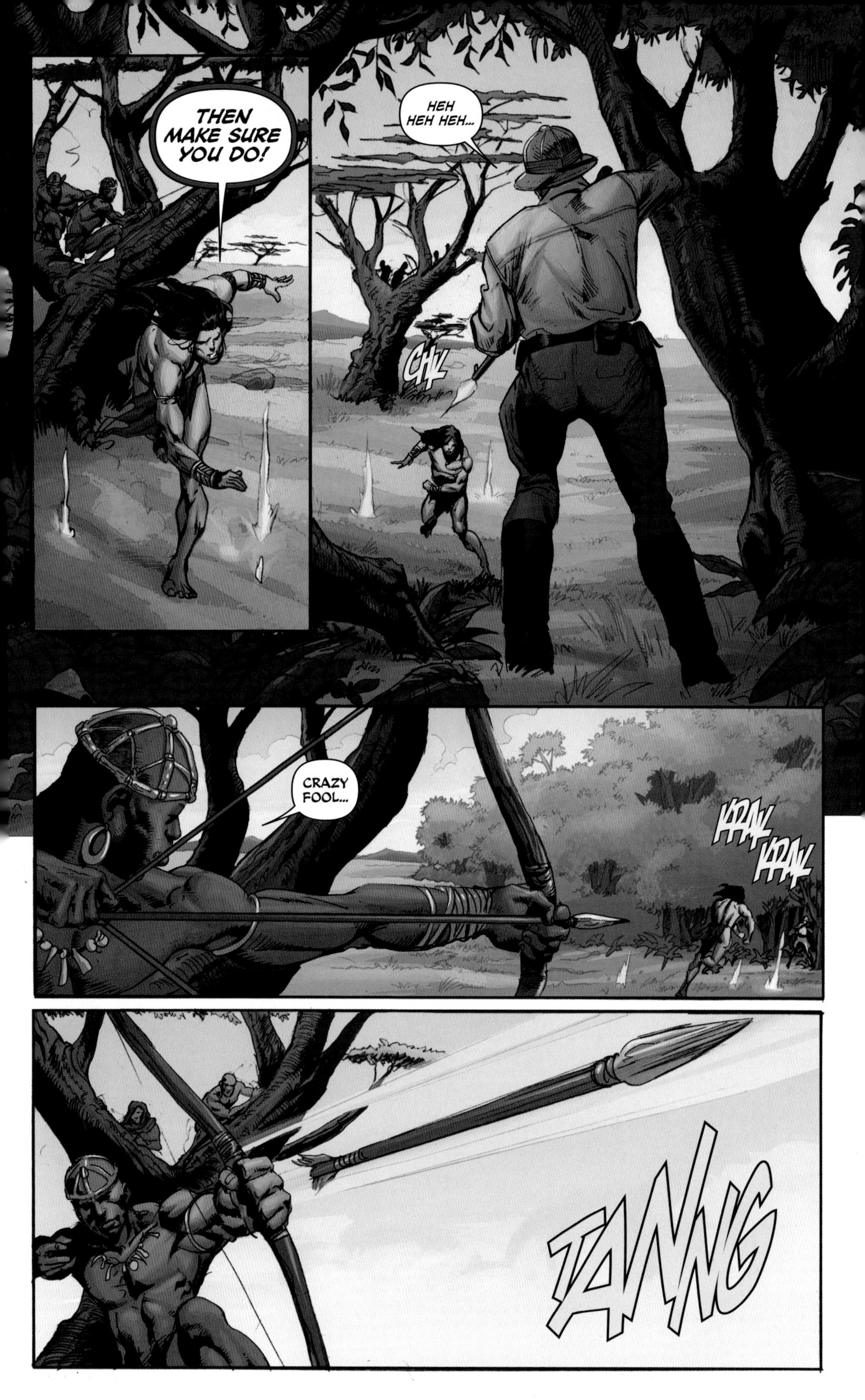
THEN MAKE SURE YOU DO!
HEH HEH HEH...
CHK
CRAZY FOOL...
KRAK
KRAK
TANNG

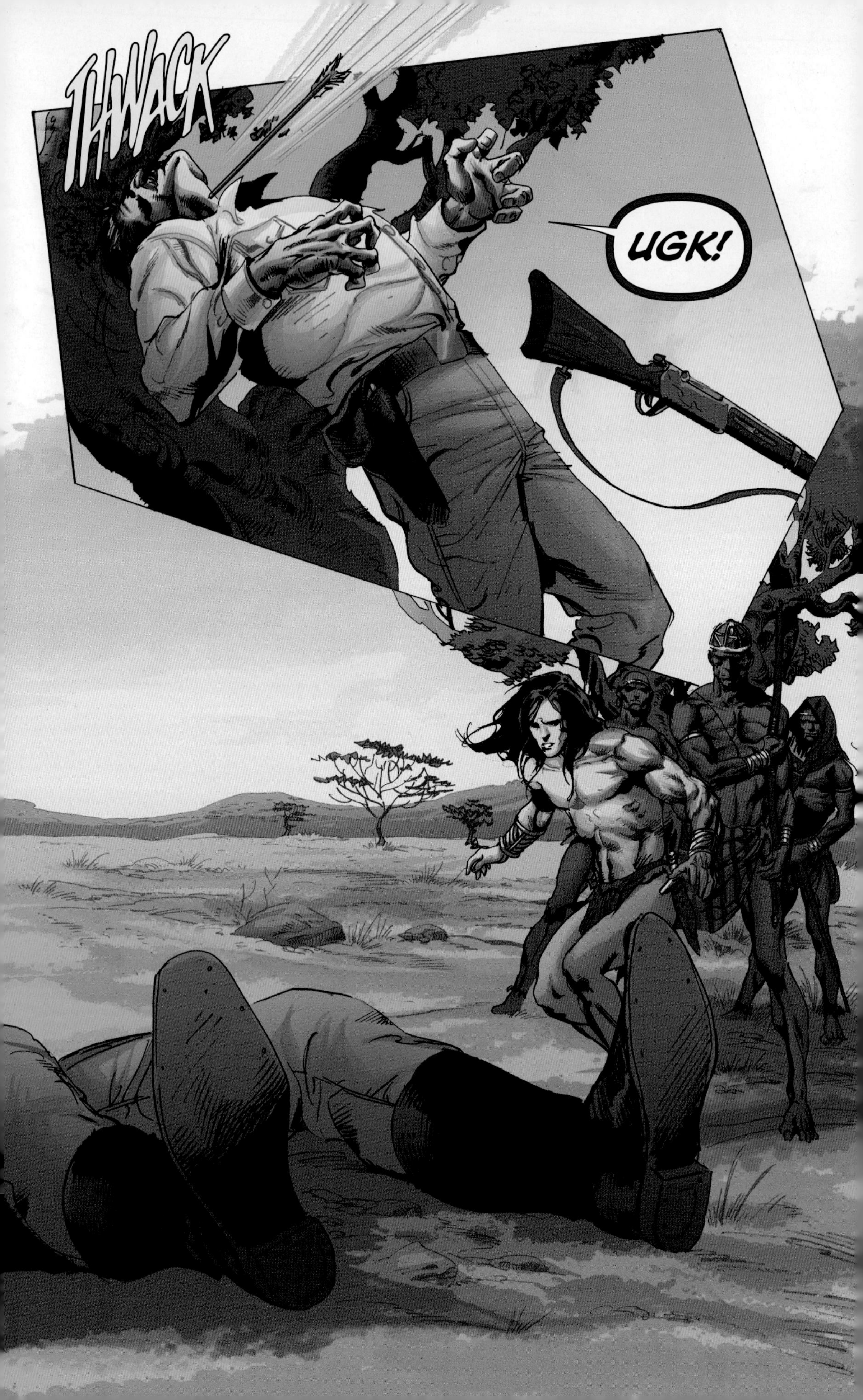
THWACK
UGK!

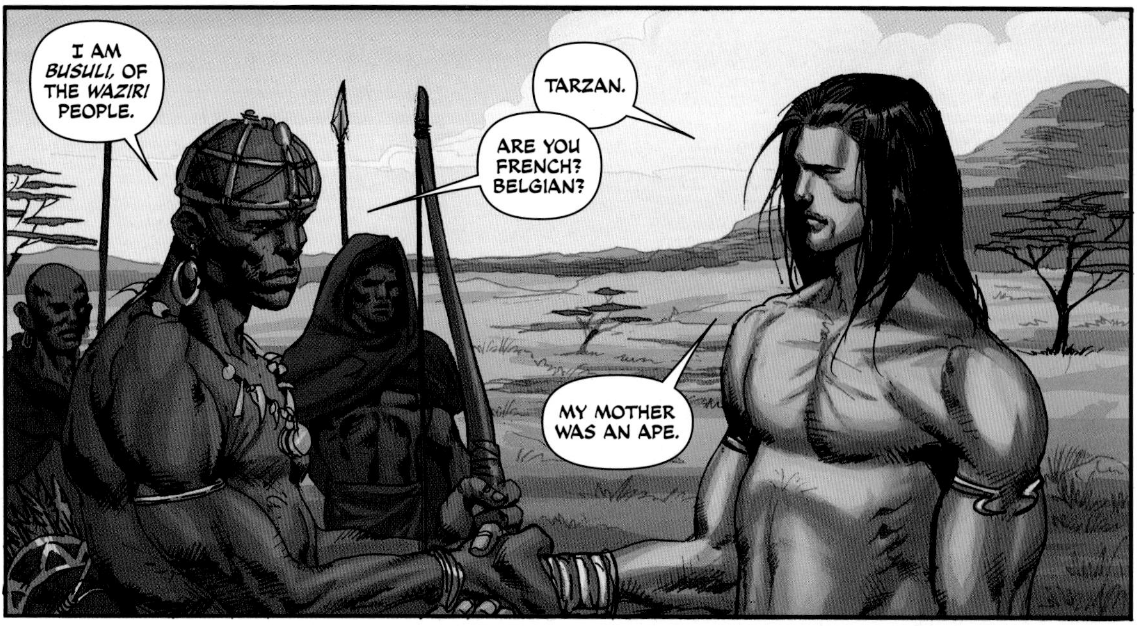
I AM *BUSULI,* OF THE *WAZIRI* PEOPLE.
TARZAN.
ARE YOU FRENCH? BELGIAN?
MY MOTHER WAS AN APE.

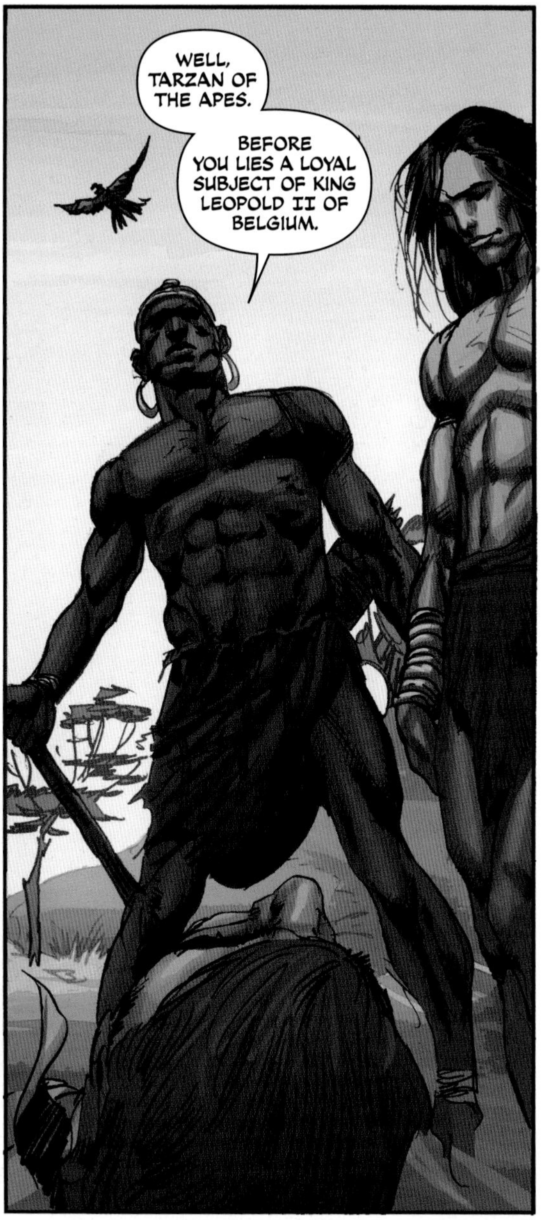
WELL, TARZAN OF THE APES.
BEFORE YOU LIES A LOYAL SUBJECT OF KING LEOPOLD II OF BELGIUM.

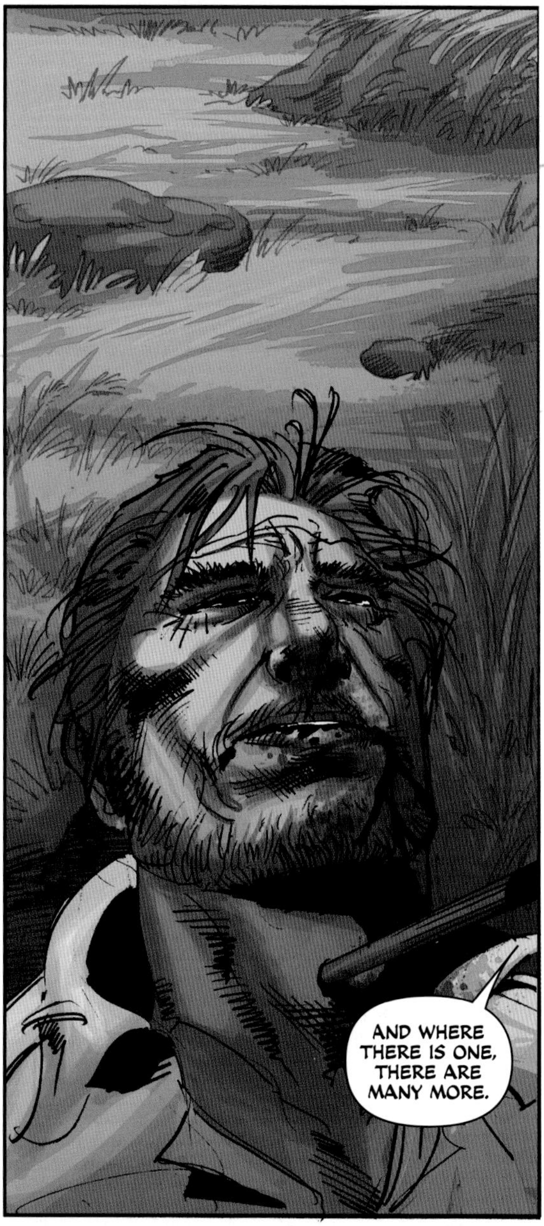
AND WHERE THERE IS ONE, THERE ARE MANY MORE.

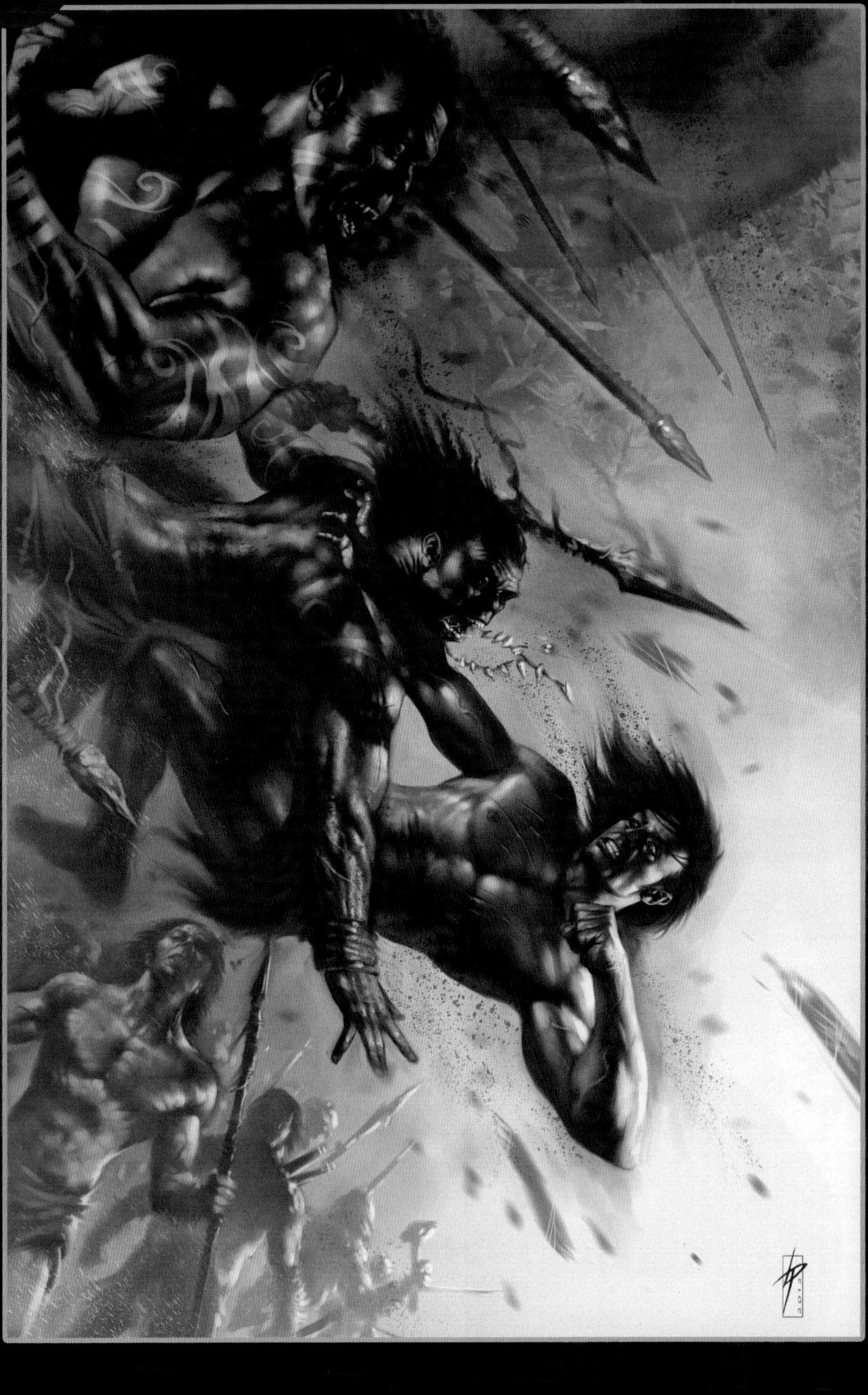

COVER BY LUCIO PARRILLO

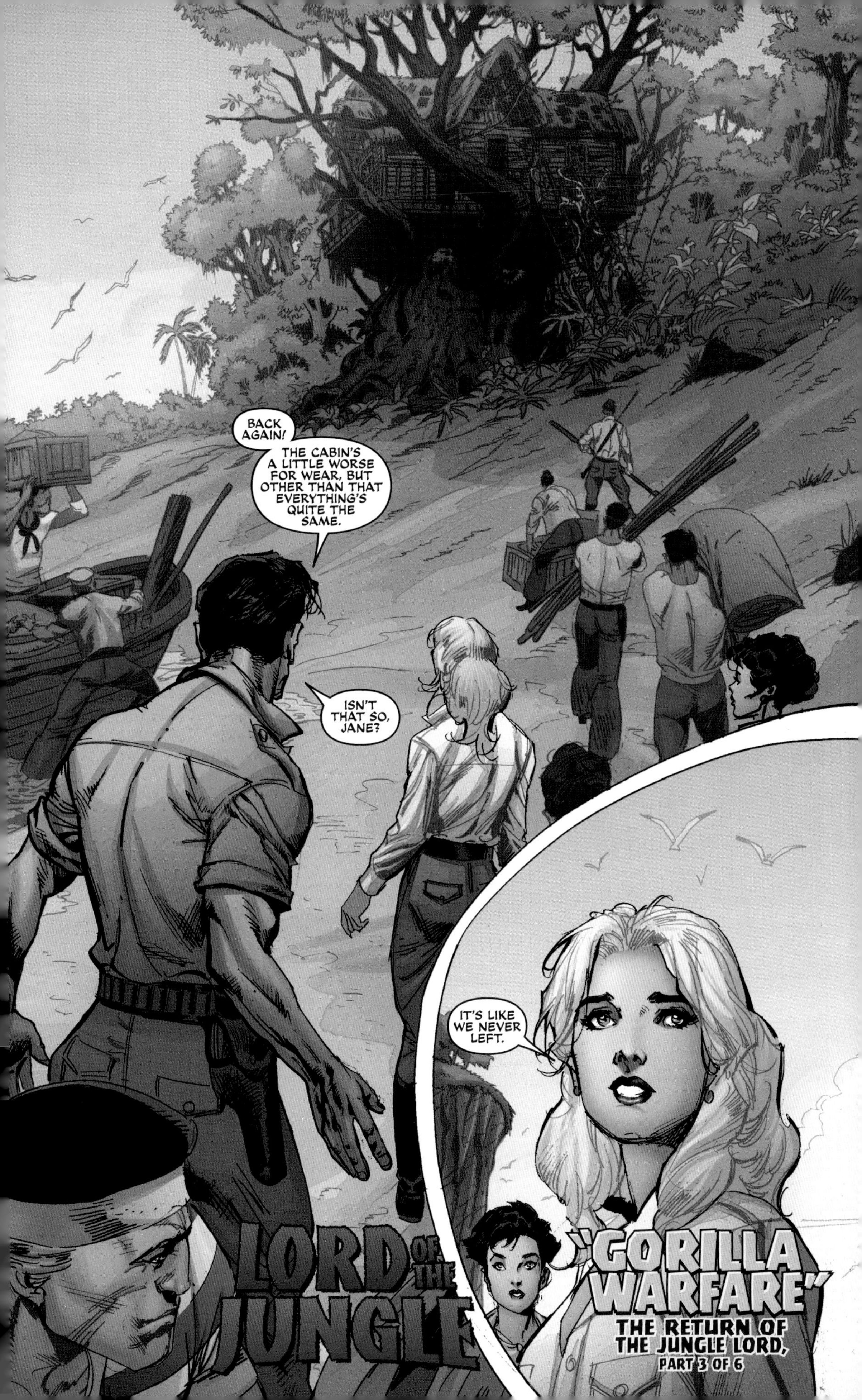
BACK AGAIN!
THE CABIN'S A LITTLE WORSE FOR WEAR, BUT OTHER THAN THAT EVERYTHING'S QUITE THE SAME.
ISN'T THAT SO, JANE?
IT'S LIKE WE NEVER LEFT.
LORD OF THE JUNGLE
"GORILLA WARFARE"
THE RETURN OF THE JUNGLE LORD,
PART 3 OF 6

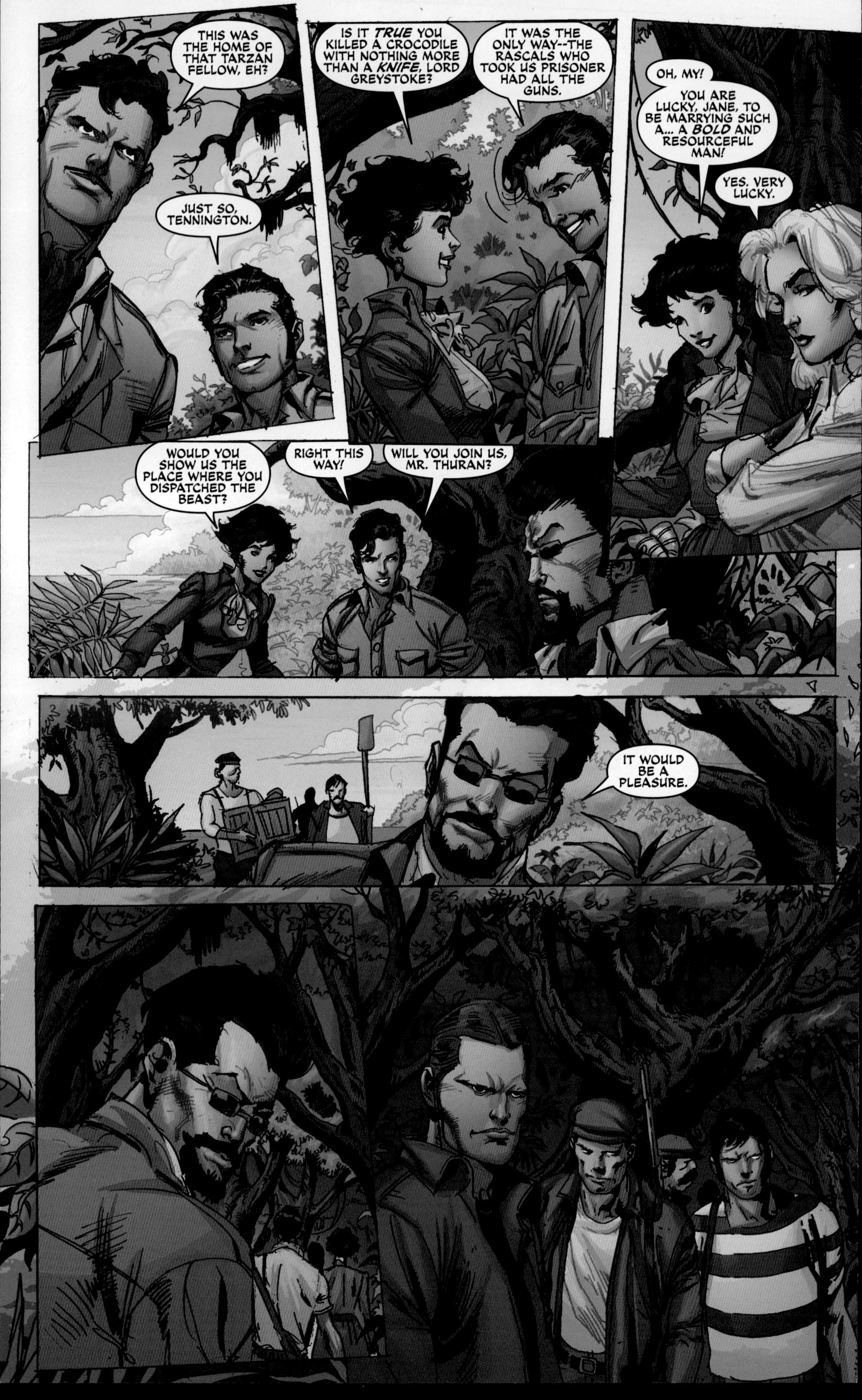
THIS WAS THE HOME OF THAT TARZAN FELLOW, EH?
JUST SO, TENNINGTON.
IS IT TRUE YOU KILLED A CROCODILE WITH NOTHING MORE THAN A KNIFE, LORD GREYSTOKE?
IT WAS THE ONLY WAY--THE RASCALS WHO TOOK US PRISONER HAD ALL THE GUNS.
OH, MY!
YOU ARE LUCKY, JANE, TO BE MARRYING SUCH A... A BOLD AND RESOURCEFUL MAN!
YES. VERY LUCKY.
WOULD YOU SHOW US THE PLACE WHERE YOU DISPATCHED THE BEAST?
RIGHT THIS WAY!
WILL YOU JOIN US, MR. THURAN?
IT WOULD BE A PLEASURE.

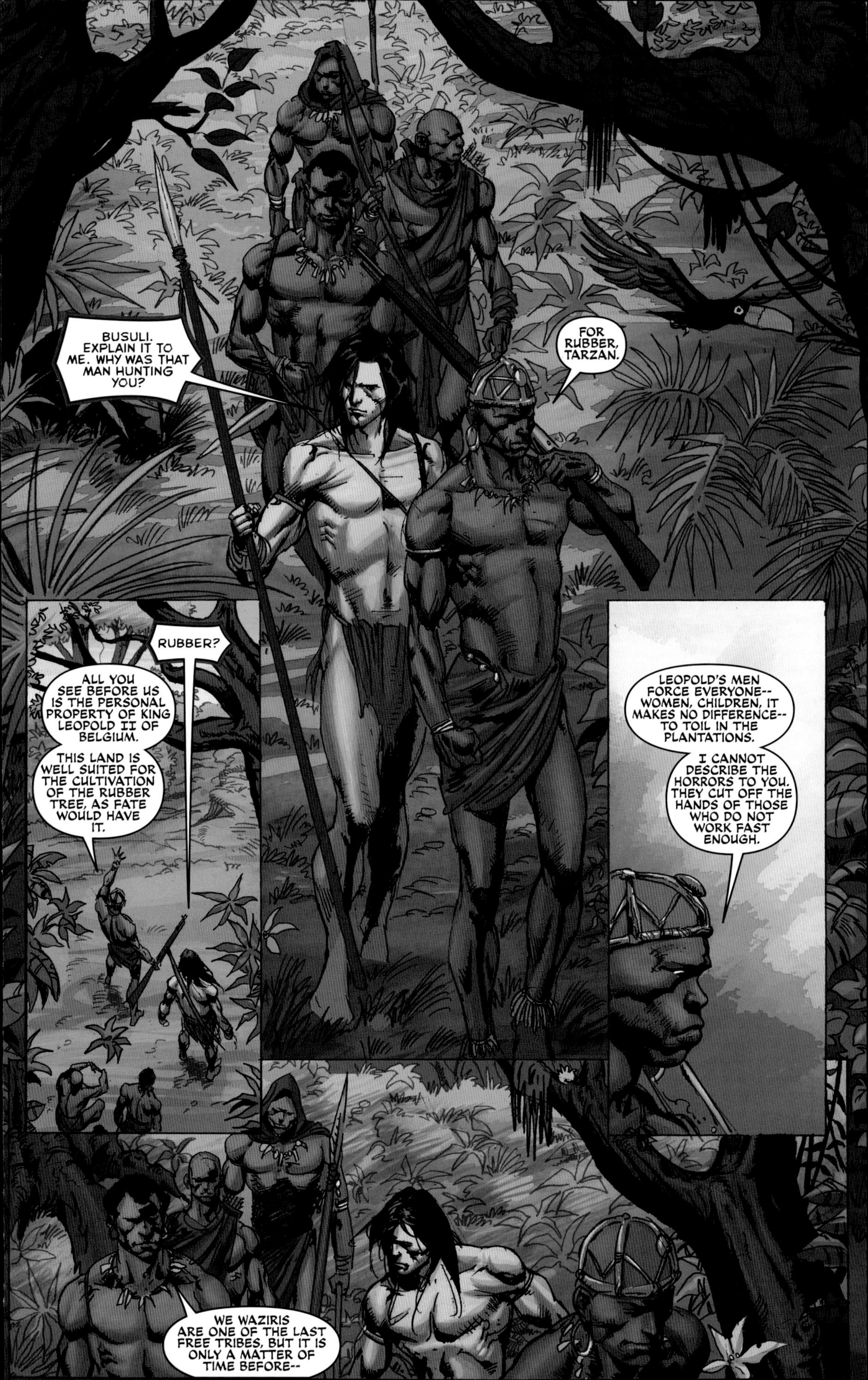

BUSULI. EXPLAIN IT TO ME. WHY WAS THAT MAN HUNTING YOU?
FOR RUBBER, TARZAN.
RUBBER?
ALL YOU SEE BEFORE US IS THE PERSONAL PROPERTY OF KING LEOPOLD II OF BELGIUM.
THIS LAND IS WELL SUITED FOR THE CULTIVATION OF THE RUBBER TREE, AS FATE WOULD HAVE IT.
LEOPOLD'S MEN FORCE EVERYONE--WOMEN, CHILDREN, IT MAKES NO DIFFERENCE--TO TOIL IN THE PLANTATIONS.
I CANNOT DESCRIBE THE HORRORS TO YOU. THEY CUT OFF THE HANDS OF THOSE WHO DO NOT WORK FAST ENOUGH.
WE WAZIRIS ARE ONE OF THE LAST FREE TRIBES, BUT IT IS ONLY A MATTER OF TIME BEFORE--

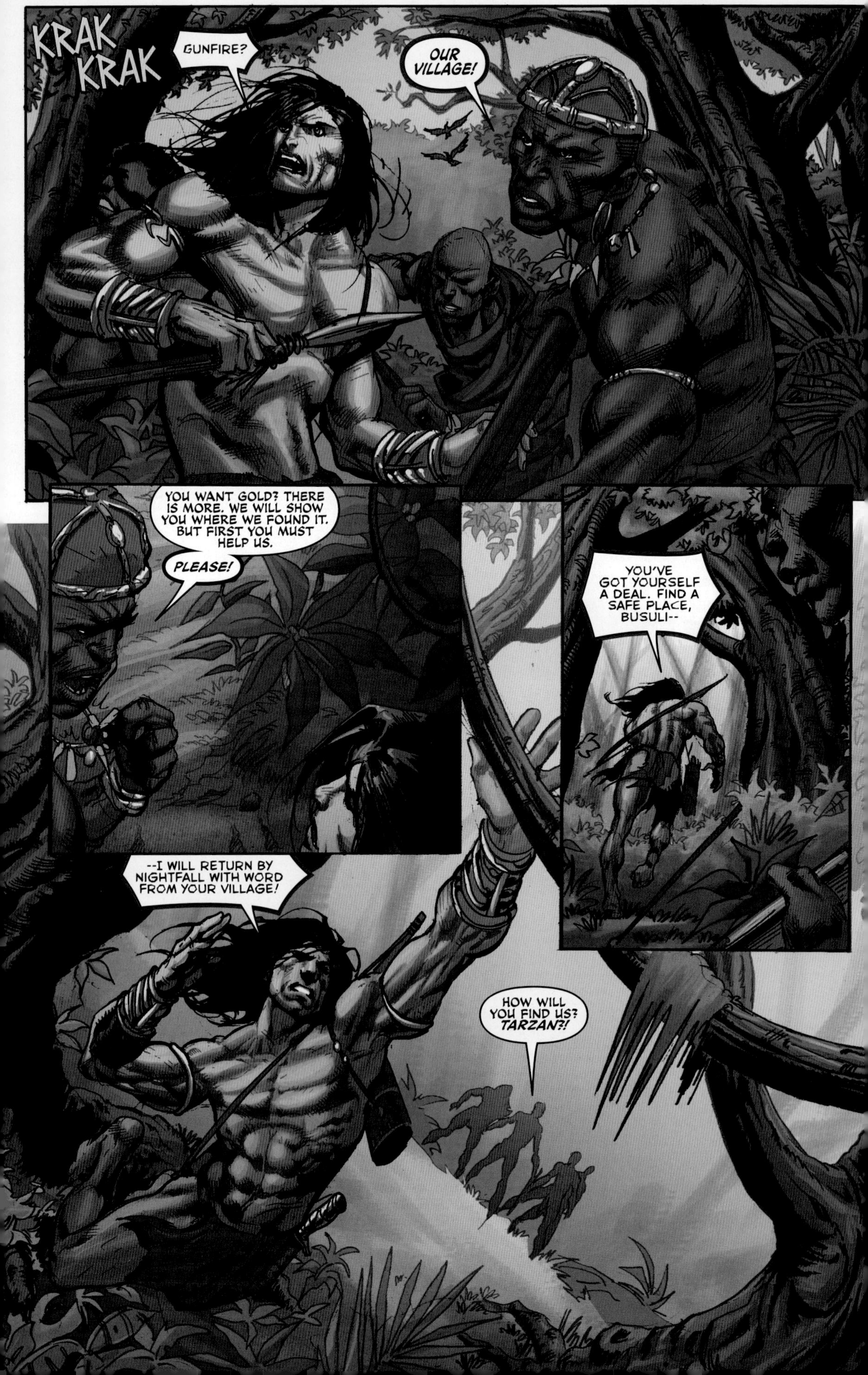
KRAK KRAK
GUNFIRE?
OUR VILLAGE!
YOU WANT GOLD? THERE IS MORE. WE WILL SHOW YOU WHERE WE FOUND IT. BUT FIRST YOU MUST HELP US.
PLEASE!
YOU'VE GOT YOURSELF A DEAL. FIND A SAFE PLACE, BUSULI--
--I WILL RETURN BY NIGHTFALL WITH WORD FROM YOUR VILLAGE!
HOW WILL YOU FIND US? TARZAN?!

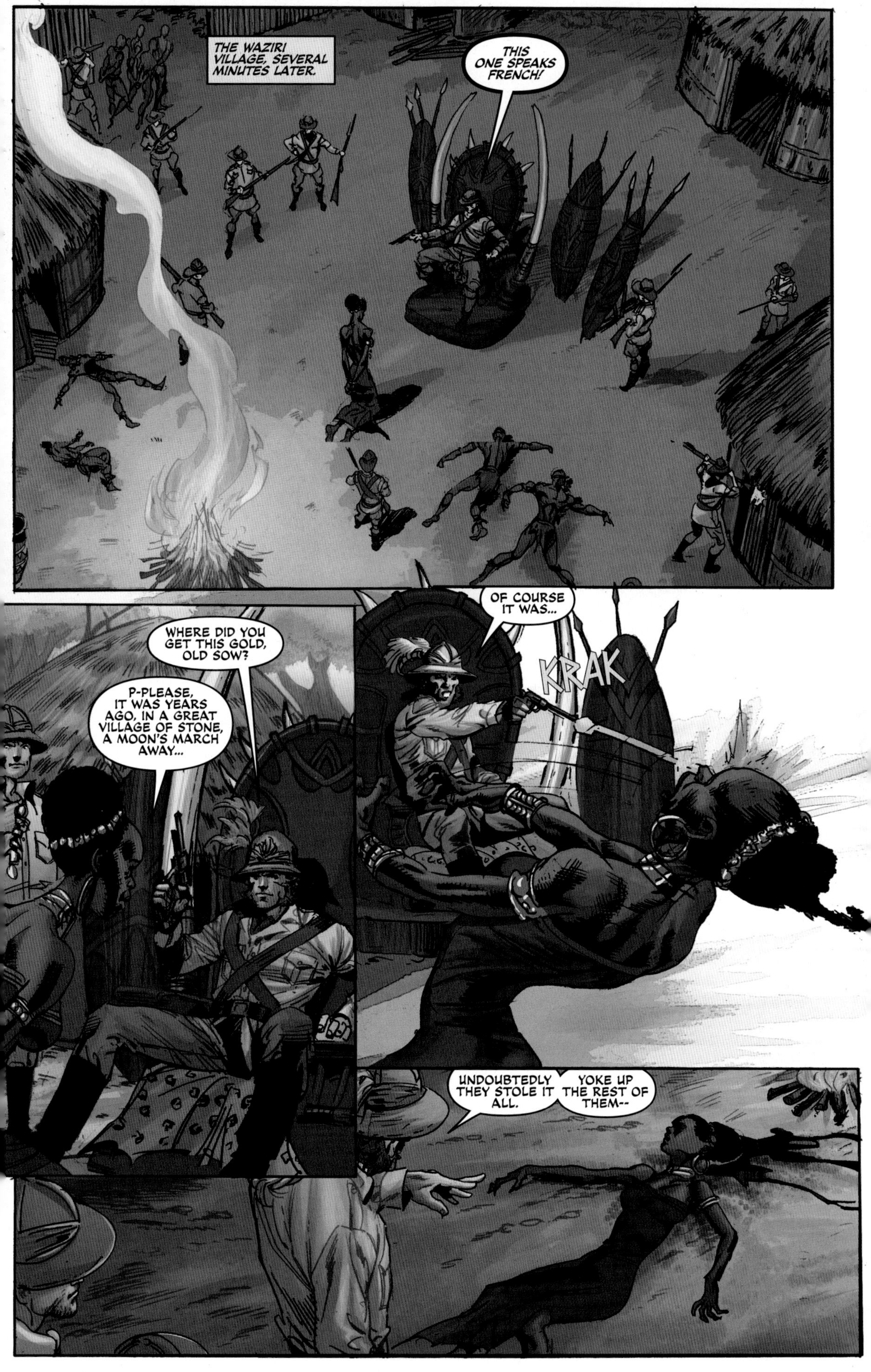
THE WAZIRI VILLAGE, SEVERAL MINUTES LATER.
THIS ONE SPEAKS FRENCH!
WHERE DID YOU GET THIS GOLD, OLD SOW?
P-PLEASE, IT WAS YEARS AGO, IN A GREAT VILLAGE OF STONE, A MOON'S MARCH AWAY...
OF COURSE IT WAS...
KRAK
UNDOUBTEDLY THEY STOLE IT ALL.
YOKE UP THE REST OF THEM--

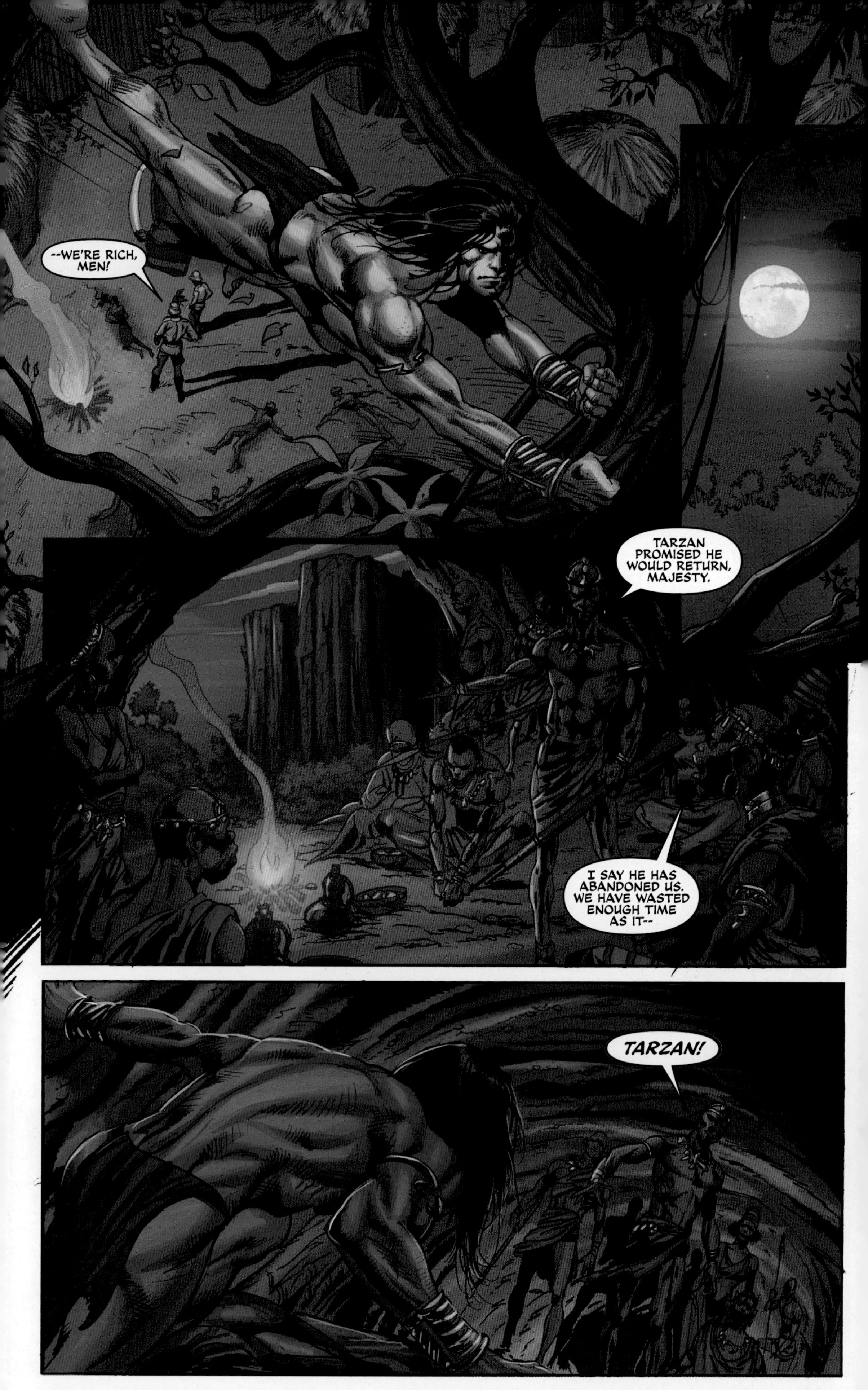
--WE'RE RICH, MEN!
TARZAN PROMISED HE WOULD RETURN, MAJESTY.
I SAY HE HAS ABANDONED US. WE HAVE WASTED ENOUGH TIME AS IT--
TARZAN!

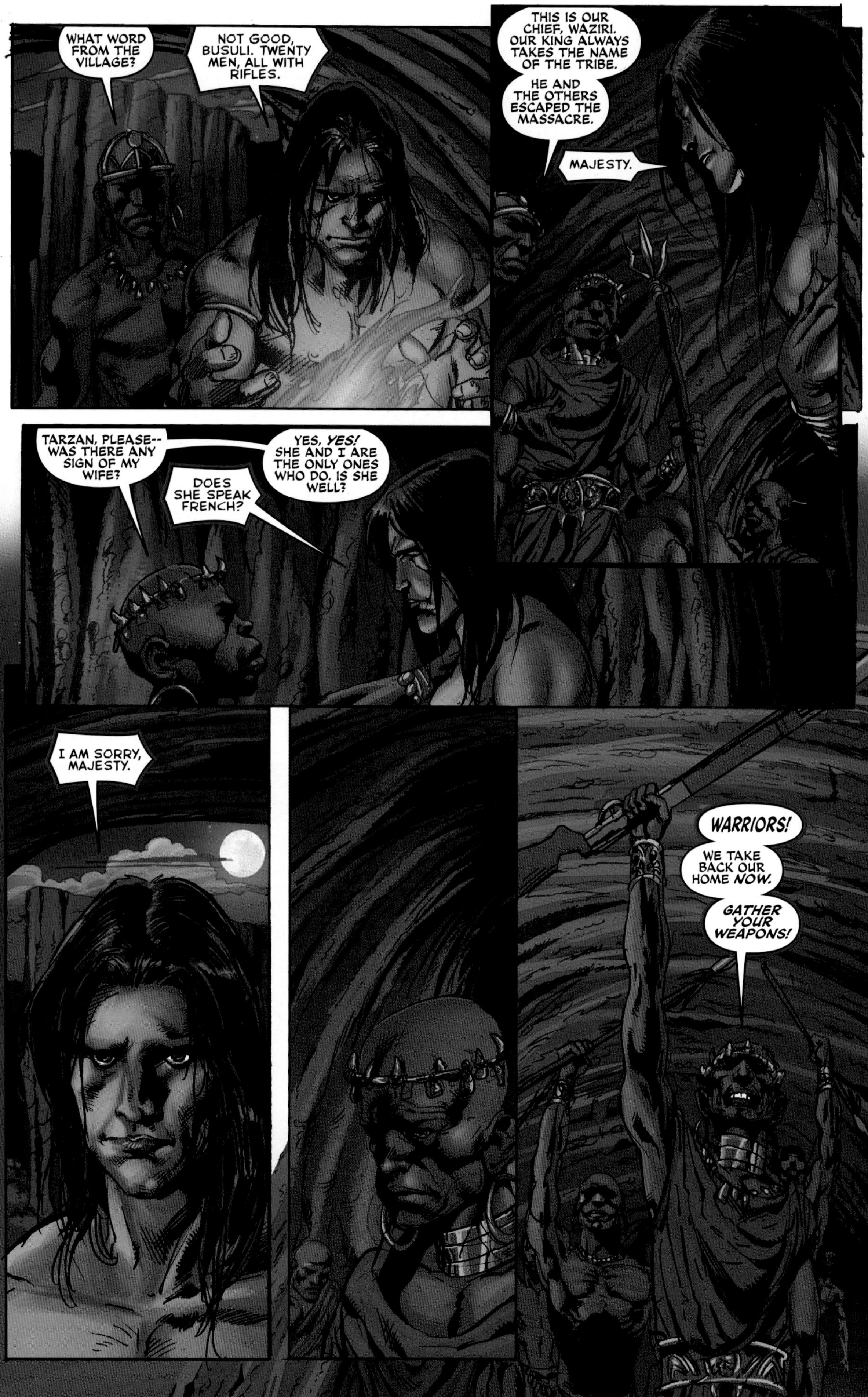

WHAT WORD FROM THE VILLAGE?
NOT GOOD, BUSULI. TWENTY MEN, ALL WITH RIFLES.
THIS IS OUR CHIEF, WAZIRI. OUR KING ALWAYS TAKES THE NAME OF THE TRIBE.
HE AND THE OTHERS ESCAPED THE MASSACRE.
MAJESTY.
TARZAN, PLEASE-- WAS THERE ANY SIGN OF MY WIFE?
DOES SHE SPEAK FRENCH?
YES, *YES!* SHE AND I ARE THE ONLY ONES WHO DO. IS SHE WELL?
I AM SORRY, MAJESTY.
WARRIORS!
WE TAKE BACK OUR HOME *NOW.*
GATHER YOUR WEAPONS!

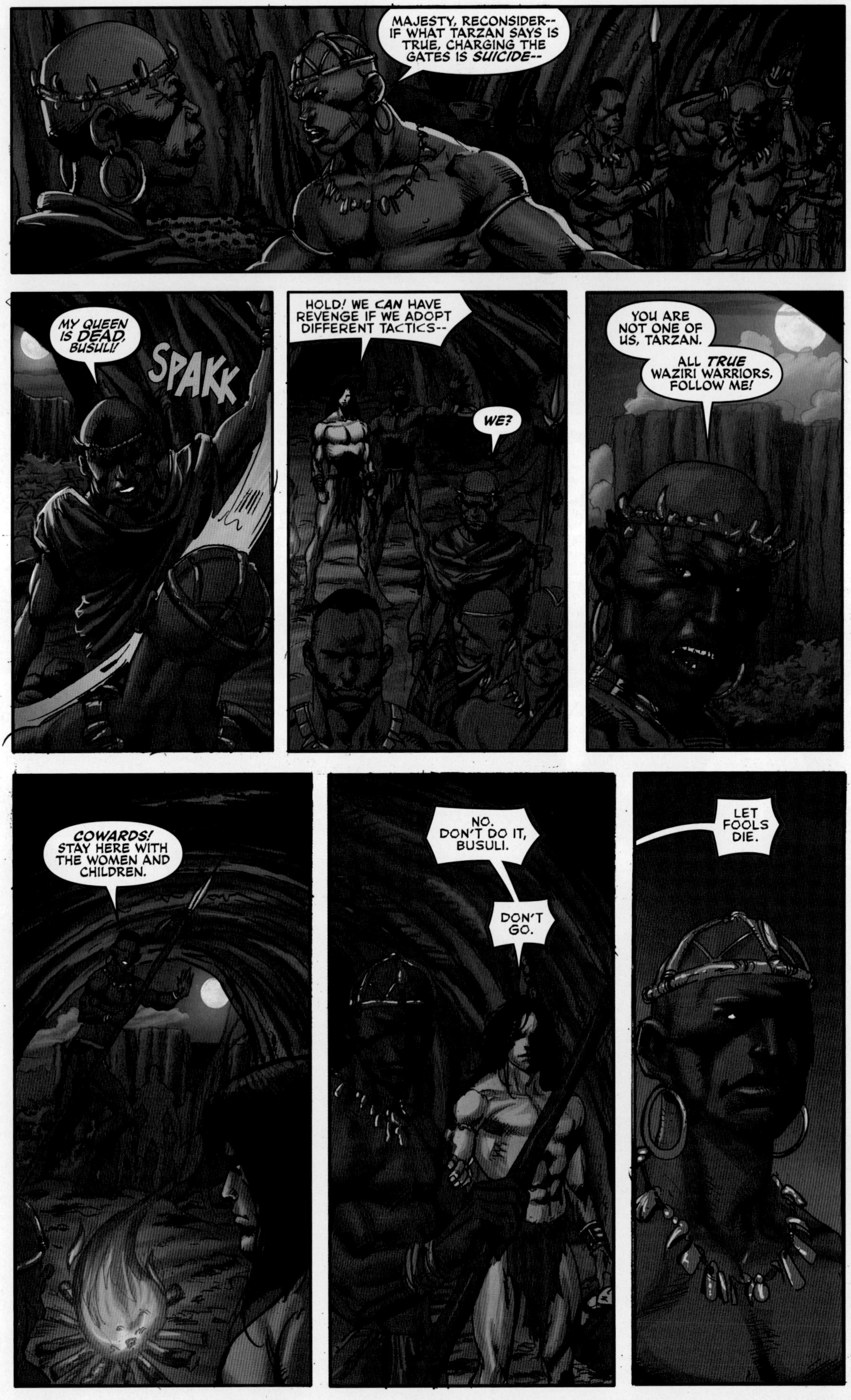
MAJESTY, RECONSIDER-- IF WHAT TARZAN SAYS IS TRUE, CHARGING THE GATES IS SUICIDE--
MY QUEEN IS DEAD, BUSULI!
SPAKK
HOLD! WE CAN HAVE REVENGE IF WE ADOPT DIFFERENT TACTICS--
WE?
YOU ARE NOT ONE OF US, TARZAN.
ALL TRUE WAZIRI WARRIORS, FOLLOW ME!
COWARDS! STAY HERE WITH THE WOMEN AND CHILDREN.
NO. DON'T DO IT, BUSULI.
DON'T GO.
LET FOOLS DIE.

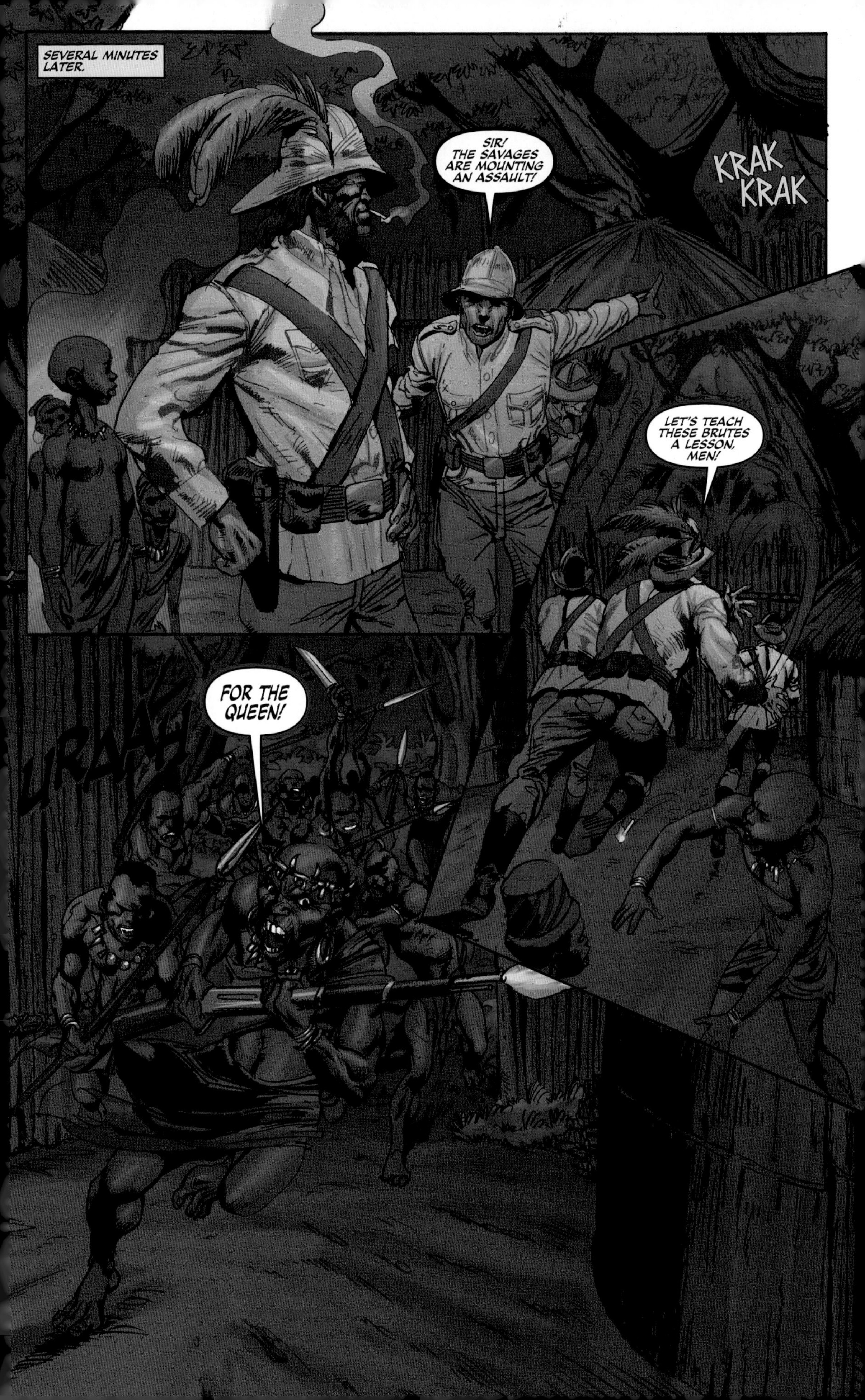
SEVERAL MINUTES LATER.
SIR! THE SAVAGES ARE MOUNTING AN ASSAULT!
KRAK KRAK
LET'S TEACH THESE BRUTES A LESSON, MEN!
FOR THE QUEEN!
URAAH

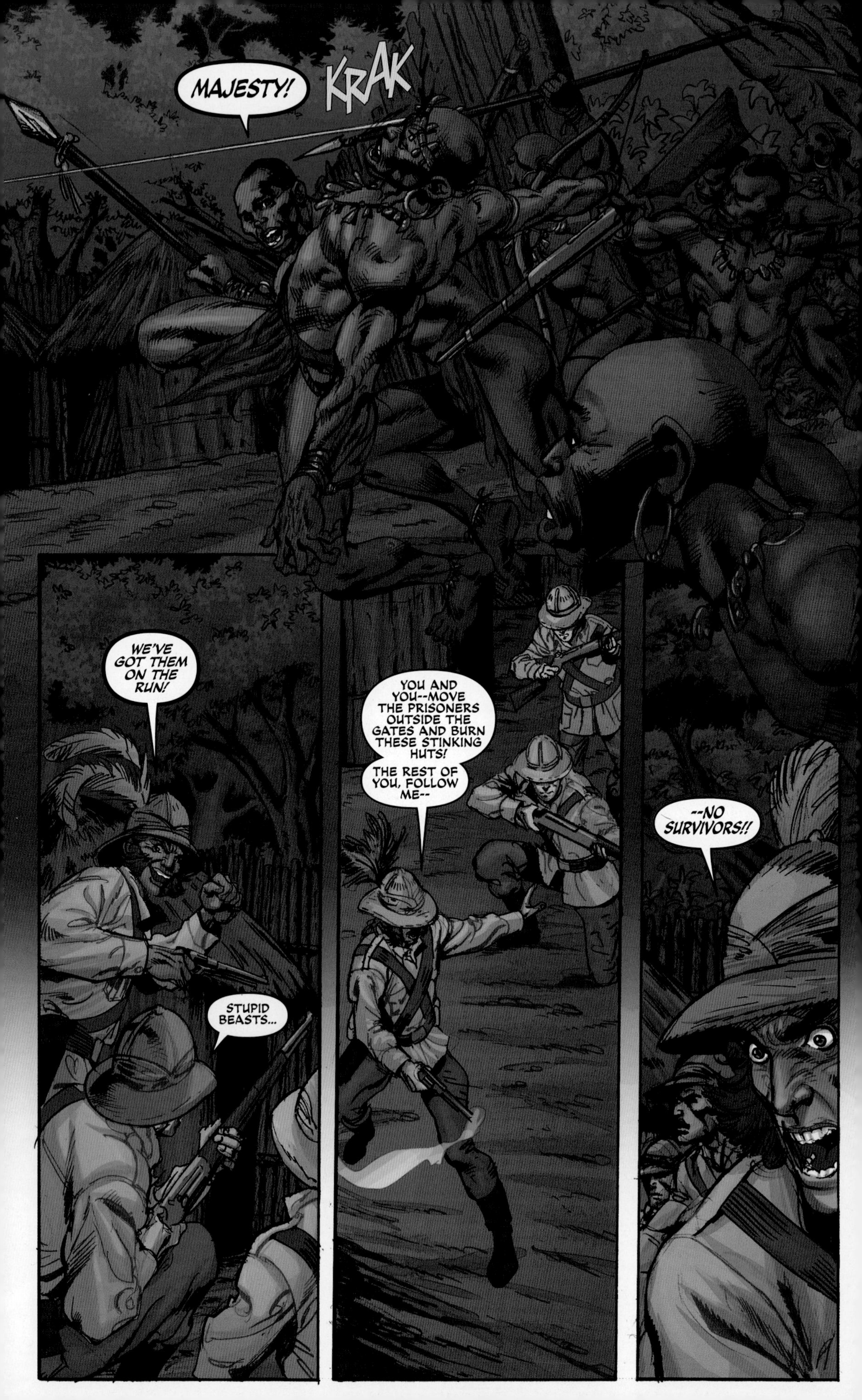
MAJESTY!
KRAK
WE'VE GOT THEM ON THE RUN!
STUPID BEASTS...
YOU AND YOU--MOVE THE PRISONERS OUTSIDE THE GATES AND BURN THESE STINKING HUTS!
THE REST OF YOU, FOLLOW ME--
--NO SURVIVORS!!

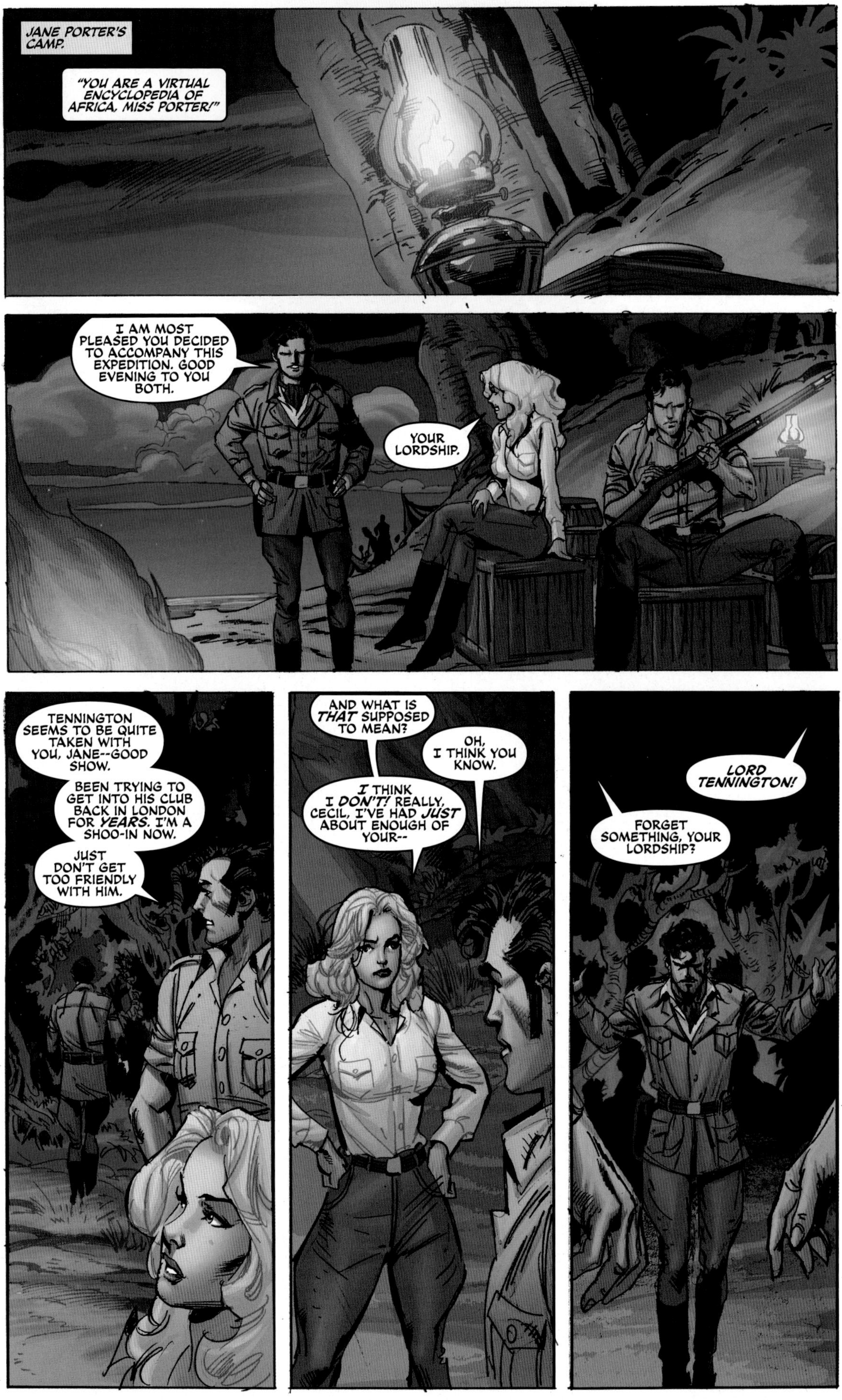
JANE PORTER'S CAMP.
"YOU ARE A VIRTUAL ENCYCLOPEDIA OF AFRICA, MISS PORTER!"
I AM MOST PLEASED YOU DECIDED TO ACCOMPANY THIS EXPEDITION. GOOD EVENING TO YOU BOTH.
YOUR LORDSHIP.
TENNINGTON SEEMS TO BE QUITE TAKEN WITH YOU, JANE--GOOD SHOW.
BEEN TRYING TO GET INTO HIS CLUB BACK IN LONDON FOR *YEARS*. I'M A SHOO-IN NOW.
JUST DON'T GET TOO FRIENDLY WITH HIM.
AND WHAT IS *THAT* SUPPOSED TO MEAN?
OH, I THINK YOU KNOW.
I THINK I *DON'T!* REALLY, CECIL, I'VE HAD *JUST* ABOUT ENOUGH OF YOUR--
LORD TENNINGTON!
FORGET SOMETHING, YOUR LORDSHIP?

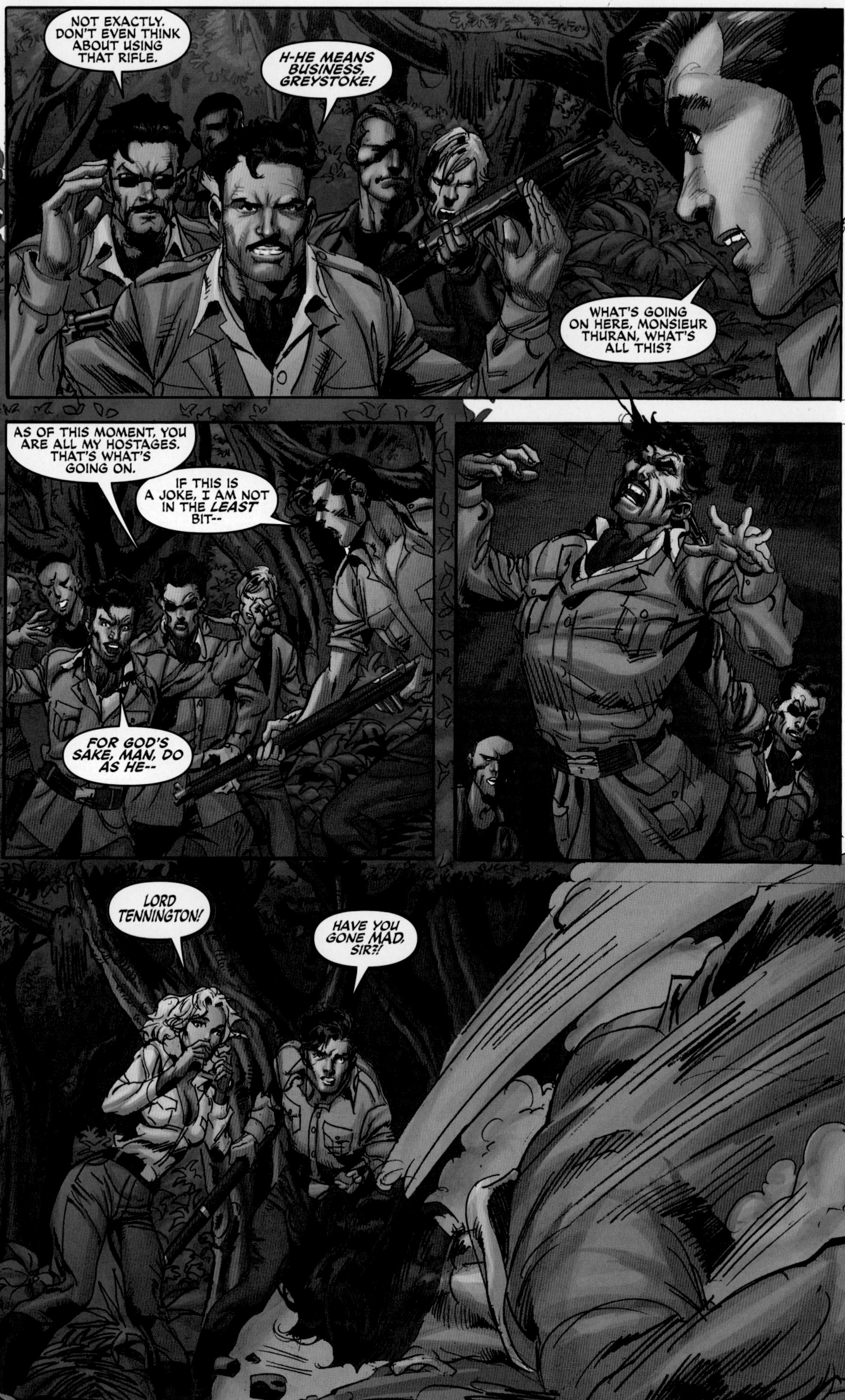

NOT EXACTLY. DON'T EVEN THINK ABOUT USING THAT RIFLE.
H-HE MEANS BUSINESS, GREYSTOKE!
WHAT'S GOING ON HERE, MONSIEUR THURAN, WHAT'S ALL THIS?
AS OF THIS MOMENT, YOU ARE ALL MY HOSTAGES. THAT'S WHAT'S GOING ON.
IF THIS IS A JOKE, I AM NOT IN THE *LEAST* BIT--
FOR GOD'S SAKE, MAN, DO AS HE--
LORD TENNINGTON!
HAVE YOU GONE MAD, SIR?!

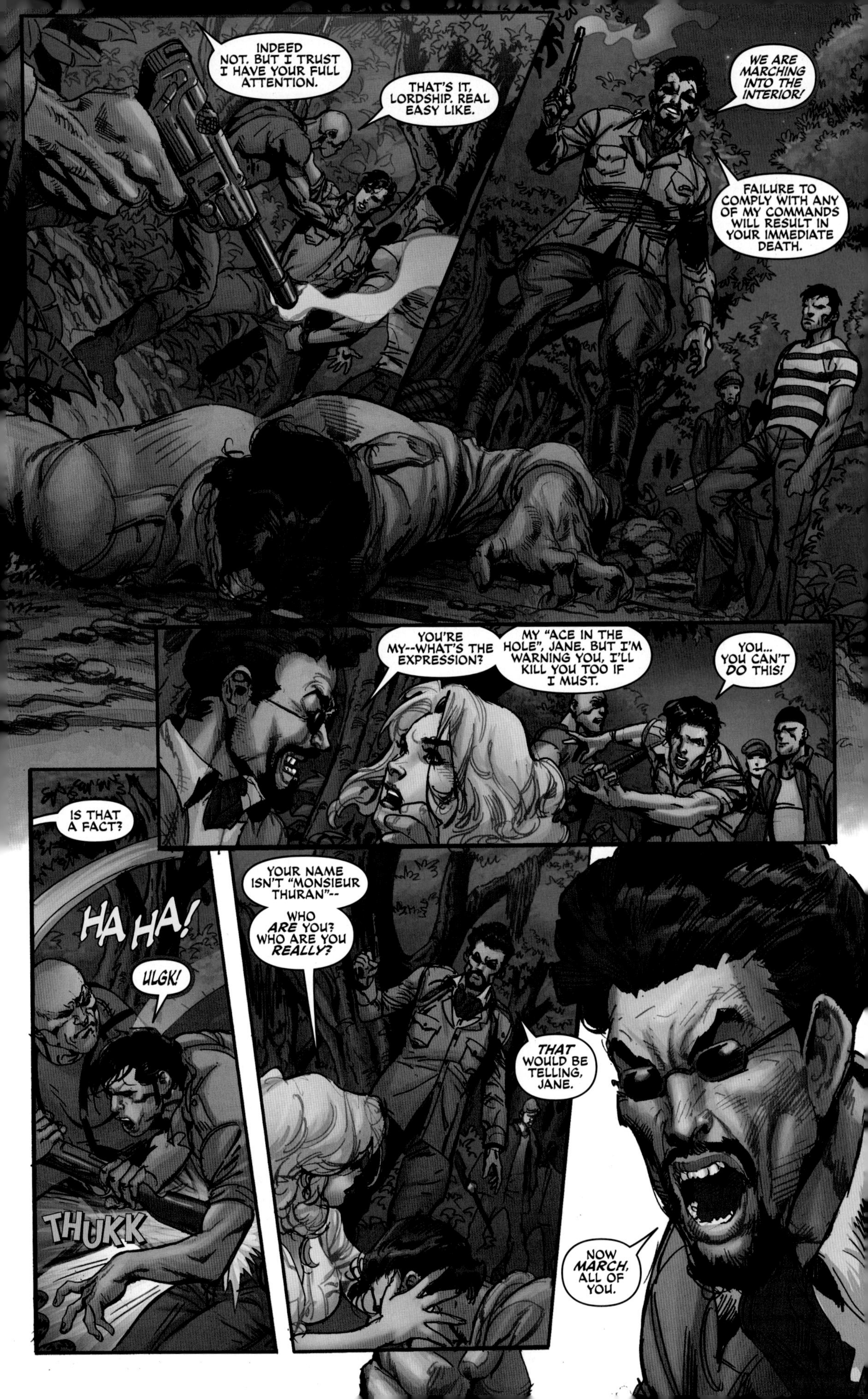
INDEED NOT. BUT I TRUST I HAVE YOUR FULL ATTENTION.
THAT'S IT, LORDSHIP. REAL EASY LIKE.
WE ARE MARCHING INTO THE INTERIOR!
FAILURE TO COMPLY WITH ANY OF MY COMMANDS WILL RESULT IN YOUR IMMEDIATE DEATH.
YOU'RE MY--WHAT'S THE EXPRESSION?
MY "ACE IN THE HOLE", JANE. BUT I'M WARNING YOU, I'LL KILL YOU TOO IF I MUST.
YOU... YOU CAN'T DO THIS!
IS THAT A FACT?
HA HA!
ULGK!
THUKK
YOUR NAME ISN'T "MONSIEUR THURAN"--
WHO ARE YOU? WHO ARE YOU REALLY?
THAT WOULD BE TELLING, JANE.
NOW MARCH, ALL OF YOU.

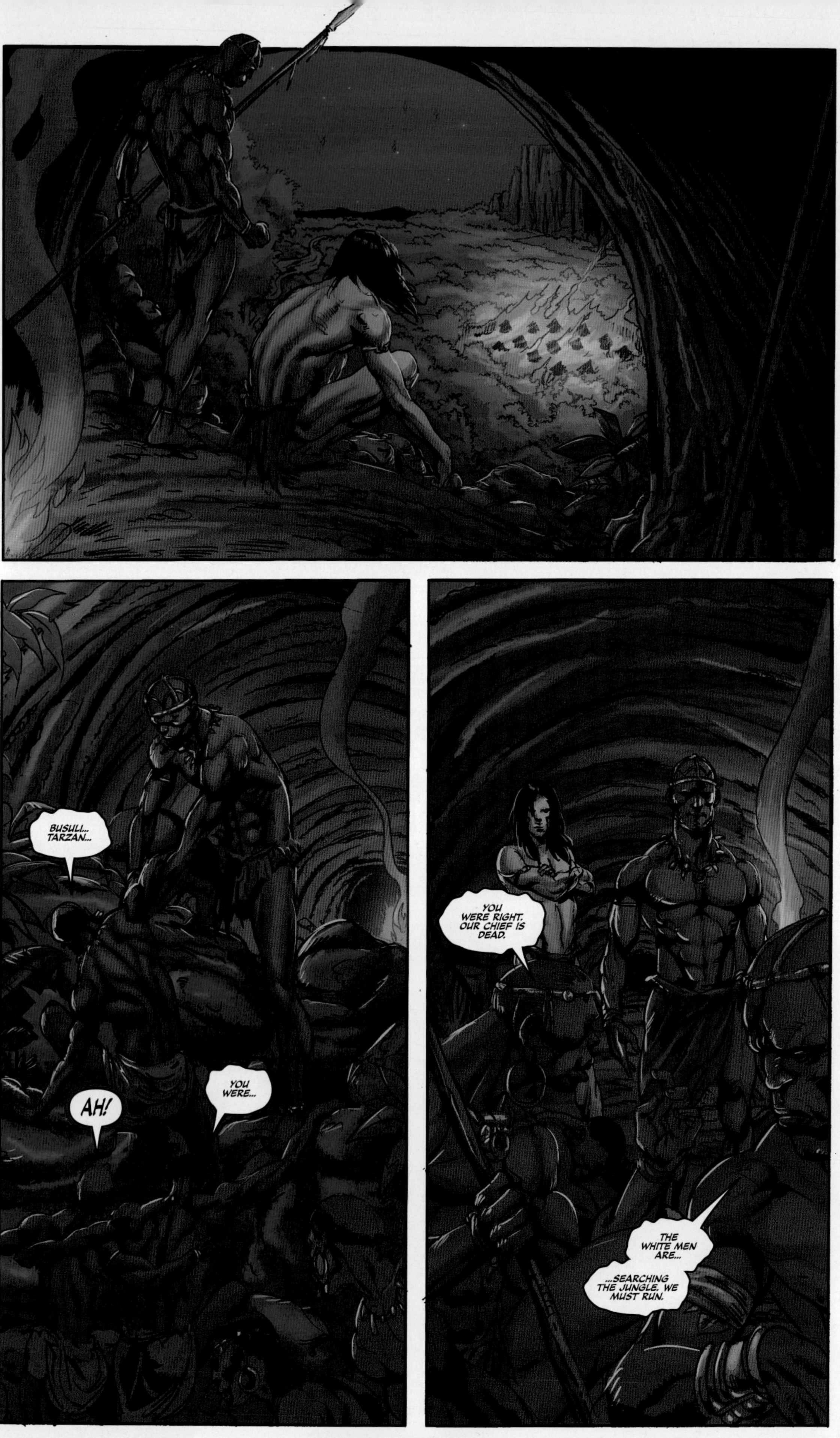
BUSULI... TARZAN...
AH!
YOU WERE...
YOU WERE RIGHT. OUR CHIEF IS DEAD.
THE WHITE MEN ARE...
...SEARCHING THE JUNGLE. WE MUST RUN.

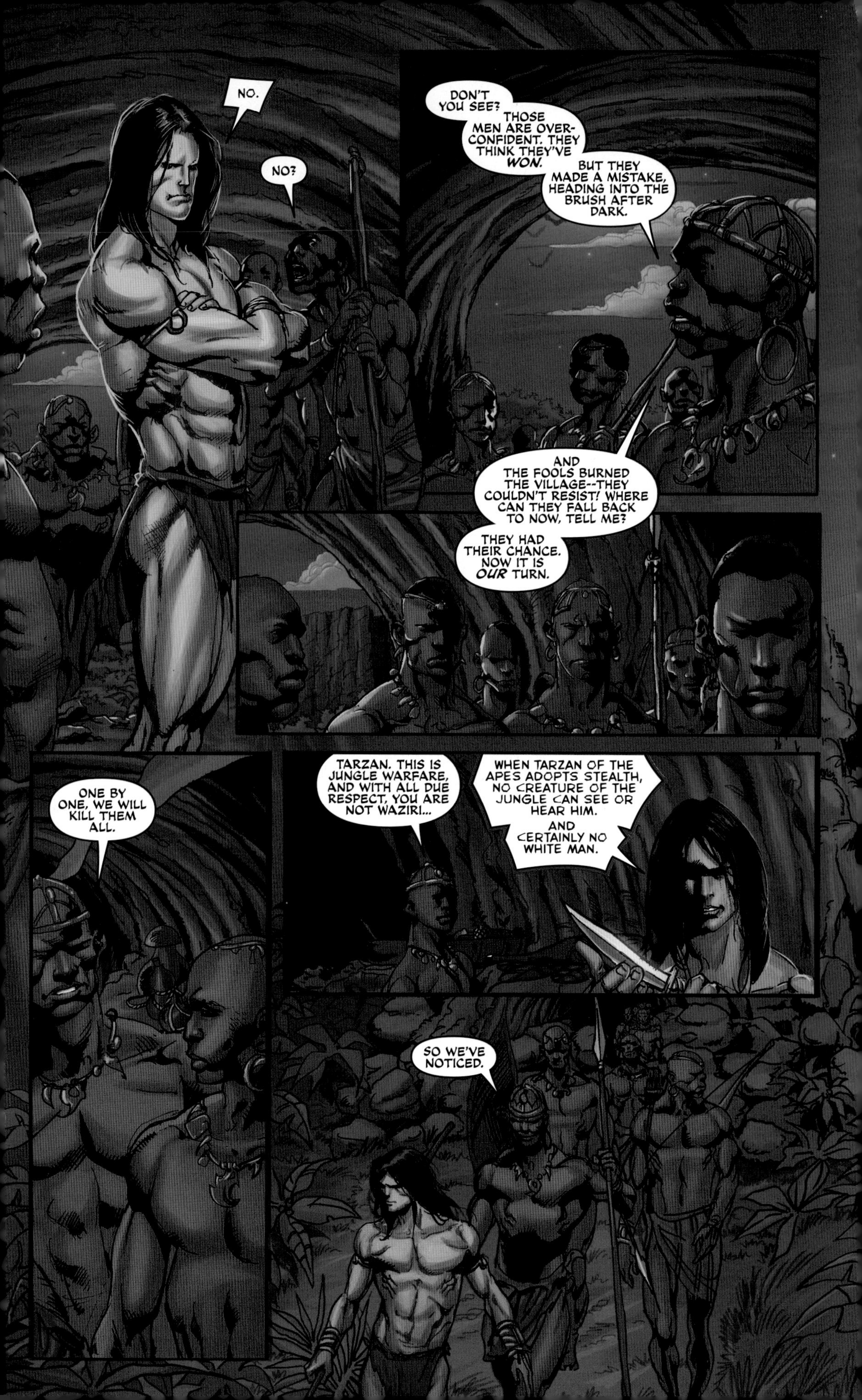
NO.
NO?
DON'T YOU SEE? THOSE MEN ARE OVER-CONFIDENT. THEY THINK THEY'VE *WON.*
BUT THEY MADE A MISTAKE, HEADING INTO THE BRUSH AFTER DARK.
AND THE FOOLS BURNED THE VILLAGE--THEY COULDN'T RESIST! WHERE CAN THEY FALL BACK TO NOW, TELL ME?
THEY HAD THEIR CHANCE. NOW IT IS *OUR* TURN.
ONE BY ONE, WE WILL KILL THEM ALL.
TARZAN. THIS IS JUNGLE WARFARE, AND WITH ALL DUE RESPECT, YOU ARE NOT WAZIRI...
WHEN TARZAN OF THE APES ADOPTS STEALTH, NO CREATURE OF THE JUNGLE CAN SEE OR HEAR HIM.
AND CERTAINLY NO WHITE MAN.
SO WE'VE NOTICED.

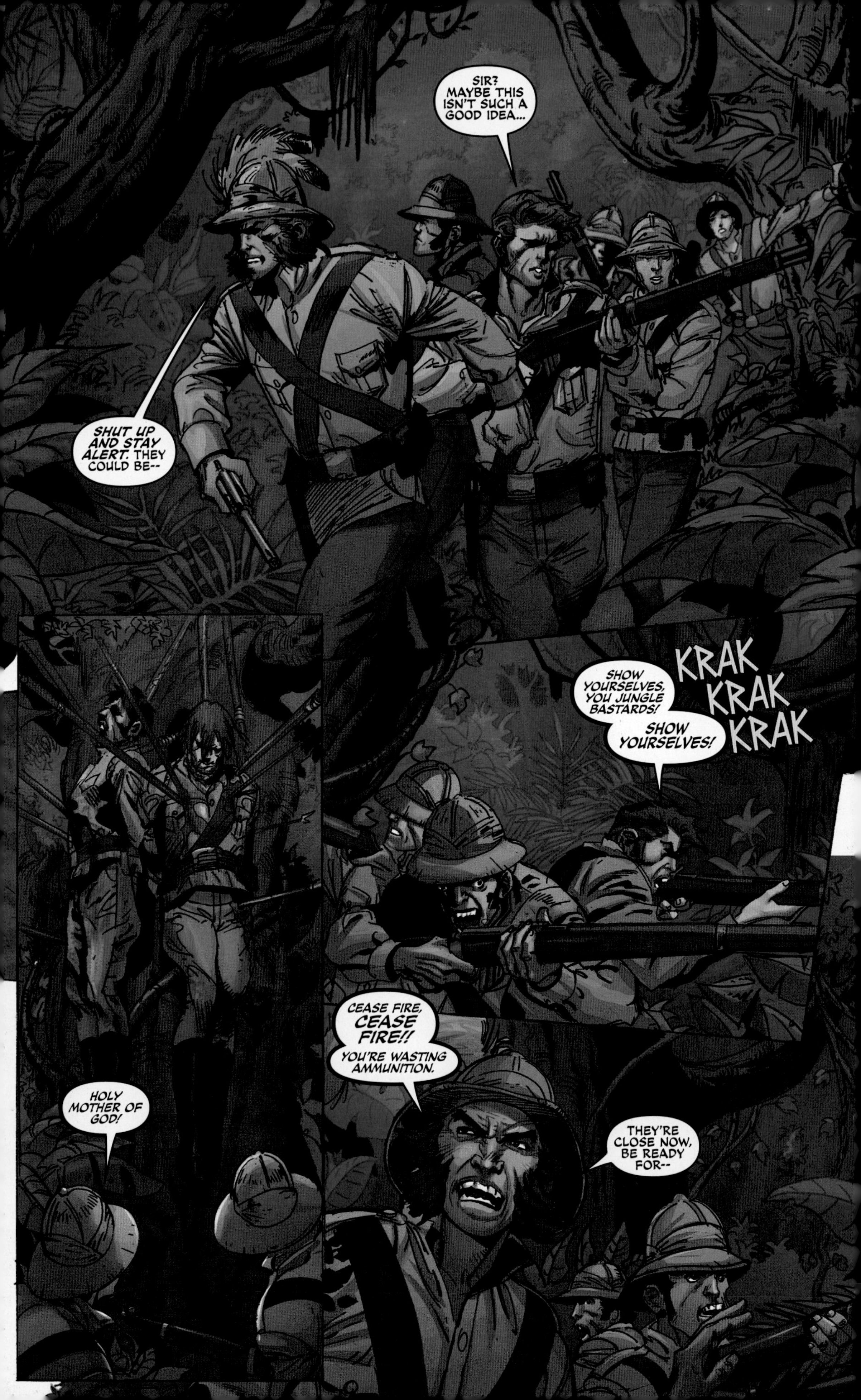
SIR? MAYBE THIS ISN'T SUCH A GOOD IDEA...
SHUT UP AND STAY ALERT. THEY COULD BE--
SHOW YOURSELVES, YOU JUNGLE BASTARDS!
SHOW YOURSELVES!
KRAK KRAK KRAK
HOLY MOTHER OF GOD!
CEASE FIRE, CEASE FIRE!!
YOU'RE WASTING AMMUNITION.
THEY'RE CLOSE NOW, BE READY FOR--

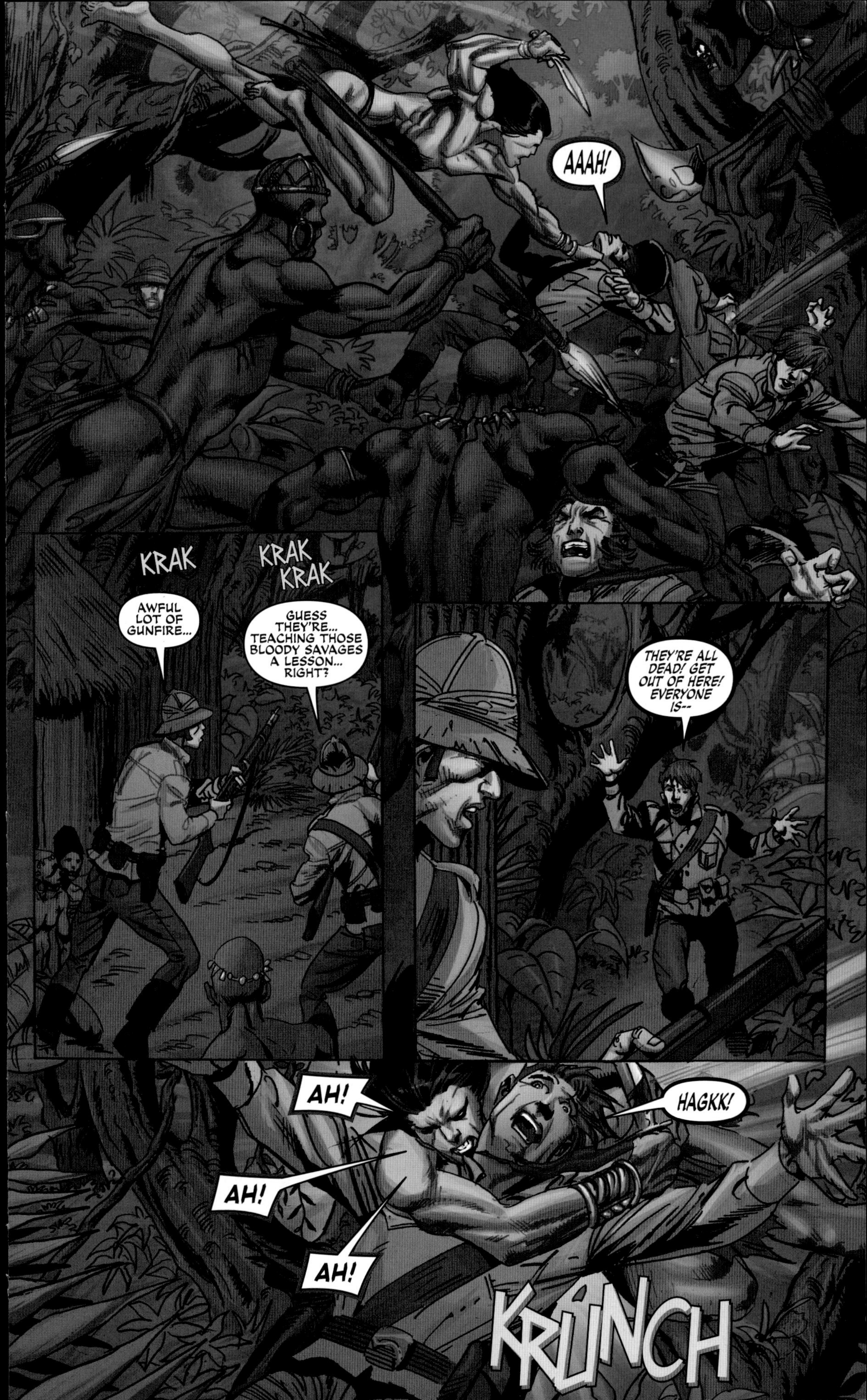
AAAH!
KRAK
KRAK KRAK
AWFUL LOT OF GUNFIRE...
GUESS THEY'RE... TEACHING THOSE BLOODY SAVAGES A LESSON... RIGHT?
THEY'RE ALL DEAD! GET OUT OF HERE! EVERYONE IS--
AH!
HAGKK!
AH!
AH!
KRUNCH

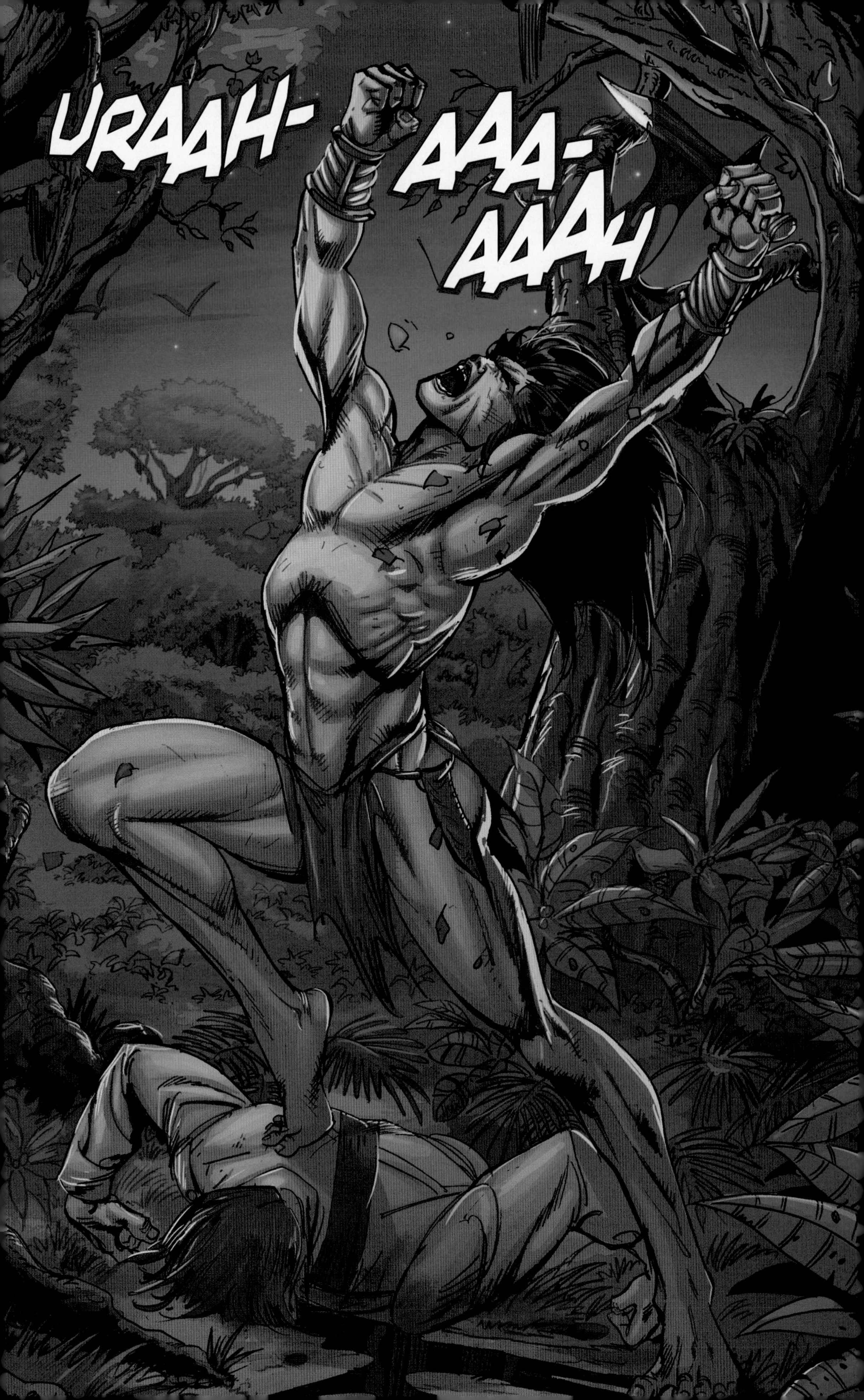
URAAH-
AAA-
AAAH

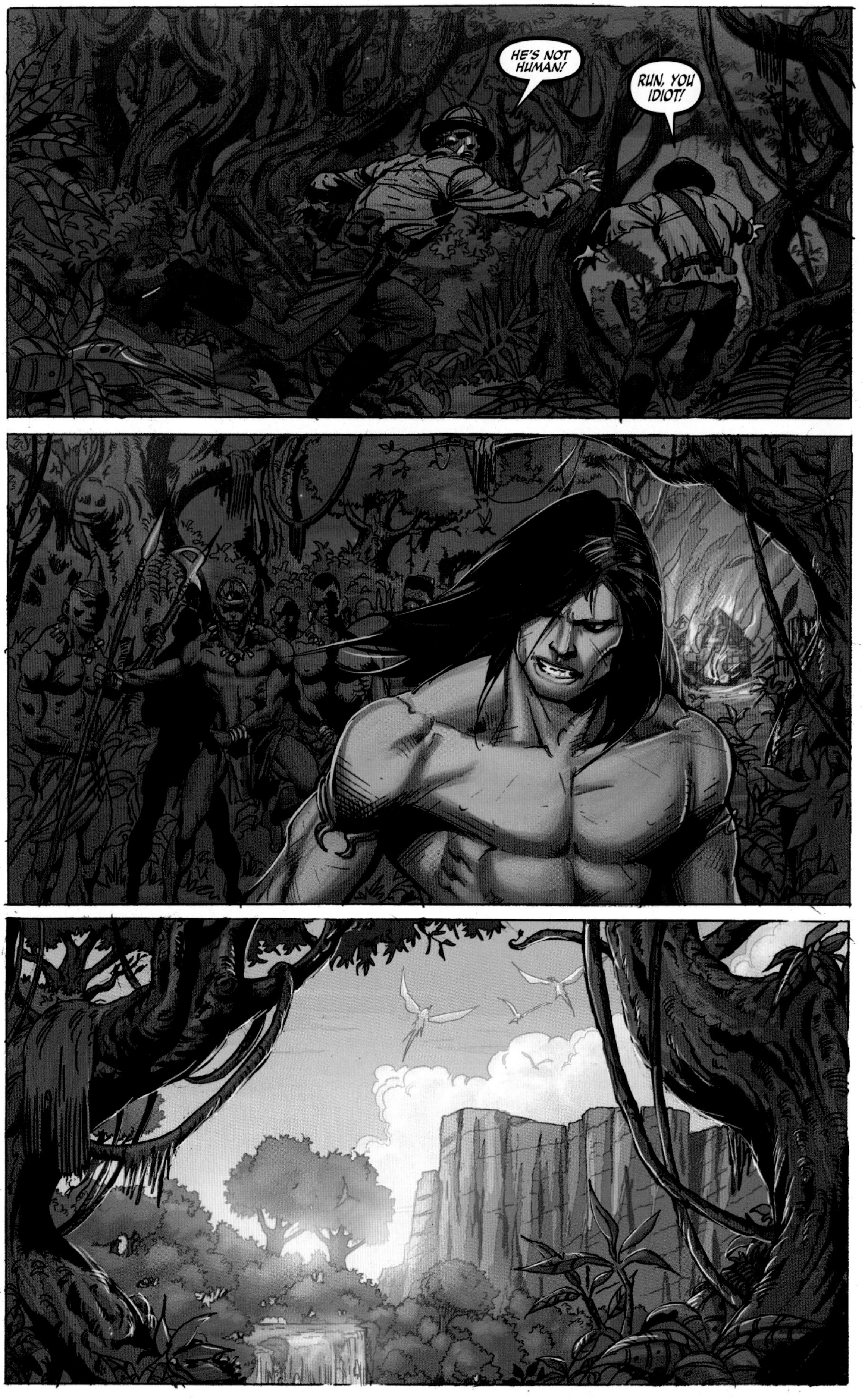
HE'S NOT HUMAN!
RUN, YOU IDIOT!

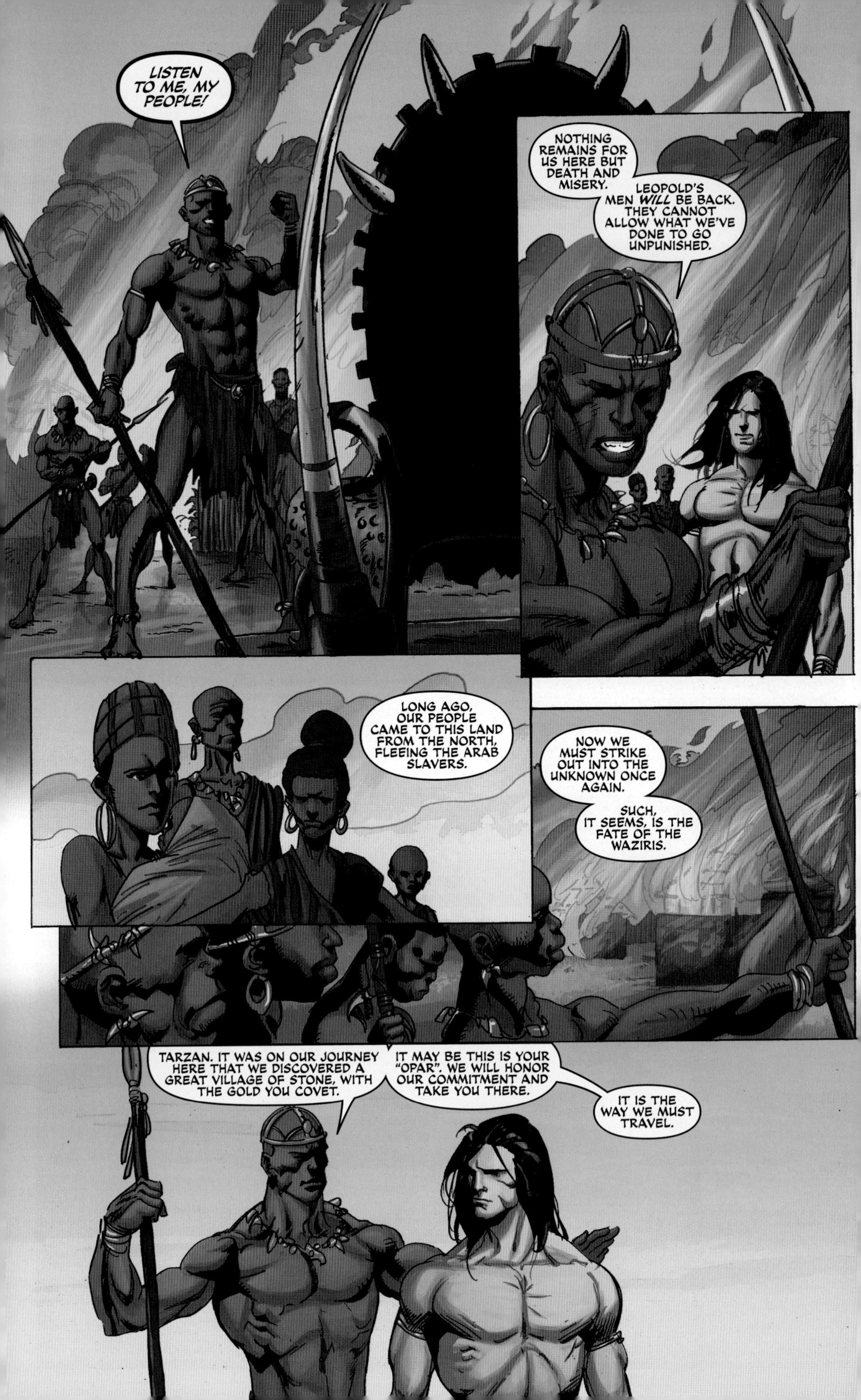
LISTEN TO ME, MY PEOPLE!
NOTHING REMAINS FOR US HERE BUT DEATH AND MISERY.
LEOPOLD'S MEN *WILL* BE BACK. THEY CANNOT ALLOW WHAT WE'VE DONE TO GO UNPUNISHED.
LONG AGO, OUR PEOPLE CAME TO THIS LAND FROM THE NORTH, FLEEING THE ARAB SLAVERS.
NOW WE MUST STRIKE OUT INTO THE UNKNOWN ONCE AGAIN.
SUCH, IT SEEMS, IS THE FATE OF THE WAZIRIS.
TARZAN. IT WAS ON OUR JOURNEY HERE THAT WE DISCOVERED A GREAT VILLAGE OF STONE, WITH THE GOLD YOU COVET.
IT MAY BE THIS IS YOUR "OPAR". WE WILL HONOR OUR COMMITMENT AND TAKE YOU THERE.
IT IS THE WAY WE MUST TRAVEL.

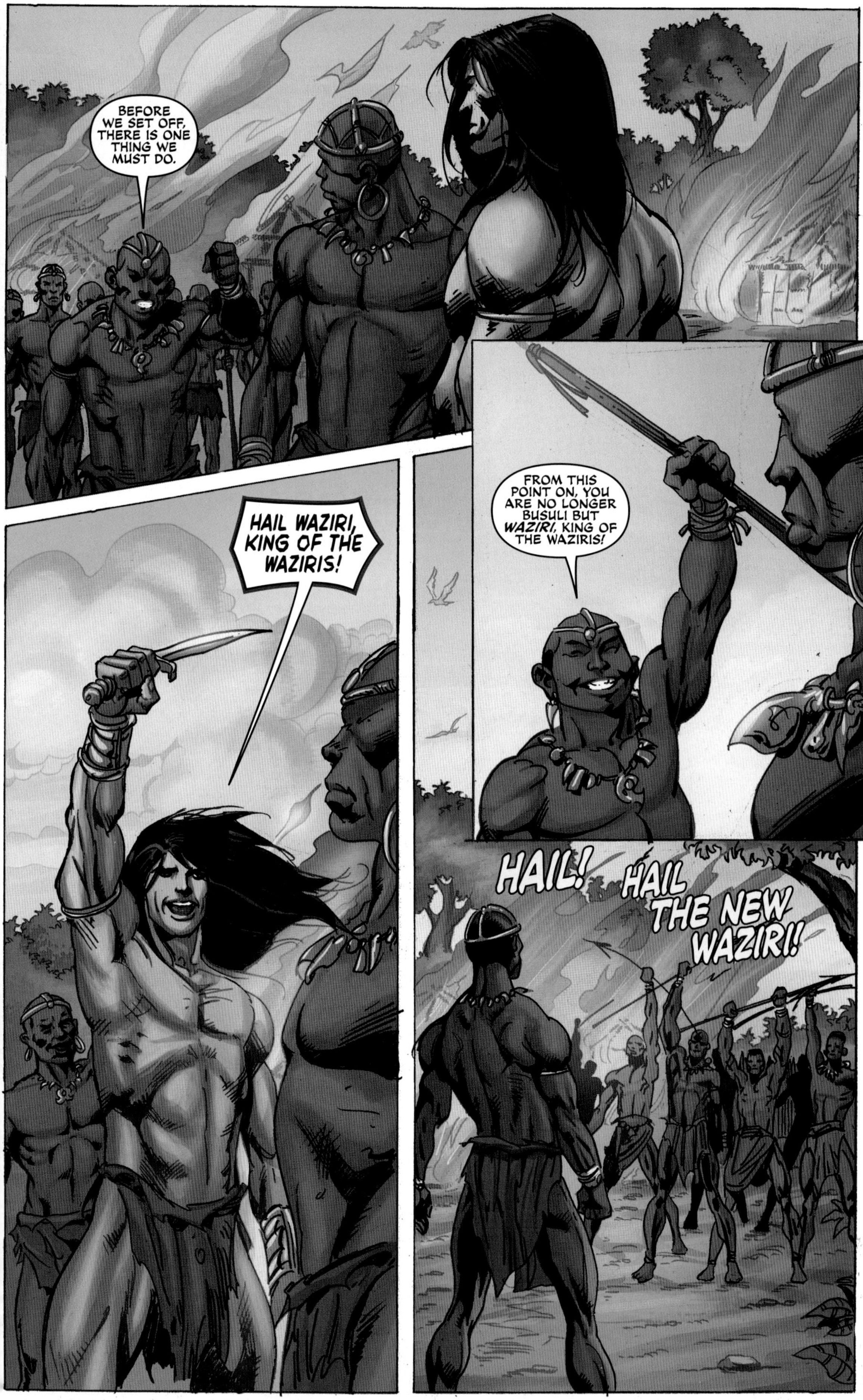
BEFORE WE SET OFF, THERE IS ONE THING WE MUST DO.
FROM THIS POINT ON, YOU ARE NO LONGER BUSULI BUT *WAZIRI*, KING OF THE WAZIRIS!
HAIL WAZIRI, KING OF THE WAZIRIS!
HAIL!
HAIL THE NEW WAZIRI!

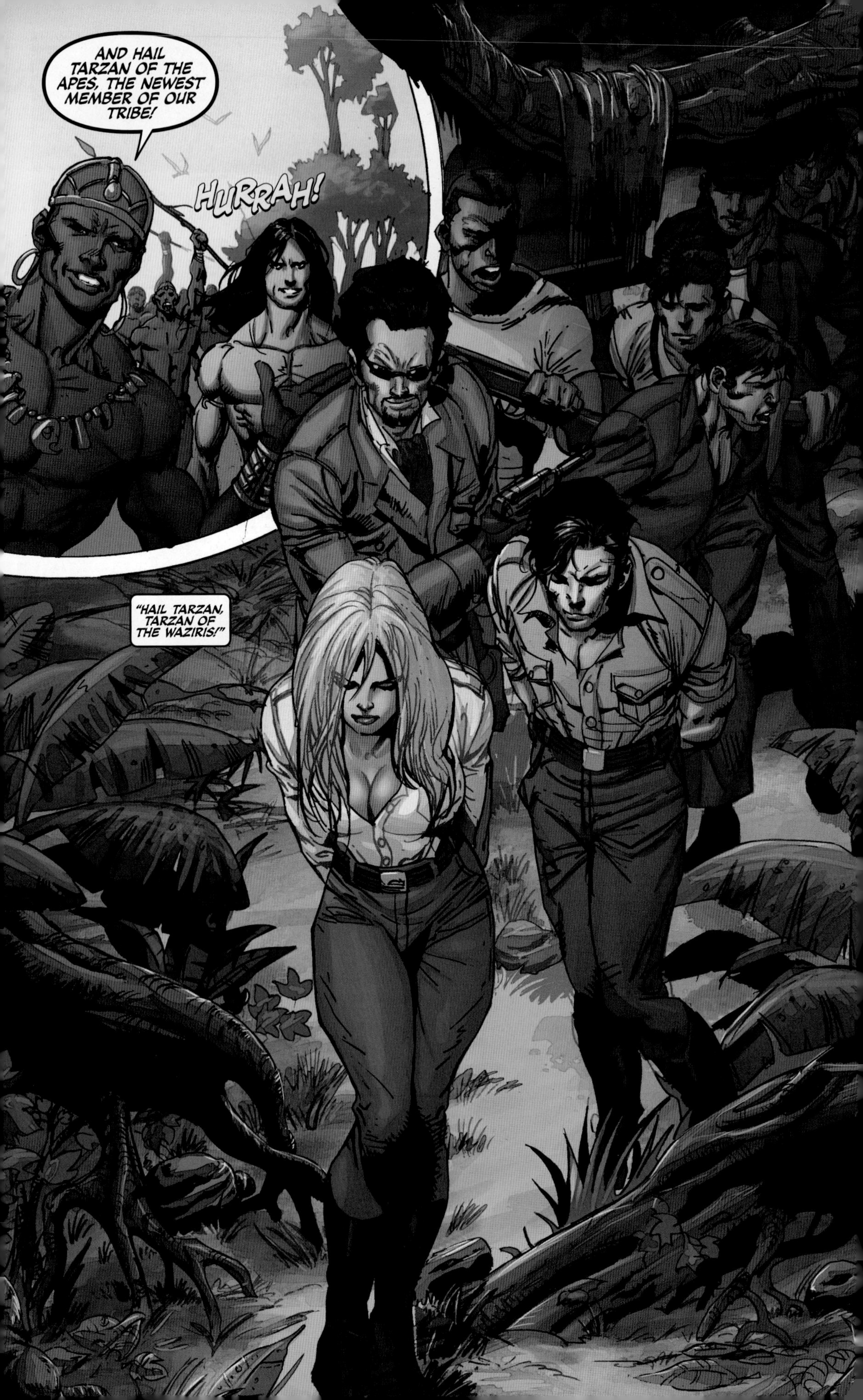
AND HAIL TARZAN OF THE APES, THE NEWEST MEMBER OF OUR TRIBE!
HURRAH!
"HAIL TARZAN, TARZAN OF THE WAZIRIS!"

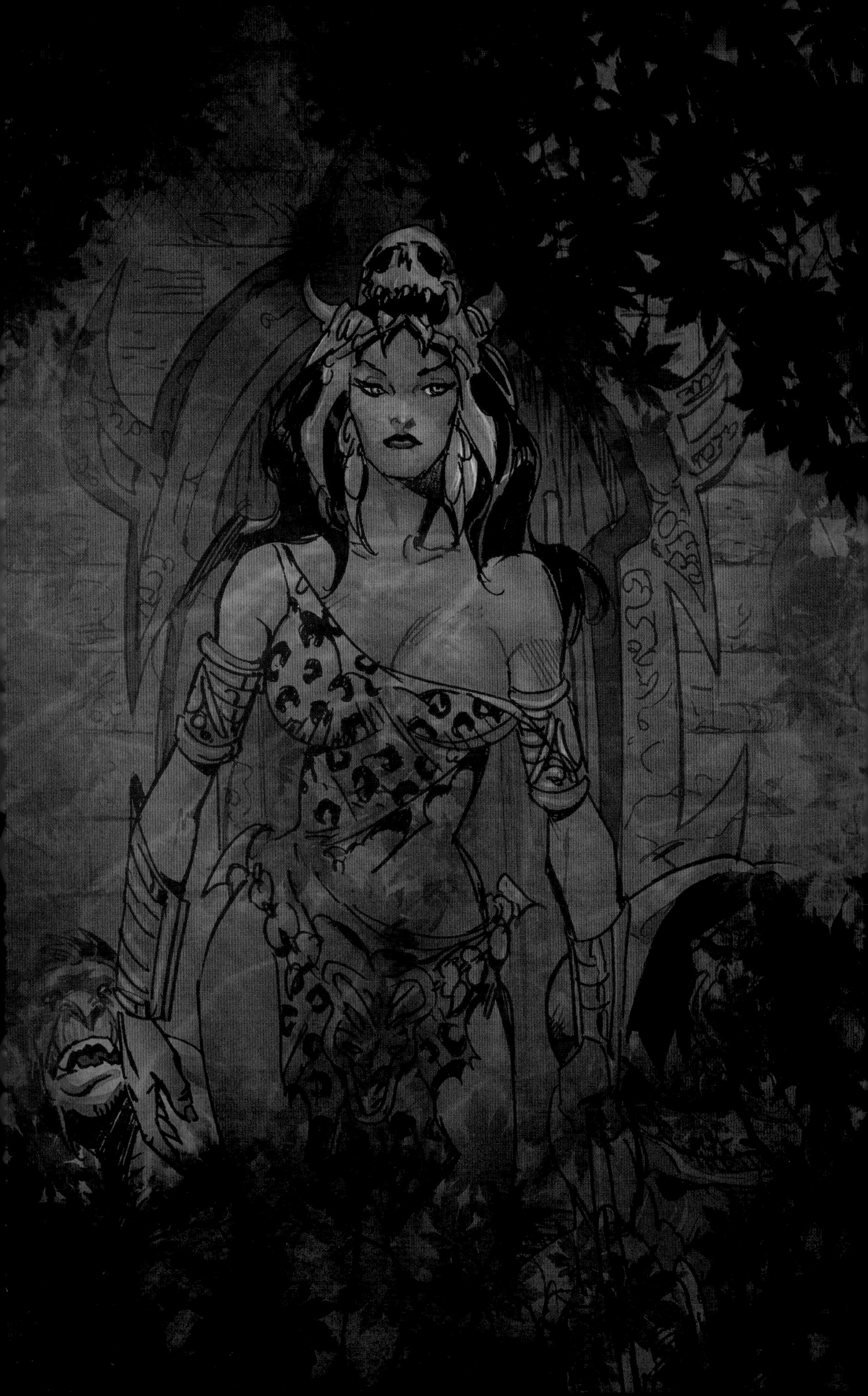

ISSUE 12

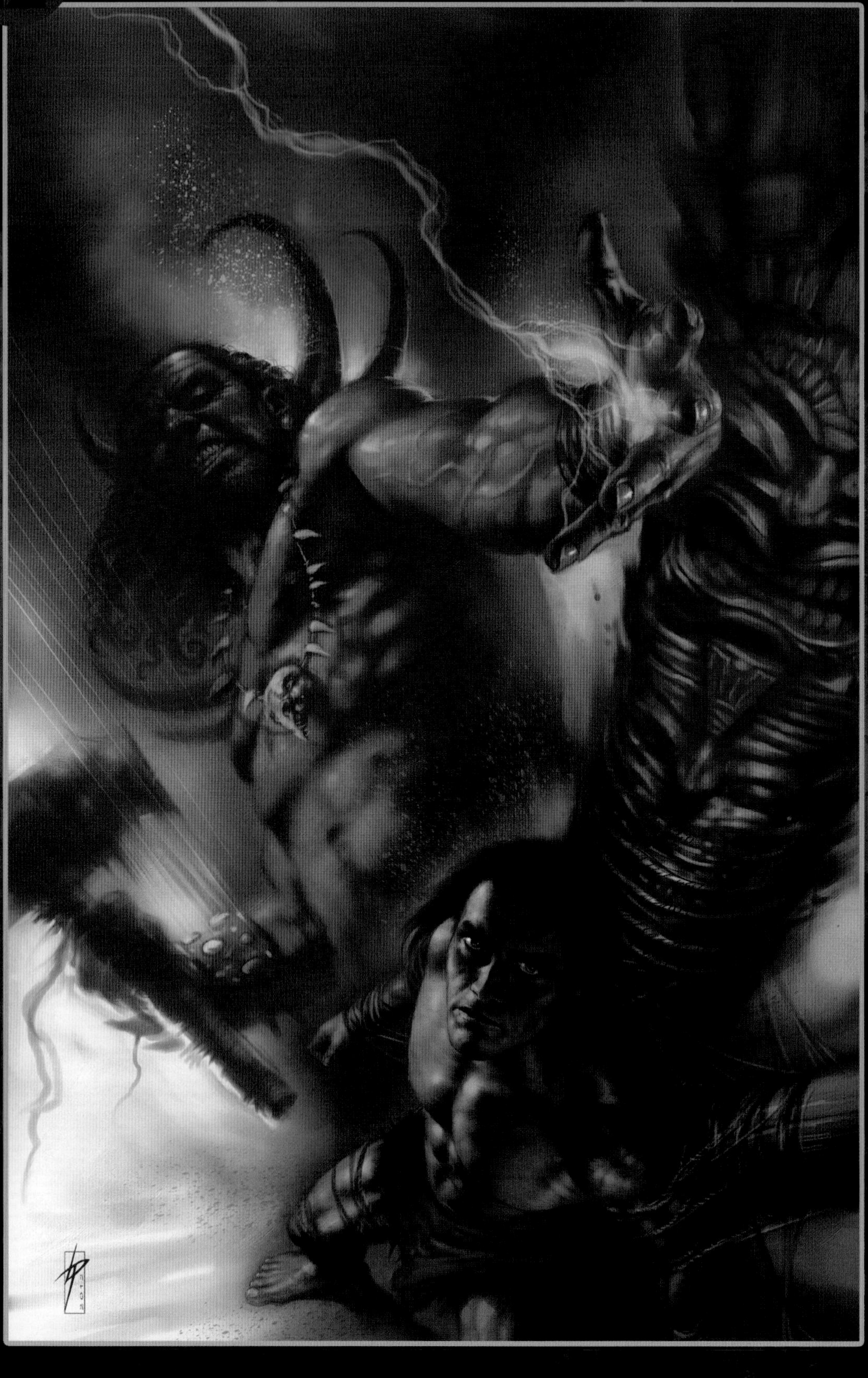

COVER BY LUCIO PARRILLO

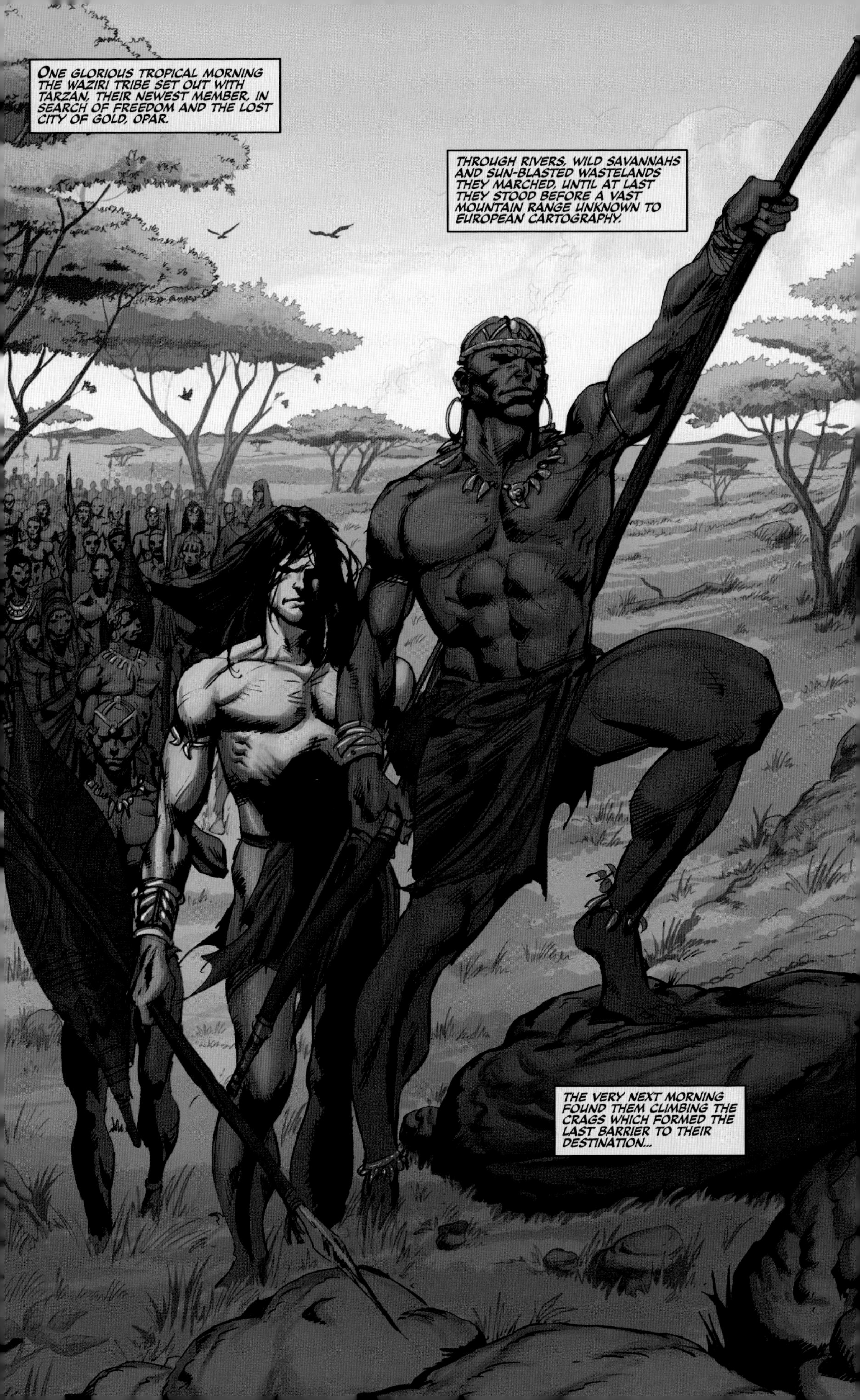
ONE GLORIOUS TROPICAL MORNING THE WAZIRI TRIBE SET OUT WITH TARZAN, THEIR NEWEST MEMBER, IN SEARCH OF FREEDOM AND THE LOST CITY OF GOLD, OPAR.
THROUGH RIVERS, WILD SAVANNAHS AND SUN-BLASTED WASTELANDS THEY MARCHED, UNTIL AT LAST THEY STOOD BEFORE A VAST MOUNTAIN RANGE UNKNOWN TO EUROPEAN CARTOGRAPHY.
THE VERY NEXT MORNING FOUND THEM CLIMBING THE CRAGS WHICH FORMED THE LAST BARRIER TO THEIR DESTINATION...

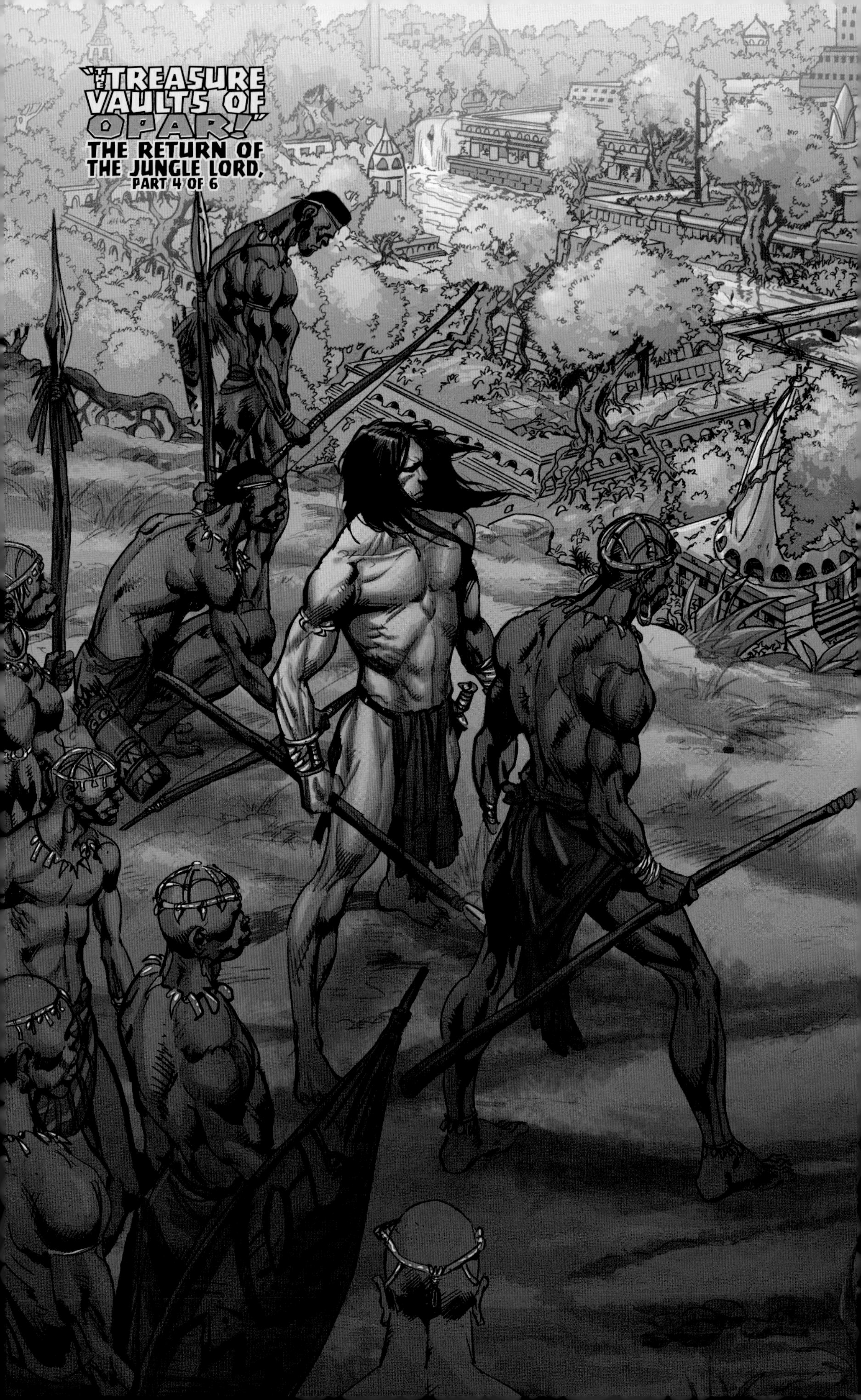
"THE TREASURE VAULTS OF OPAR!"
THE RETURN OF THE JUNGLE LORD, PART 4 OF 6

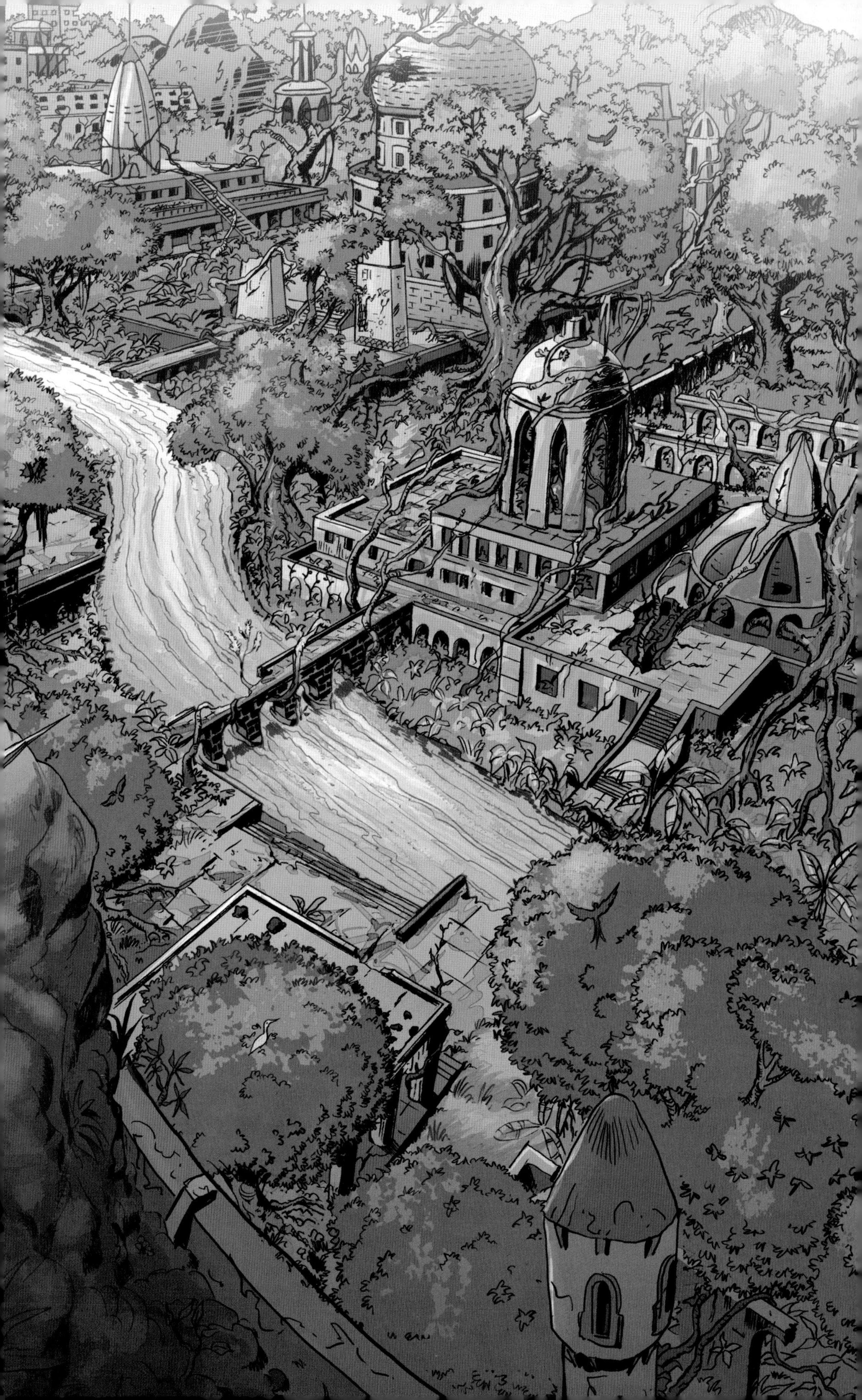

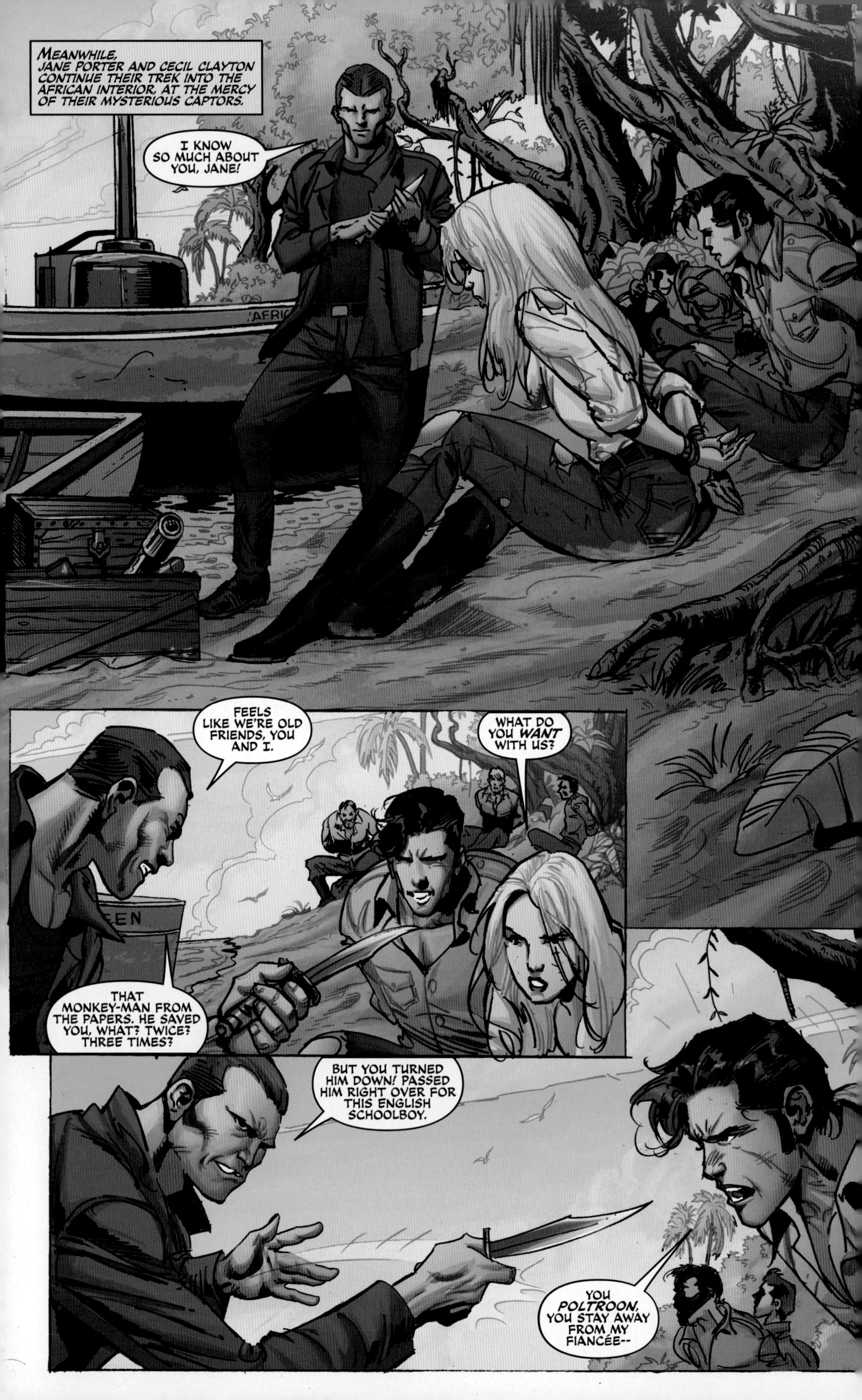
MEANWHILE, JANE PORTER AND CECIL CLAYTON CONTINUE THEIR TREK INTO THE AFRICAN INTERIOR, AT THE MERCY OF THEIR MYSTERIOUS CAPTORS.
I KNOW SO MUCH ABOUT YOU, JANE!
FEELS LIKE WE'RE OLD FRIENDS, YOU AND I.
WHAT DO YOU *WANT* WITH US?
THAT MONKEY-MAN FROM THE PAPERS. HE SAVED YOU, WHAT? TWICE? THREE TIMES?
BUT YOU TURNED HIM DOWN! PASSED HIM RIGHT OVER FOR THIS ENGLISH SCHOOLBOY.
YOU *POLTROON*, YOU STAY AWAY FROM MY FIANCÉE--

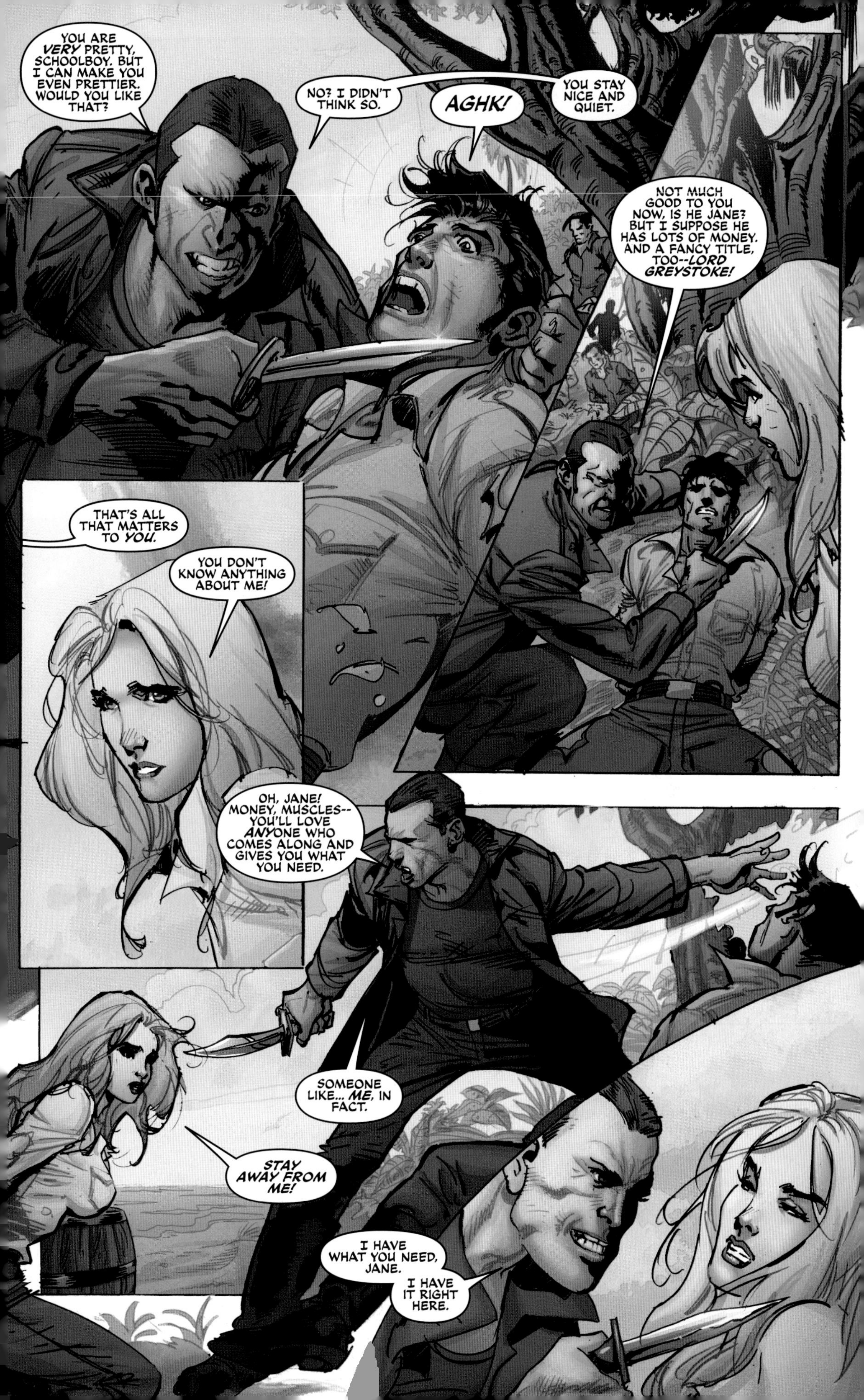

YOU ARE VERY PRETTY, SCHOOLBOY. BUT I CAN MAKE YOU EVEN PRETTIER. WOULD YOU LIKE THAT?
NO? I DIDN'T THINK SO.
AGHK!
YOU STAY NICE AND QUIET.
NOT MUCH GOOD TO YOU NOW, IS HE JANE? BUT I SUPPOSE HE HAS LOTS OF MONEY. AND A FANCY TITLE, TOO--LORD GREYSTOKE!
THAT'S ALL THAT MATTERS TO YOU.
YOU DON'T KNOW ANYTHING ABOUT ME!
OH, JANE! MONEY, MUSCLES-- YOU'LL LOVE ANYONE WHO COMES ALONG AND GIVES YOU WHAT YOU NEED.
SOMEONE LIKE... ME, IN FACT.
STAY AWAY FROM ME!
I HAVE WHAT YOU NEED, JANE.
I HAVE IT RIGHT HERE.

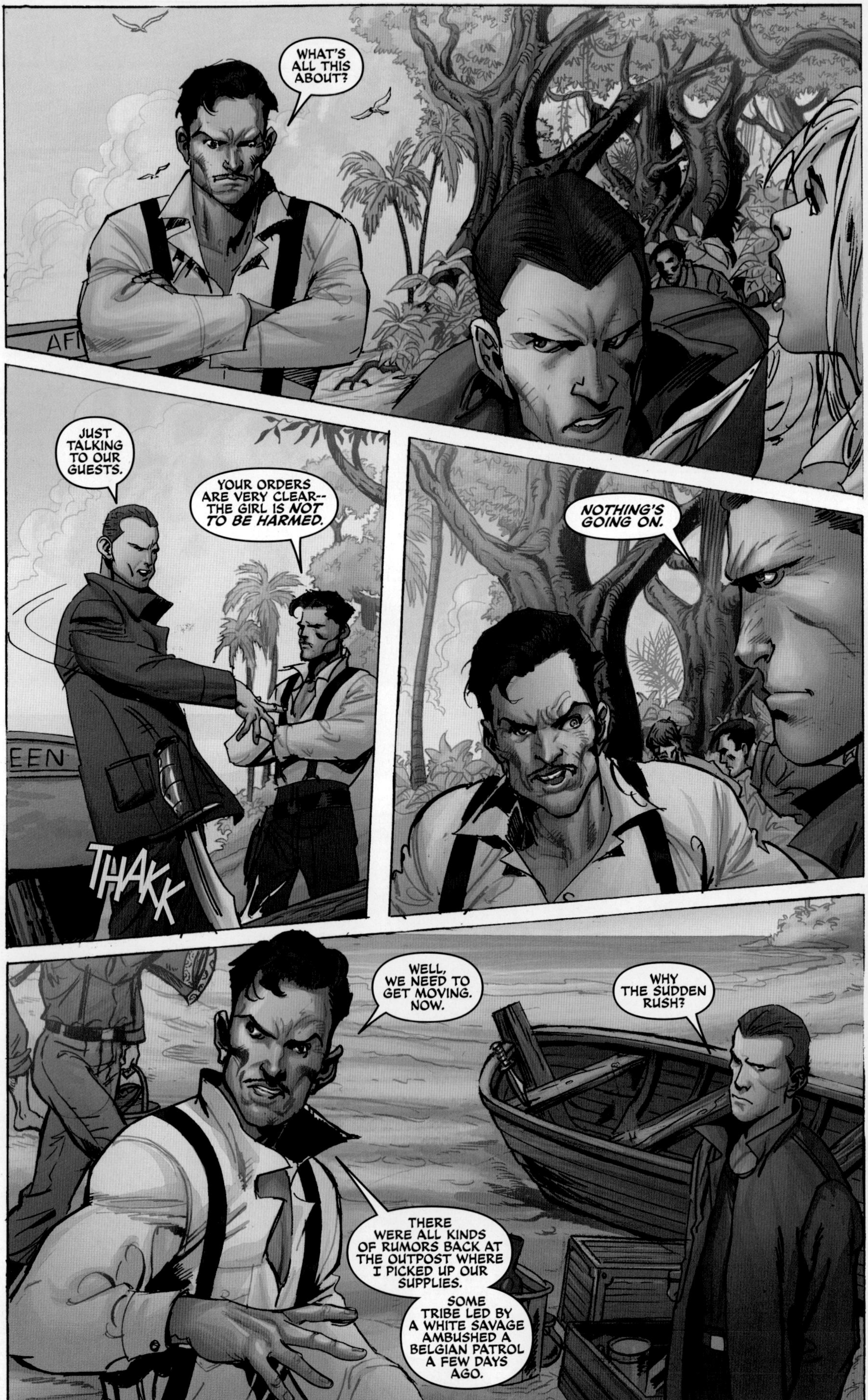
WHAT'S ALL THIS ABOUT?
AFI
JUST TALKING TO OUR GUESTS.
YOUR ORDERS ARE VERY CLEAR-- THE GIRL IS NOT TO BE HARMED.
EEN
THAKK
NOTHING'S GOING ON.
WELL, WE NEED TO GET MOVING. NOW.
WHY THE SUDDEN RUSH?
THERE WERE ALL KINDS OF RUMORS BACK AT THE OUTPOST WHERE I PICKED UP OUR SUPPLIES.
SOME TRIBE LED BY A WHITE SAVAGE AMBUSHED A BELGIAN PATROL A FEW DAYS AGO.

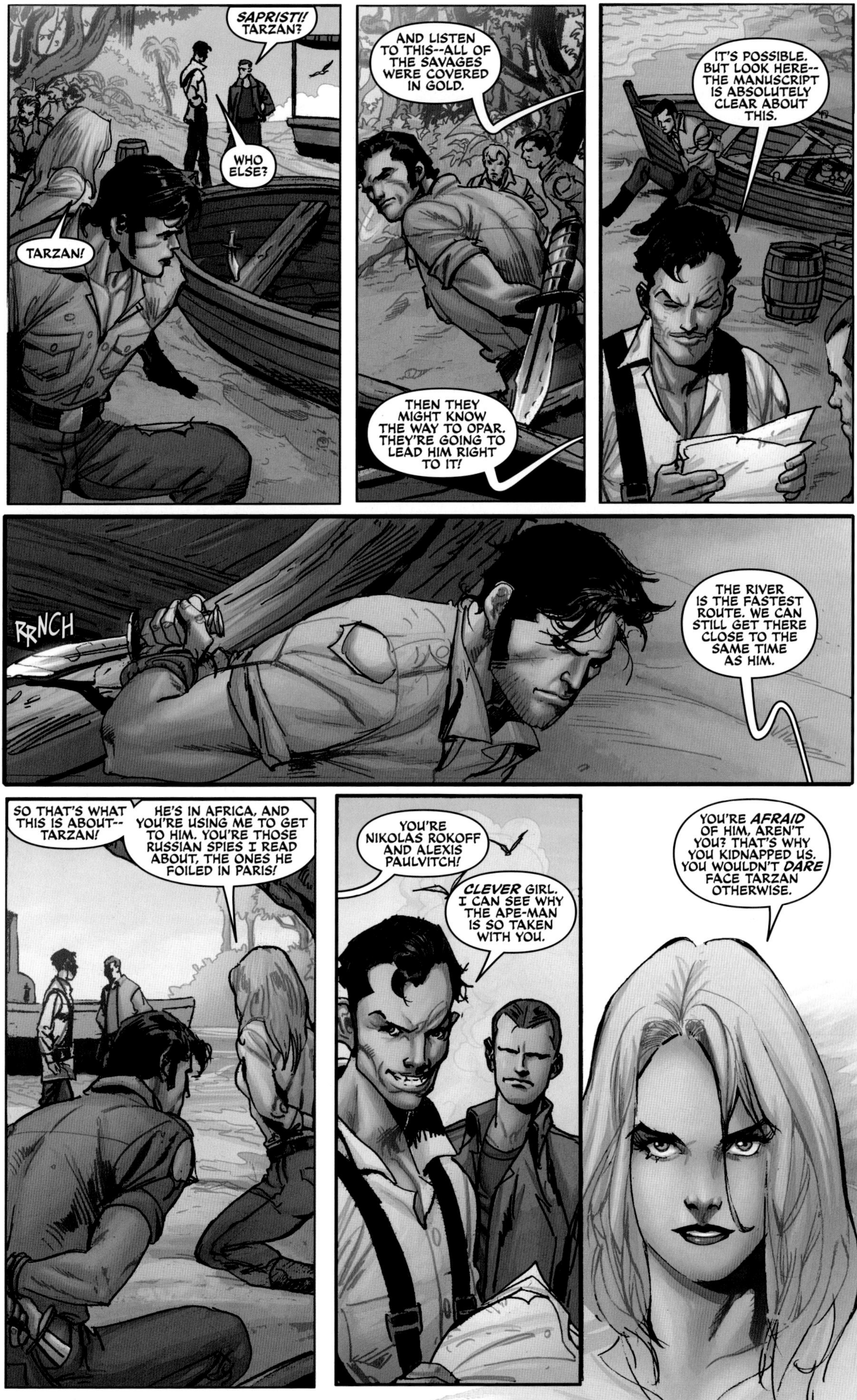
SAPRISTI!! TARZAN?
WHO ELSE?
TARZAN!
AND LISTEN TO THIS--ALL OF THE SAVAGES WERE COVERED IN GOLD.
THEN THEY MIGHT KNOW THE WAY TO OPAR. THEY'RE GOING TO LEAD HIM RIGHT TO IT!
IT'S POSSIBLE. BUT LOOK HERE-- THE MANUSCRIPT IS ABSOLUTELY CLEAR ABOUT THIS.
RRNCH
THE RIVER IS THE FASTEST ROUTE. WE CAN STILL GET THERE CLOSE TO THE SAME TIME AS HIM.
SO THAT'S WHAT THIS IS ABOUT-- TARZAN!
HE'S IN AFRICA, AND YOU'RE USING ME TO GET TO HIM. YOU'RE THOSE RUSSIAN SPIES I READ ABOUT, THE ONES HE FOILED IN PARIS!
YOU'RE NIKOLAS ROKOFF AND ALEXIS PAULVITCH!
CLEVER GIRL. I CAN SEE WHY THE APE-MAN IS SO TAKEN WITH YOU.
YOU'RE AFRAID OF HIM, AREN'T YOU? THAT'S WHY YOU KIDNAPPED US. YOU WOULDN'T DARE FACE TARZAN OTHERWISE.

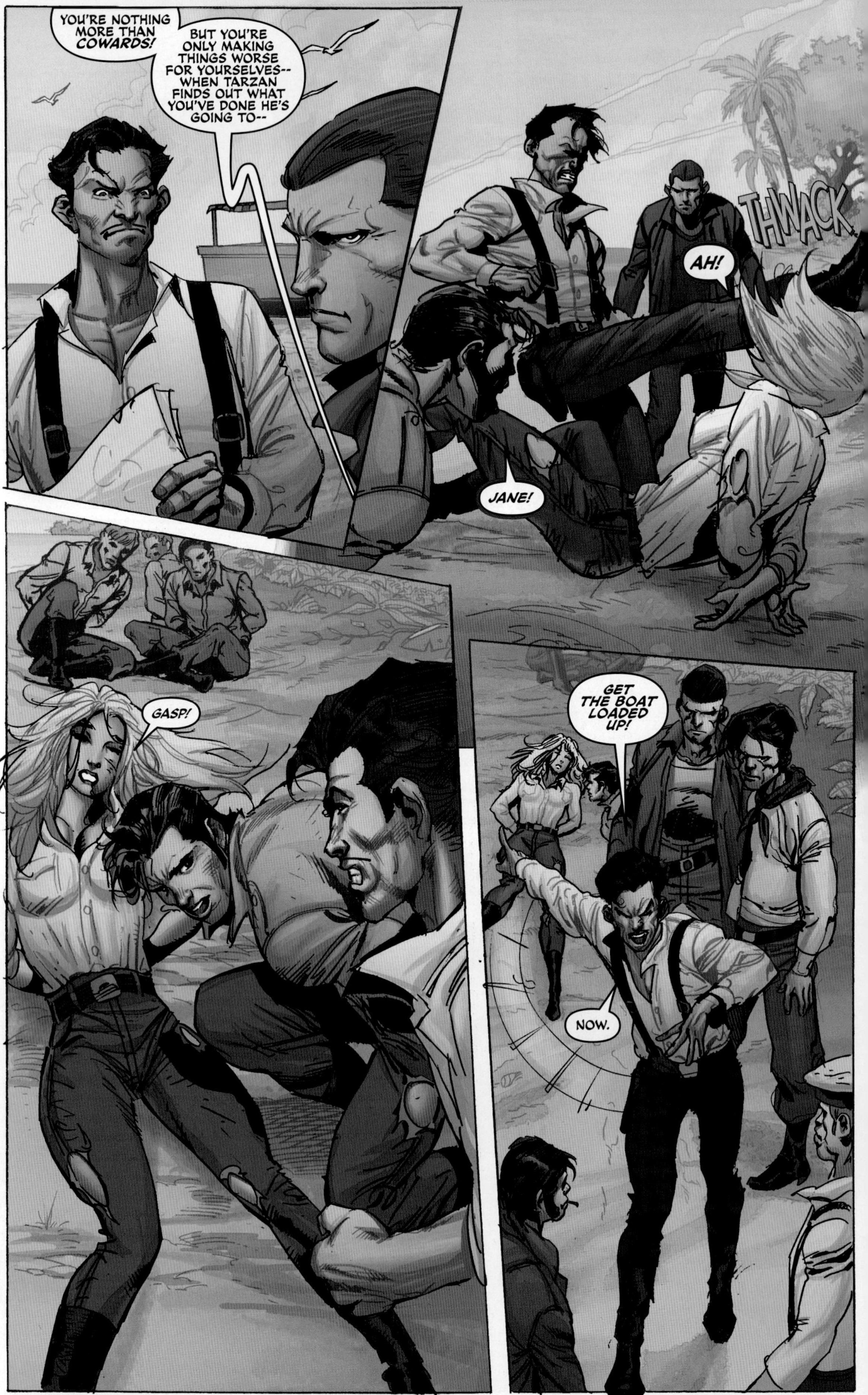
YOU'RE NOTHING MORE THAN COWARDS!
BUT YOU'RE ONLY MAKING THINGS WORSE FOR YOURSELVES-- WHEN TARZAN FINDS OUT WHAT YOU'VE DONE HE'S GOING TO--
THWACK
AH!
JANE!
GASP!
GET THE BOAT LOADED UP!
NOW.

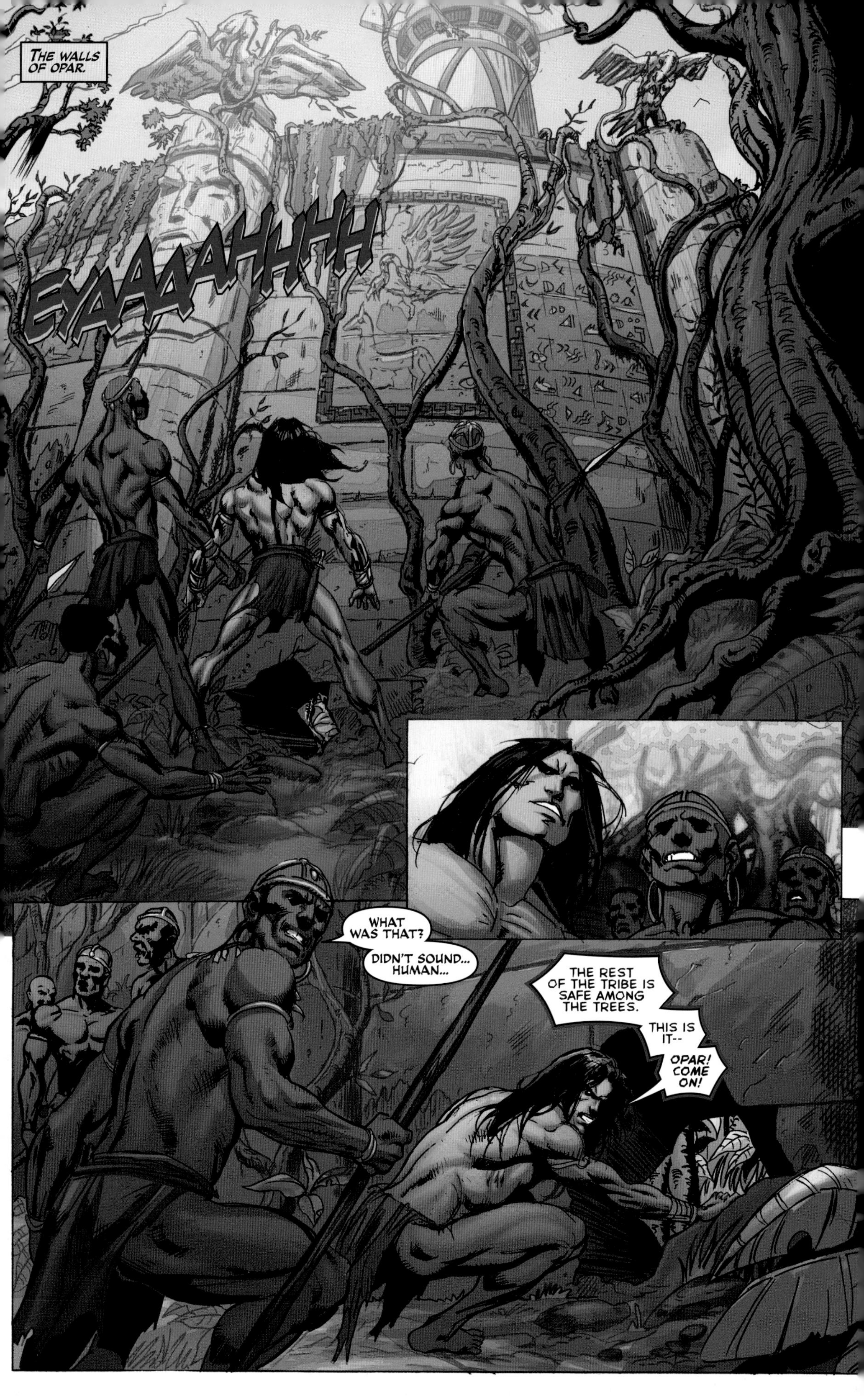
THE WALLS OF OPAR.
EYAAAAHHHH
WHAT WAS THAT?
DIDN'T SOUND... HUMAN...
THE REST OF THE TRIBE IS SAFE AMONG THE TREES.
THIS IS IT--
OPAR! COME ON!

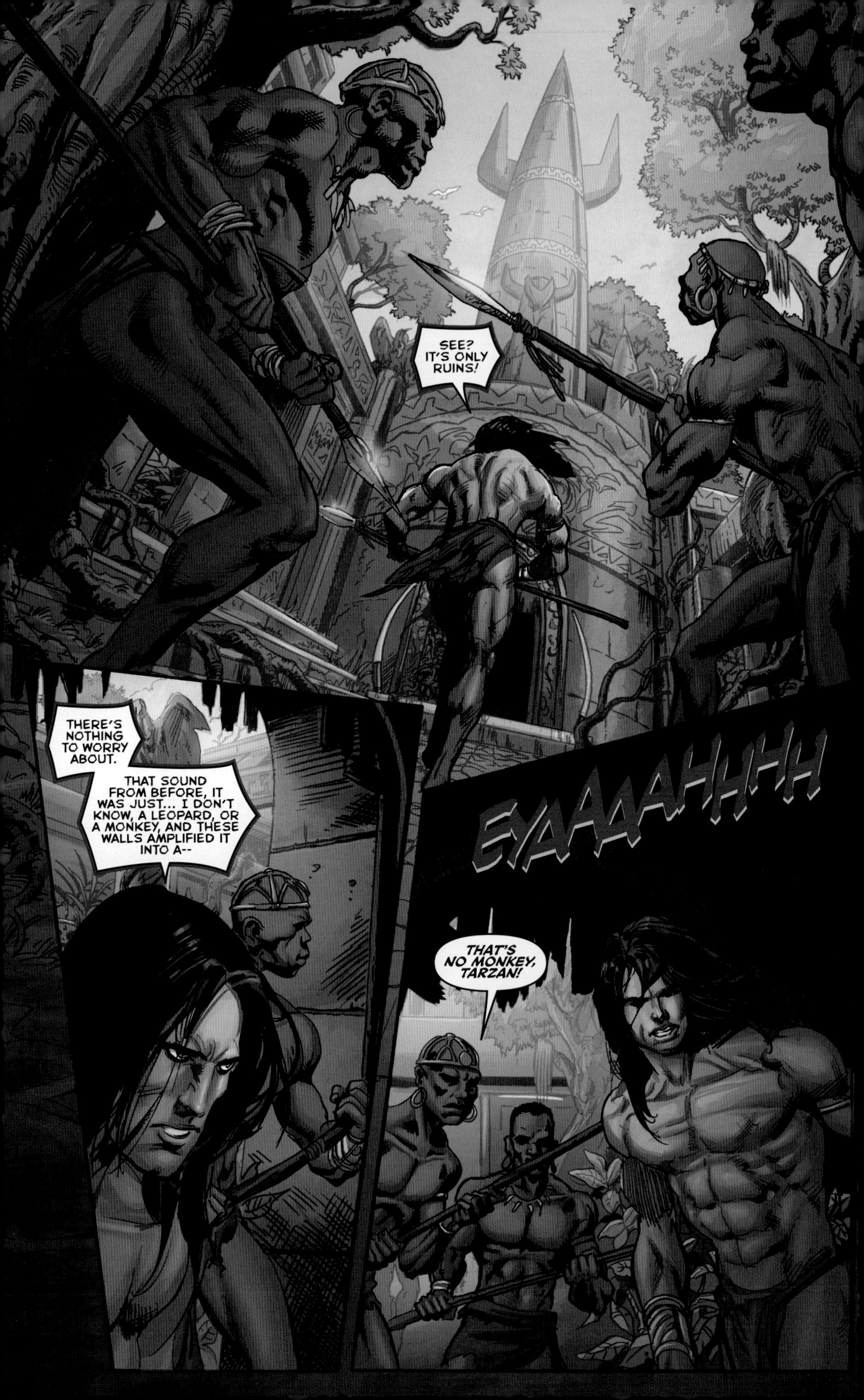
SEE? IT'S ONLY RUINS!
THERE'S NOTHING TO WORRY ABOUT.
THAT SOUND FROM BEFORE, IT WAS JUST... I DON'T KNOW, A LEOPARD, OR A MONKEY, AND THESE WALLS AMPLIFIED IT INTO A--
EYAAAAHHHH
THAT'S NO MONKEY, TARZAN!

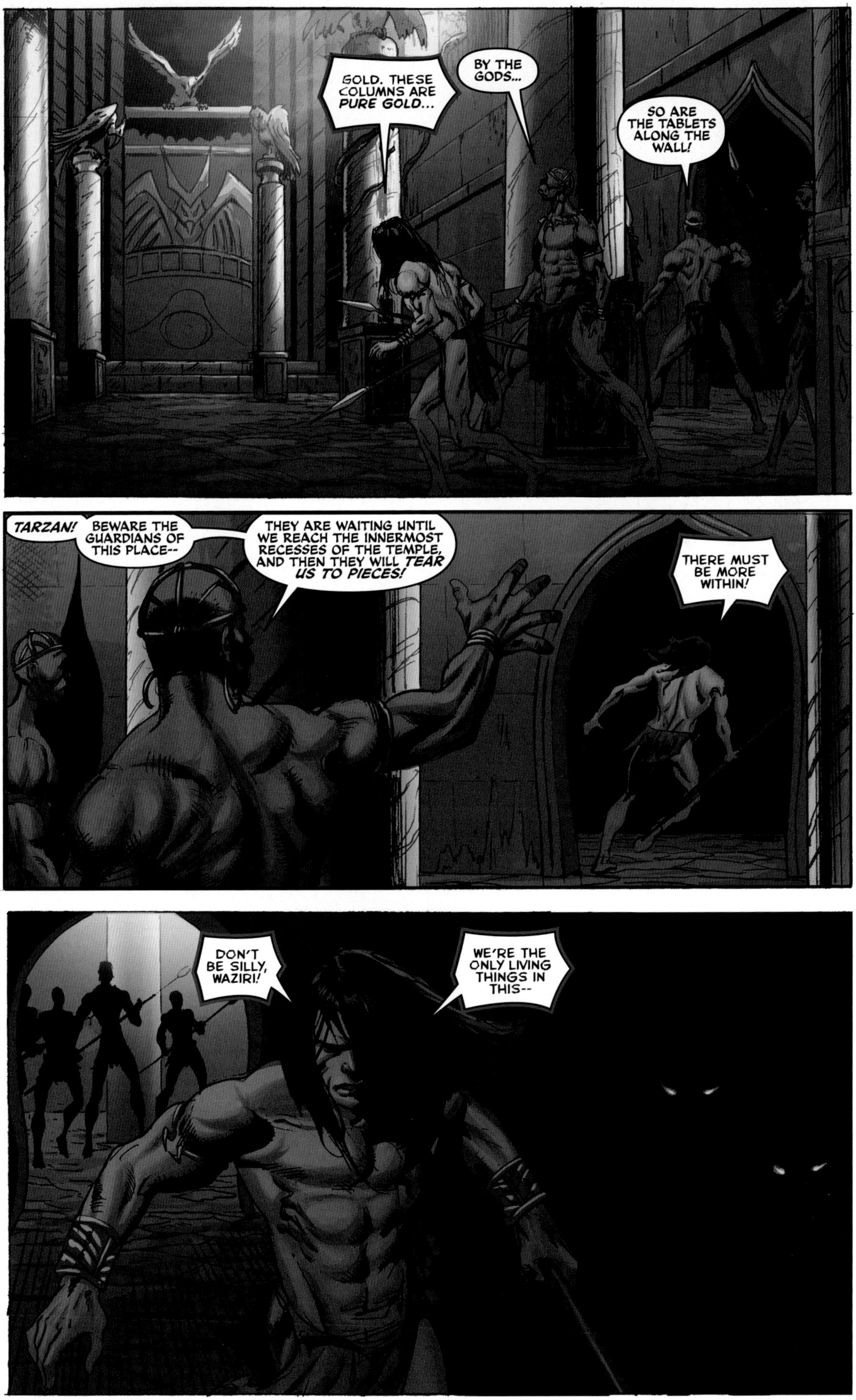
GOLD. THESE COLUMNS ARE *PURE GOLD...*
BY THE GODS...
SO ARE THE TABLETS ALONG THE WALL!
TARZAN!
BEWARE THE GUARDIANS OF THIS PLACE--
THEY ARE WAITING UNTIL WE REACH THE INNERMOST RECESSES OF THE TEMPLE, AND THEN THEY WILL *TEAR US TO PIECES!*
THERE MUST BE MORE WITHIN!
DON'T BE SILLY, WAZIRI!
WE'RE THE ONLY LIVING THINGS IN THIS--

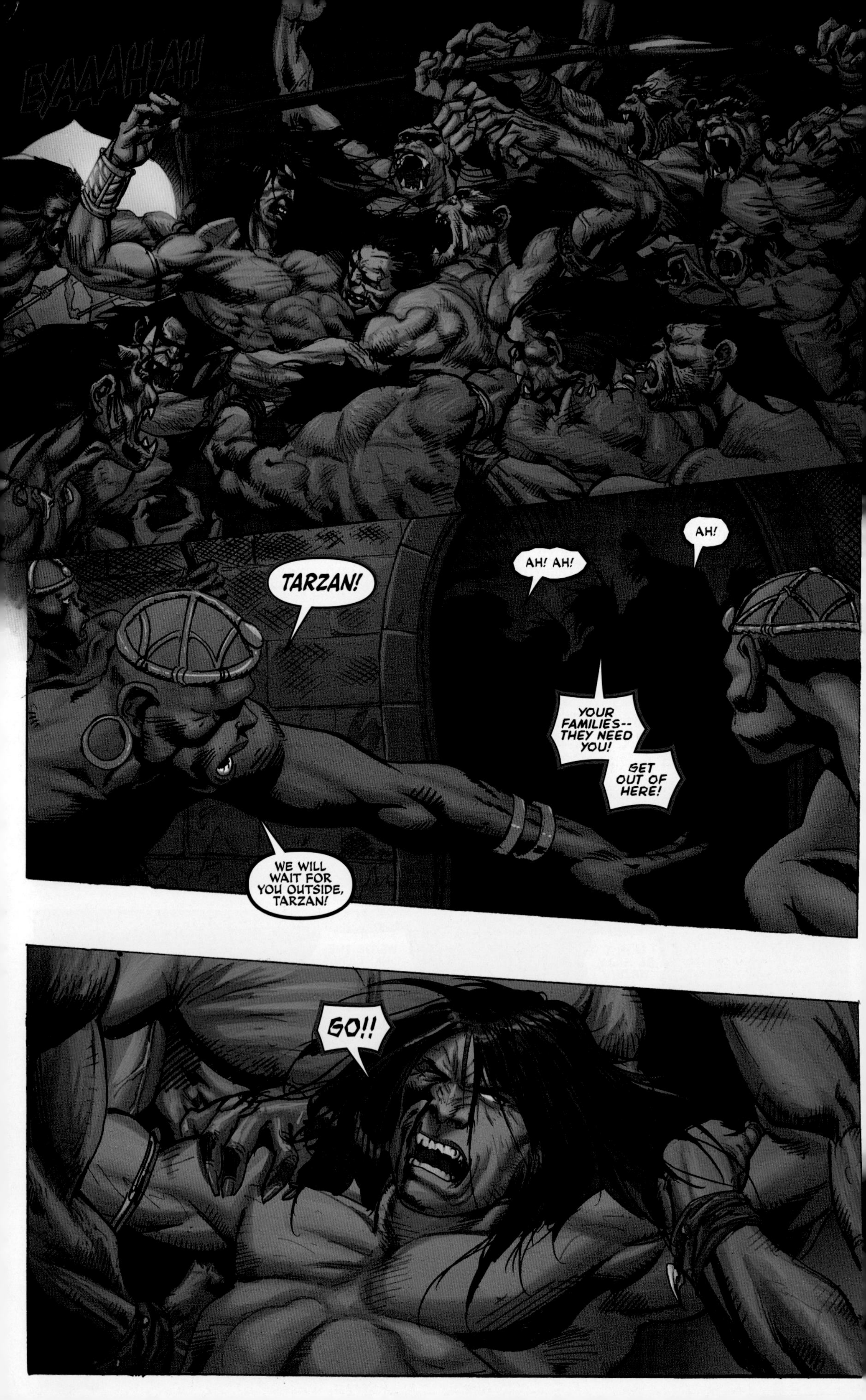
EYAAAHAH
TARZAN!
AH! AH!
AH!
YOUR FAMILIES-- THEY NEED YOU!
GET OUT OF HERE!
WE WILL WAIT FOR YOU OUTSIDE, TARZAN!
GO!!

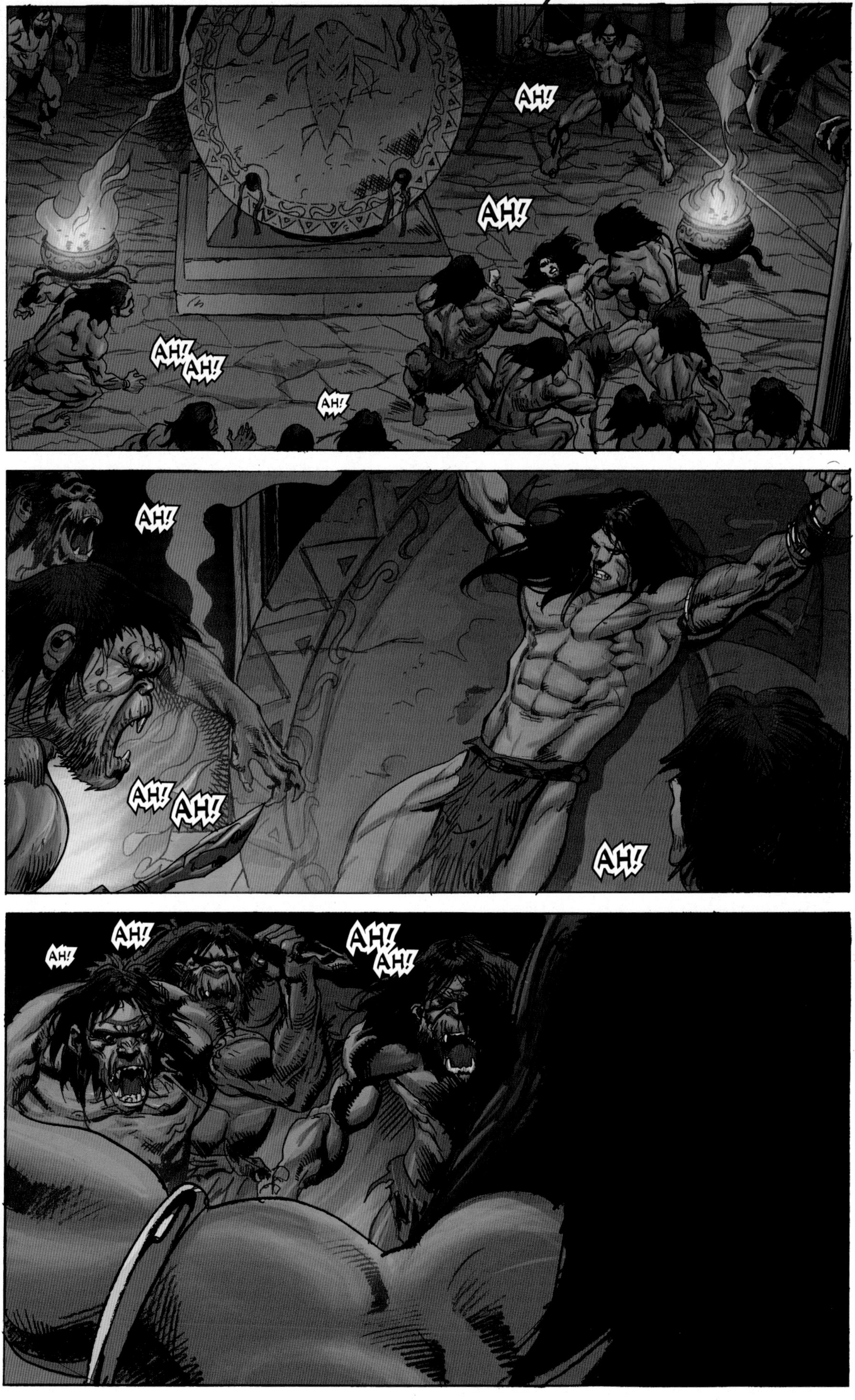
AH!
AH!
AH!
AH!
AH!
AH!
AH!
AH!
AH!
AH!
AH!
AH!
AH!

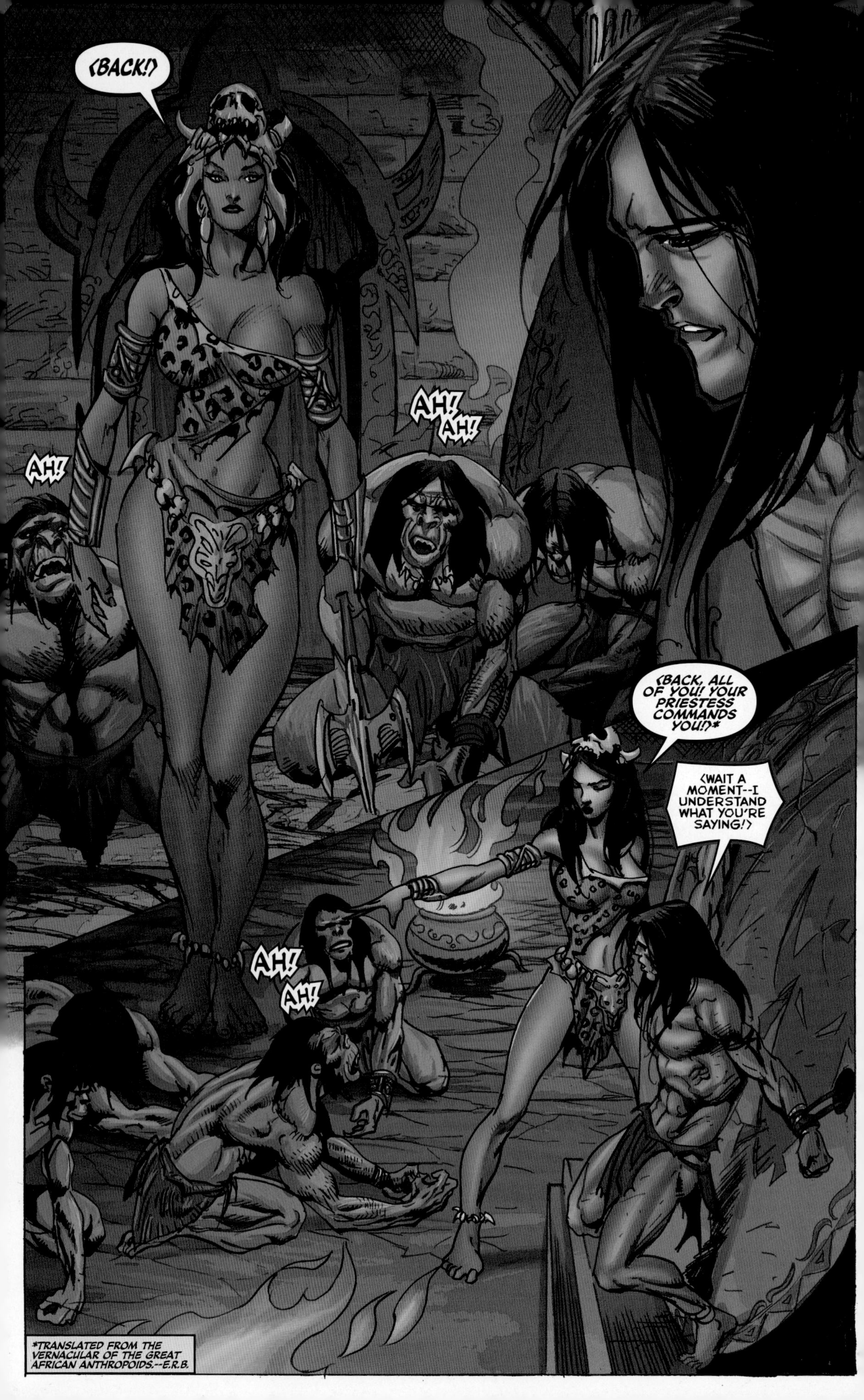
‹BACK!›
AH!
AH! AH!
‹BACK, ALL OF YOU! YOUR PRIESTESS COMMANDS YOU!›*
‹WAIT A MOMENT--I UNDERSTAND WHAT YOU'RE SAYING!›
AH! AH!
*TRANSLATED FROM THE VERNACULAR OF THE GREAT AFRICAN ANTHROPOIDS.--E.R.B.

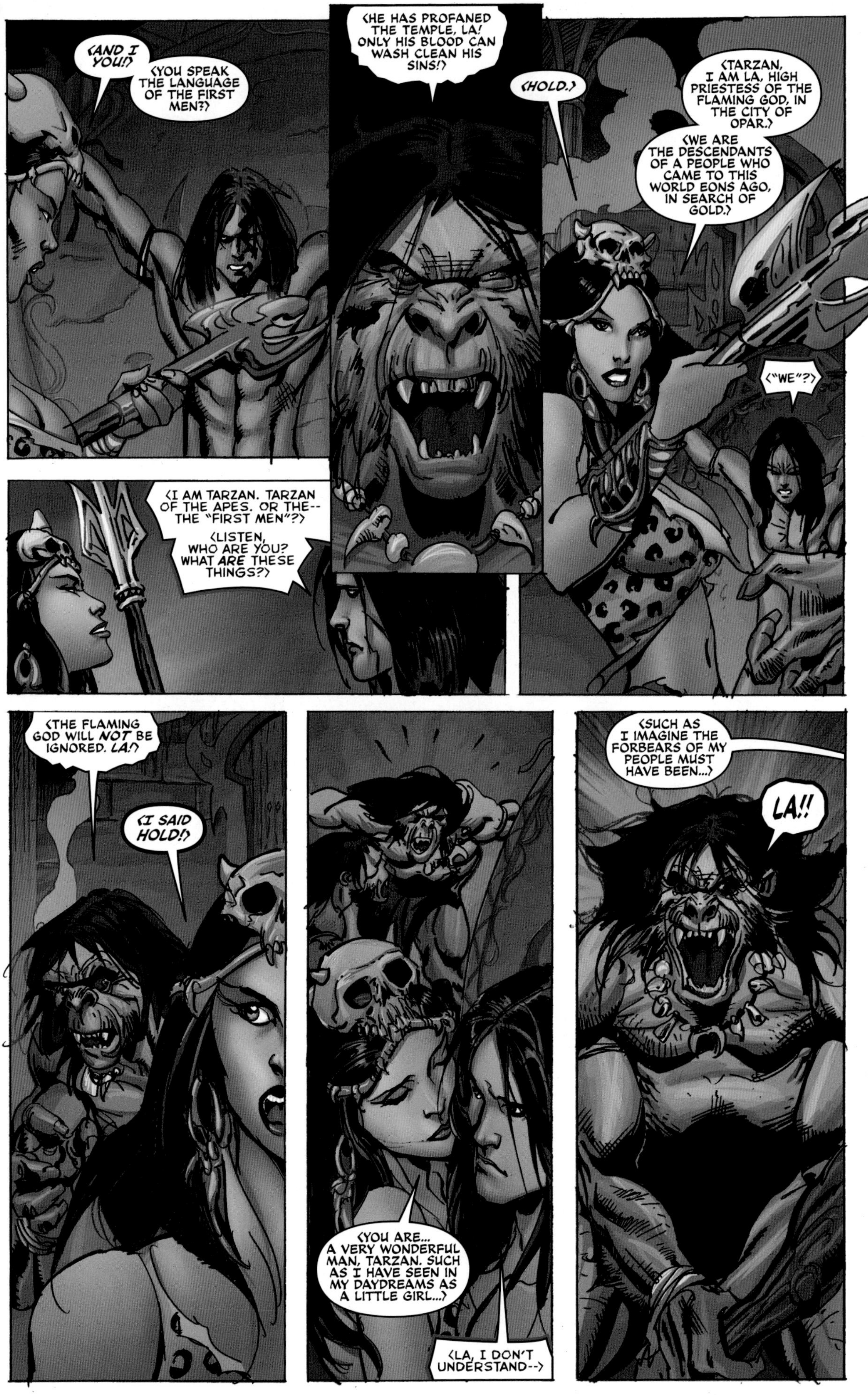
‹AND I YOU!›
‹YOU SPEAK THE LANGUAGE OF THE FIRST MEN?›
‹HE HAS PROFANED THE TEMPLE, LA! ONLY HIS BLOOD CAN WASH CLEAN HIS SINS!›
‹HOLD.›
‹TARZAN, I AM LA, HIGH PRIESTESS OF THE FLAMING GOD, IN THE CITY OF OPAR.›
‹WE ARE THE DESCENDANTS OF A PEOPLE WHO CAME TO THIS WORLD EONS AGO, IN SEARCH OF GOLD.›
‹"WE"?›
‹I AM TARZAN. TARZAN OF THE APES. OR THE-- THE "FIRST MEN"?›
‹LISTEN, WHO ARE YOU? WHAT ARE THESE THINGS?›
‹THE FLAMING GOD WILL NOT BE IGNORED. LA!›
‹I SAID HOLD!›
‹YOU ARE... A VERY WONDERFUL MAN, TARZAN. SUCH AS I HAVE SEEN IN MY DAYDREAMS AS A LITTLE GIRL...›
‹LA, I DON'T UNDERSTAND--›
‹SUCH AS I IMAGINE THE FORBEARS OF MY PEOPLE MUST HAVE BEEN...›
LA!!

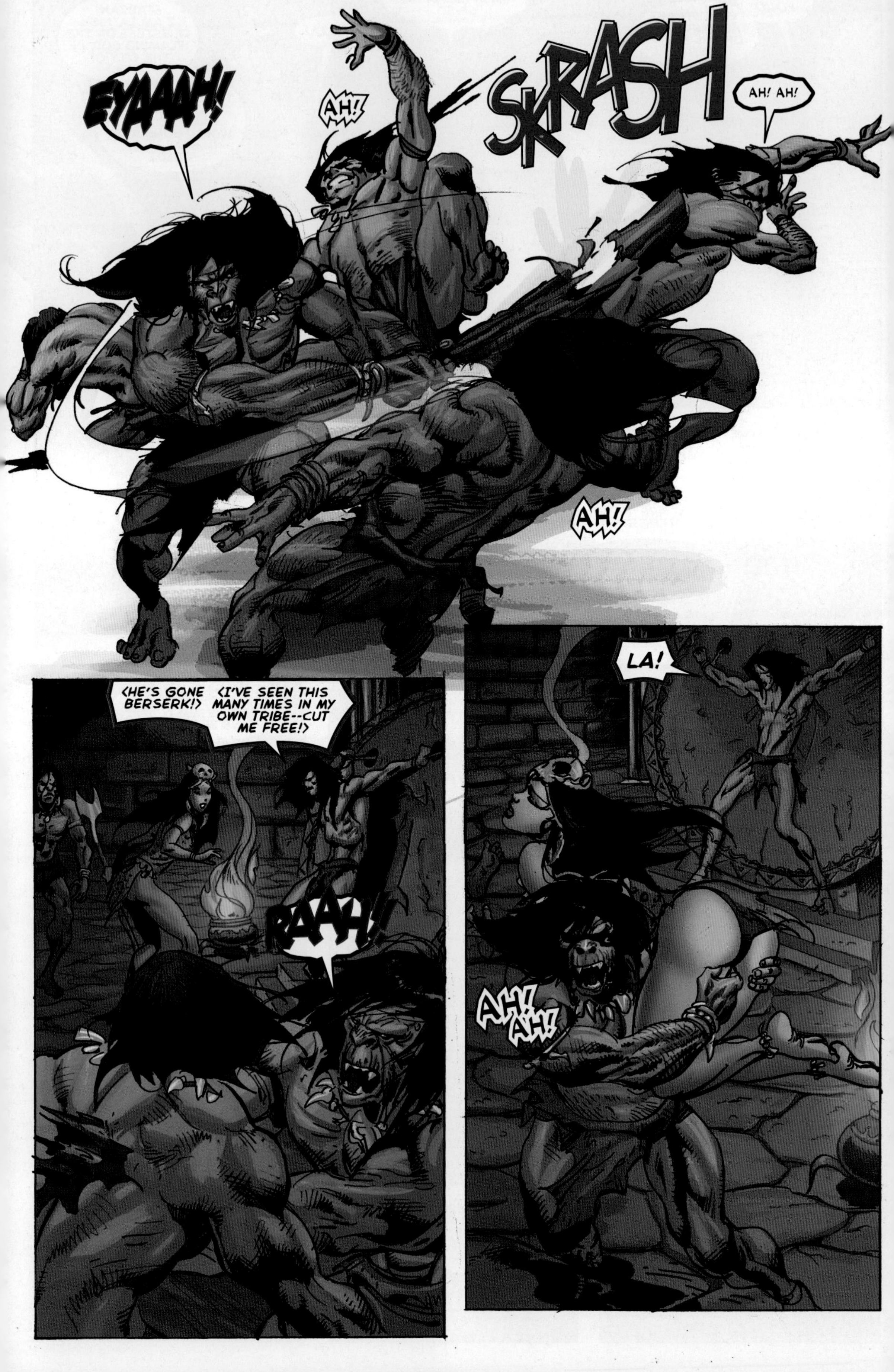
EYAAAH!
AH!
SKRASH
AH! AH!
AH!
<HE'S GONE BERSERK!>
<I'VE SEEN THIS MANY TIMES IN MY OWN TRIBE--CUT ME FREE!>
RAAH!
LA!
AH! AH!

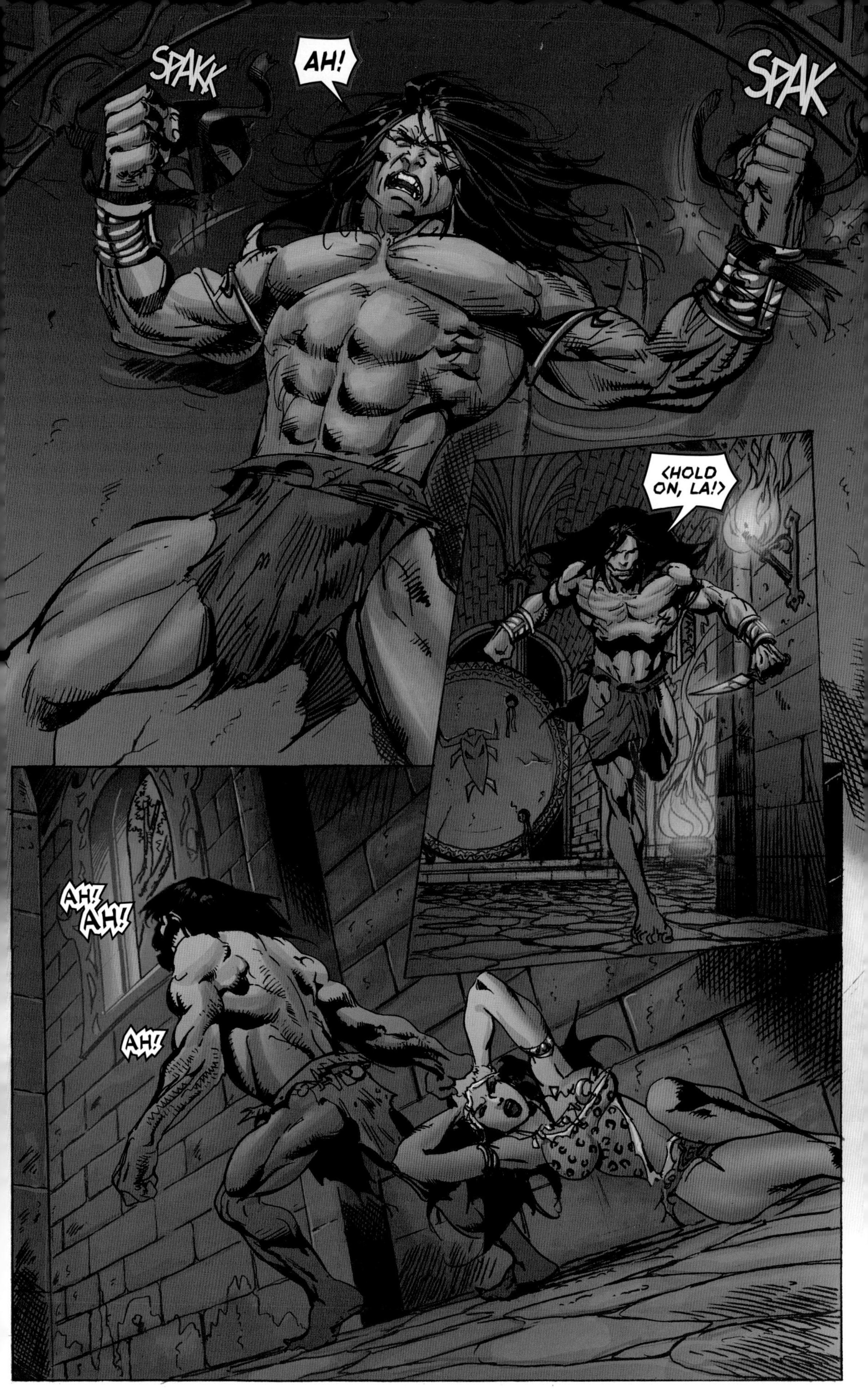
SPAKK
AH!
SPAK
<HOLD ON, LA!>
AH! AH!
AH!

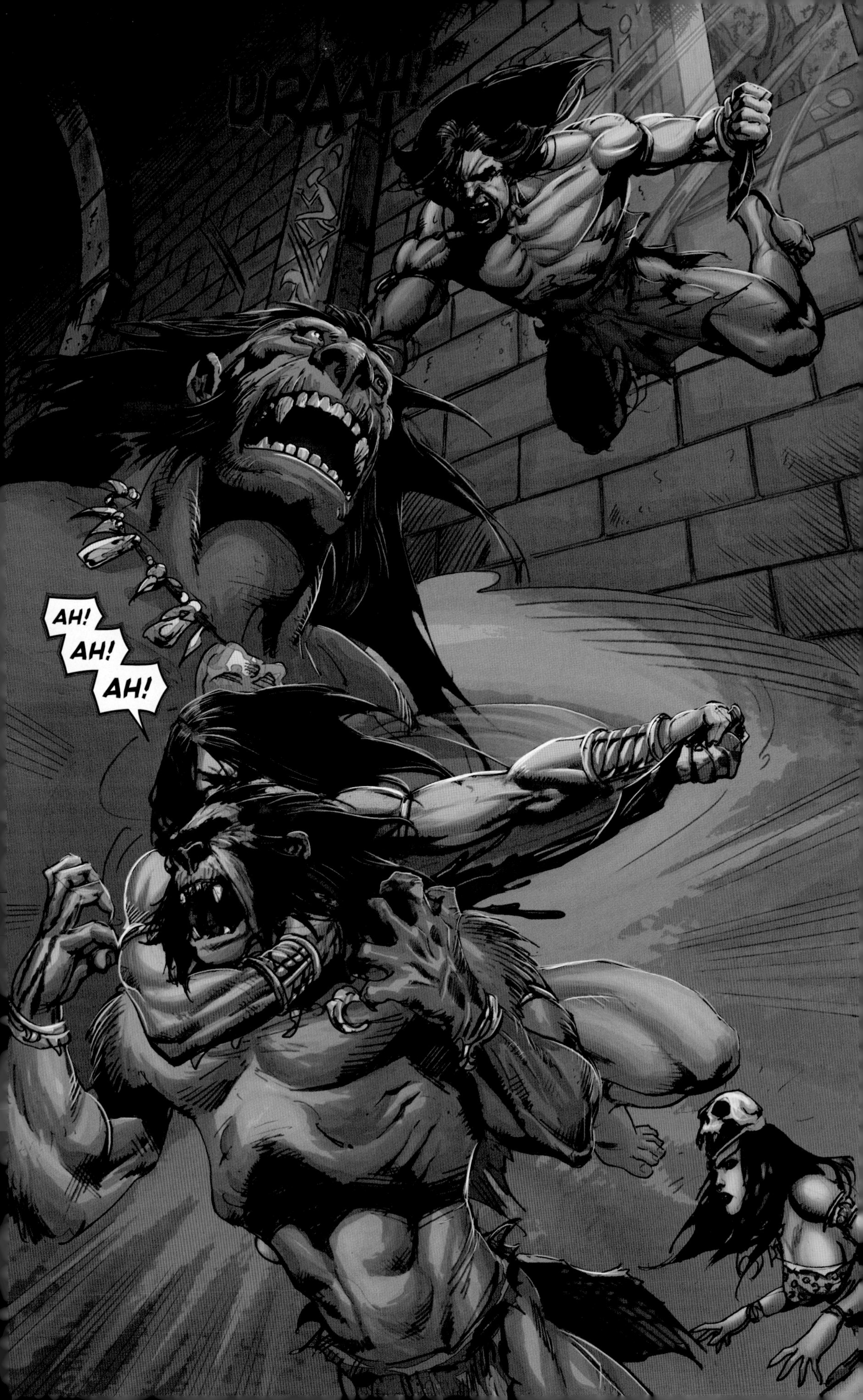
URAAH!
AH! AH! AH!

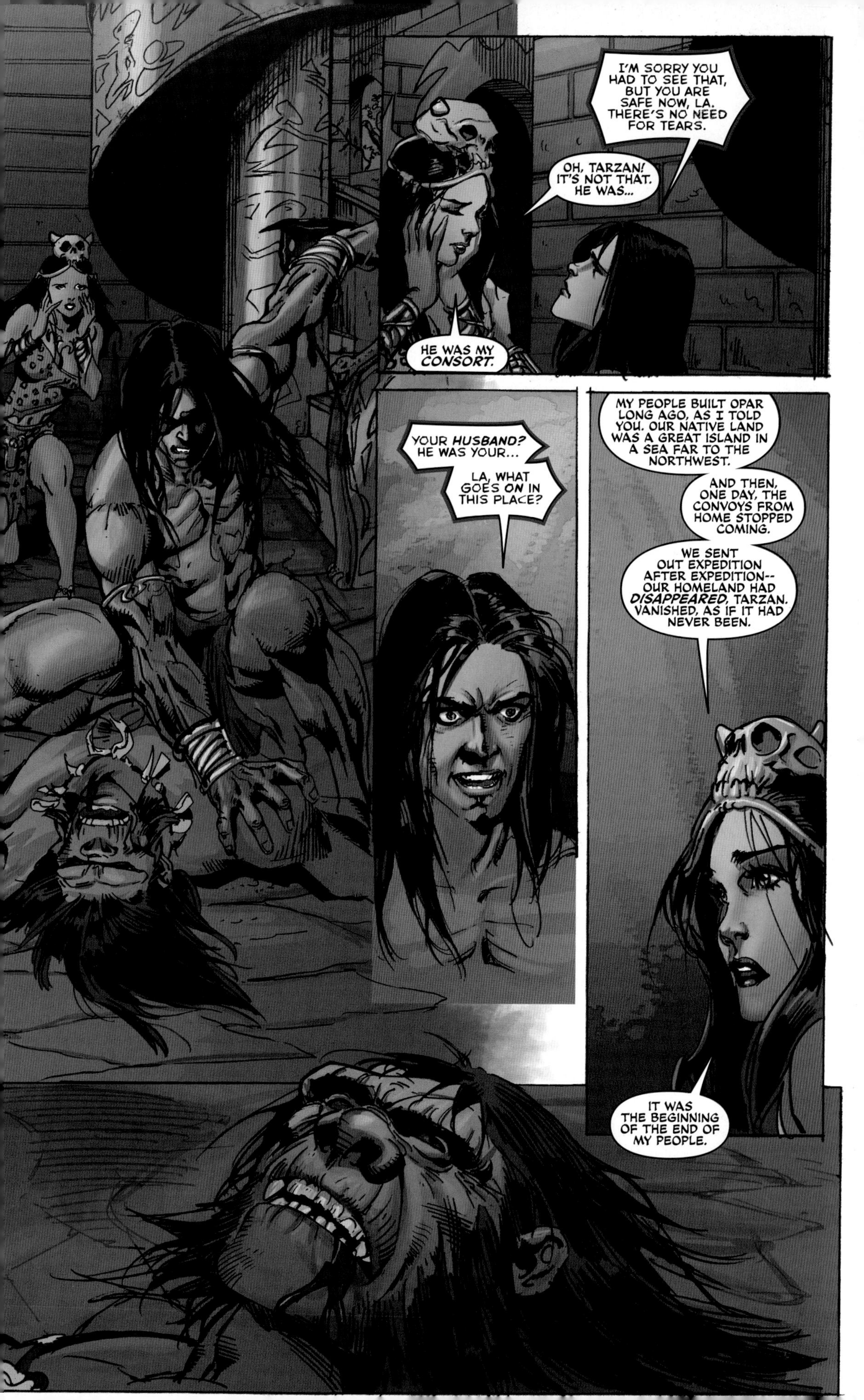
I'M SORRY YOU HAD TO SEE THAT, BUT YOU ARE SAFE NOW, LA. THERE'S NO NEED FOR TEARS.
OH, TARZAN! IT'S NOT THAT. HE WAS...
HE WAS MY *CONSORT.*
YOUR **HUSBAND?** HE WAS YOUR...
LA, WHAT GOES **ON** IN THIS PLACE?
MY PEOPLE BUILT OPAR LONG AGO, AS I TOLD YOU. OUR NATIVE LAND WAS A GREAT ISLAND IN A SEA FAR TO THE NORTHWEST.
AND THEN, ONE DAY, THE CONVOYS FROM HOME STOPPED COMING.
WE SENT OUT EXPEDITION AFTER EXPEDITION-- OUR HOMELAND HAD ***DISAPPEARED***, TARZAN. VANISHED, AS IF IT HAD NEVER BEEN.
IT WAS THE BEGINNING OF THE END OF MY PEOPLE.

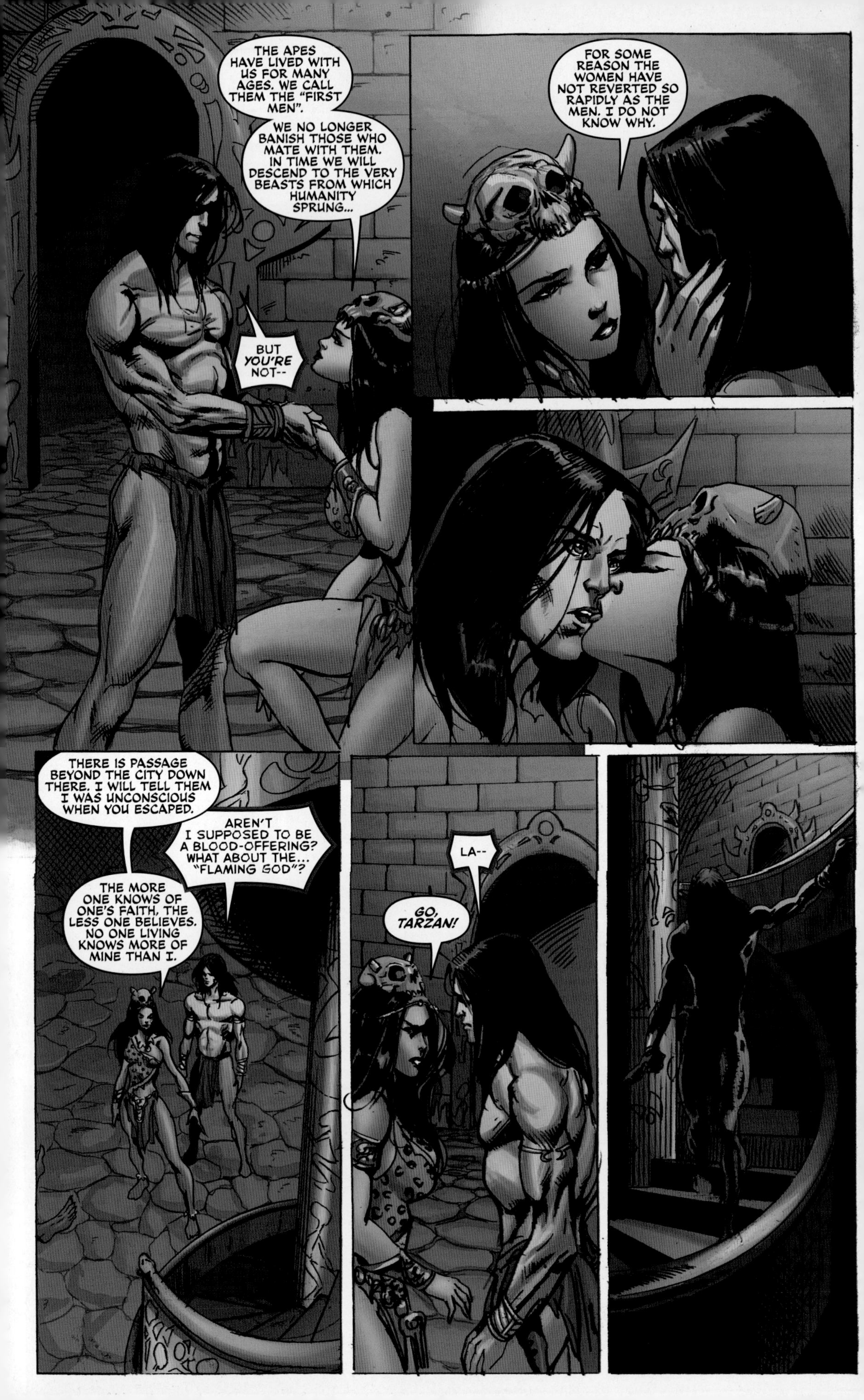
THE APES HAVE LIVED WITH US FOR MANY AGES. WE CALL THEM THE "FIRST MEN".
WE NO LONGER BANISH THOSE WHO MATE WITH THEM. IN TIME WE WILL DESCEND TO THE VERY BEASTS FROM WHICH HUMANITY SPRUNG...
BUT *YOU'RE* NOT--
FOR SOME REASON THE WOMEN HAVE NOT REVERTED SO RAPIDLY AS THE MEN. I DO NOT KNOW WHY.
THERE IS PASSAGE BEYOND THE CITY DOWN THERE. I WILL TELL THEM I WAS UNCONSCIOUS WHEN YOU ESCAPED.
AREN'T I SUPPOSED TO BE A BLOOD-OFFERING? WHAT ABOUT THE... "FLAMING GOD"?
THE MORE ONE KNOWS OF ONE'S FAITH, THE LESS ONE BELIEVES. NO ONE LIVING KNOWS MORE OF MINE THAN I.
LA--
GO, TARZAN!

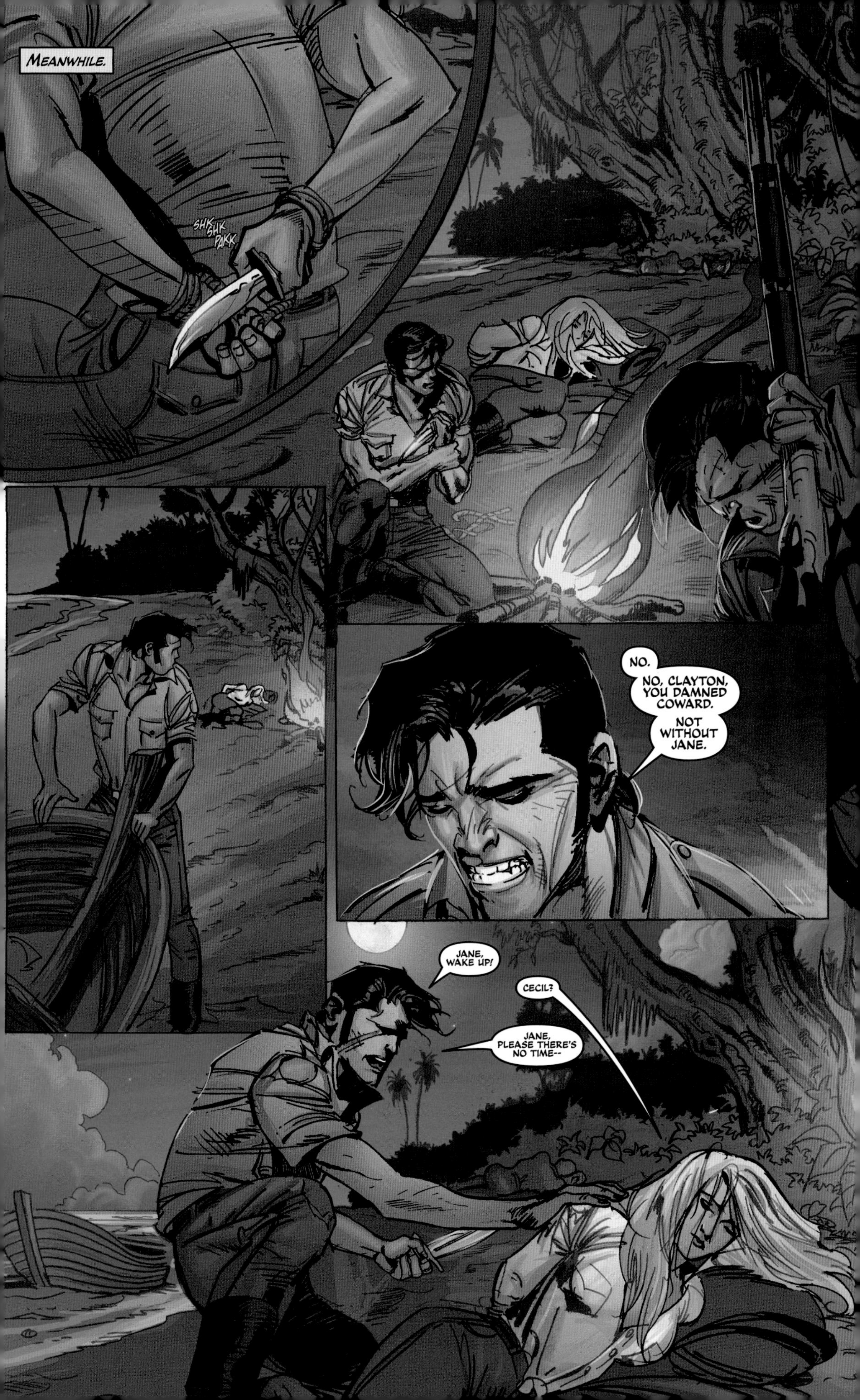
MEANWHILE.
SHK SHK PAKK
NO.
NO, CLAYTON, YOU DAMNED COWARD.
NOT WITHOUT JANE.
JANE, WAKE UP!
CECIL?
JANE, PLEASE THERE'S NO TIME--

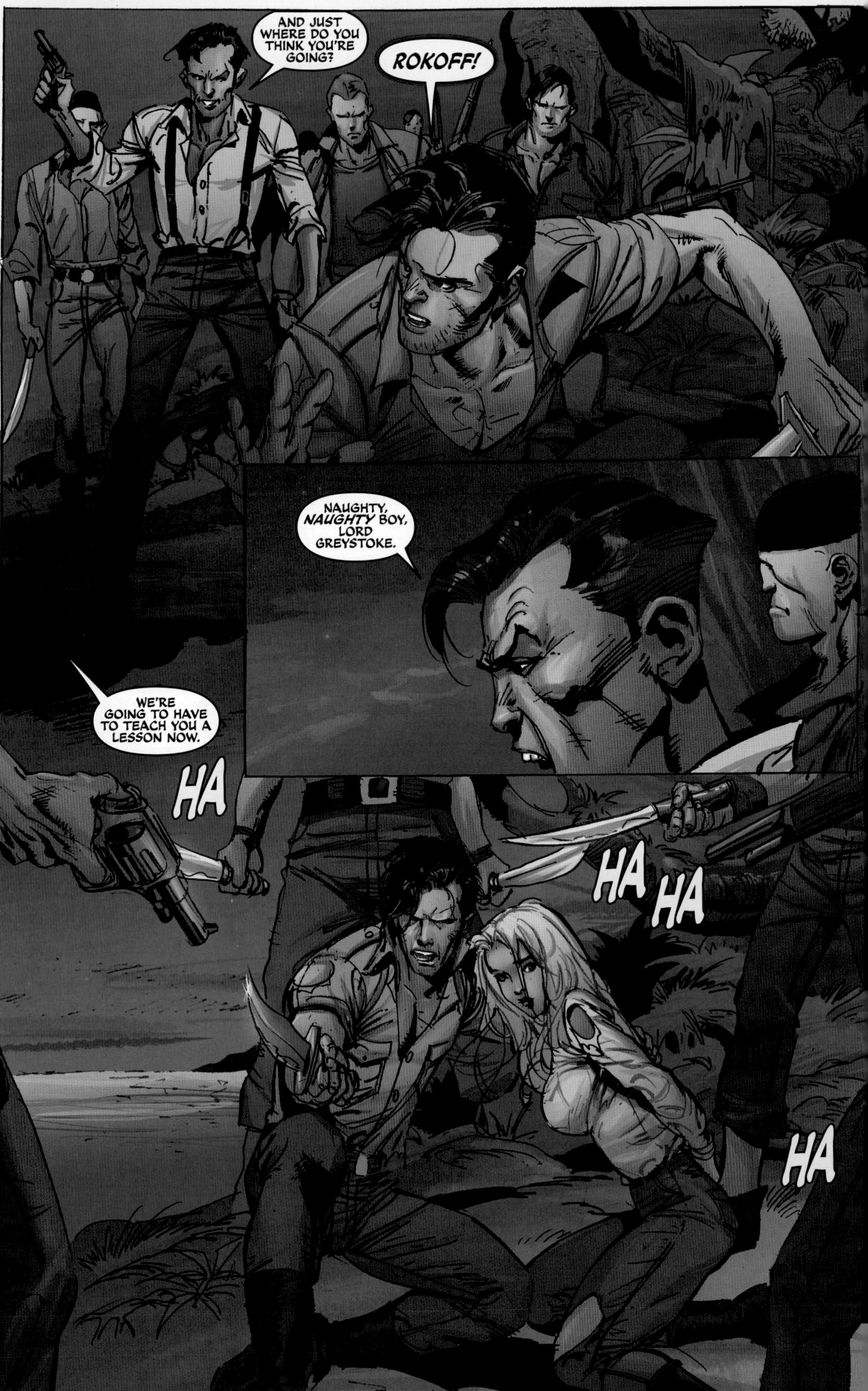
AND JUST WHERE DO YOU THINK YOU'RE GOING?
ROKOFF!
NAUGHTY, NAUGHTY BOY, LORD GREYSTOKE.
WE'RE GOING TO HAVE TO TEACH YOU A LESSON NOW.
HA
HA HA
HA

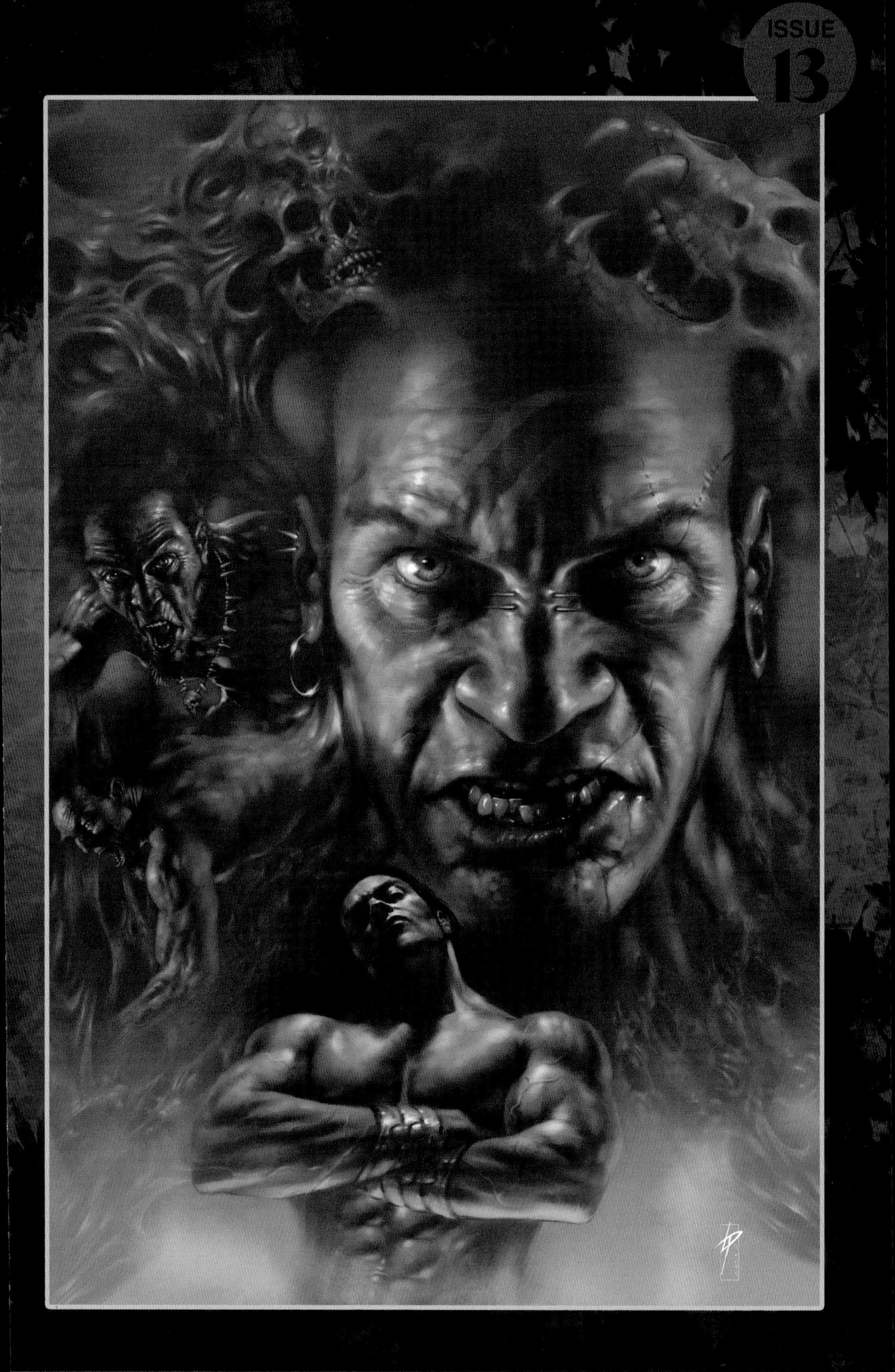
ISSUE
13

COVER BY LUCIO PARRILLO

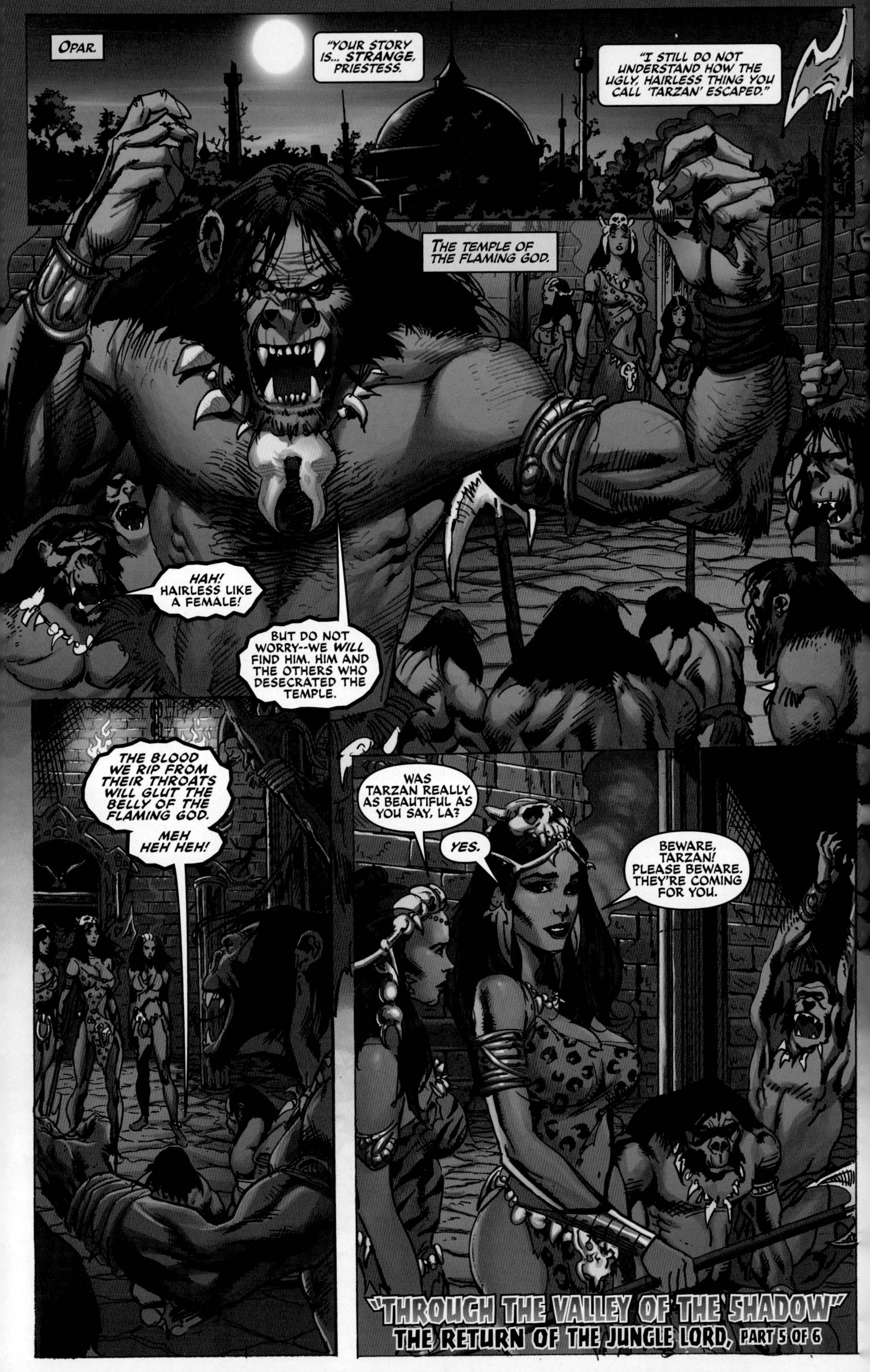
OPAR.
"YOUR STORY IS... STRANGE, PRIESTESS.
"I STILL DO NOT UNDERSTAND HOW THE UGLY, HAIRLESS THING YOU CALL 'TARZAN' ESCAPED."
THE TEMPLE OF THE FLAMING GOD.
HAH! HAIRLESS LIKE A FEMALE!
BUT DO NOT WORRY--WE WILL FIND HIM. HIM AND THE OTHERS WHO DESECRATED THE TEMPLE.
THE BLOOD WE RIP FROM THEIR THROATS WILL GLUT THE BELLY OF THE FLAMING GOD.
MEH HEH HEH!
WAS TARZAN REALLY AS BEAUTIFUL AS YOU SAY, LA?
YES.
BEWARE, TARZAN! PLEASE BEWARE. THEY'RE COMING FOR YOU.
"THROUGH THE VALLEY OF THE SHADOW"
THE RETURN OF THE JUNGLE LORD, PART 5 OF 6

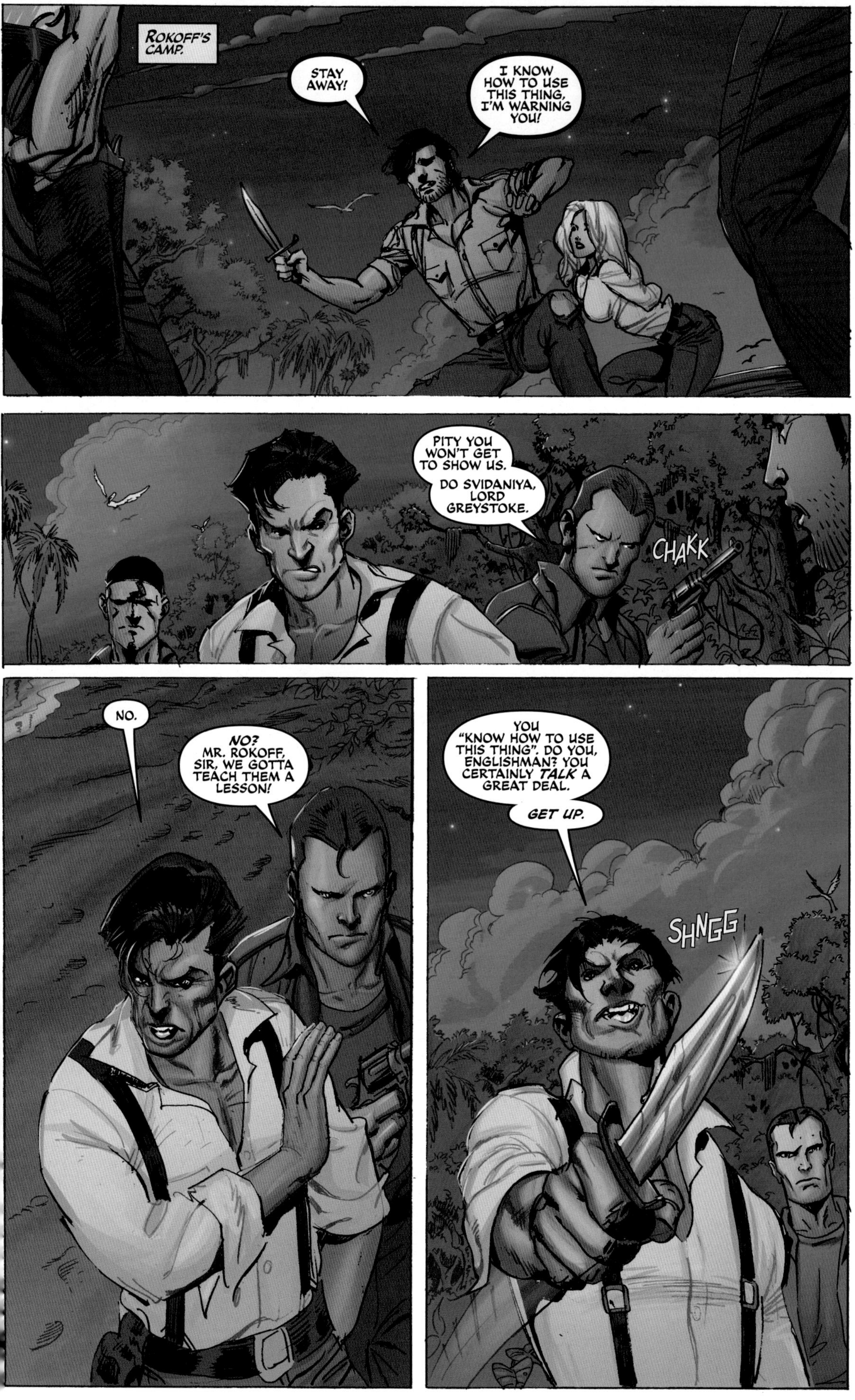
ROKOFF'S CAMP.
STAY AWAY!
I KNOW HOW TO USE THIS THING, I'M WARNING YOU!
PITY YOU WON'T GET TO SHOW US.
DO SVIDANIYA, LORD GREYSTOKE.
CHAKK
NO.
NO? MR. ROKOFF, SIR, WE GOTTA TEACH THEM A LESSON!
YOU "KNOW HOW TO USE THIS THING". DO YOU, ENGLISHMAN? YOU CERTAINLY TALK A GREAT DEAL.
GET UP.
SHNGG

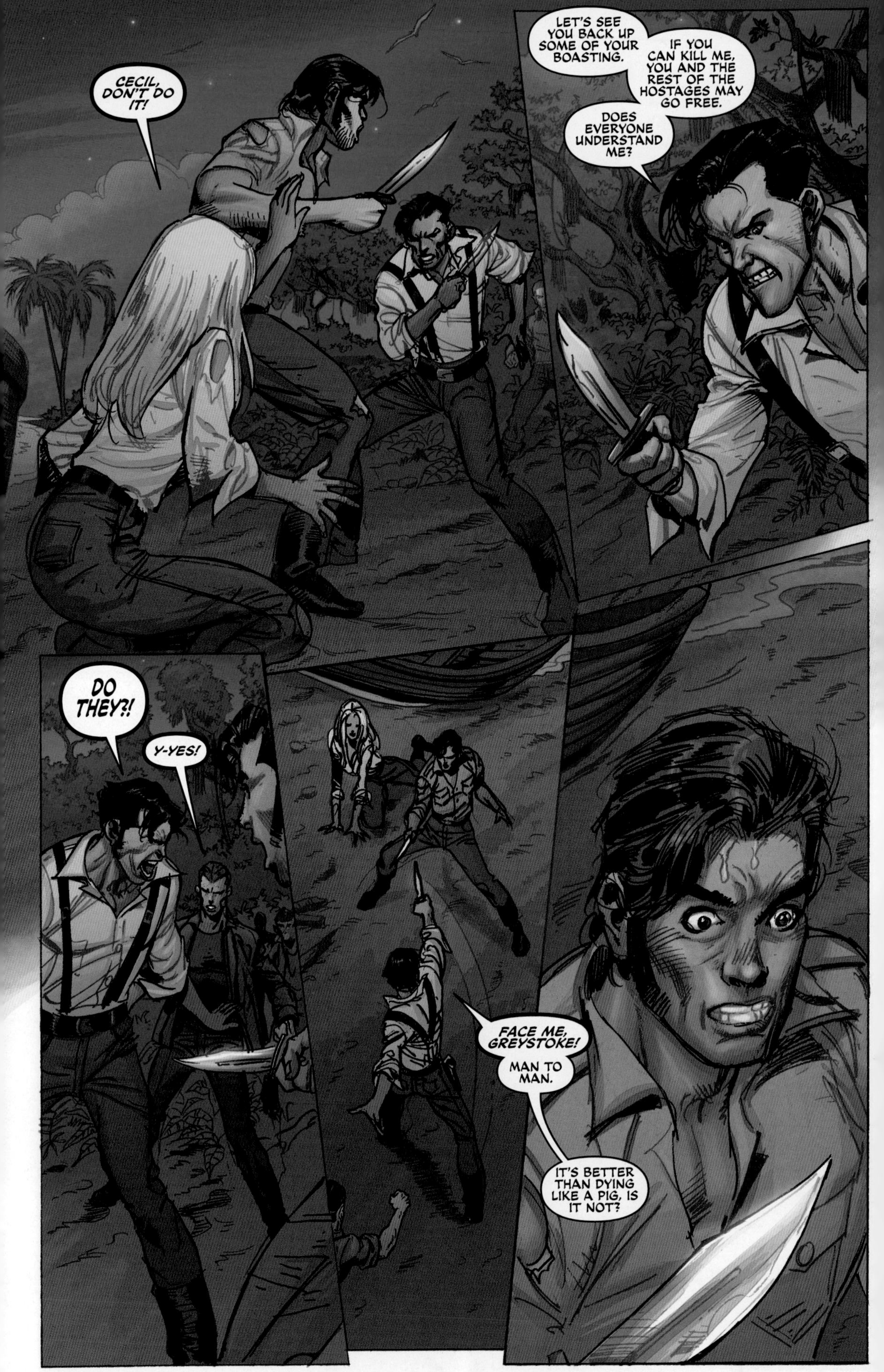
CECIL, DON'T DO IT!
LET'S SEE YOU BACK UP SOME OF YOUR BOASTING.
IF YOU CAN KILL ME, YOU AND THE REST OF THE HOSTAGES MAY GO FREE.
DOES EVERYONE UNDERSTAND ME?
DO THEY?!
Y-YES!
FACE ME, GREYSTOKE!
MAN TO MAN.
IT'S BETTER THAN DYING LIKE A PIG, IS IT NOT?

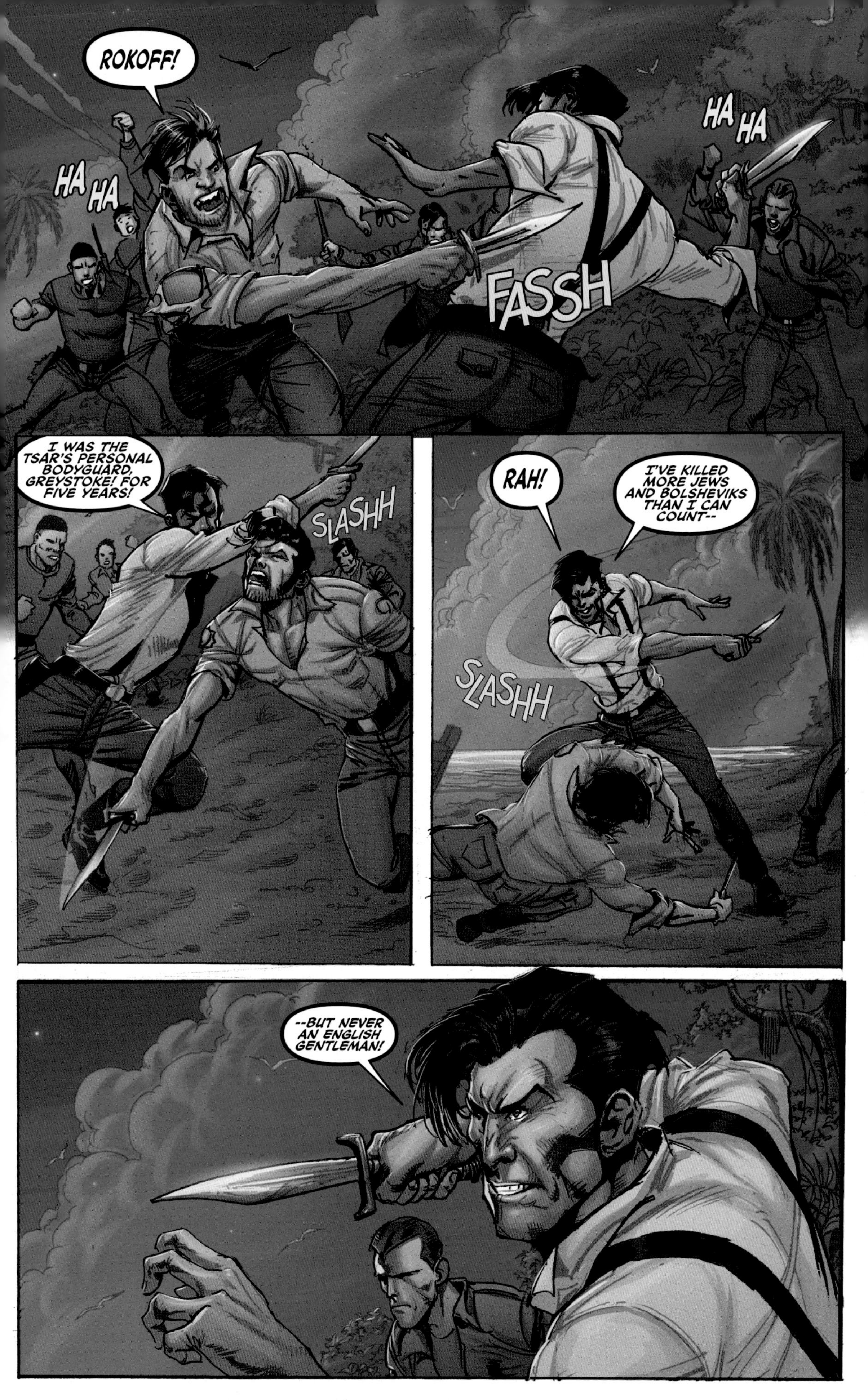
ROKOFF!
HA HA
HA HA
FASSH
I WAS THE TSAR'S PERSONAL BODYGUARD, GREYSTOKE! FOR FIVE YEARS!
SLASHH
RAH!
I'VE KILLED MORE JEWS AND BOLSHEVIKS THAN I CAN COUNT--
SLASHH
--BUT NEVER AN ENGLISH GENTLEMAN!

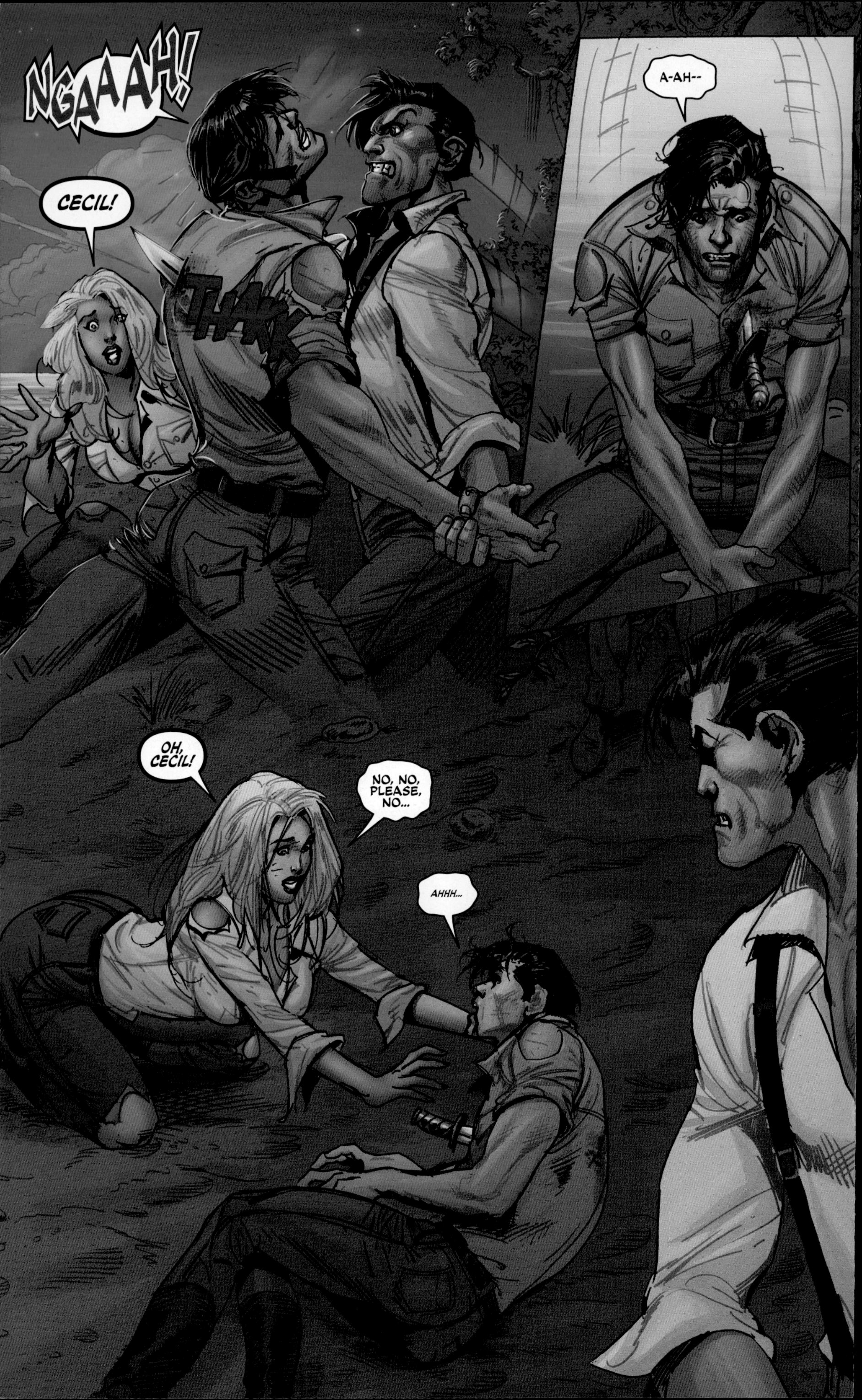
NGAAAH!
CECIL!
THAKK
A-AH--
OH, CECIL!
NO, NO, PLEASE, NO...
AHHH...

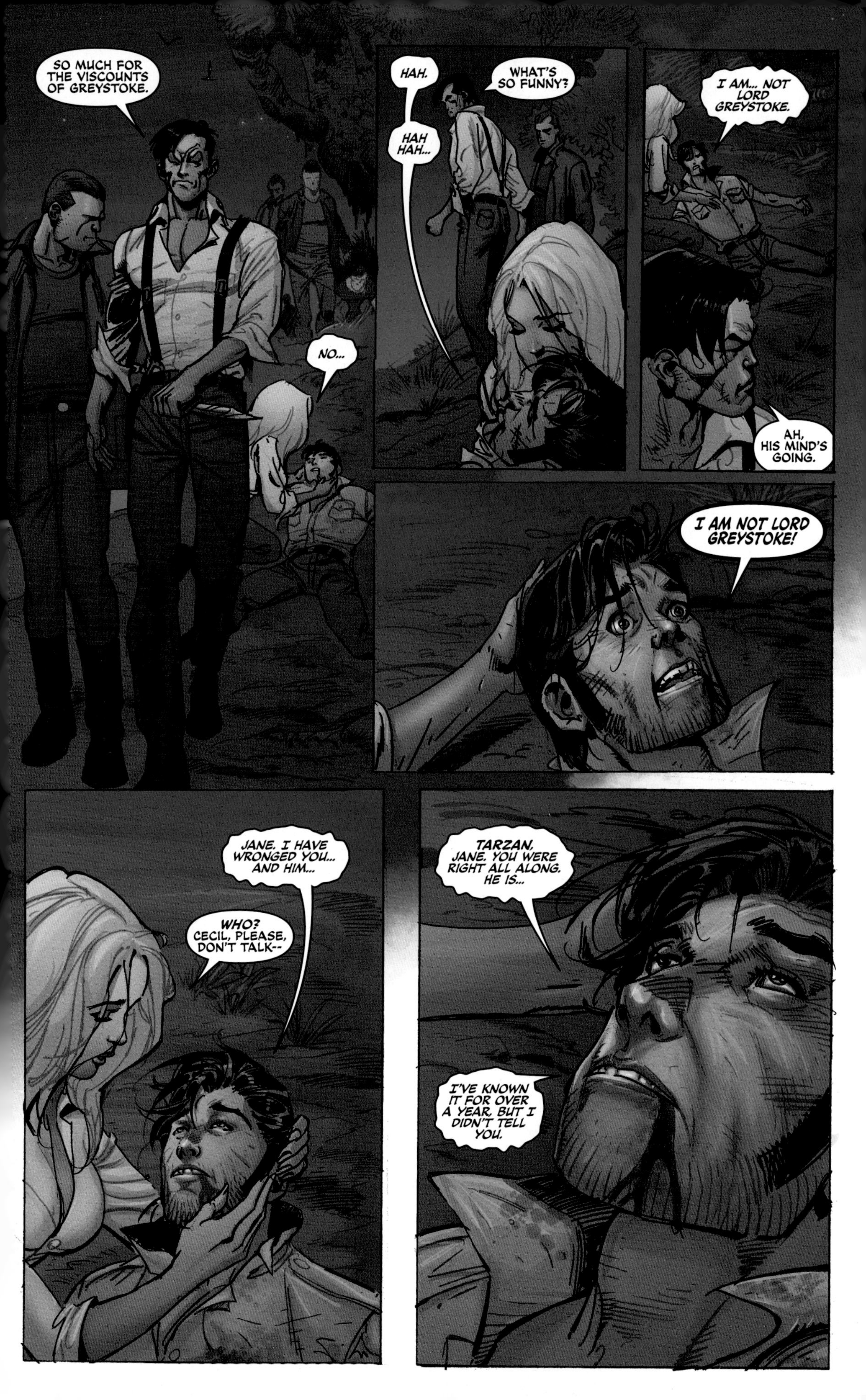
SO MUCH FOR THE VISCOUNTS OF GREYSTOKE.
NO...
HAH.
HAH HAH...
WHAT'S SO FUNNY?
I AM... NOT LORD GREYSTOKE.
AH, HIS MIND'S GOING.
I AM NOT LORD GREYSTOKE!
JANE. I HAVE WRONGED YOU... AND HIM...
WHO? CECIL, PLEASE, DON'T TALK--
TARZAN, JANE. YOU WERE RIGHT ALL ALONG. HE IS...
I'VE KNOWN IT FOR OVER A YEAR, BUT I DIDN'T TELL YOU.

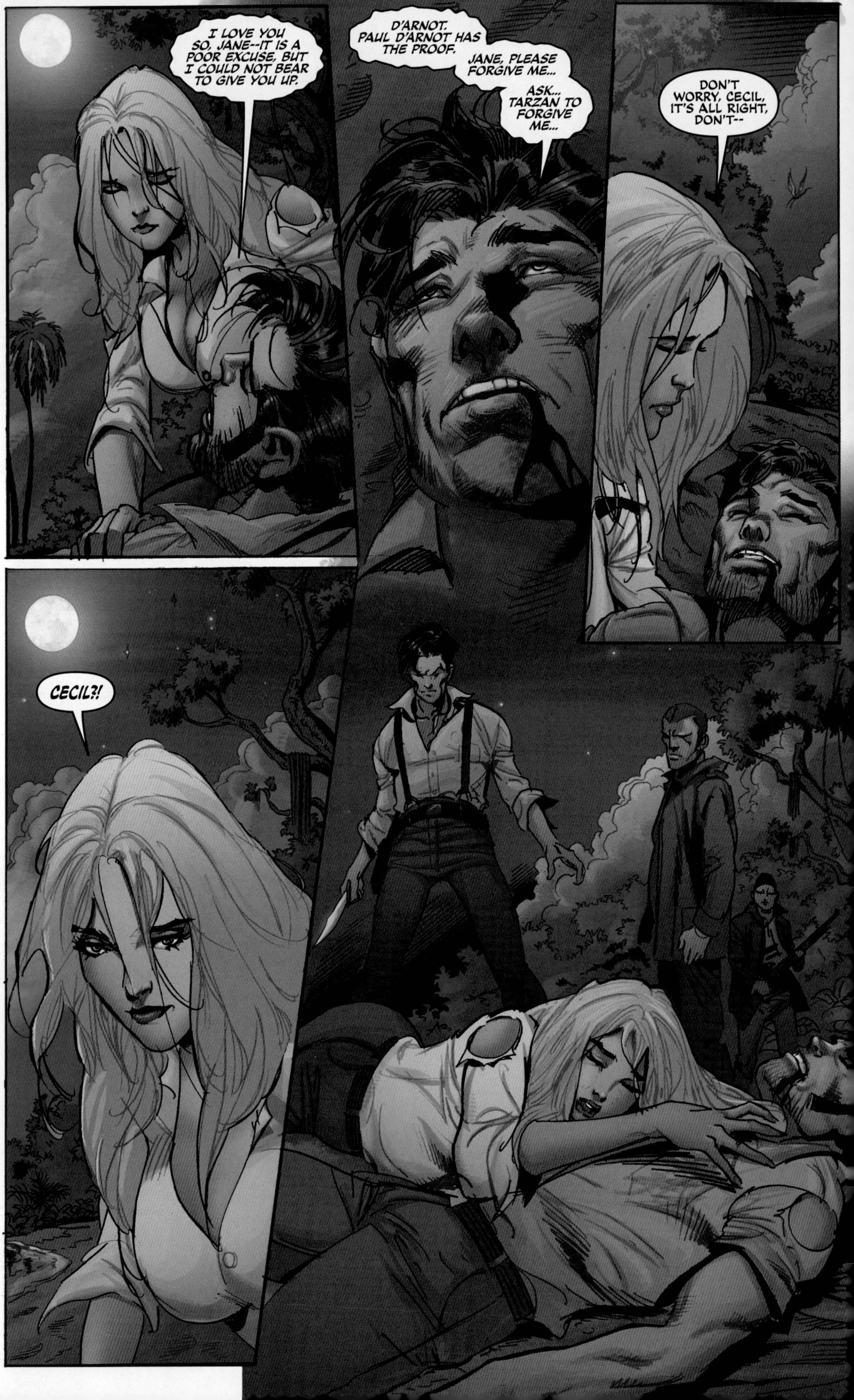
I LOVE YOU SO, JANE--IT IS A POOR EXCUSE, BUT I COULD NOT BEAR TO GIVE YOU UP.
D'ARNOT. PAUL D'ARNOT HAS THE PROOF.
JANE, PLEASE FORGIVE ME...
ASK... TARZAN TO FORGIVE ME...
DON'T WORRY, CECIL, IT'S ALL RIGHT, DON'T--
CECIL?!

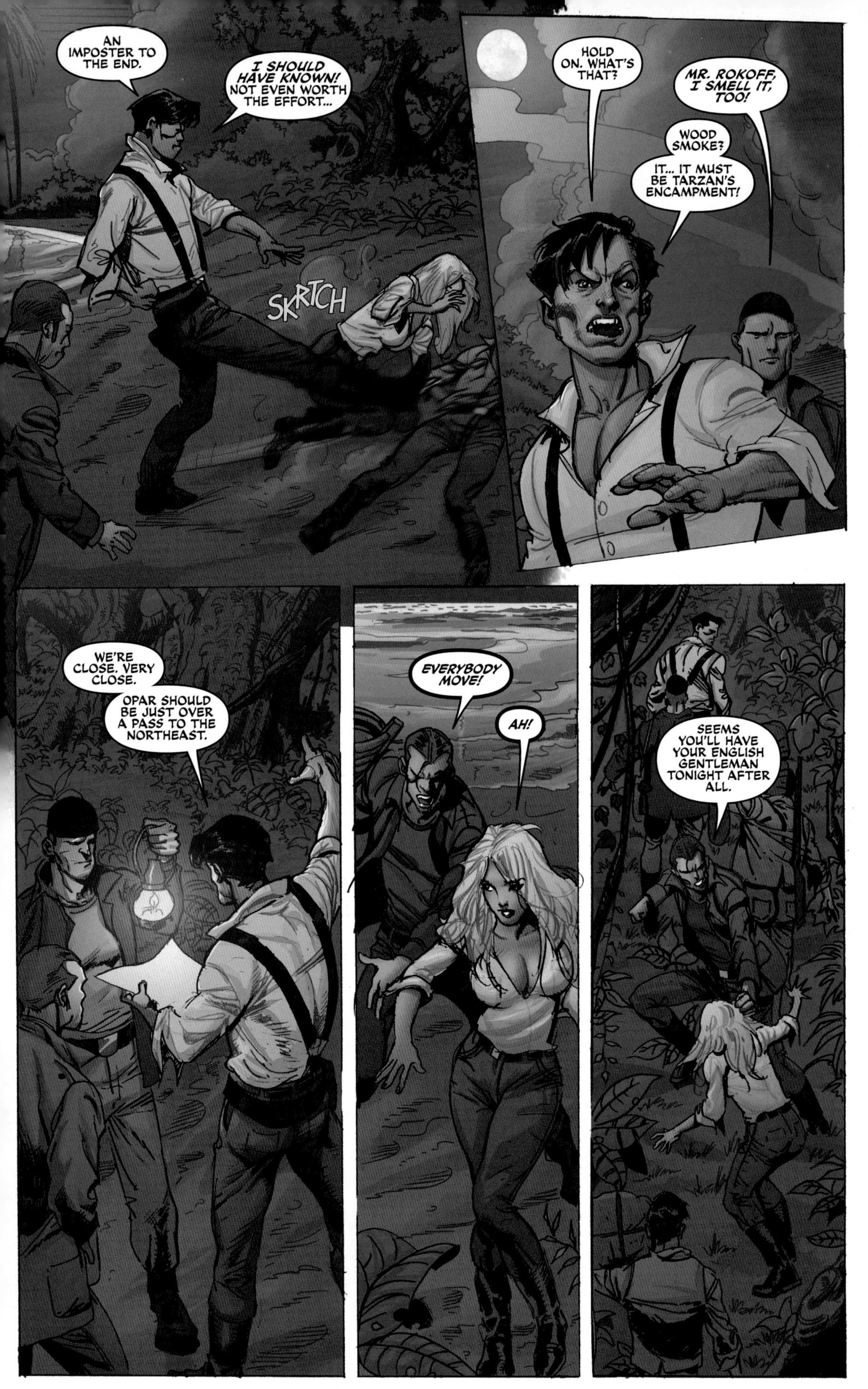
AN IMPOSTER TO THE END.
I SHOULD HAVE KNOWN! NOT EVEN WORTH THE EFFORT...
SKRTCH
HOLD ON. WHAT'S THAT?
MR. ROKOFF, I SMELL IT, TOO!
WOOD SMOKE?
IT... IT MUST BE TARZAN'S ENCAMPMENT!
WE'RE CLOSE. VERY CLOSE.
OPAR SHOULD BE JUST OVER A PASS TO THE NORTHEAST.
EVERYBODY MOVE!
AH!
SEEMS YOU'LL HAVE YOUR ENGLISH GENTLEMAN TONIGHT AFTER ALL.

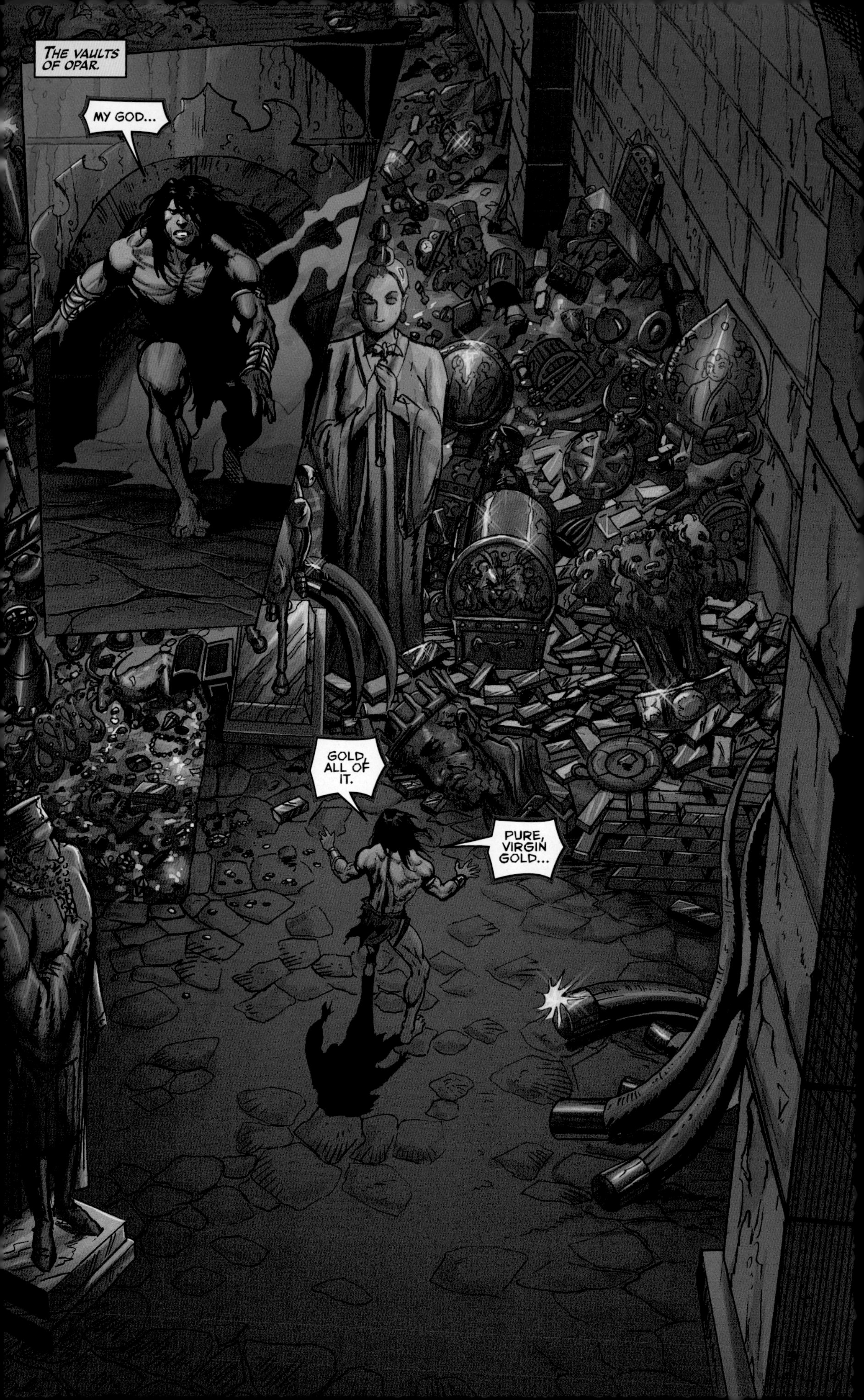
THE VAULTS OF OPAR.
MY GOD...
GOLD, ALL OF IT.
PURE, VIRGIN GOLD...

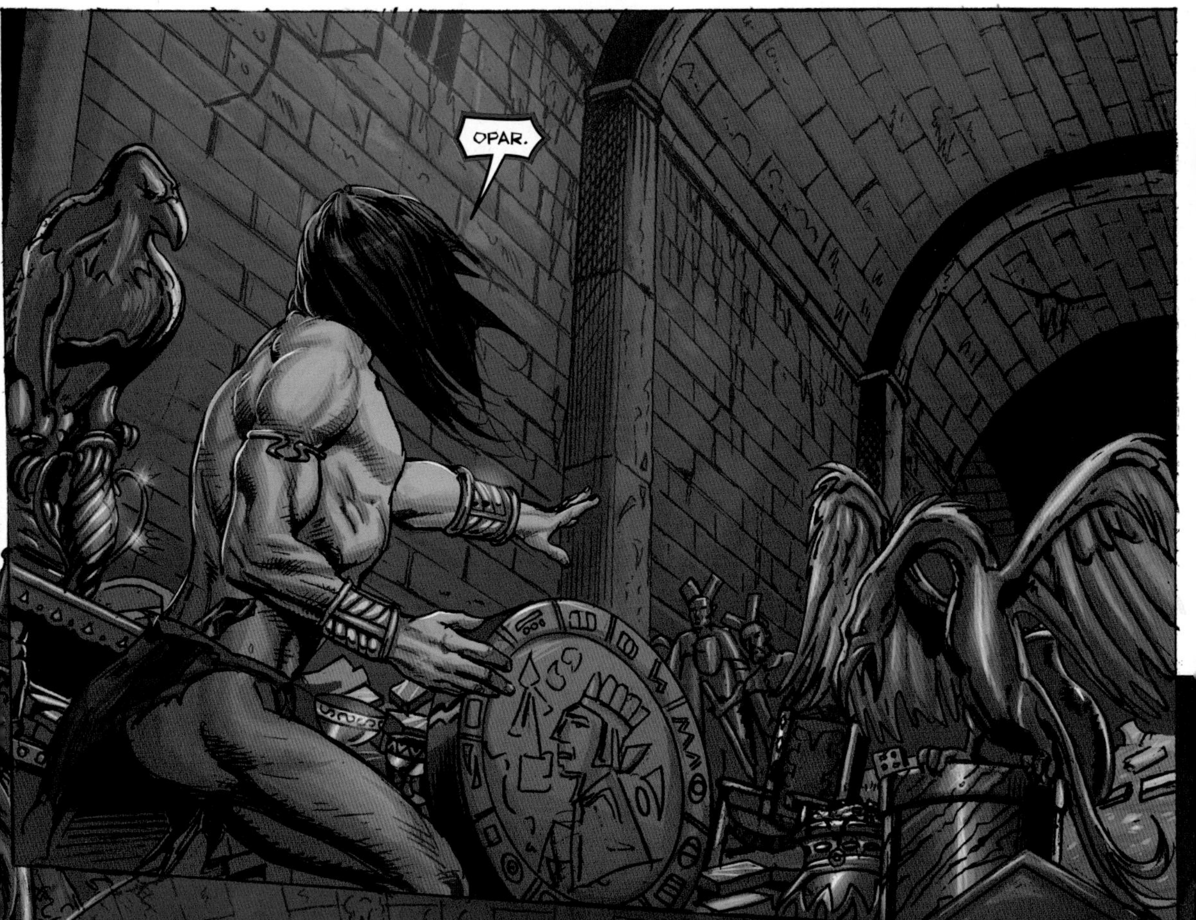
OPAR.

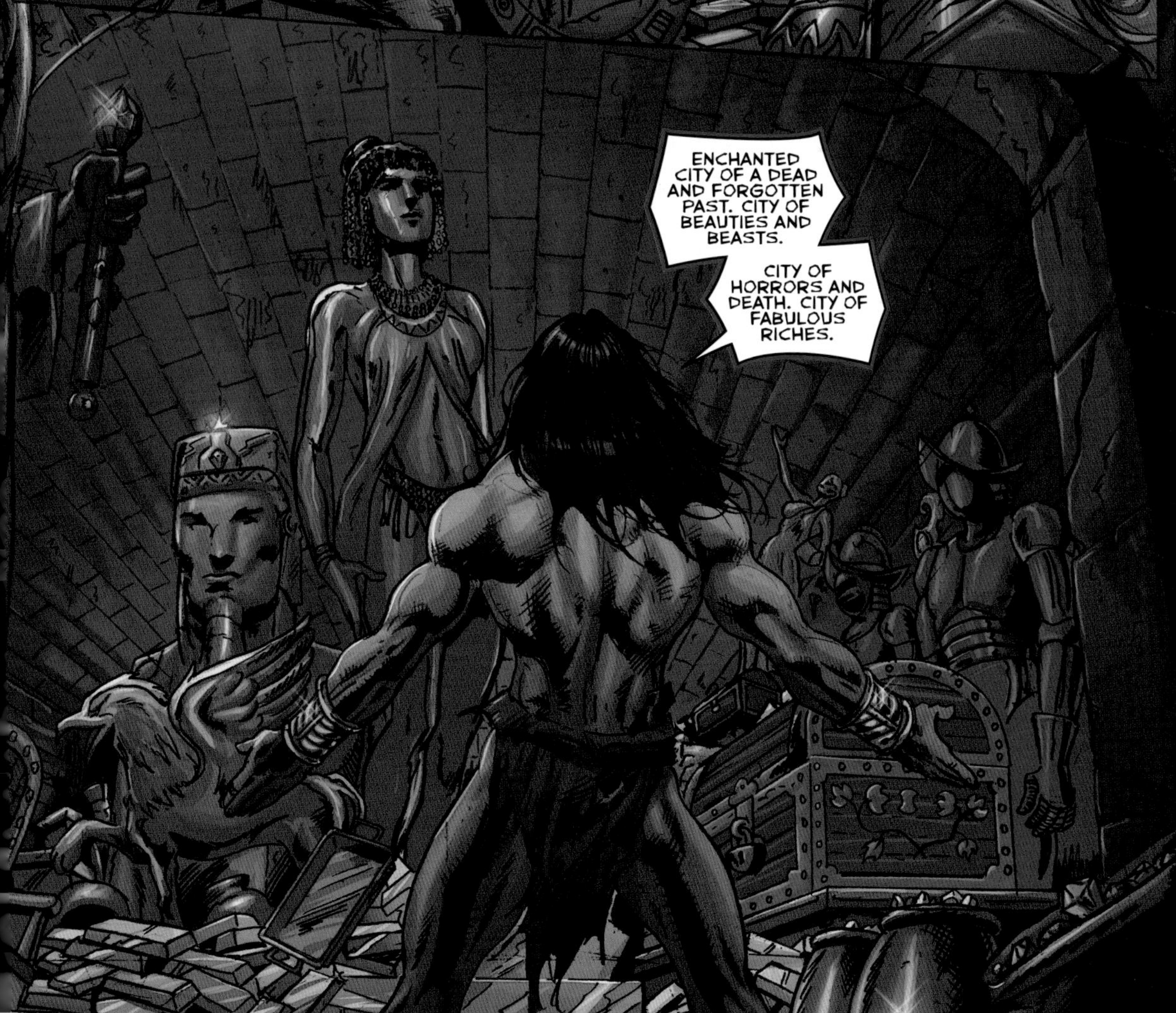
ENCHANTED CITY OF A DEAD AND FORGOTTEN PAST. CITY OF BEAUTIES AND BEASTS.
CITY OF HORRORS AND DEATH. CITY OF FABULOUS RICHES.

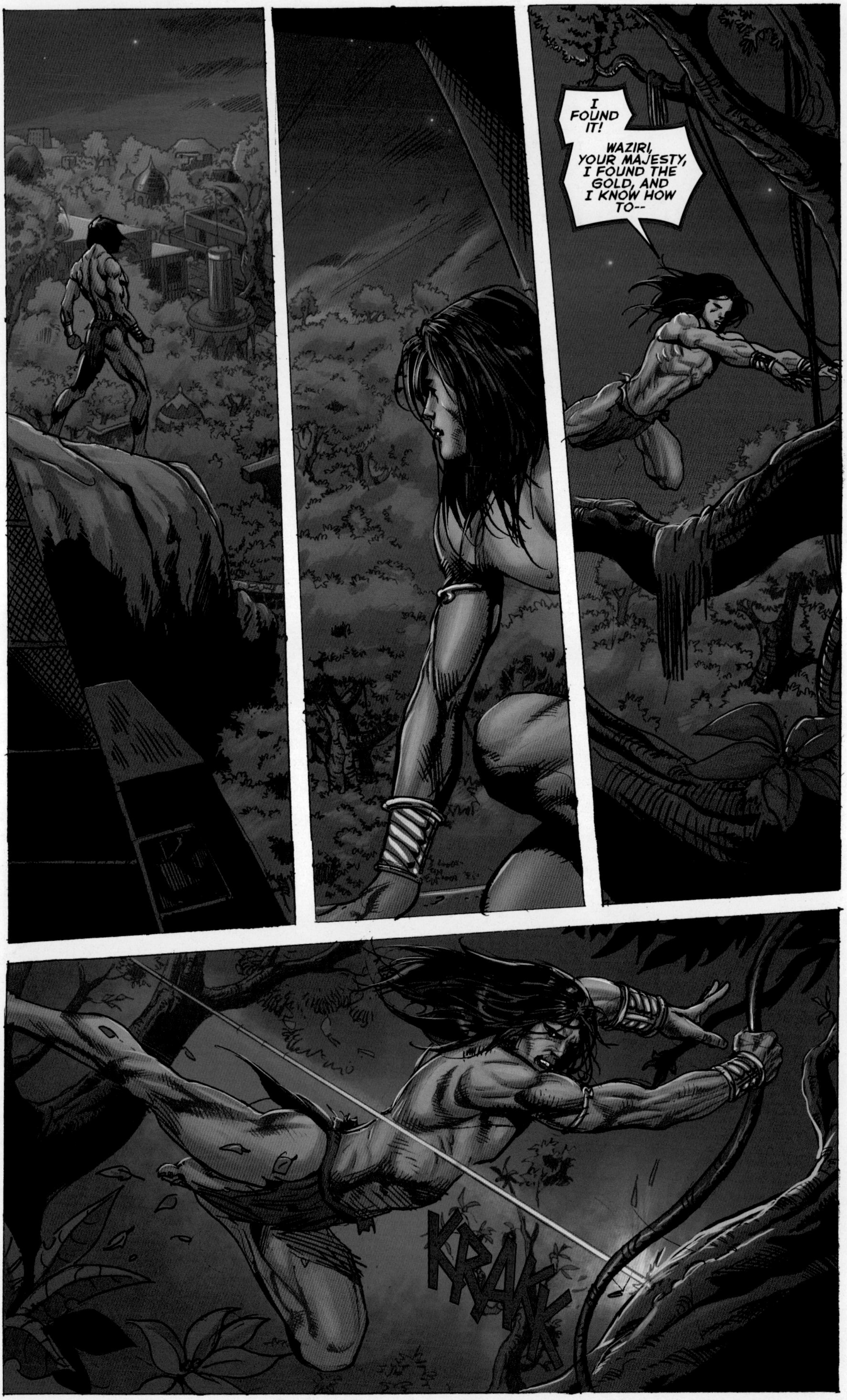
I FOUND IT!
WAZIRI, YOUR MAJESTY, I FOUND THE GOLD, AND I KNOW HOW TO--
KRAKK

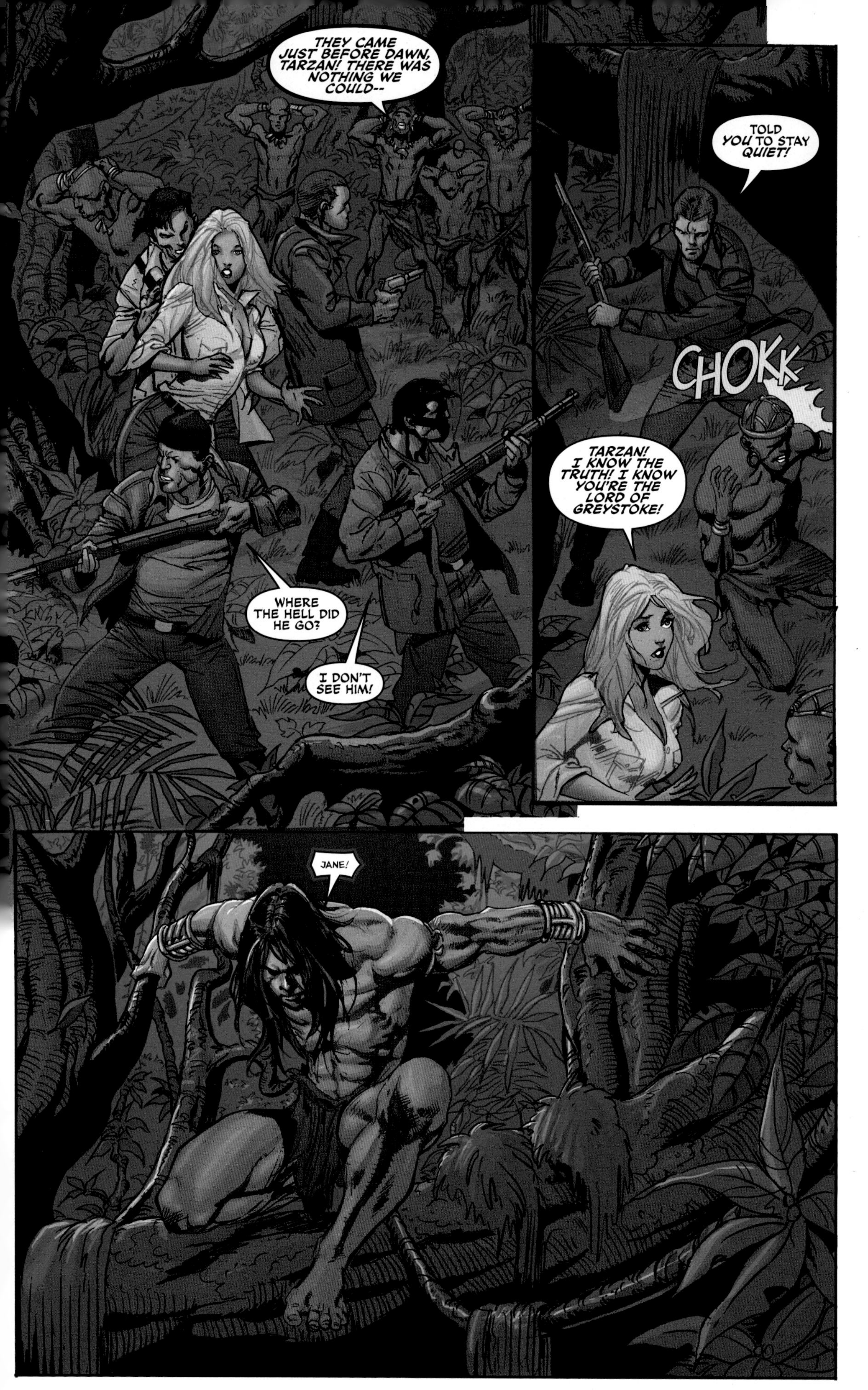
THEY CAME JUST BEFORE DAWN, TARZAN! THERE WAS NOTHING WE COULD--
WHERE THE HELL DID HE GO?
I DON'T SEE HIM!
TOLD YOU TO STAY QUIET!
CHOKK
TARZAN! I KNOW THE TRUTH! I KNOW YOU'RE THE LORD OF GREYSTOKE!
JANE!

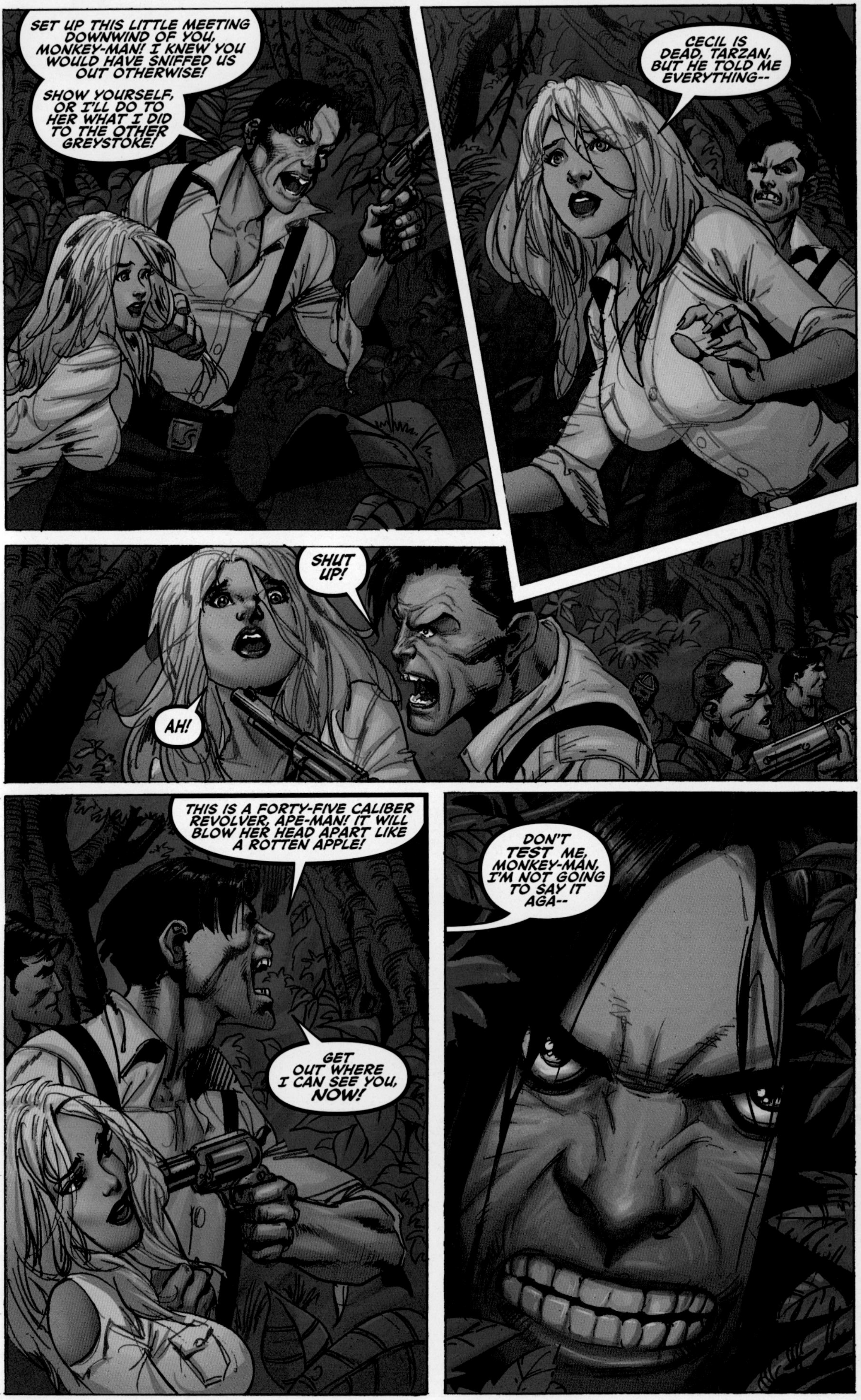
SET UP THIS LITTLE MEETING DOWNWIND OF YOU, MONKEY-MAN! I KNEW YOU WOULD HAVE SNIFFED US OUT OTHERWISE!
SHOW YOURSELF, OR I'LL DO TO HER WHAT I DID TO THE OTHER GREYSTOKE!
CECIL IS DEAD, TARZAN, BUT HE TOLD ME EVERYTHING--
SHUT UP!
AH!
THIS IS A FORTY-FIVE CALIBER REVOLVER, APE-MAN! IT WILL BLOW HER HEAD APART LIKE A ROTTEN APPLE!
GET OUT WHERE I CAN SEE YOU, NOW!
DON'T TEST ME, MONKEY-MAN, I'M NOT GOING TO SAY IT AGA--

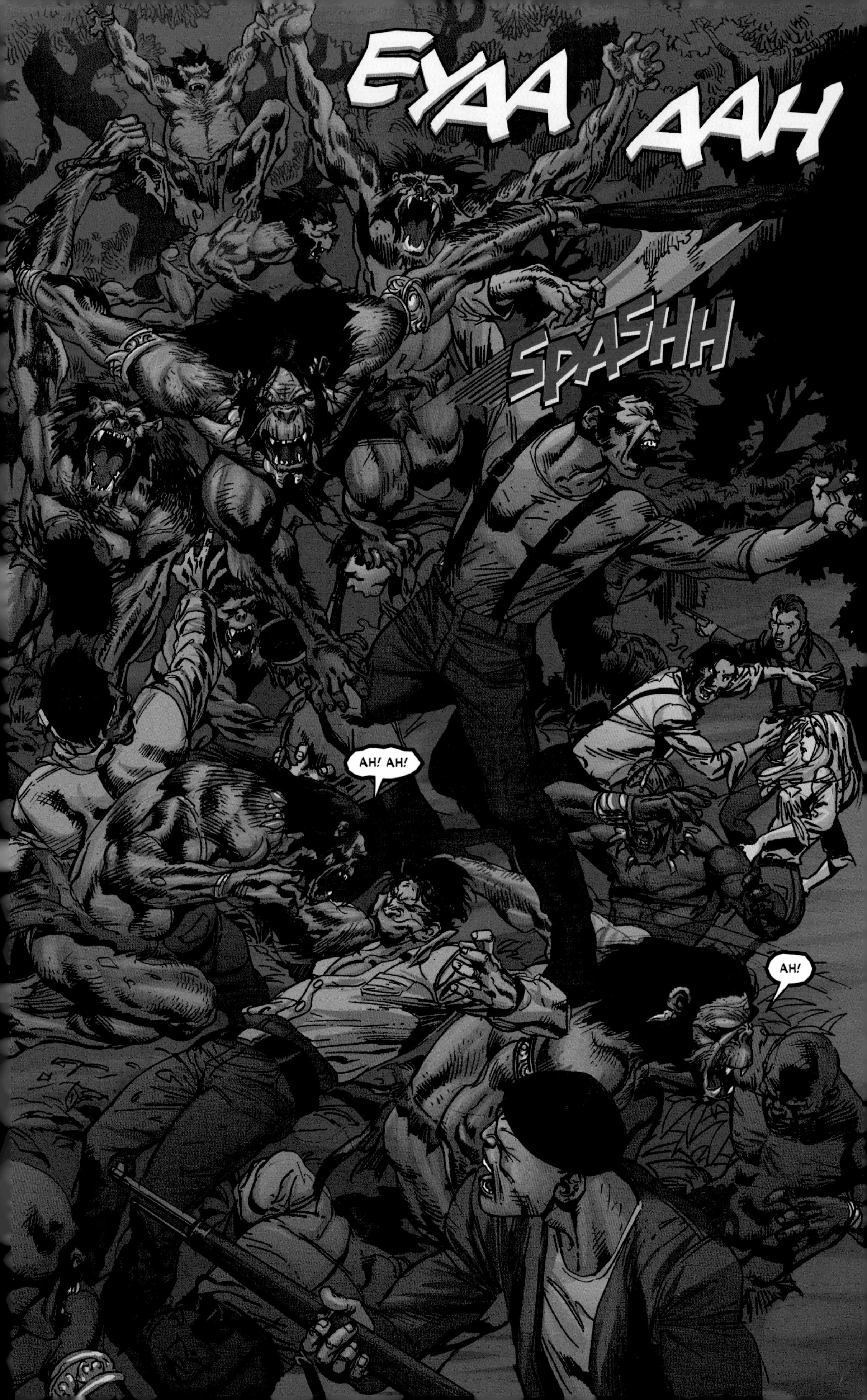
EYAA AAH
SPASHH
AH! AH!
AH!

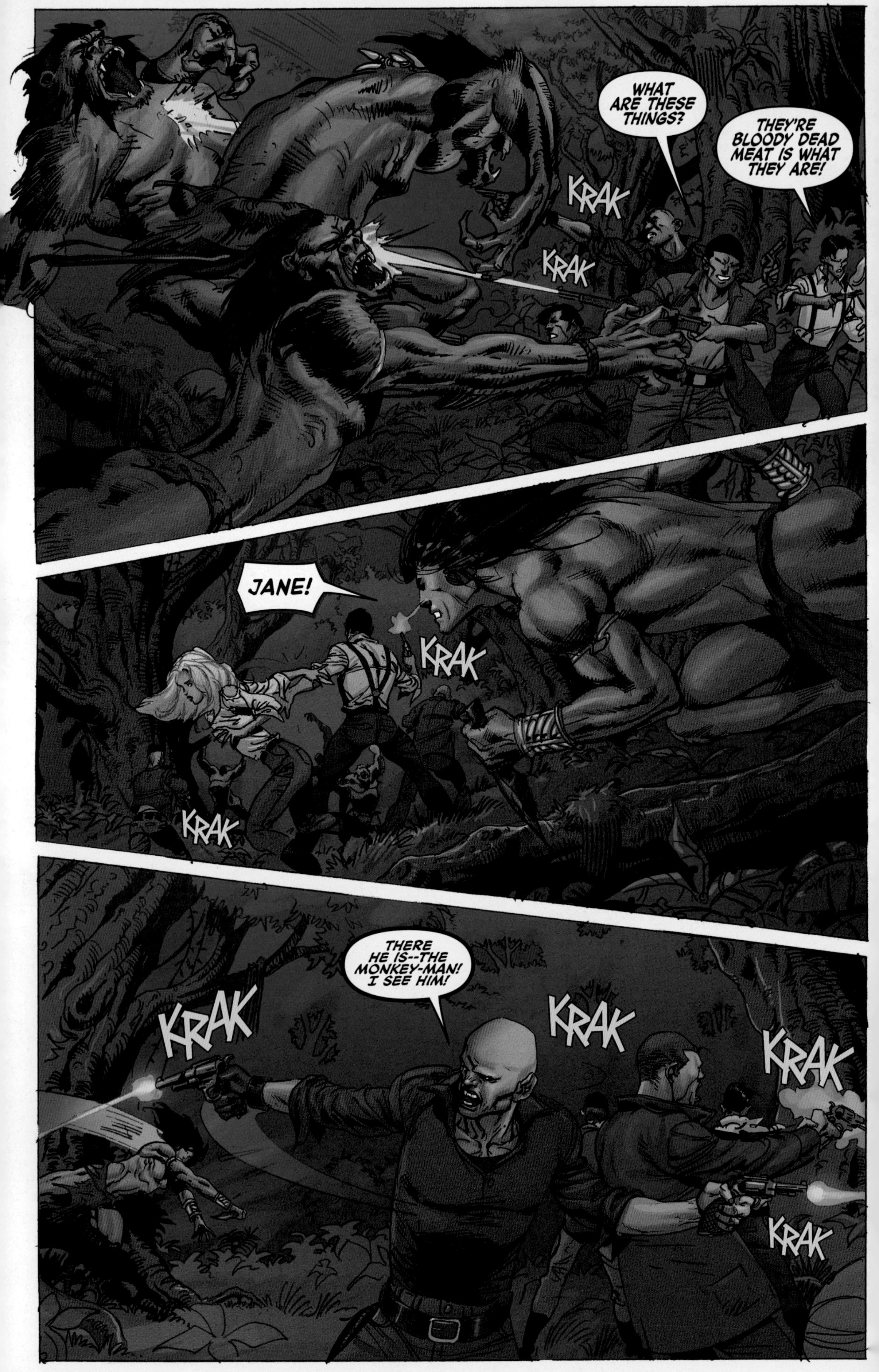
WHAT ARE THESE THINGS?
THEY'RE BLOODY DEAD MEAT IS WHAT THEY ARE!
KRAK
KRAK
JANE!
KRAK
KRAK
THERE HE IS--THE MONKEY-MAN! I SEE HIM!
KRAK
KRAK
KRAK
KRAK

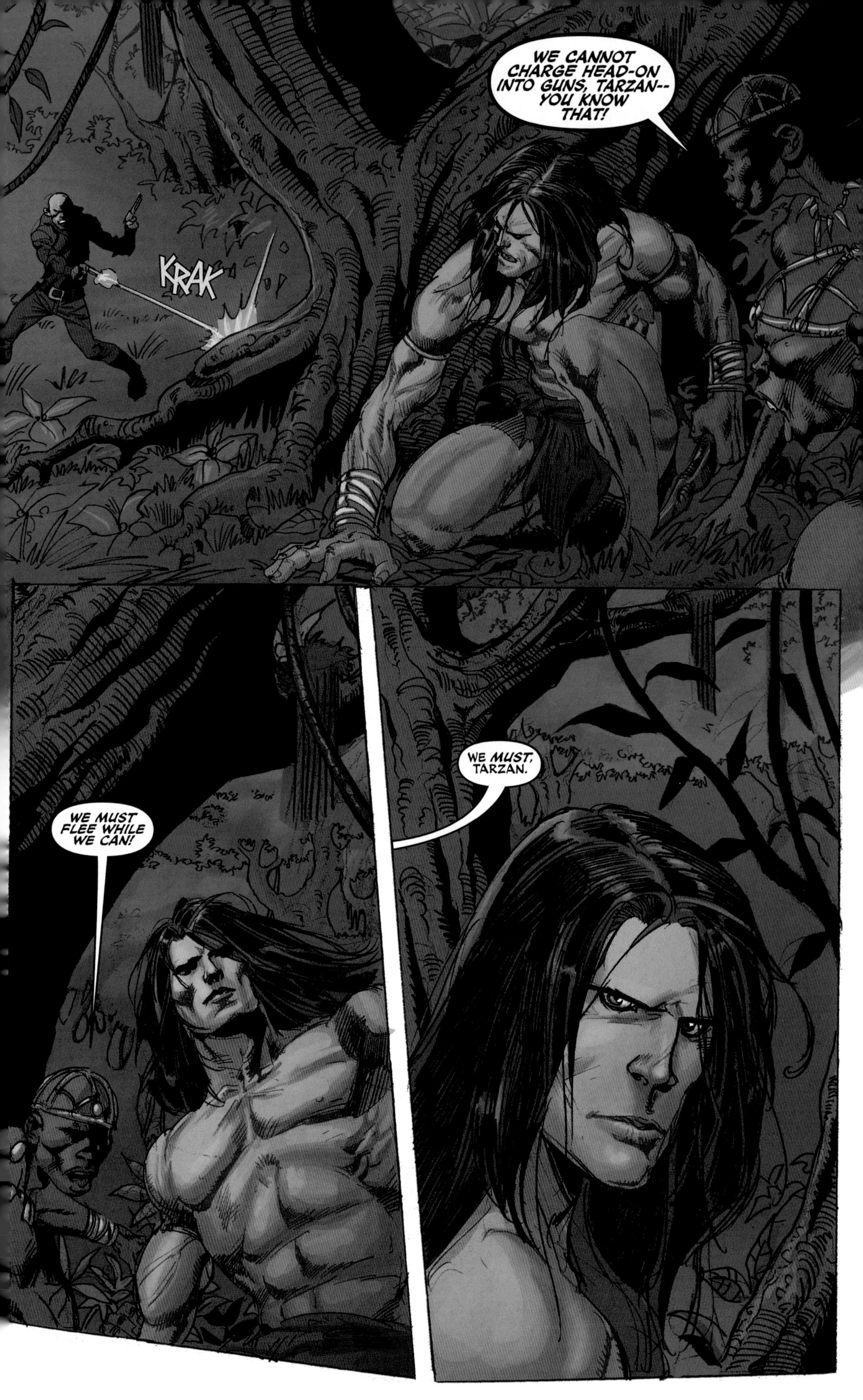
KRAK
WE CANNOT CHARGE HEAD-ON INTO GUNS, TARZAN-- YOU KNOW THAT!
WE MUST FLEE WHILE WE CAN!
WE MUST, TARZAN.

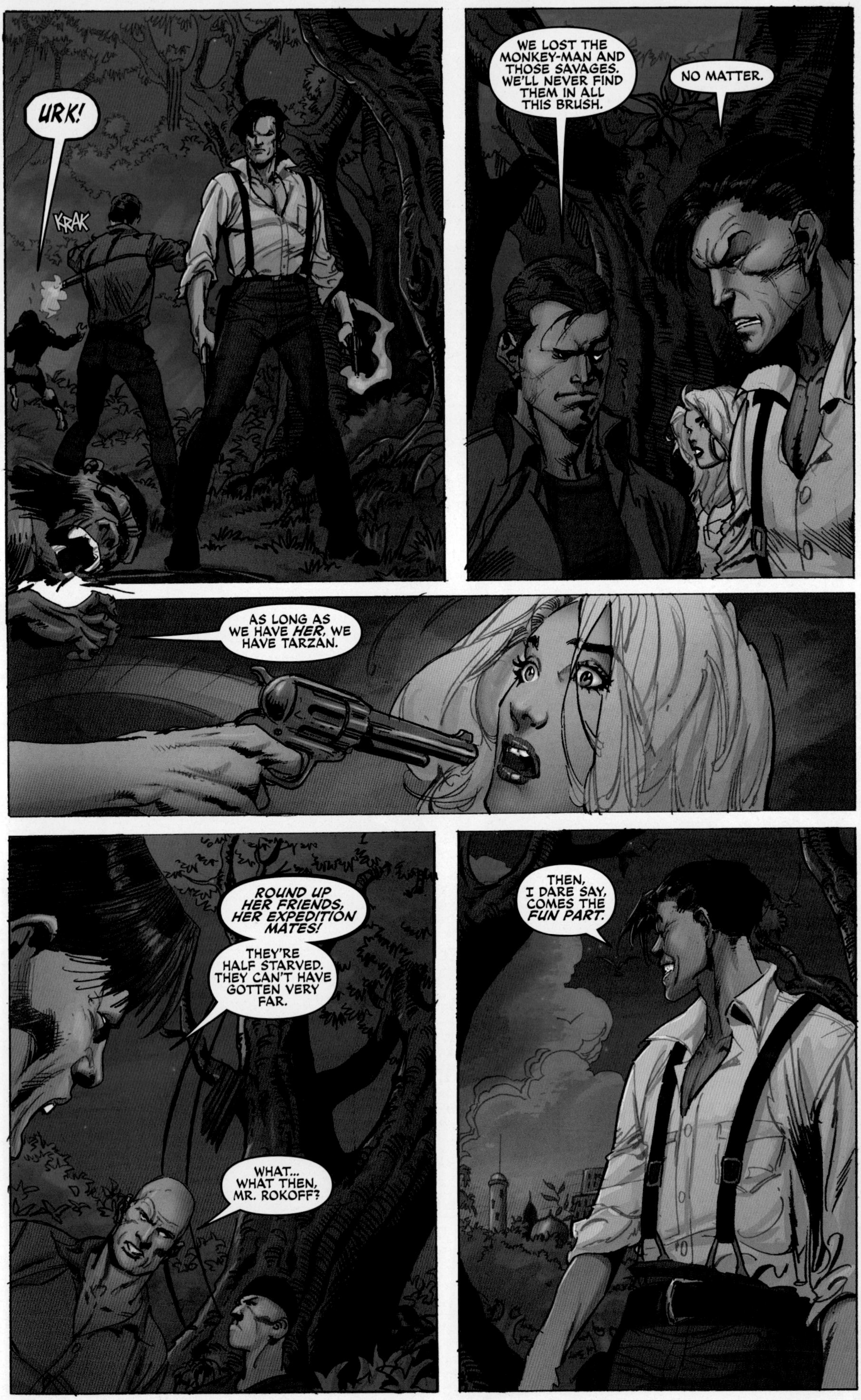
URK!
KRAK
WE LOST THE MONKEY-MAN AND THOSE SAVAGES. WE'LL NEVER FIND THEM IN ALL THIS BRUSH.
NO MATTER.
AS LONG AS WE HAVE HER, WE HAVE TARZAN.
ROUND UP HER FRIENDS, HER EXPEDITION MATES!
THEY'RE HALF STARVED. THEY CAN'T HAVE GOTTEN VERY FAR.
WHAT... WHAT THEN, MR. ROKOFF?
THEN, I DARE SAY, COMES THE FUN PART.

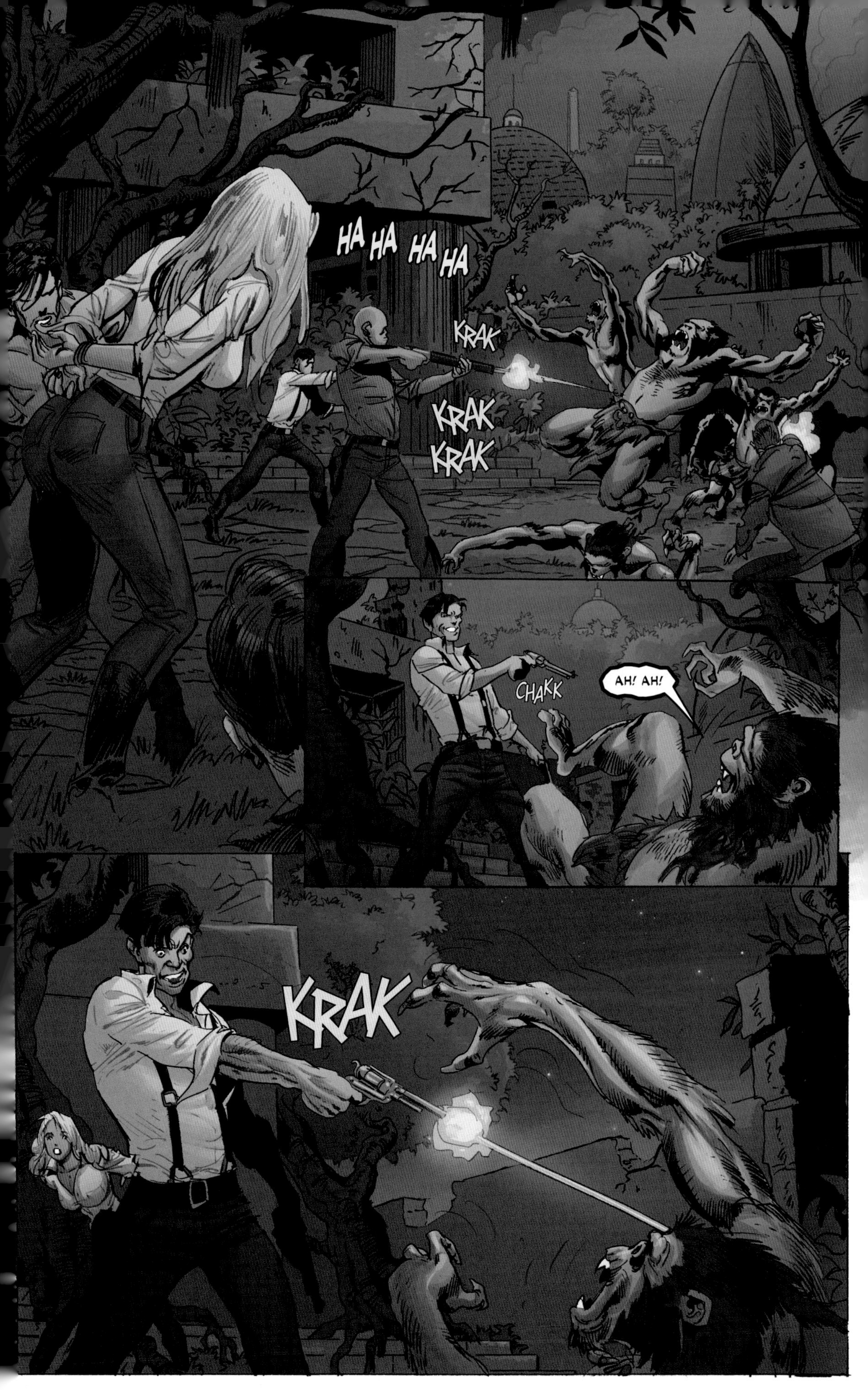

HA HA HA HA
KRAK
KRAK
KRAK
CHAKK
AH! AH!
KRAK

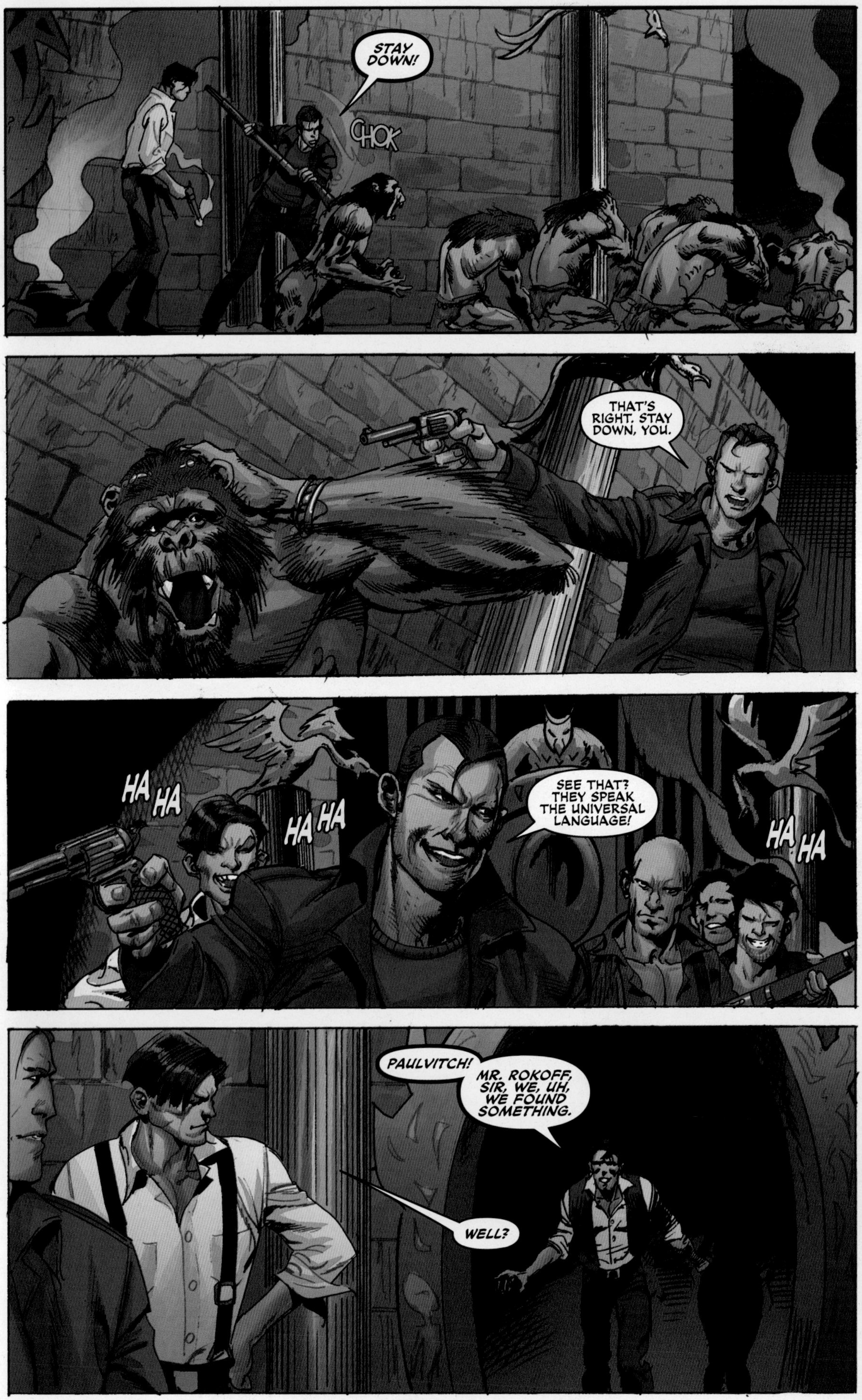
STAY DOWN!
CHOK
THAT'S RIGHT. STAY DOWN, YOU.
HA HA
HA HA
SEE THAT? THEY SPEAK THE UNIVERSAL LANGUAGE!
HA HA
PAULVITCH!
MR. ROKOFF, SIR, WE, UH, WE FOUND SOMETHING.
WELL?

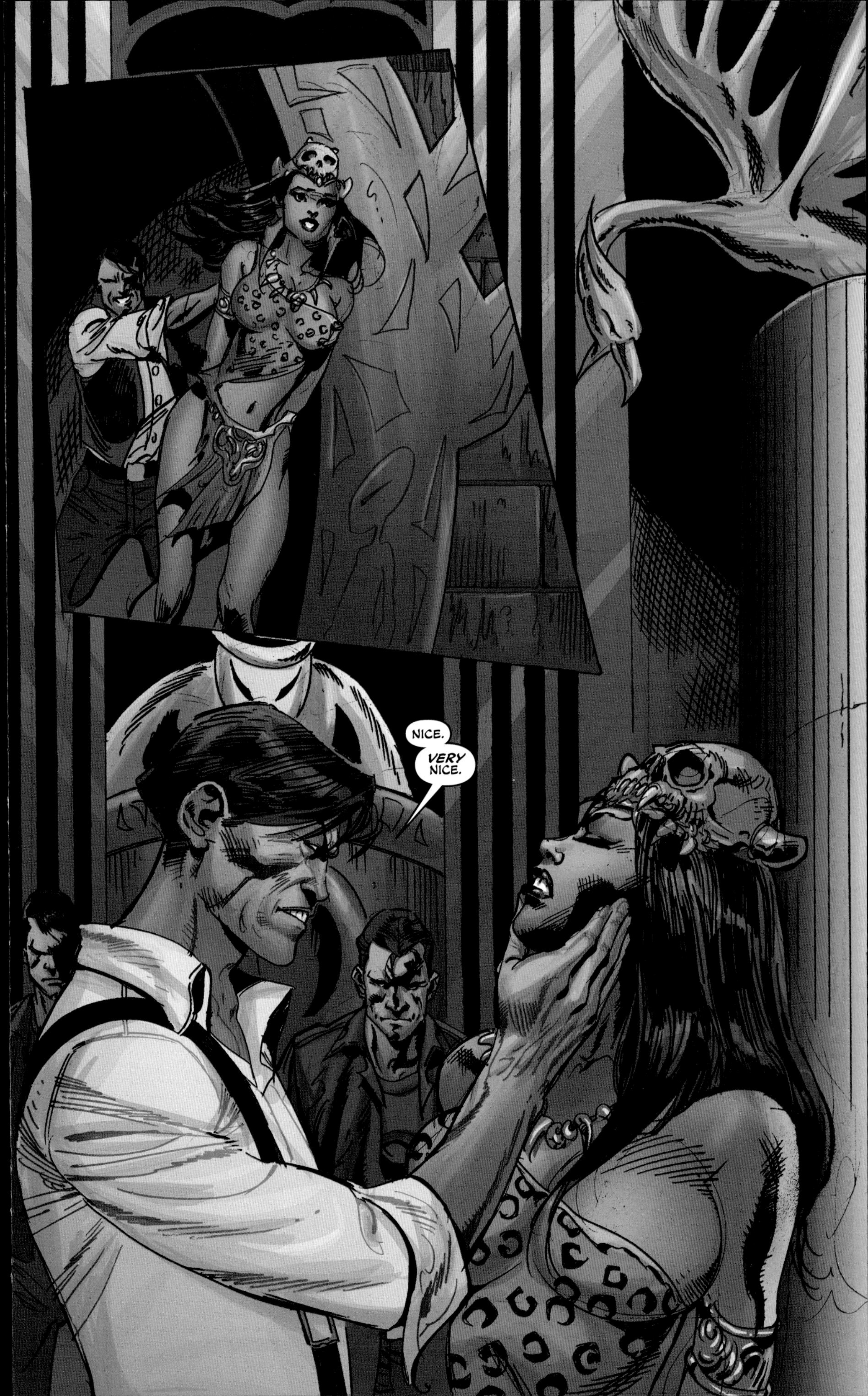
NICE.
VERY NICE.

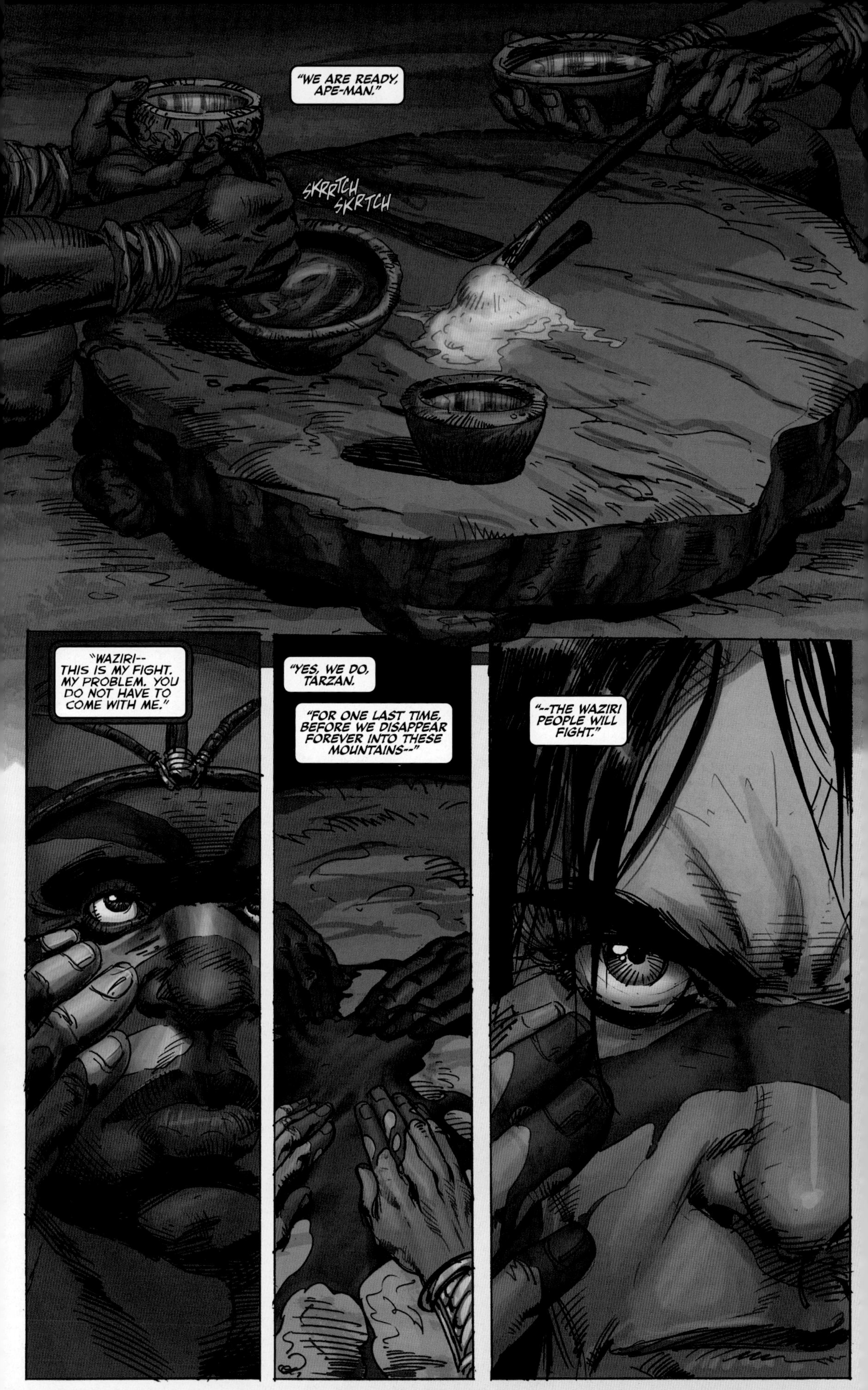
"WE ARE READY, APE-MAN."
SKRRTCH SKRTCH
"WAZIRI-- THIS IS MY FIGHT. MY PROBLEM. YOU DO NOT HAVE TO COME WITH ME."
"YES, WE DO, TARZAN.
"FOR ONE LAST TIME, BEFORE WE DISAPPEAR FOREVER INTO THESE MOUNTAINS--"
"--THE WAZIRI PEOPLE WILL FIGHT."

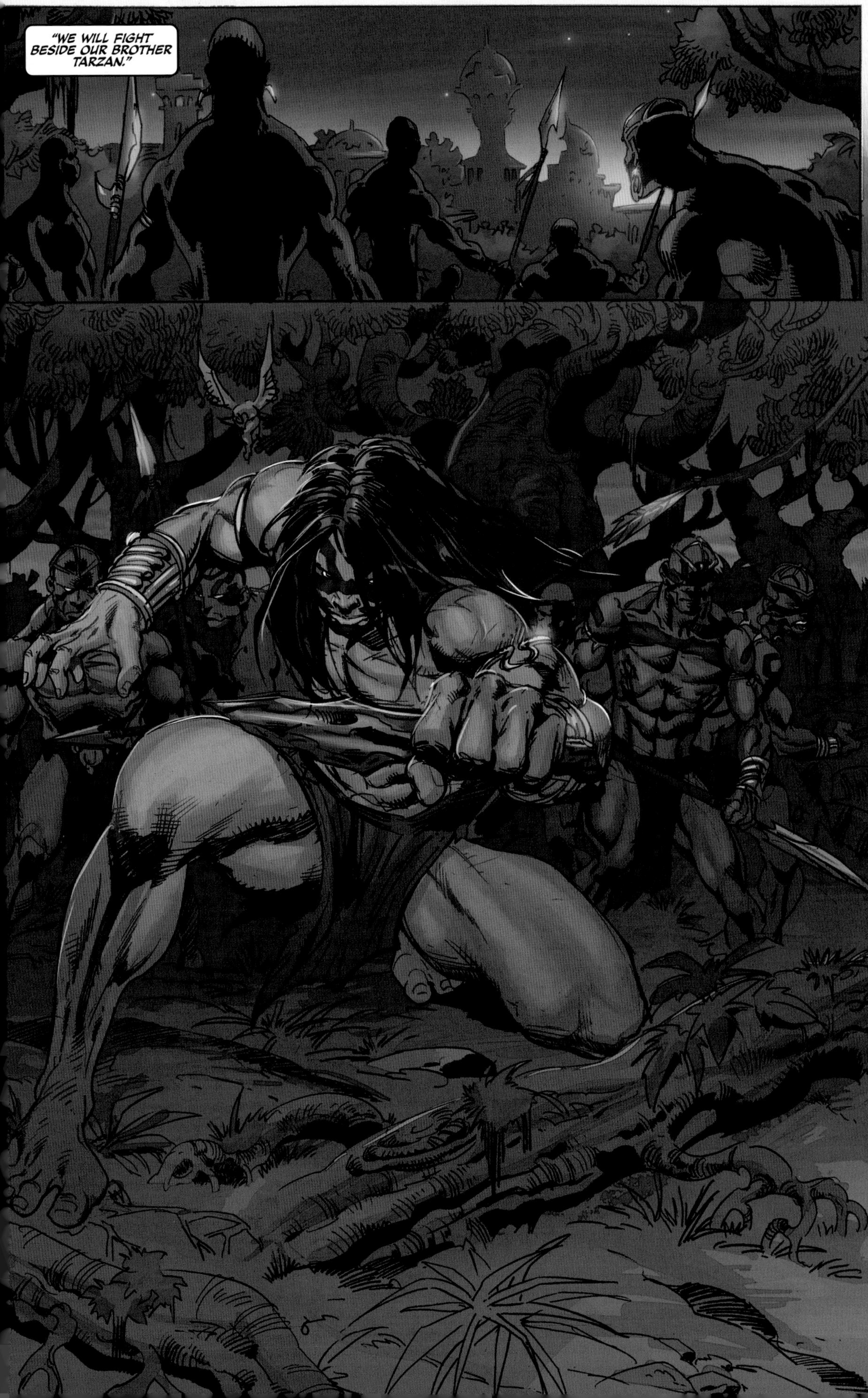
"WE WILL FIGHT BESIDE OUR BROTHER TARZAN."

ISSUE 14

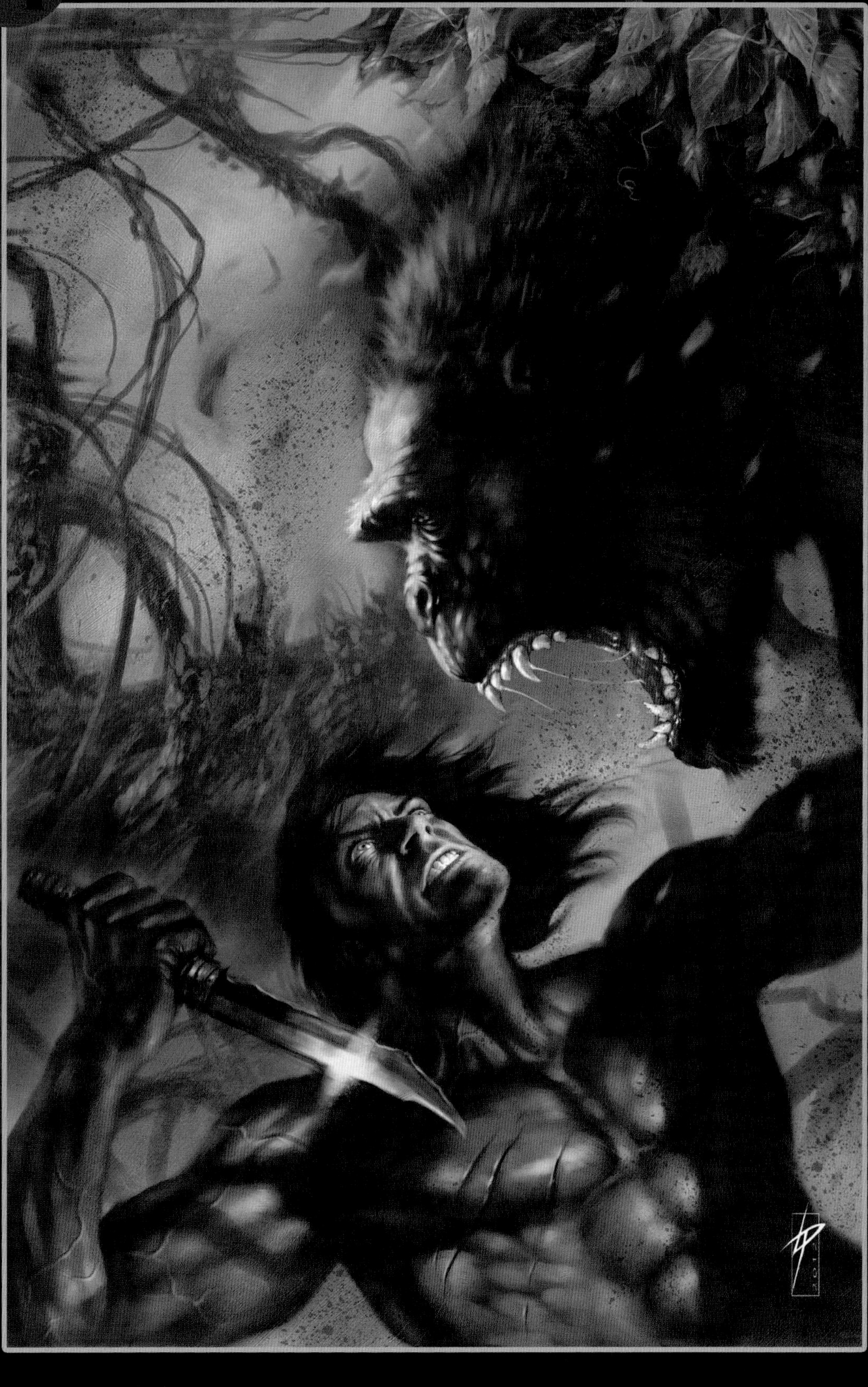

COVER BY LUCIO PARRILLO

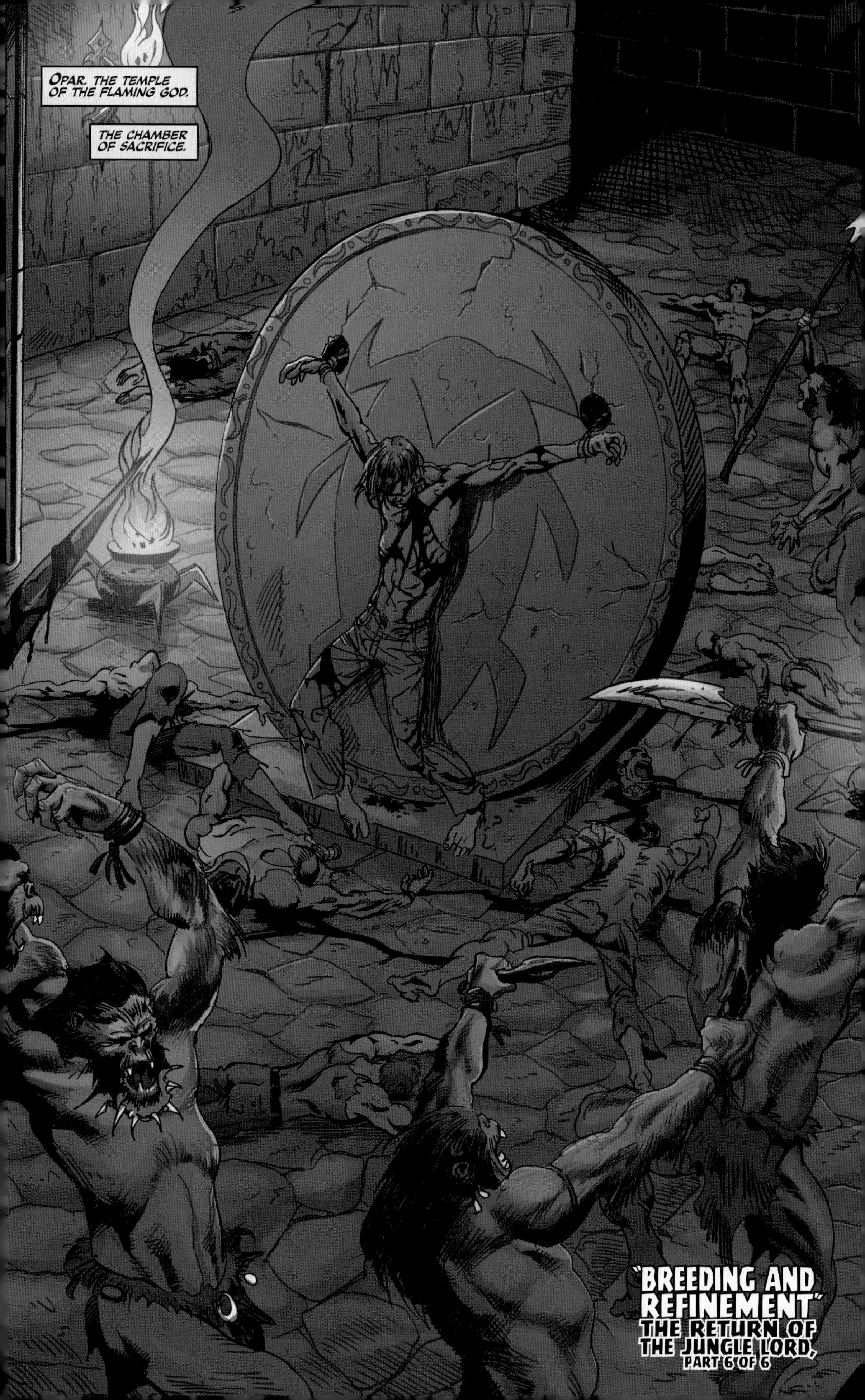
OPAR. THE TEMPLE OF THE FLAMING GOD.
THE CHAMBER OF SACRIFICE.
"BREEDING AND REFINEMENT"
THE RETURN OF THE JUNGLE LORD,
PART 6 OF 6

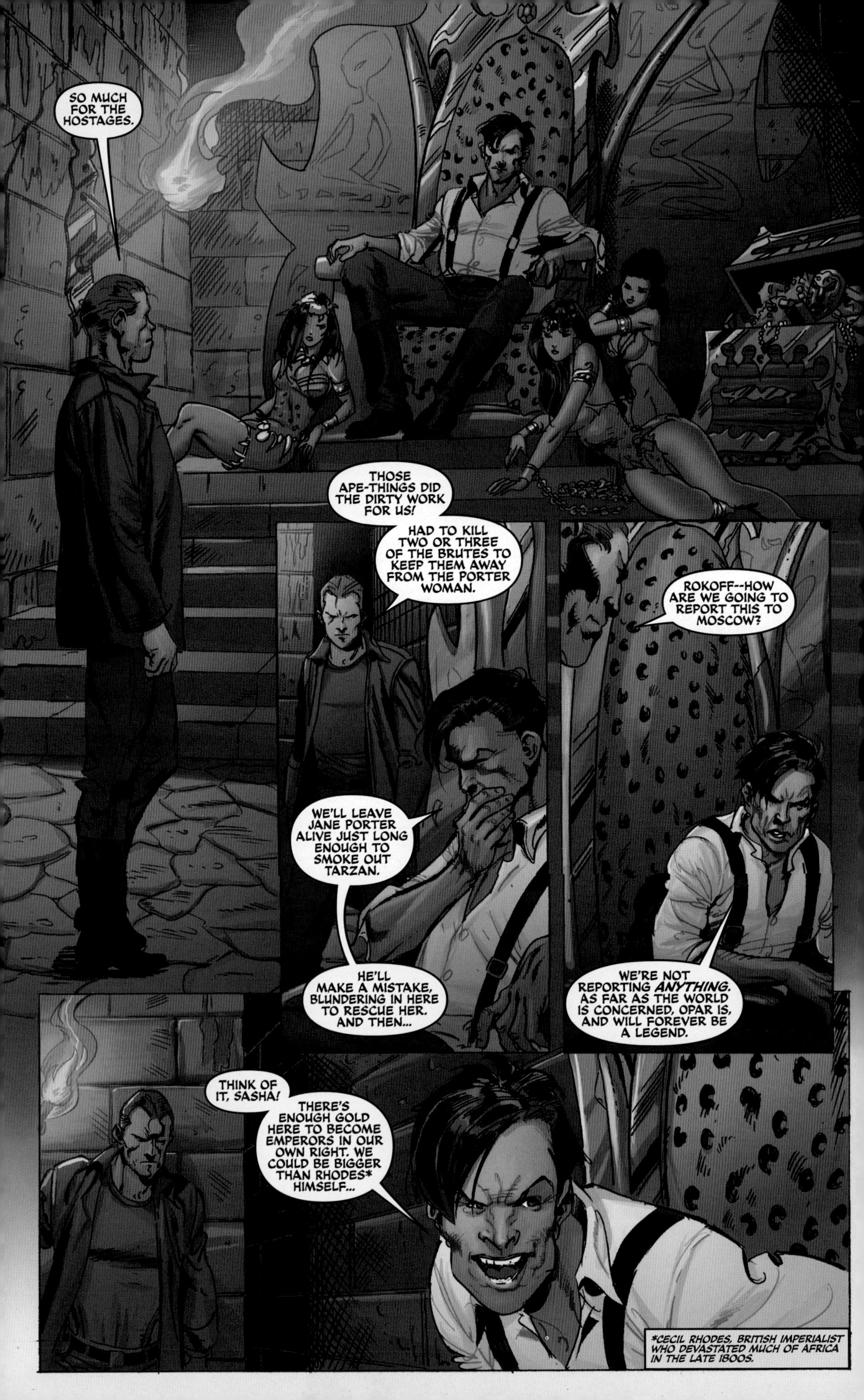
SO MUCH FOR THE HOSTAGES.
THOSE APE-THINGS DID THE DIRTY WORK FOR US!
HAD TO KILL TWO OR THREE OF THE BRUTES TO KEEP THEM AWAY FROM THE PORTER WOMAN.
WE'LL LEAVE JANE PORTER ALIVE JUST LONG ENOUGH TO SMOKE OUT TARZAN.
HE'LL MAKE A MISTAKE, BLUNDERING IN HERE TO RESCUE HER. AND THEN...
ROKOFF--HOW ARE WE GOING TO REPORT THIS TO MOSCOW?
WE'RE NOT REPORTING *ANYTHING*. AS FAR AS THE WORLD IS CONCERNED, OPAR IS, AND WILL FOREVER BE A LEGEND.
THINK OF IT, SASHA!
THERE'S ENOUGH GOLD HERE TO BECOME EMPERORS IN OUR OWN RIGHT. WE COULD BE BIGGER THAN RHODES* HIMSELF...
*CECIL RHODES, BRITISH IMPERIALIST WHO DEVASTATED MUCH OF AFRICA IN THE LATE 1800S.

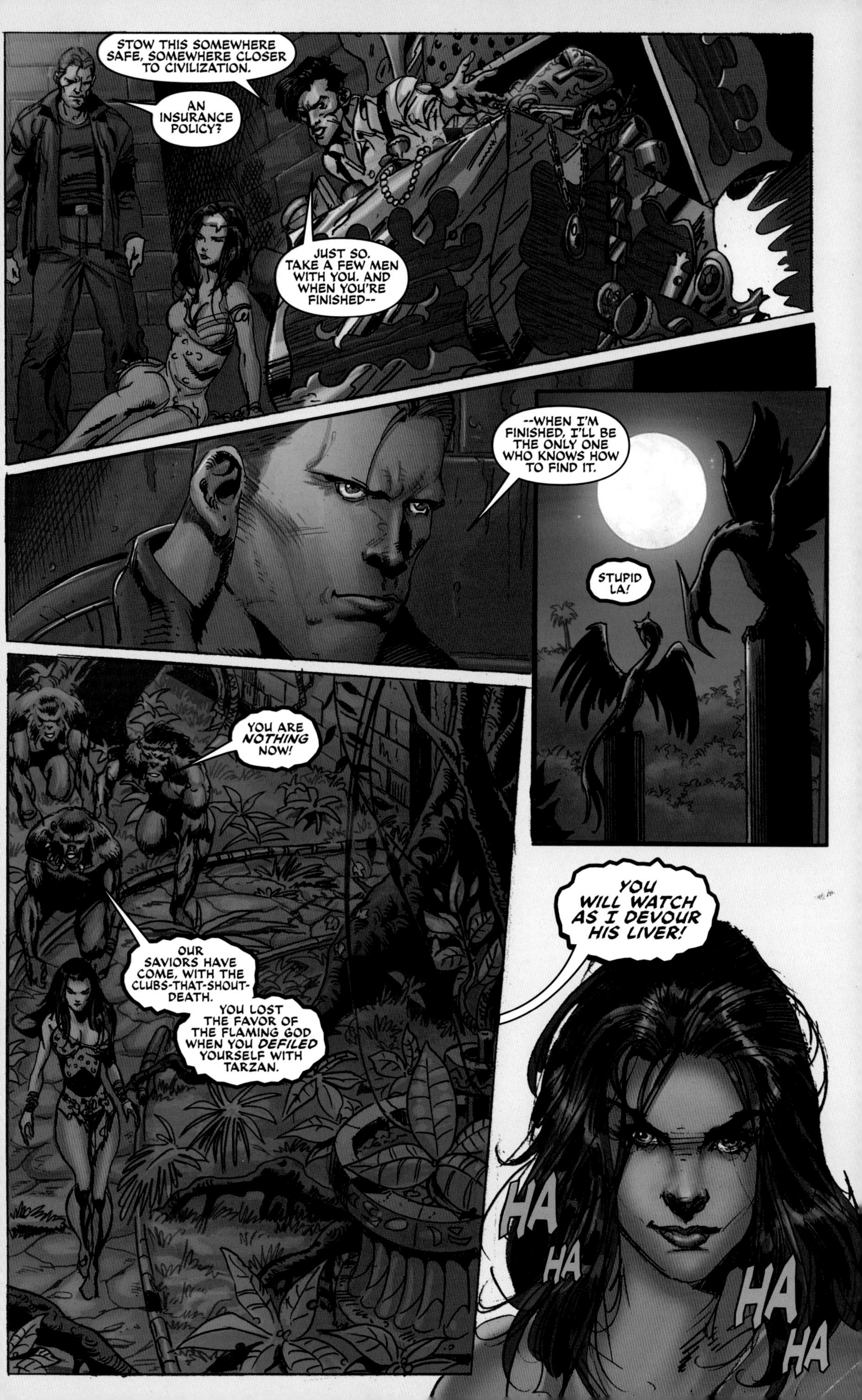
STOW THIS SOMEWHERE SAFE, SOMEWHERE CLOSER TO CIVILIZATION.
AN INSURANCE POLICY?
JUST SO. TAKE A FEW MEN WITH YOU. AND WHEN YOU'RE FINISHED--
--WHEN I'M FINISHED, I'LL BE THE ONLY ONE WHO KNOWS HOW TO FIND IT.
STUPID LA!
YOU ARE NOTHING NOW!
OUR SAVIORS HAVE COME, WITH THE CLUBS-THAT-SHOUT-DEATH.
YOU LOST THE FAVOR OF THE FLAMING GOD WHEN YOU DEFILED YOURSELF WITH TARZAN.
YOU WILL WATCH AS I DEVOUR HIS LIVER!
HA HA HA HA

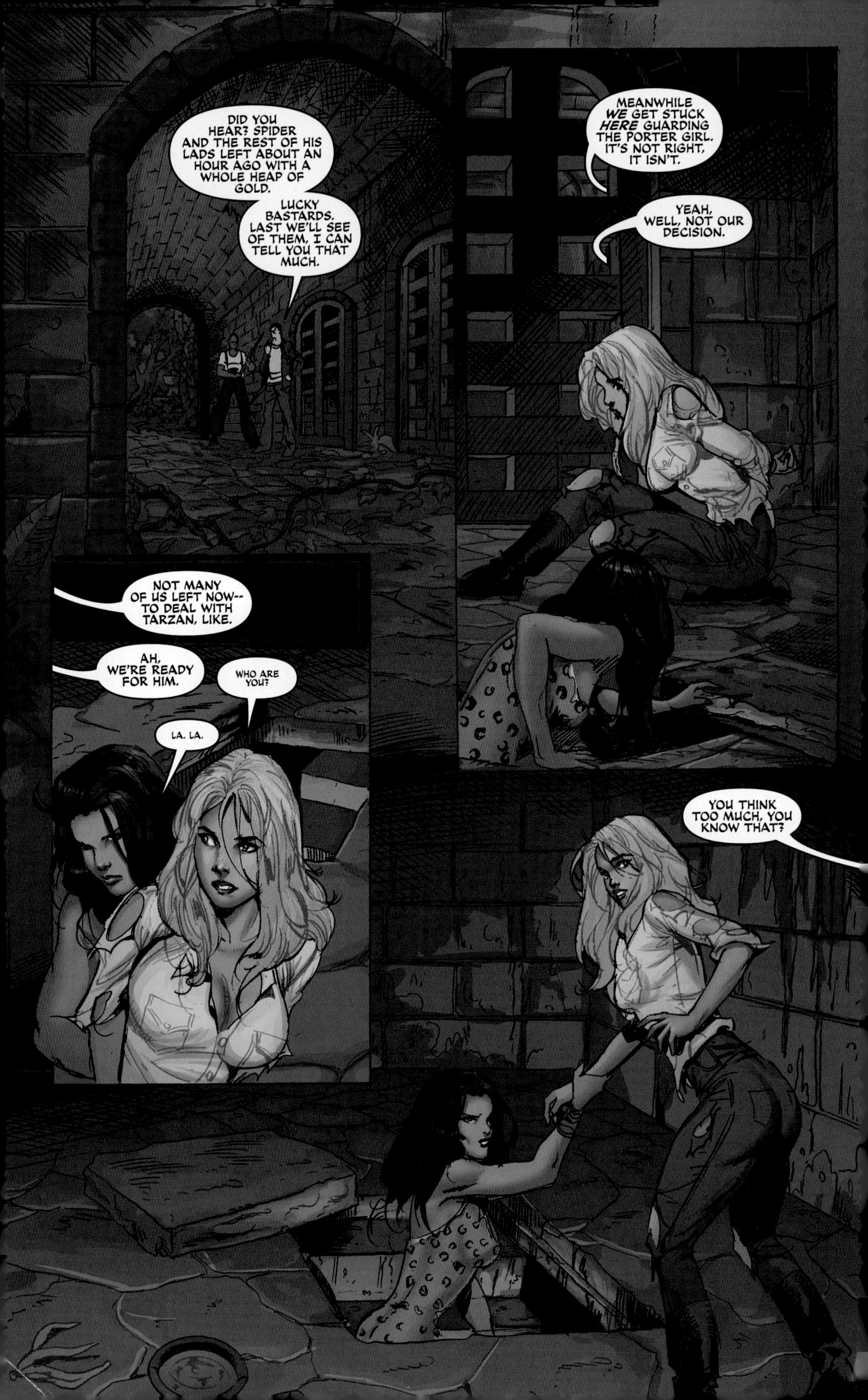
DID YOU HEAR? SPIDER AND THE REST OF HIS LADS LEFT ABOUT AN HOUR AGO WITH A WHOLE HEAP OF GOLD.
LUCKY BASTARDS. LAST WE'LL SEE OF THEM, I CAN TELL YOU THAT MUCH.
MEANWHILE *WE* GET STUCK *HERE* GUARDING THE PORTER GIRL. IT'S NOT RIGHT, IT ISN'T.
YEAH, WELL, NOT OUR DECISION.
NOT MANY OF US LEFT NOW-- TO DEAL WITH TARZAN, LIKE.
AH, WE'RE READY FOR HIM.
WHO ARE YOU?
LA. LA.
YOU THINK TOO MUCH, YOU KNOW THAT?

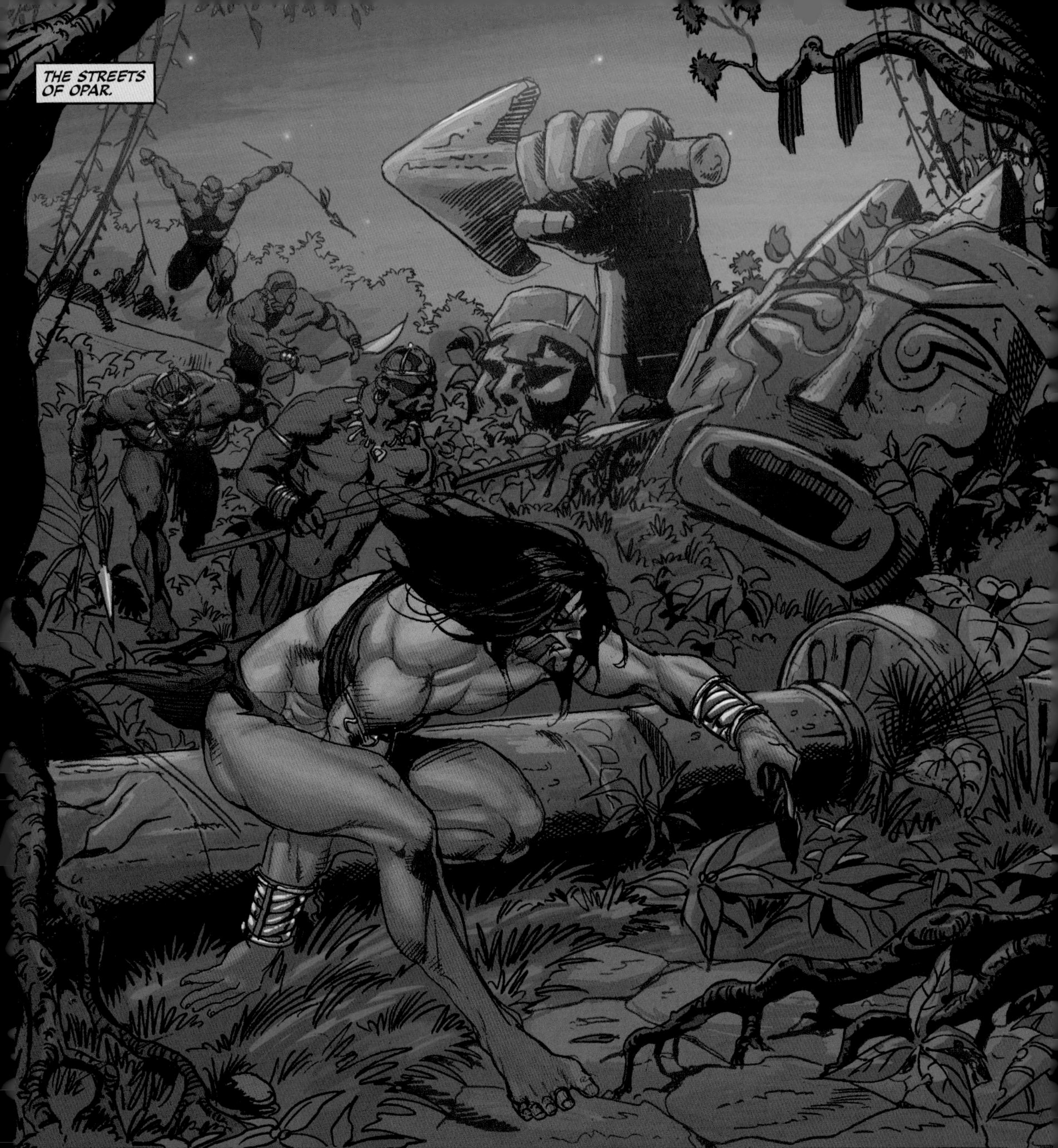
THE STREETS OF OPAR.

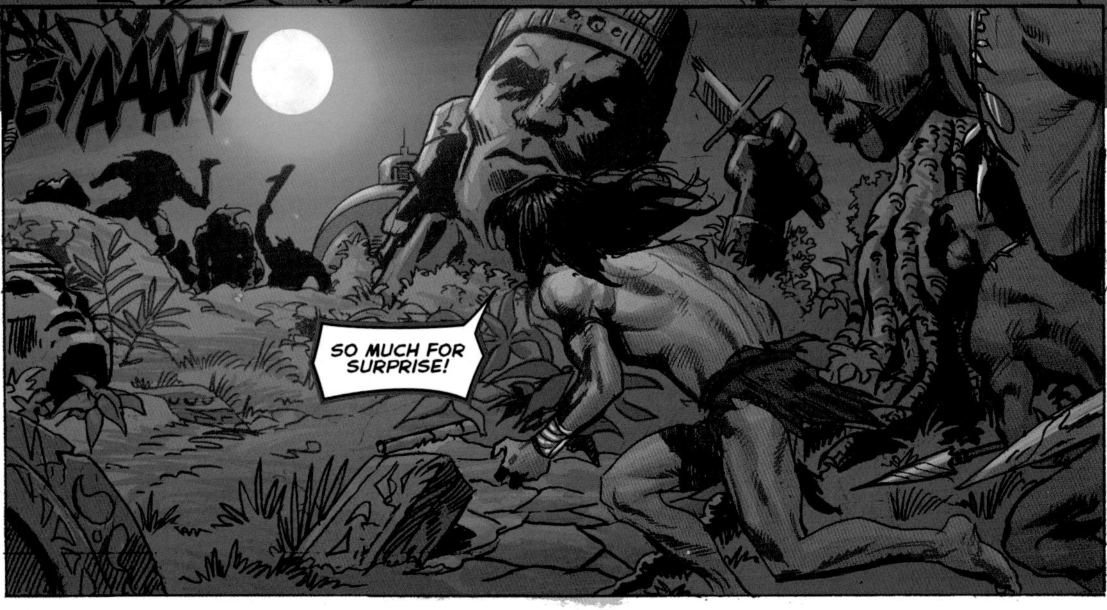
EYAAAH!
SO MUCH FOR SURPRISE!

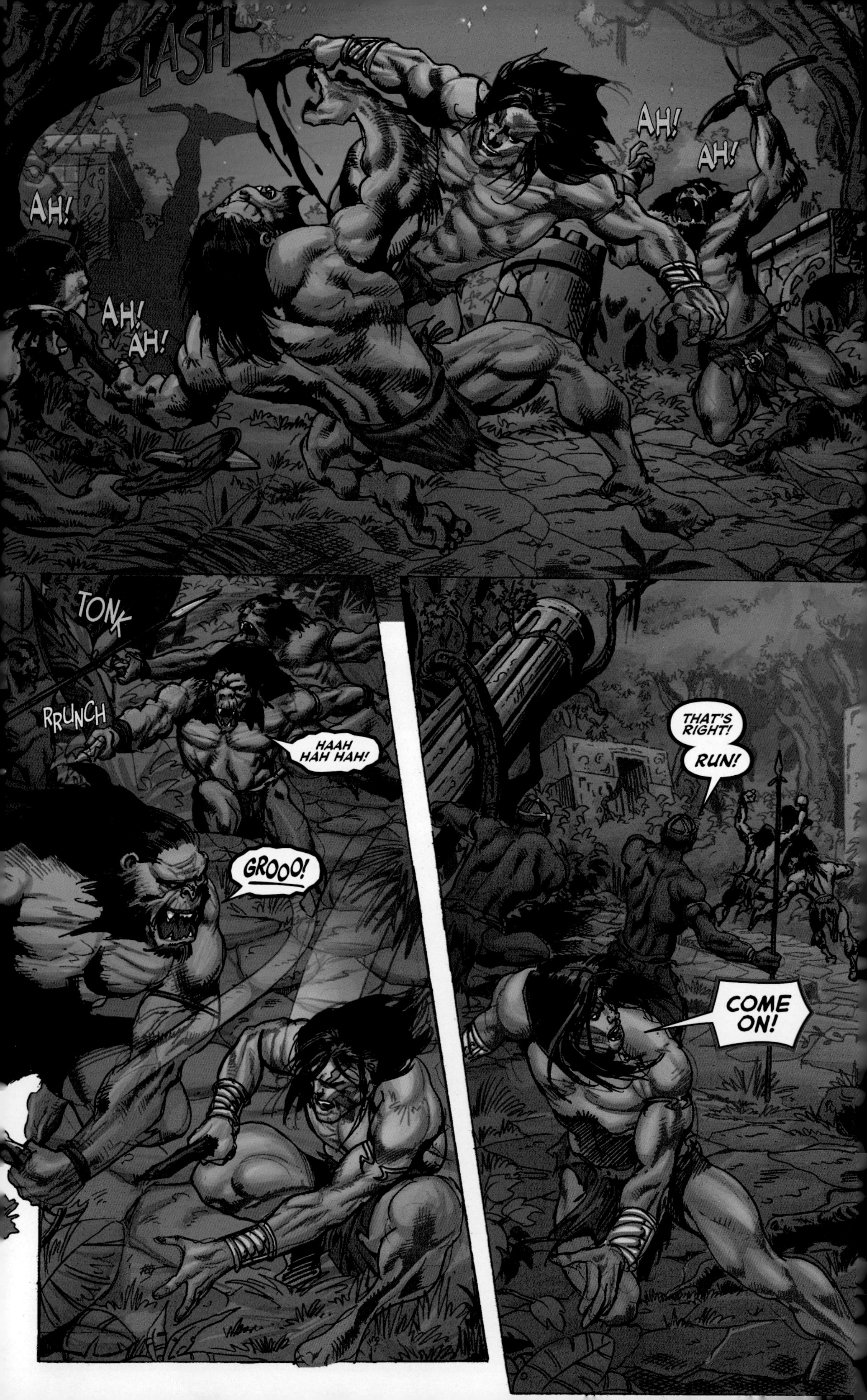
SLASH
AH!
AH!
AH!
AH!
AH!
TONK
RRUNCH
HAAH HAH HAH!
GROOO!
THAT'S RIGHT!
RUN!
COME ON!

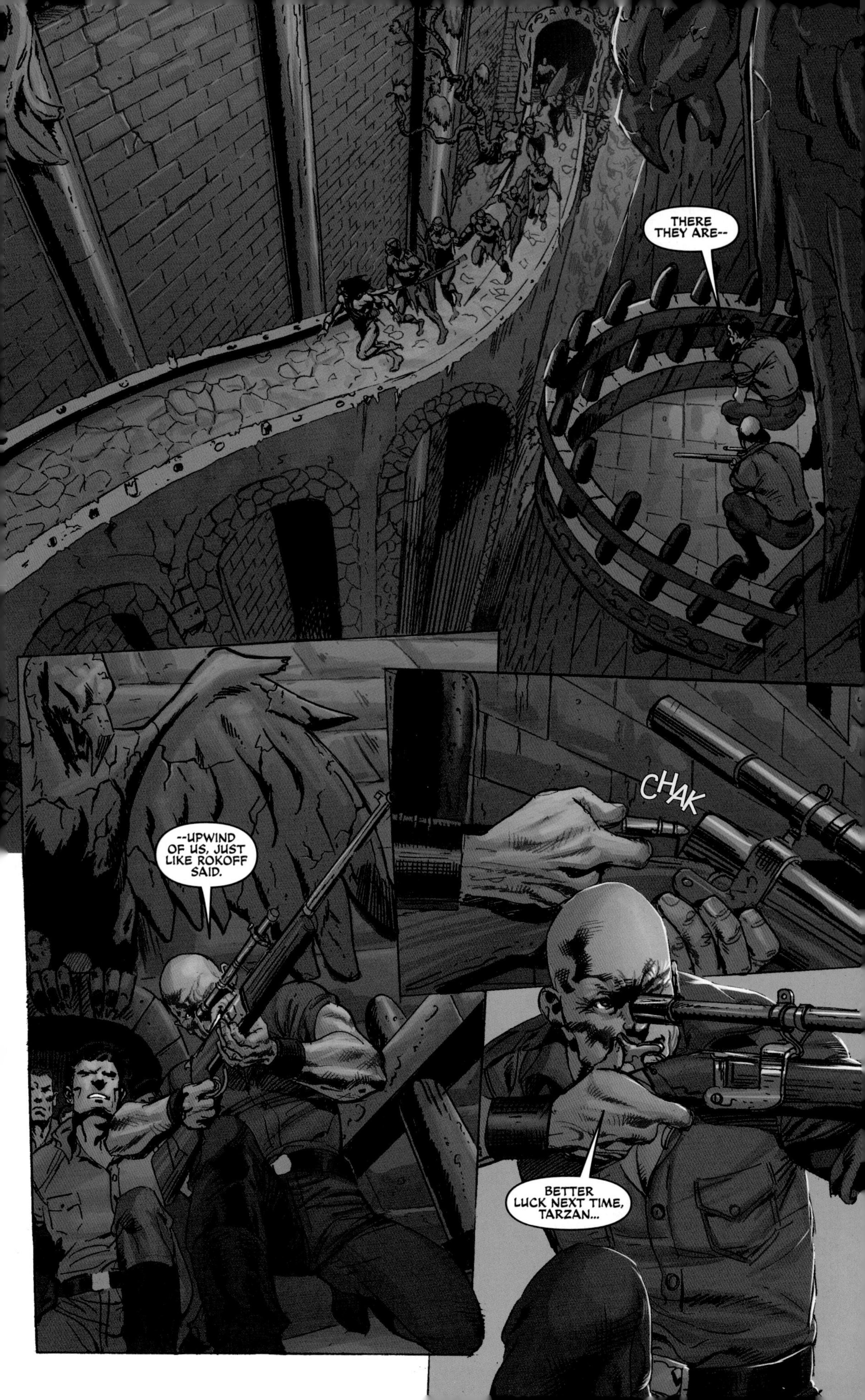
THERE THEY ARE--
CHAK
--UPWIND OF US, JUST LIKE ROKOFF SAID.
BETTER LUCK NEXT TIME, TARZAN...

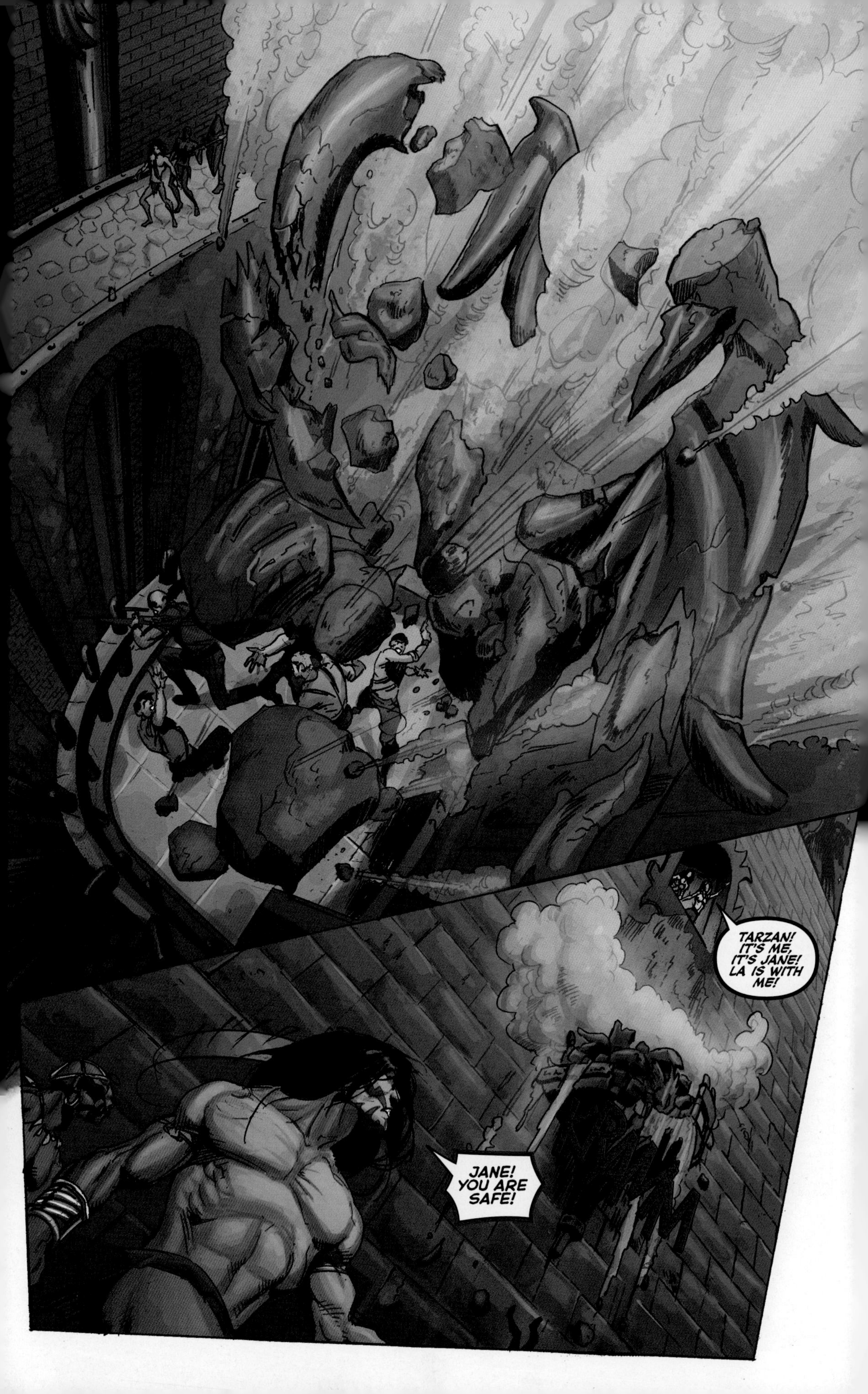
TARZAN! IT'S ME, IT'S JANE! LA IS WITH ME!
JANE! YOU ARE SAFE!

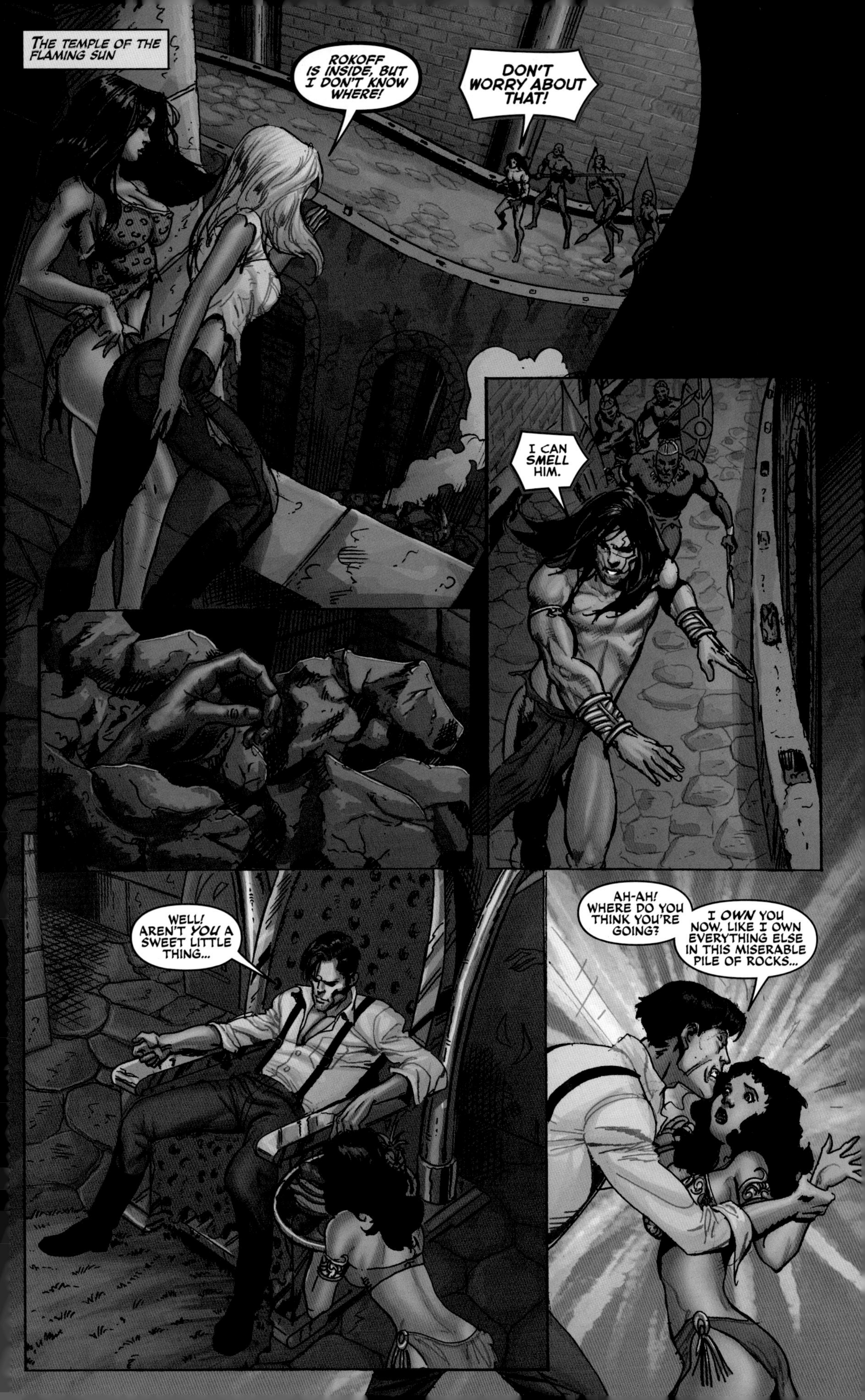
THE TEMPLE OF THE FLAMING SUN
ROKOFF IS INSIDE, BUT I DON'T KNOW WHERE!
DON'T WORRY ABOUT THAT!
I CAN SMELL HIM.
WELL! AREN'T YOU A SWEET LITTLE THING...
AH-AH! WHERE DO YOU THINK YOU'RE GOING?
I OWN YOU NOW, LIKE I OWN EVERYTHING ELSE IN THIS MISERABLE PILE OF ROCKS...

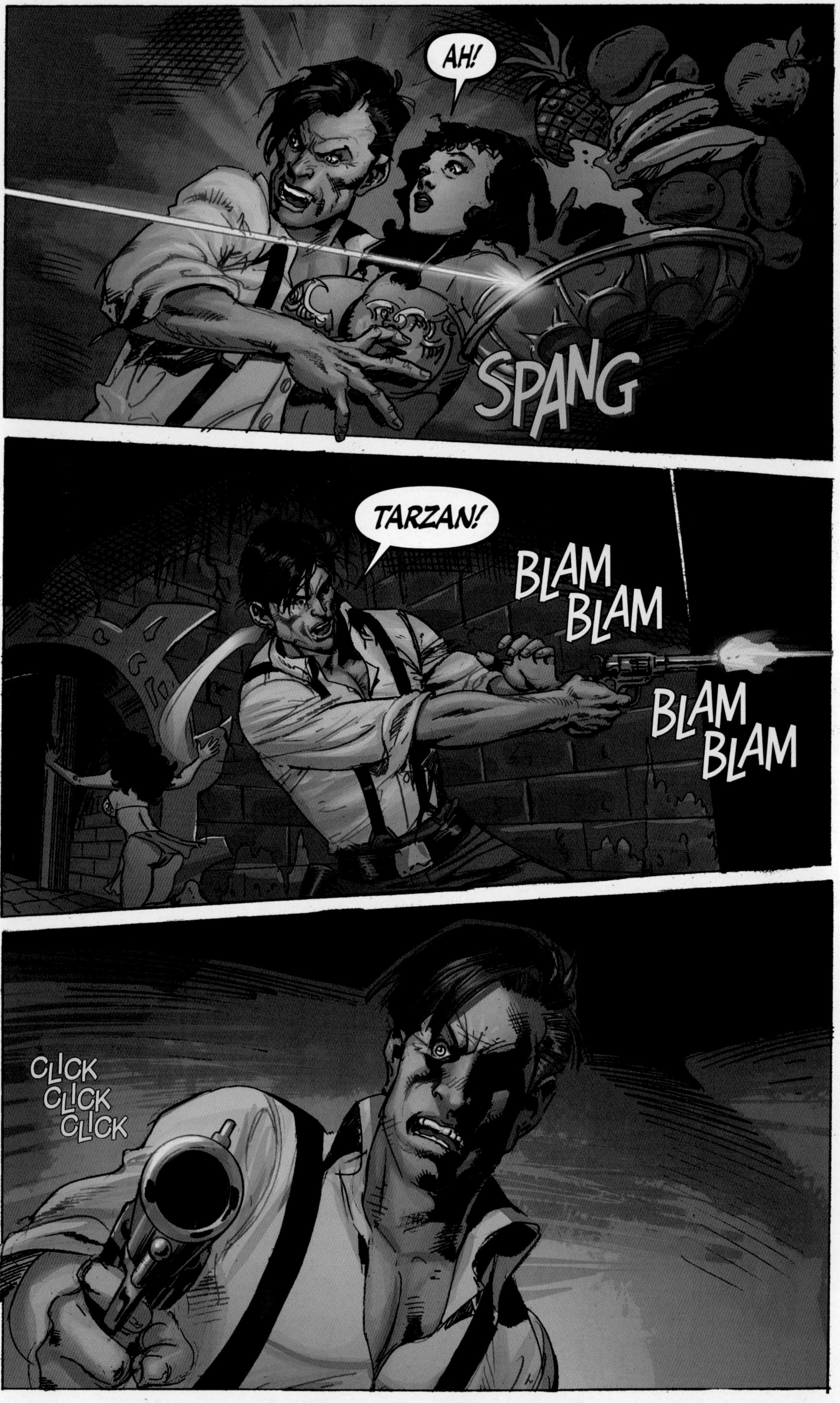
AH!
SPANG
TARZAN!
BLAM BLAM
BLAM BLAM
CLICK CLICK CLICK

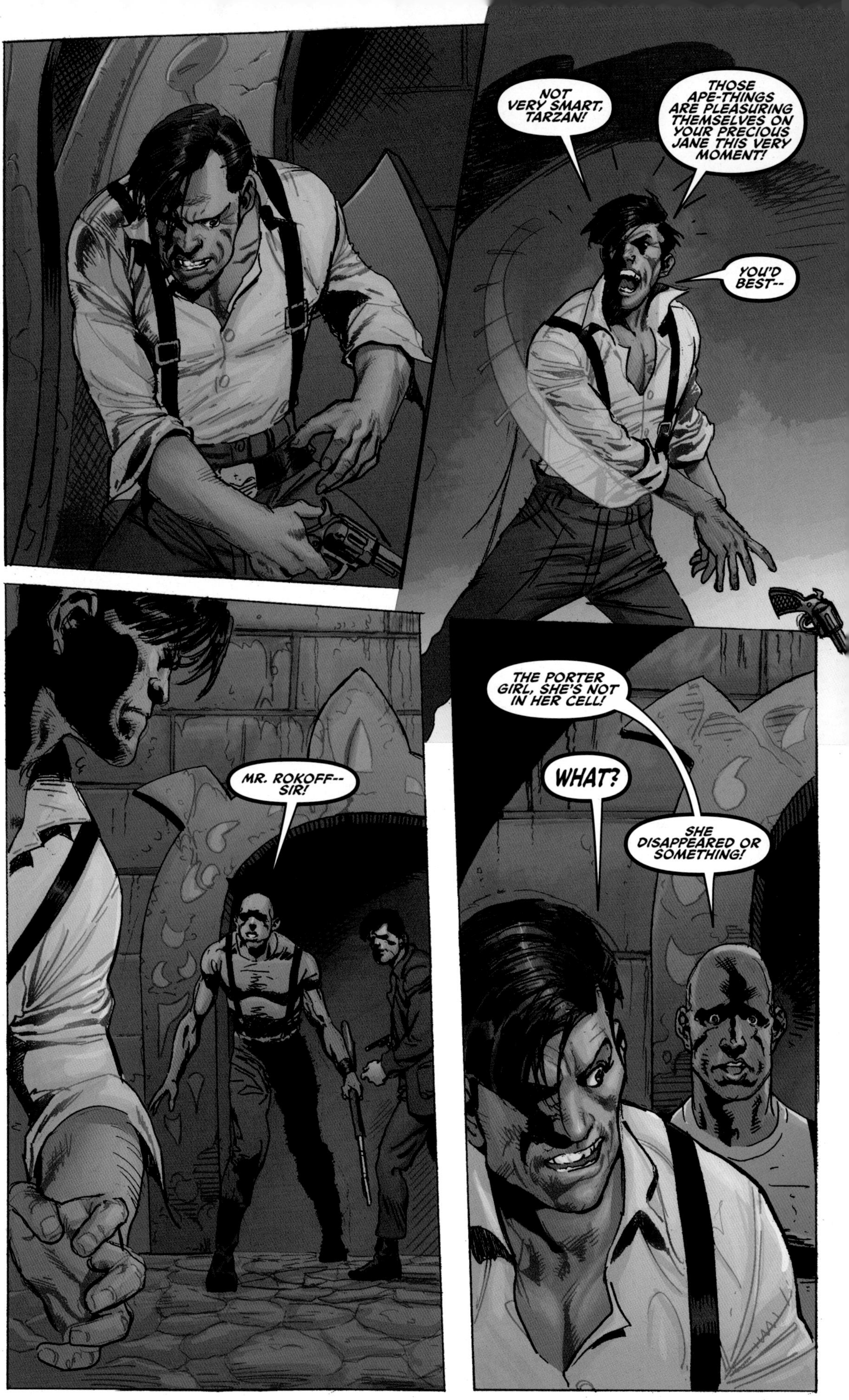
NOT VERY SMART, TARZAN!
THOSE APE-THINGS ARE PLEASURING THEMSELVES ON YOUR PRECIOUS JANE THIS VERY MOMENT!
YOU'D BEST--
MR. ROKOFF--SIR!
THE PORTER GIRL, SHE'S NOT IN HER CELL!
WHAT?
SHE DISAPPEARED OR SOMETHING!

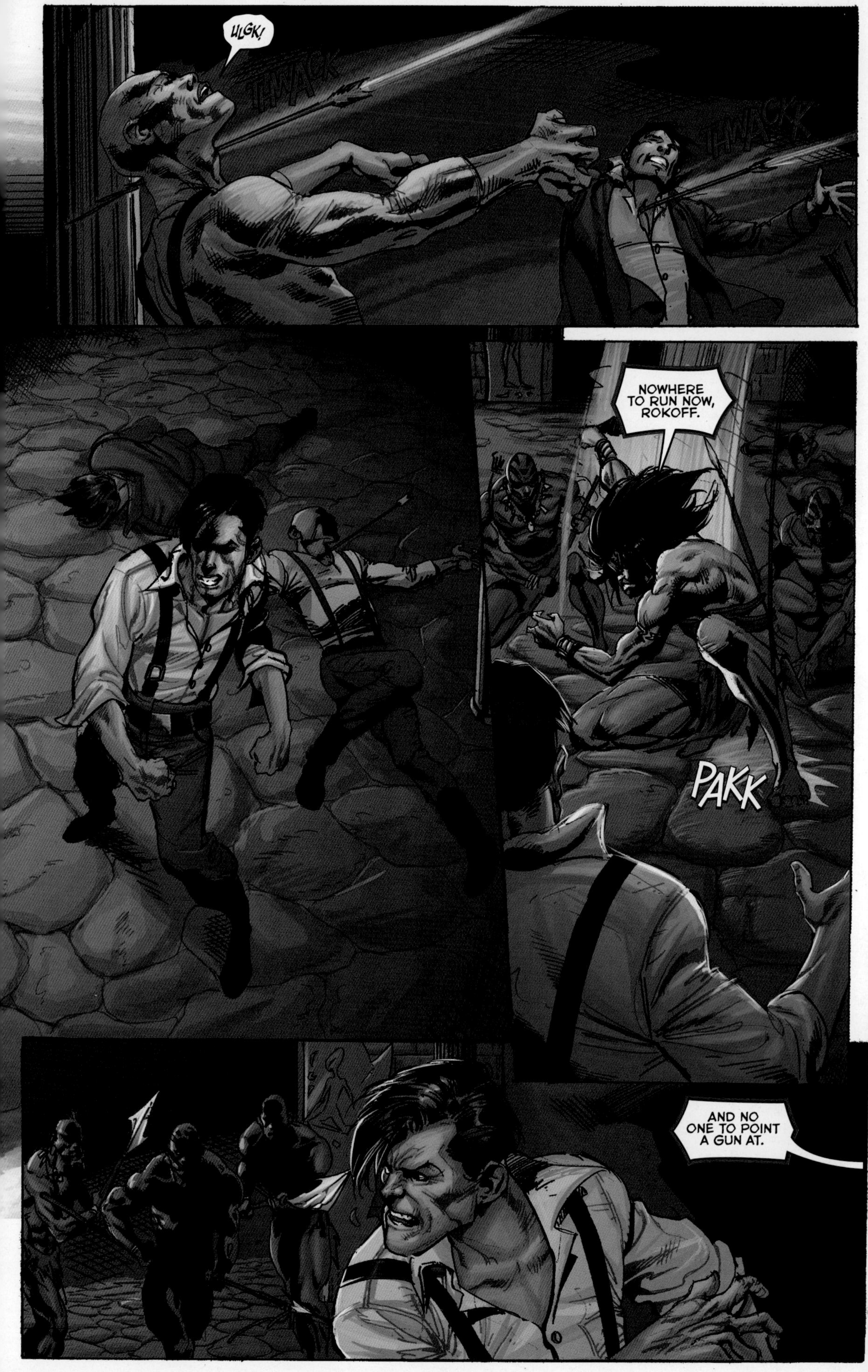
ULGK!
THWACK
THWACK
NOWHERE TO RUN NOW, ROKOFF.
PAKK
AND NO ONE TO POINT A GUN AT.

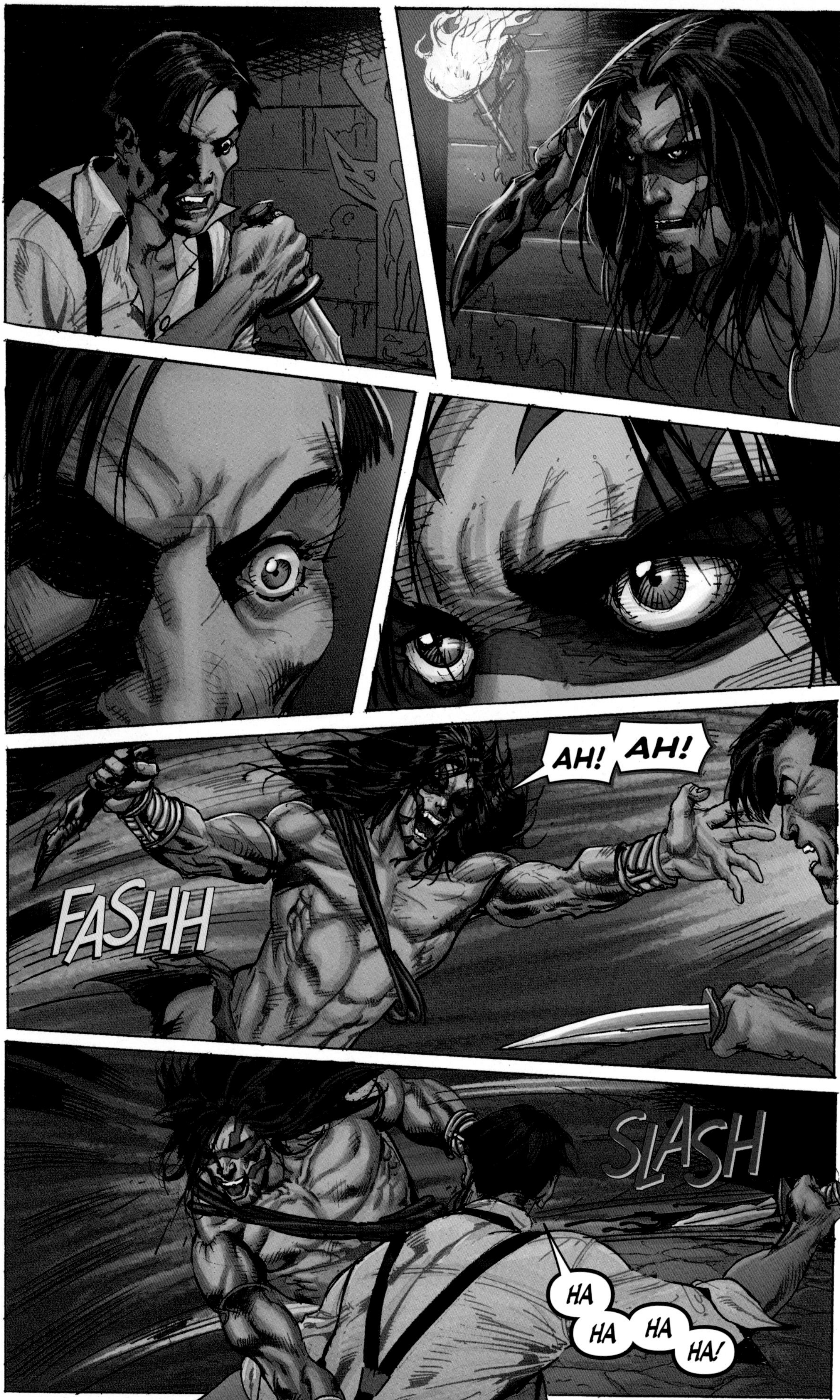
AH! AH!
FASHH
SLASH
HA HA HA HA!

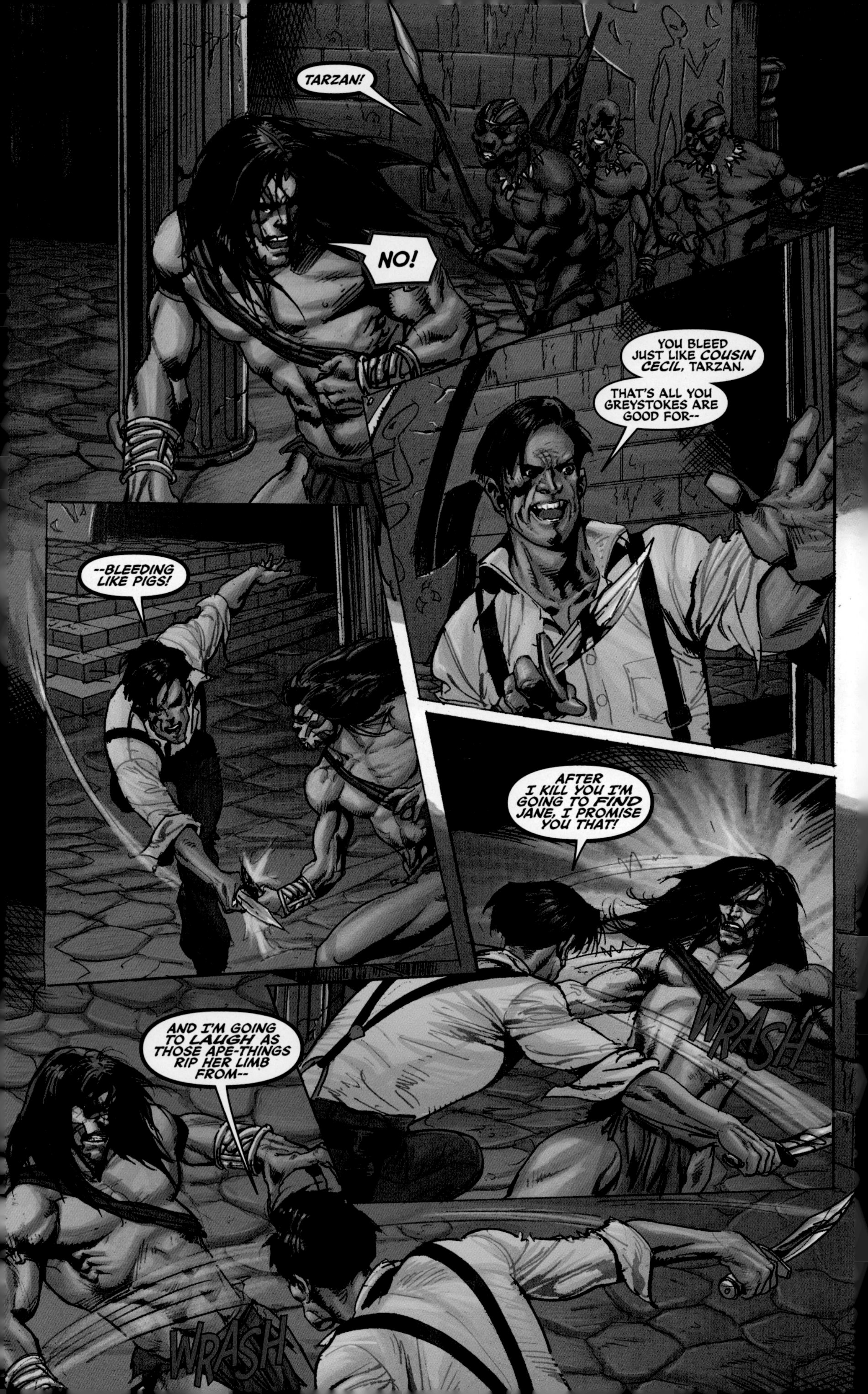
TARZAN!
NO!
YOU BLEED JUST LIKE COUSIN CECIL, TARZAN.
THAT'S ALL YOU GREYSTOKES ARE GOOD FOR--
--BLEEDING LIKE PIGS!
AFTER I KILL YOU I'M GOING TO FIND JANE, I PROMISE YOU THAT!
WRASH
AND I'M GOING TO LAUGH AS THOSE APE-THINGS RIP HER LIMB FROM--
WRASH

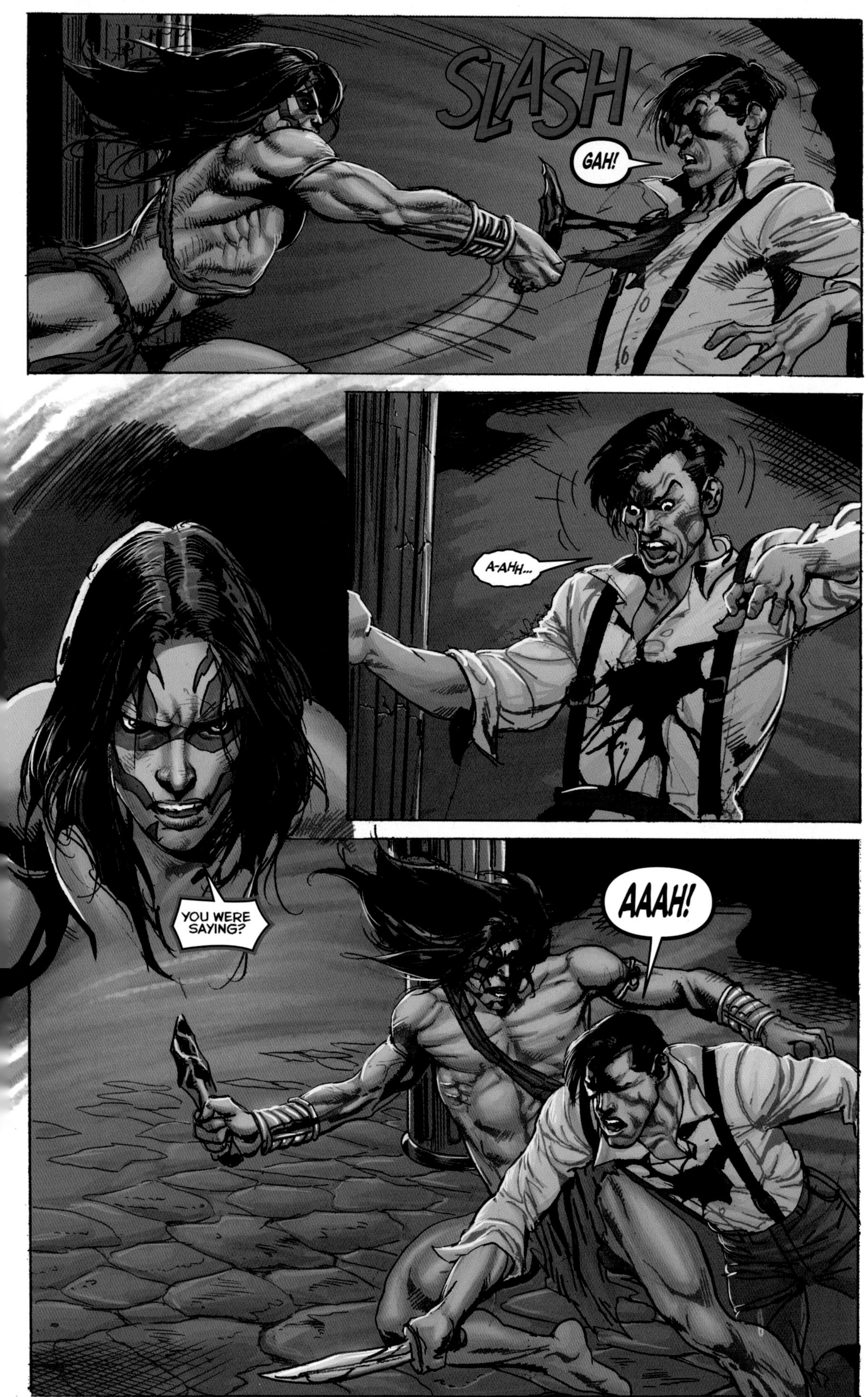
SLASH
GAH!
A-AHH...
YOU WERE SAYING?
AAAH!

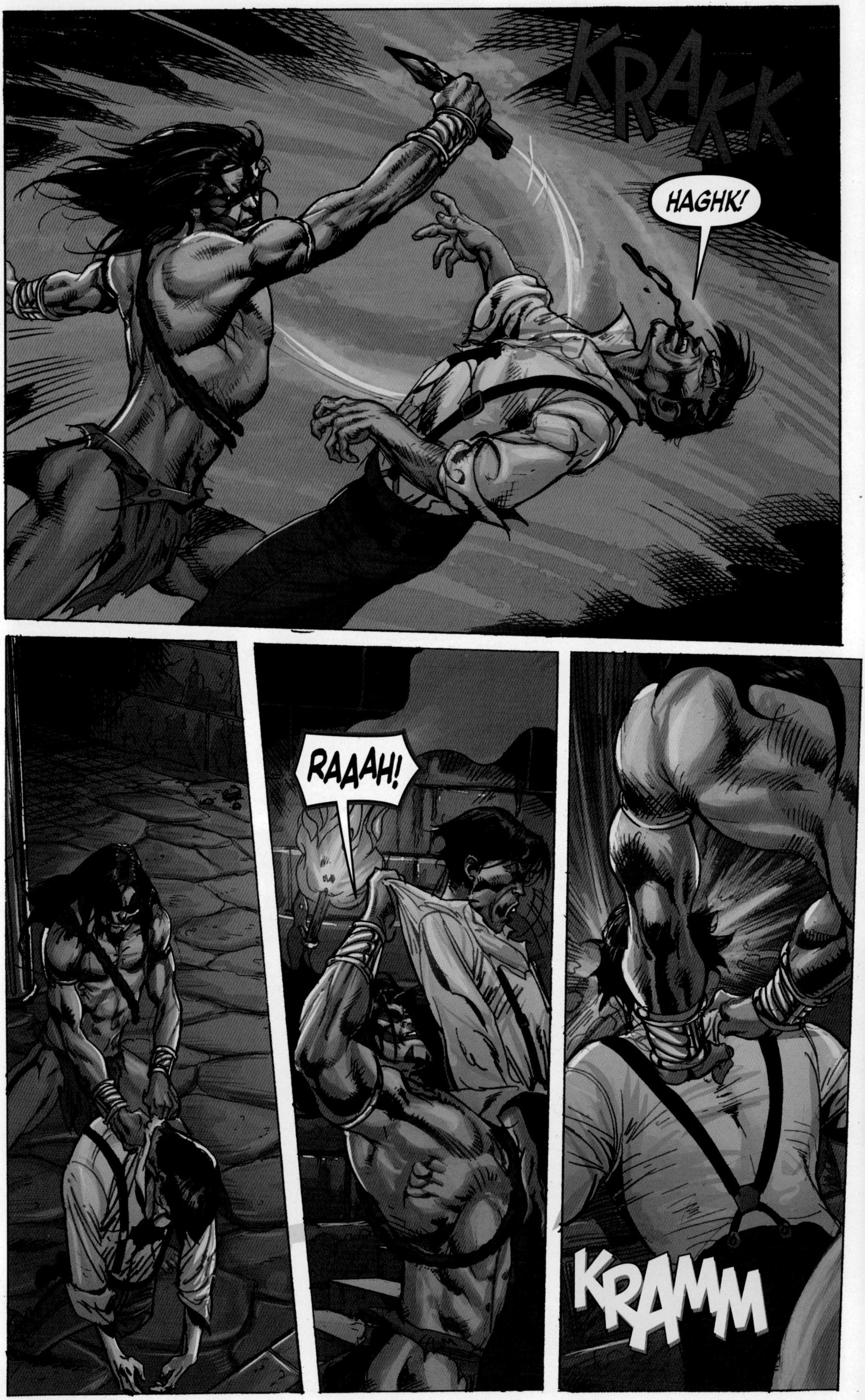
KRAKK
HAGHK!
RAAAH!
KRAMM

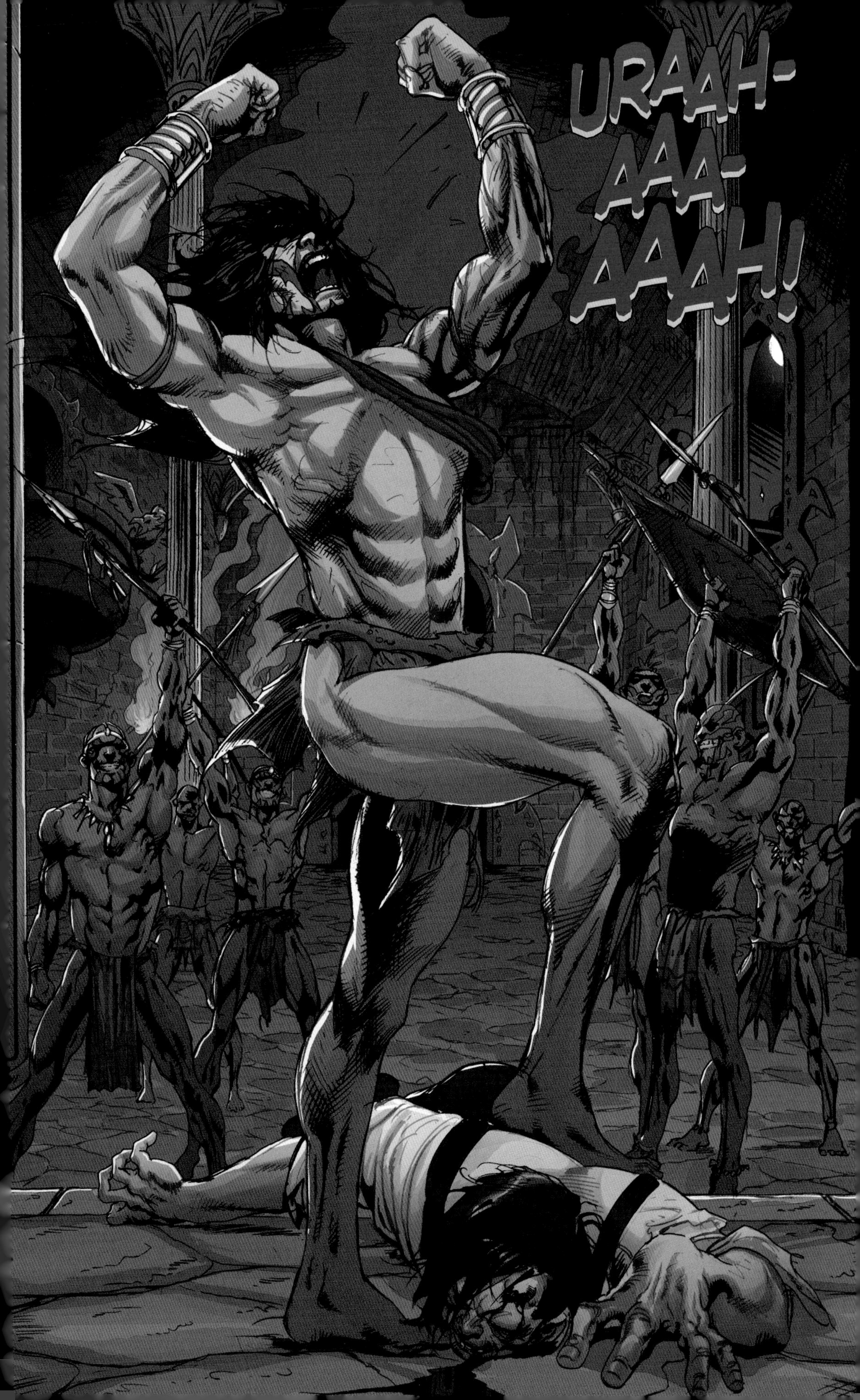
URAAH-AAA-AAAH!

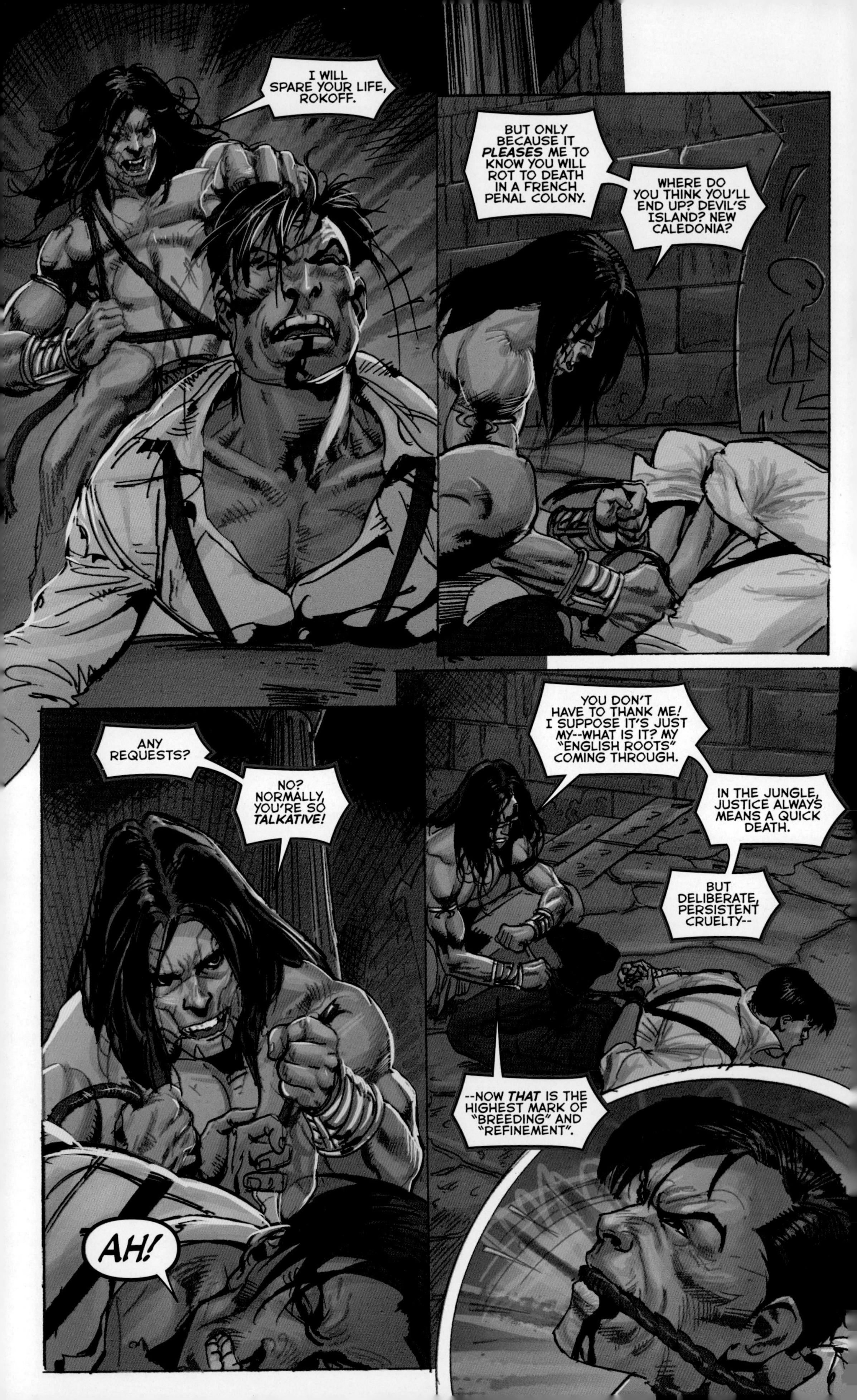
I WILL SPARE YOUR LIFE, ROKOFF.
BUT ONLY BECAUSE IT *PLEASES* ME TO KNOW YOU WILL ROT TO DEATH IN A FRENCH PENAL COLONY.
WHERE DO YOU THINK YOU'LL END UP? DEVIL'S ISLAND? NEW CALEDONIA?
ANY REQUESTS?
NO? NORMALLY, YOU'RE SO *TALKATIVE!*
AH!
YOU DON'T HAVE TO THANK ME! I SUPPOSE IT'S JUST MY--WHAT IS IT? MY "ENGLISH ROOTS" COMING THROUGH.
IN THE JUNGLE, JUSTICE ALWAYS MEANS A QUICK DEATH.
BUT DELIBERATE, PERSISTENT CRUELTY--
--NOW *THAT* IS THE HIGHEST MARK OF "BREEDING" AND "REFINEMENT".

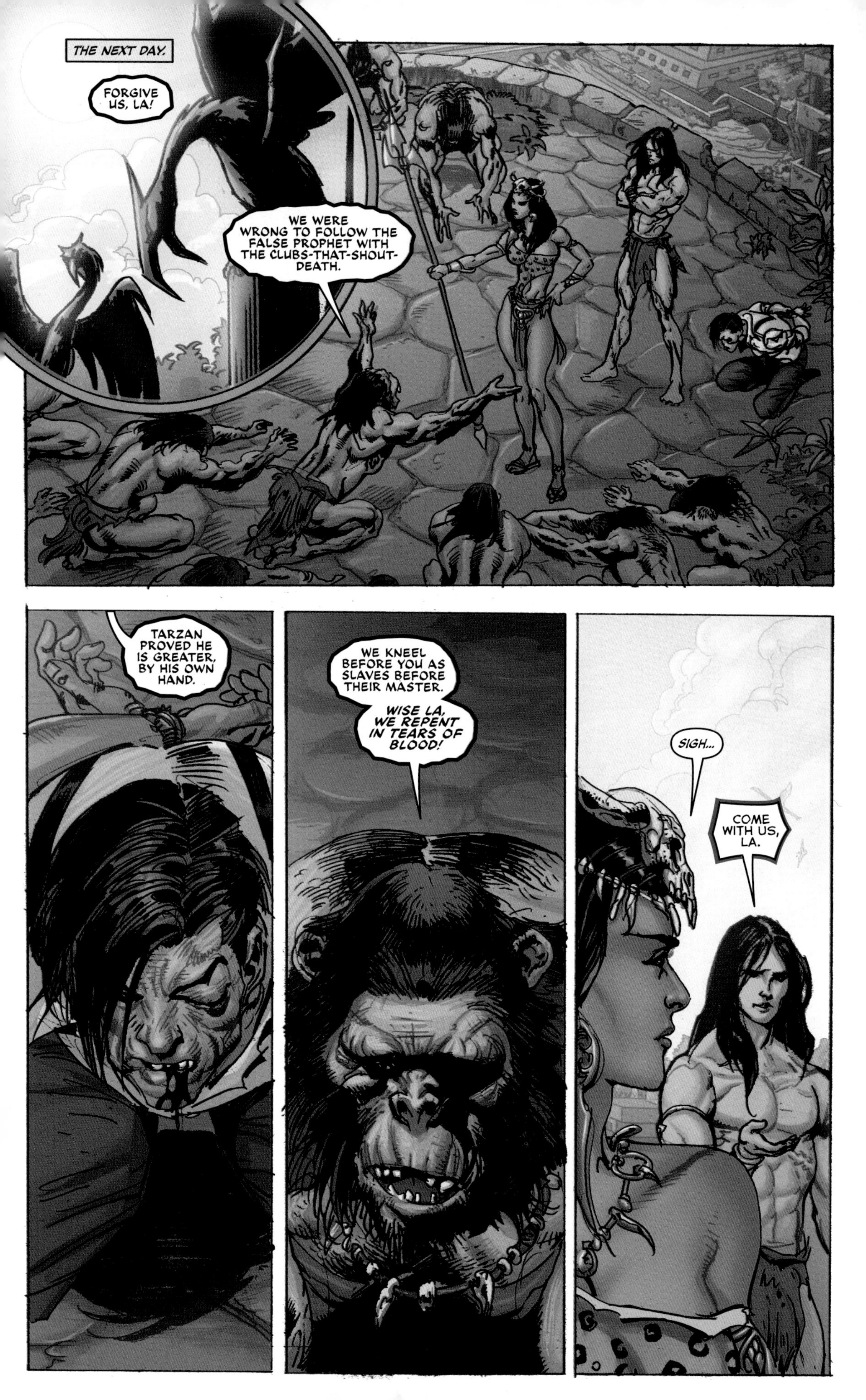
THE NEXT DAY.
FORGIVE US, LA!
WE WERE WRONG TO FOLLOW THE FALSE PROPHET WITH THE CLUBS-THAT-SHOUT-DEATH.
TARZAN PROVED HE IS GREATER, BY HIS OWN HAND.
WE KNEEL BEFORE YOU AS SLAVES BEFORE THEIR MASTER.
WISE LA, WE REPENT IN TEARS OF BLOOD!
SIGH...
COME WITH US, LA.

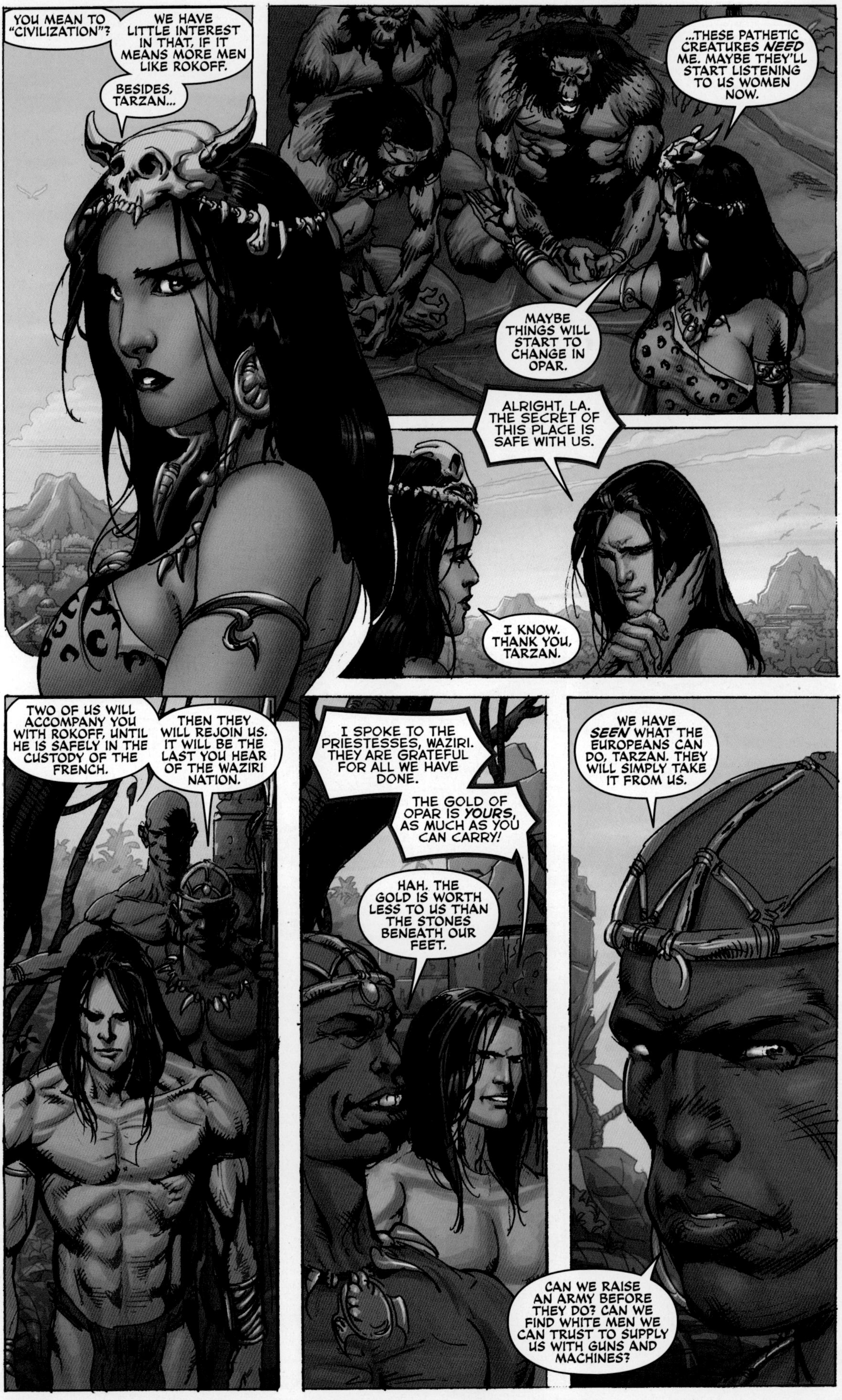
YOU MEAN TO "CIVILIZATION"?
WE HAVE LITTLE INTEREST IN THAT, IF IT MEANS MORE MEN LIKE ROKOFF.
BESIDES, TARZAN...
...THESE PATHETIC CREATURES NEED ME. MAYBE THEY'LL START LISTENING TO US WOMEN NOW.
MAYBE THINGS WILL START TO CHANGE IN OPAR.
ALRIGHT, LA. THE SECRET OF THIS PLACE IS SAFE WITH US.
I KNOW. THANK YOU, TARZAN.
TWO OF US WILL ACCOMPANY YOU WITH ROKOFF, UNTIL HE IS SAFELY IN THE CUSTODY OF THE FRENCH.
THEN THEY WILL REJOIN US. IT WILL BE THE LAST YOU HEAR OF THE WAZIRI NATION.
I SPOKE TO THE PRIESTESSES, WAZIRI. THEY ARE GRATEFUL FOR ALL WE HAVE DONE.
THE GOLD OF OPAR IS YOURS, AS MUCH AS YOU CAN CARRY!
HAH. THE GOLD IS WORTH LESS TO US THAN THE STONES BENEATH OUR FEET.
WE HAVE SEEN WHAT THE EUROPEANS CAN DO, TARZAN. THEY WILL SIMPLY TAKE IT FROM US.
CAN WE RAISE AN ARMY BEFORE THEY DO? CAN WE FIND WHITE MEN WE CAN TRUST TO SUPPLY US WITH GUNS AND MACHINES?

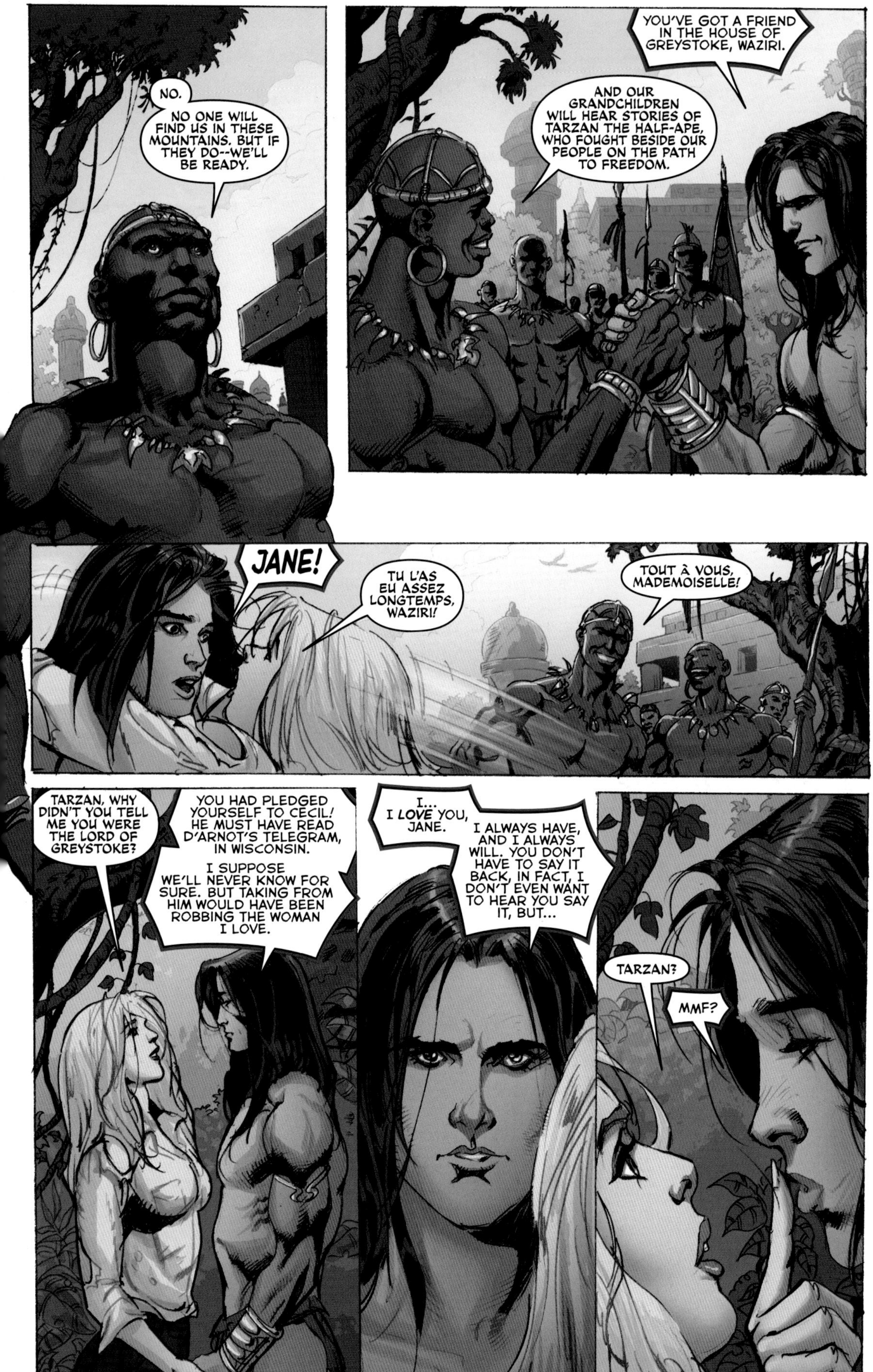
NO.
NO ONE WILL FIND US IN THESE MOUNTAINS. BUT IF THEY DO--WE'LL BE READY.
YOU'VE GOT A FRIEND IN THE HOUSE OF GREYSTOKE, WAZIRI.
AND OUR GRANDCHILDREN WILL HEAR STORIES OF TARZAN THE HALF-APE, WHO FOUGHT BESIDE OUR PEOPLE ON THE PATH TO FREEDOM.
JANE!
TU L'AS EU ASSEZ LONGTEMPS, WAZIRI!
TOUT À VOUS, MADEMOISELLE!
TARZAN, WHY DIDN'T YOU TELL ME YOU WERE THE LORD OF GREYSTOKE?
YOU HAD PLEDGED YOURSELF TO CECIL! HE MUST HAVE READ D'ARNOT'S TELEGRAM, IN WISCONSIN.
I SUPPOSE WE'LL NEVER KNOW FOR SURE. BUT TAKING FROM HIM WOULD HAVE BEEN ROBBING THE WOMAN I LOVE.
I... I *LOVE* YOU, JANE.
I ALWAYS HAVE, AND I ALWAYS WILL. YOU DON'T HAVE TO SAY IT BACK, IN FACT, I DON'T EVEN WANT TO HEAR YOU SAY IT, BUT...
TARZAN?
MMF?

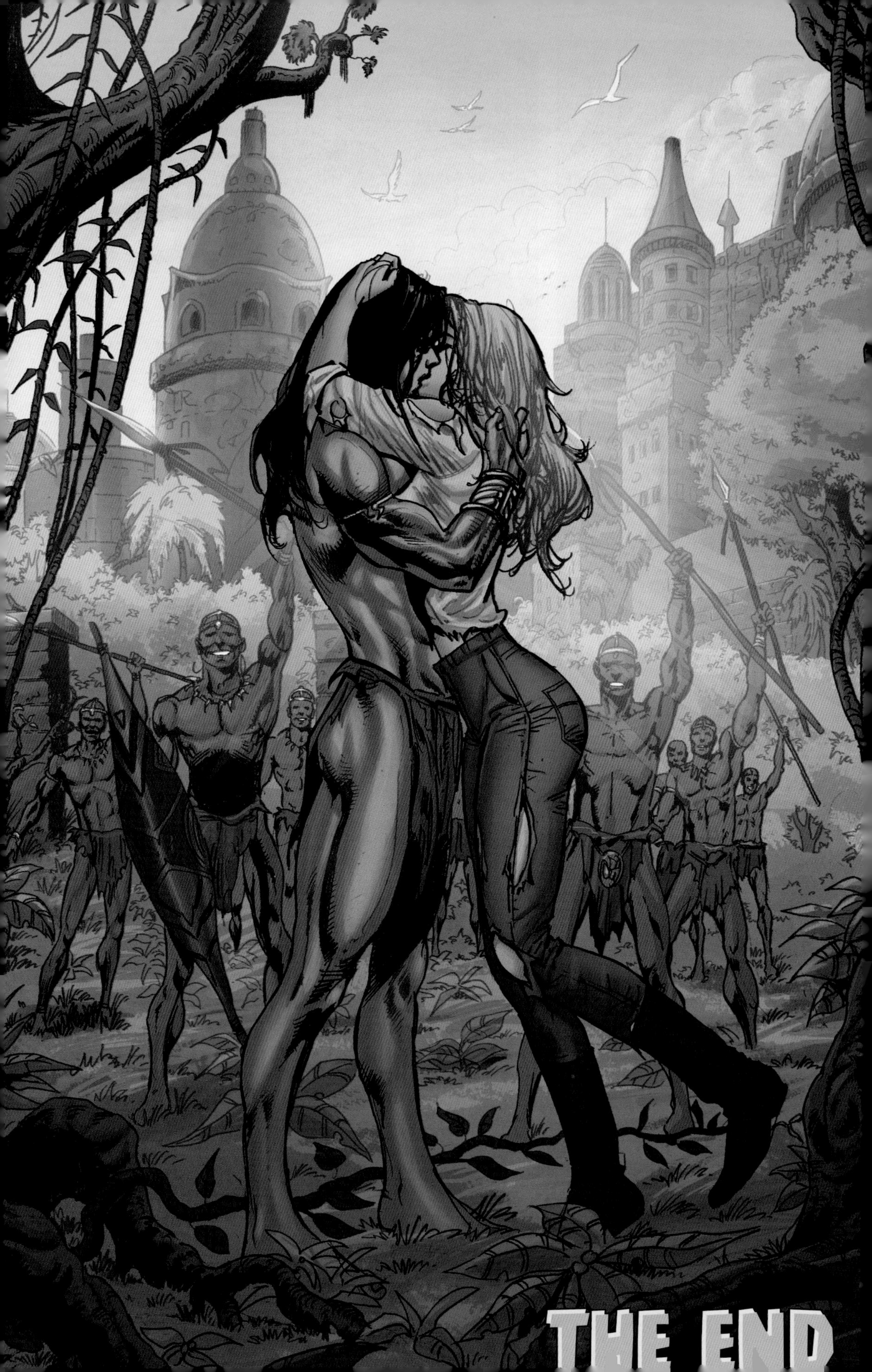
THE END

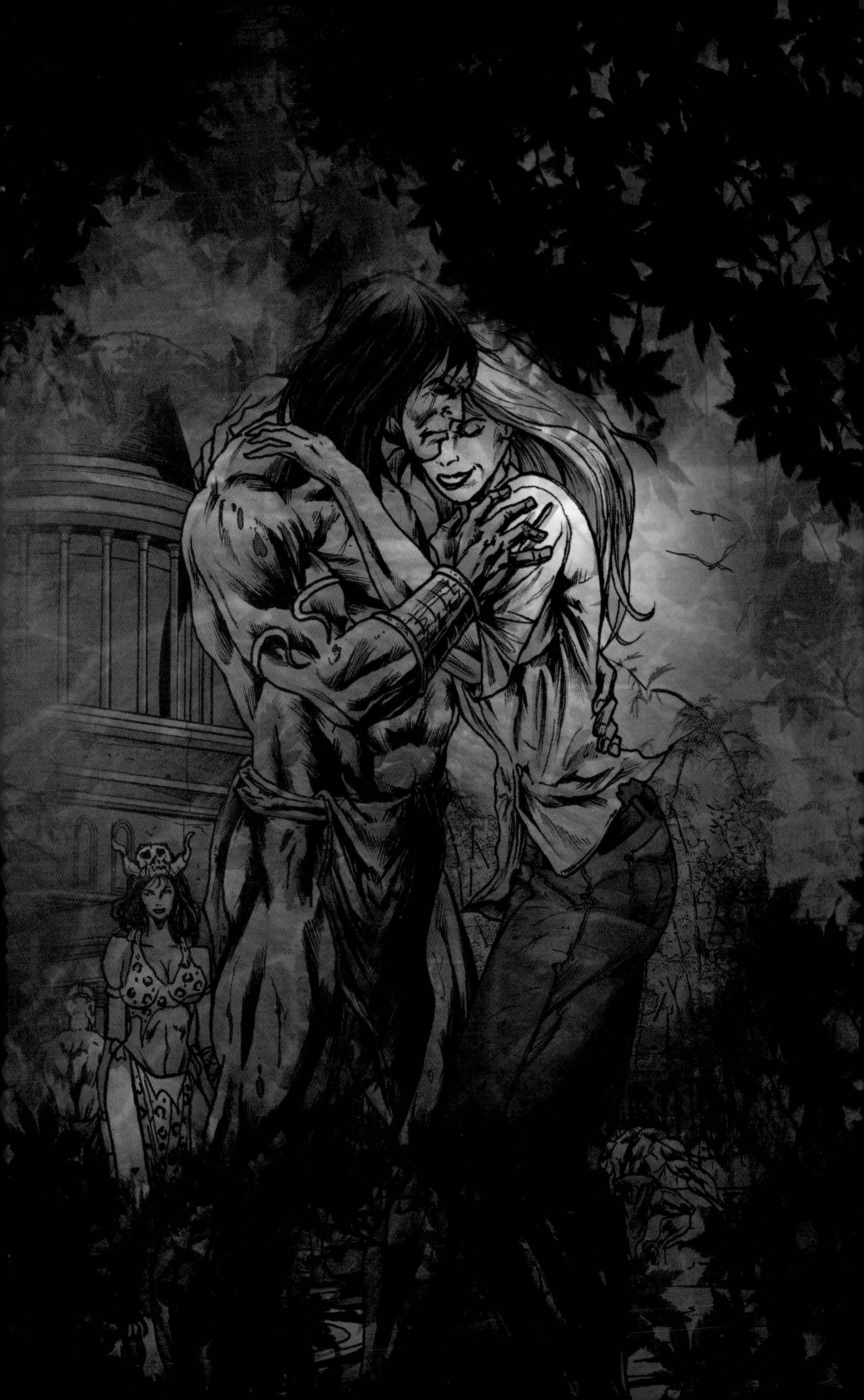

ISSUE 15

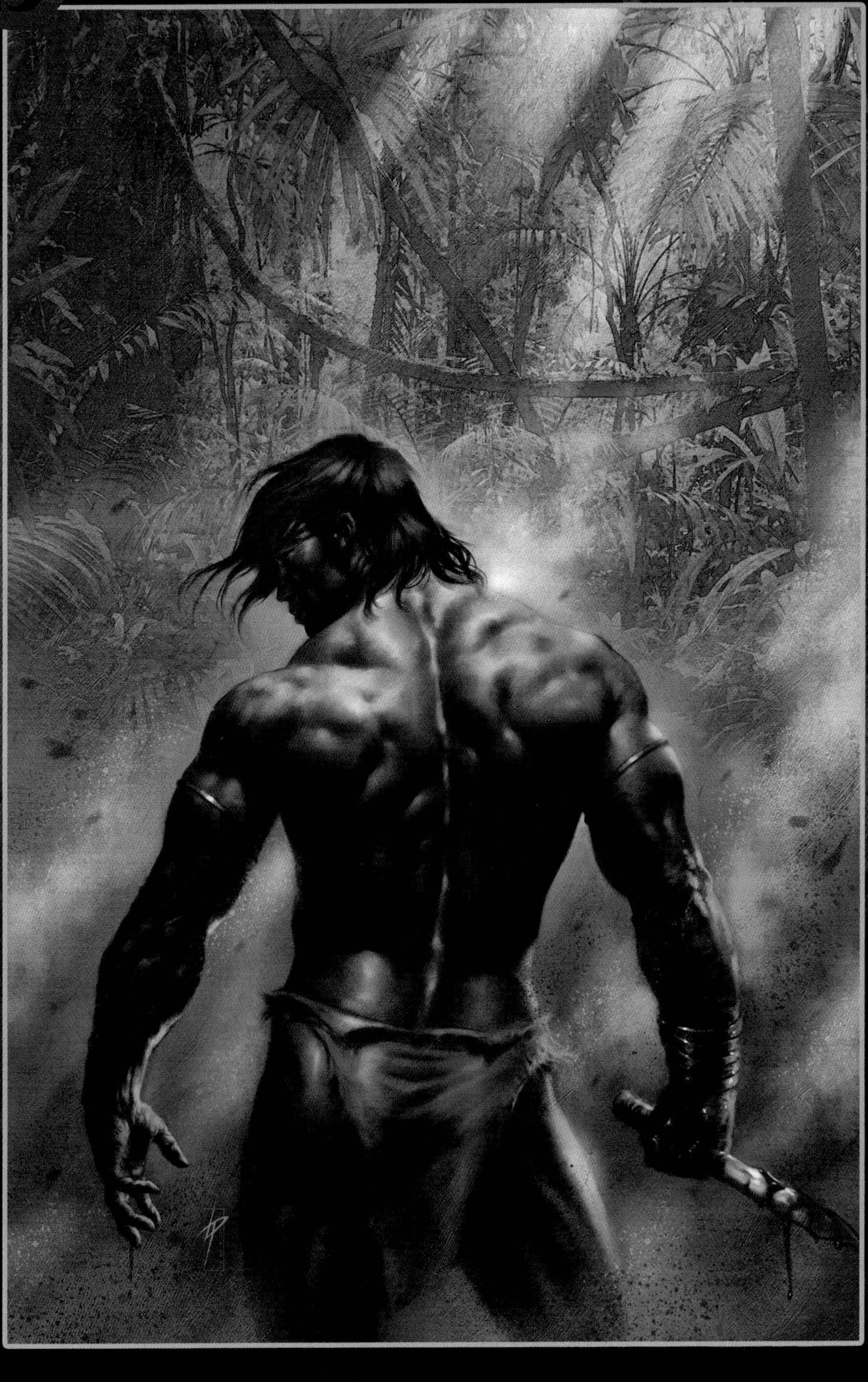

COVER BY LUCIO PARRILLO

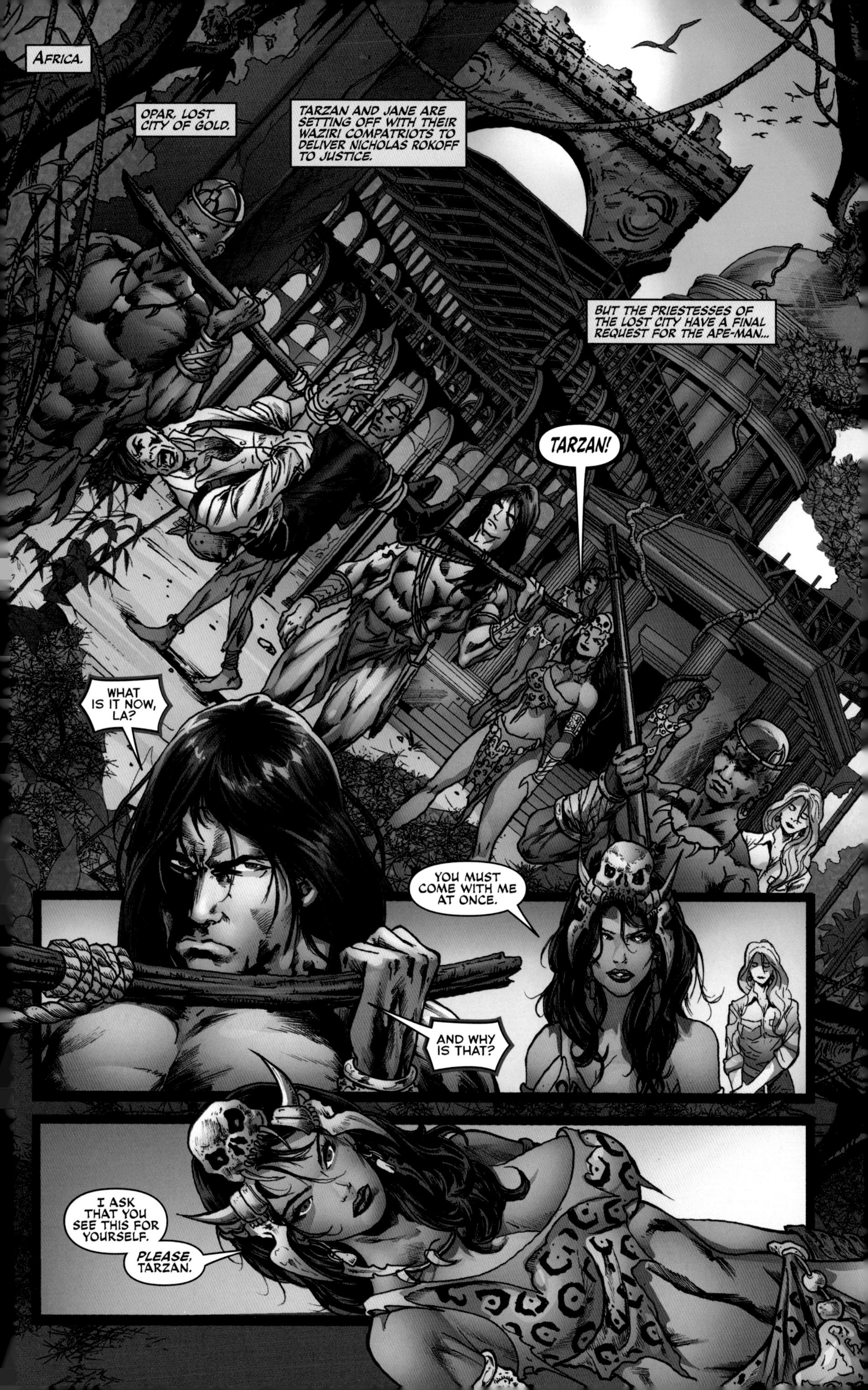
AFRICA.
OPAR, LOST CITY OF GOLD.
TARZAN AND JANE ARE SETTING OFF WITH THEIR WAZIRI COMPATRIOTS TO DELIVER NICHOLAS ROKOFF TO JUSTICE.
BUT THE PRIESTESSES OF THE LOST CITY HAVE A FINAL REQUEST FOR THE APE-MAN...
TARZAN!
WHAT IS IT NOW, LA?
YOU MUST COME WITH ME AT ONCE.
AND WHY IS THAT?
I ASK THAT YOU SEE THIS FOR YOURSELF.
PLEASE, TARZAN.

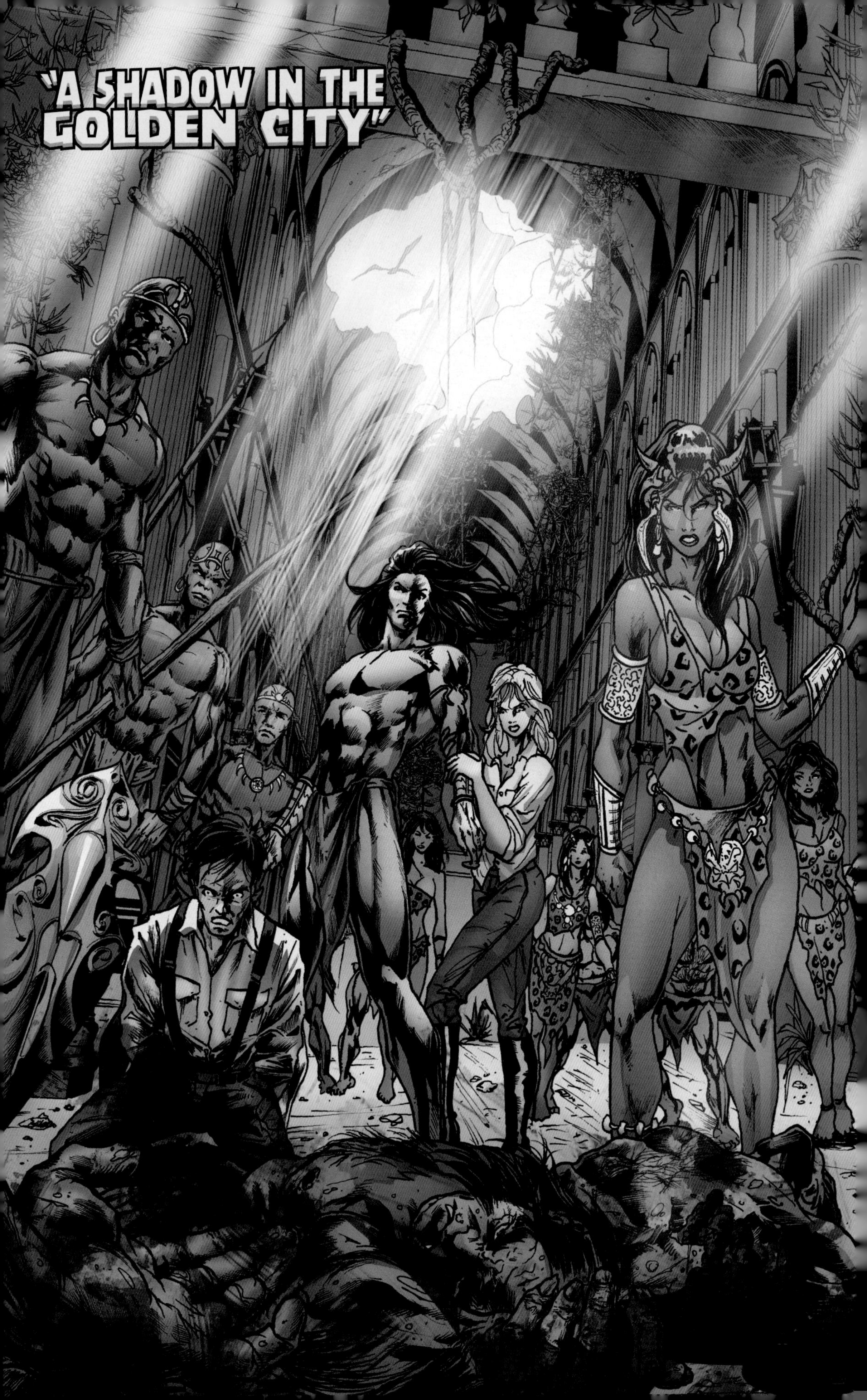
"A SHADOW IN THE GOLDEN CITY"

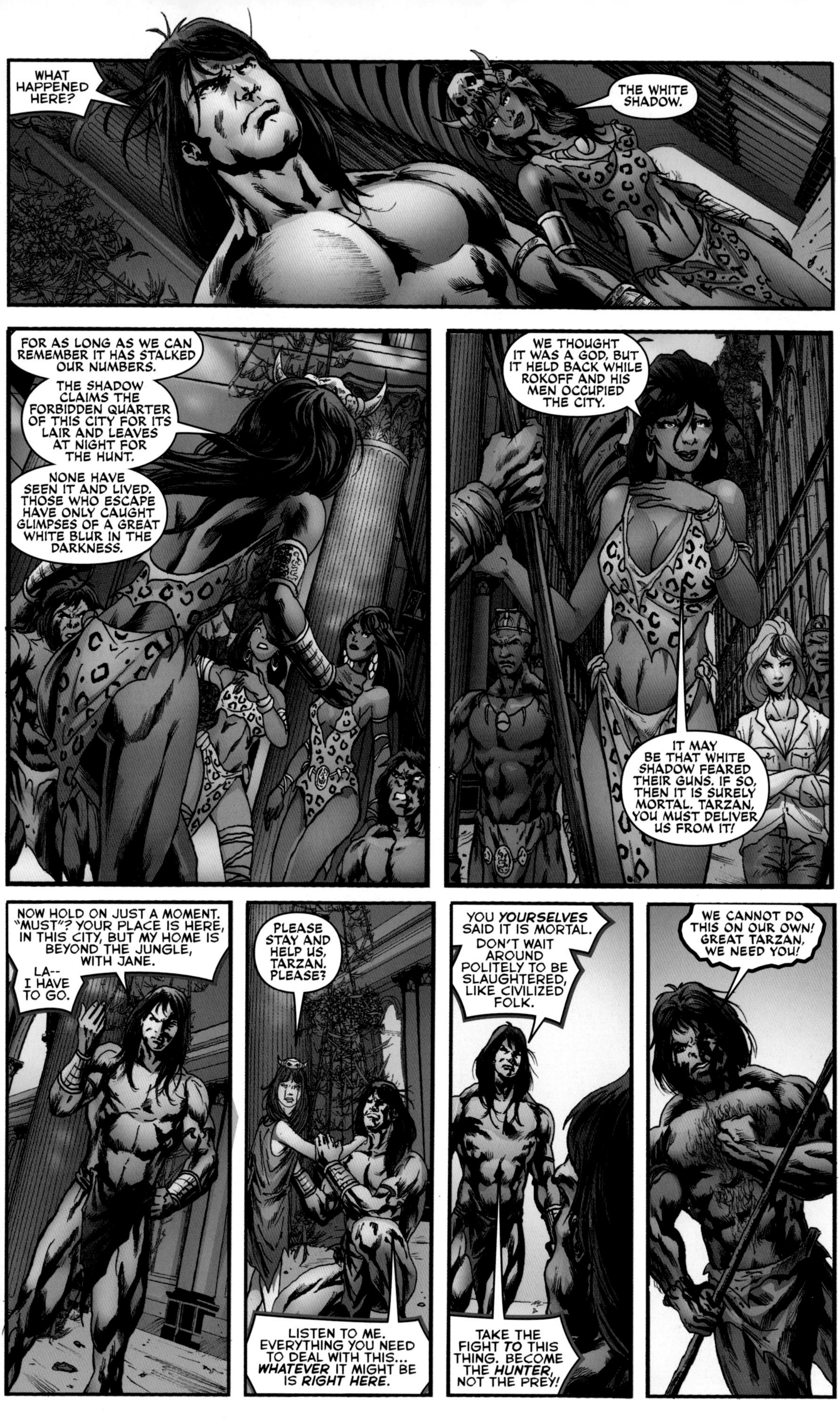
WHAT HAPPENED HERE?
THE WHITE SHADOW.
FOR AS LONG AS WE CAN REMEMBER IT HAS STALKED OUR NUMBERS.
THE SHADOW CLAIMS THE FORBIDDEN QUARTER OF THIS CITY FOR ITS LAIR AND LEAVES AT NIGHT FOR THE HUNT.
NONE HAVE SEEN IT AND LIVED. THOSE WHO ESCAPE HAVE ONLY CAUGHT GLIMPSES OF A GREAT WHITE BLUR IN THE DARKNESS.
WE THOUGHT IT WAS A GOD, BUT IT HELD BACK WHILE ROKOFF AND HIS MEN OCCUPIED THE CITY.
IT MAY BE THAT WHITE SHADOW FEARED THEIR GUNS. IF SO, THEN IT IS SURELY MORTAL. TARZAN, YOU MUST DELIVER US FROM IT!
NOW HOLD ON JUST A MOMENT. "MUST"? YOUR PLACE IS HERE, IN THIS CITY, BUT MY HOME IS BEYOND THE JUNGLE, WITH JANE.
LA-- I HAVE TO GO.
PLEASE STAY AND HELP US, TARZAN. PLEASE?
LISTEN TO ME. EVERYTHING YOU NEED TO DEAL WITH THIS... WHATEVER IT MIGHT BE IS RIGHT HERE.
YOU YOURSELVES SAID IT IS MORTAL.
DON'T WAIT AROUND POLITELY TO BE SLAUGHTERED, LIKE CIVILIZED FOLK.
TAKE THE FIGHT TO THIS THING. BECOME THE HUNTER, NOT THE PREY!
WE CANNOT DO THIS ON OUR OWN! GREAT TARZAN, WE NEED YOU!

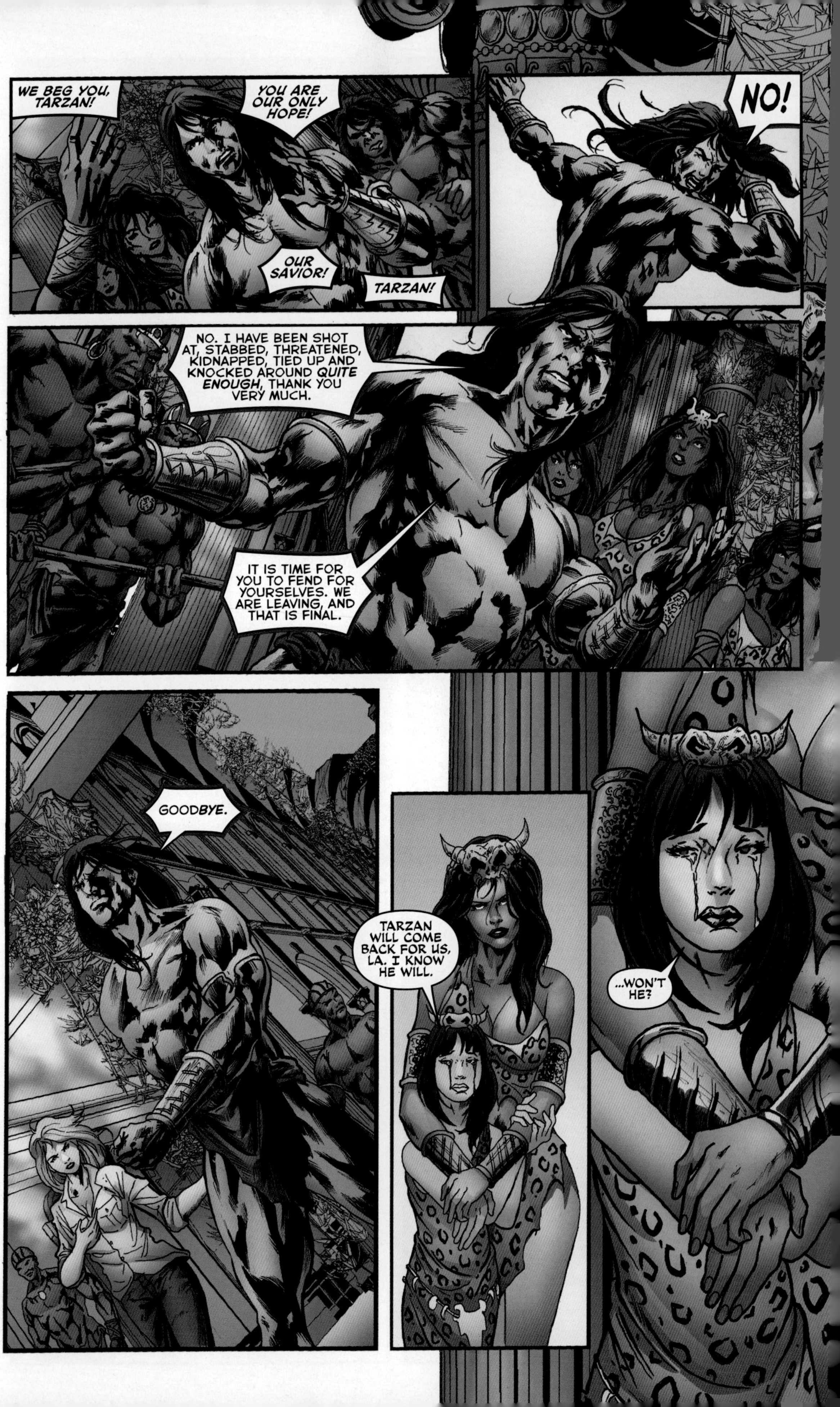
WE BEG YOU, TARZAN!
YOU ARE OUR ONLY HOPE!
OUR SAVIOR!
TARZAN!
NO!
NO. I HAVE BEEN SHOT AT, STABBED, THREATENED, KIDNAPPED, TIED UP AND KNOCKED AROUND QUITE ENOUGH, THANK YOU VERY MUCH.
IT IS TIME FOR YOU TO FEND FOR YOURSELVES. WE ARE LEAVING, AND THAT IS FINAL.
GOODBYE.
TARZAN WILL COME BACK FOR US, LA. I KNOW HE WILL.
...WON'T HE?

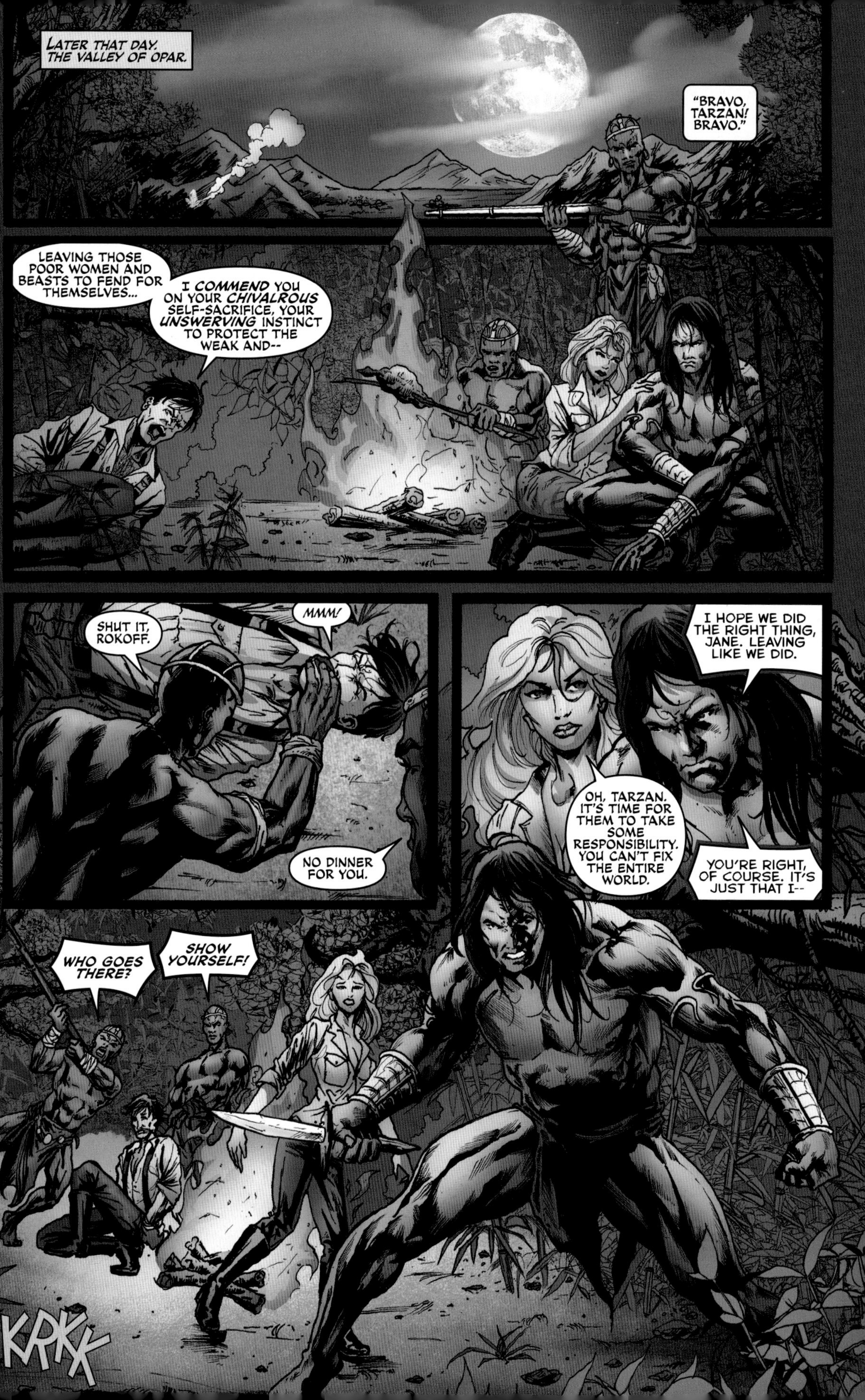
LATER THAT DAY. THE VALLEY OF OPAR.
"BRAVO, TARZAN! BRAVO."
LEAVING THOSE POOR WOMEN AND BEASTS TO FEND FOR THEMSELVES...
I COMMEND YOU ON YOUR CHIVALROUS SELF-SACRIFICE, YOUR UNSWERVING INSTINCT TO PROTECT THE WEAK AND--
SHUT IT, ROKOFF.
MMM!
NO DINNER FOR YOU.
I HOPE WE DID THE RIGHT THING, JANE. LEAVING LIKE WE DID.
OH, TARZAN. IT'S TIME FOR THEM TO TAKE SOME RESPONSIBILITY. YOU CAN'T FIX THE ENTIRE WORLD.
YOU'RE RIGHT, OF COURSE. IT'S JUST THAT I--
WHO GOES THERE?
SHOW YOURSELF!
KRKK

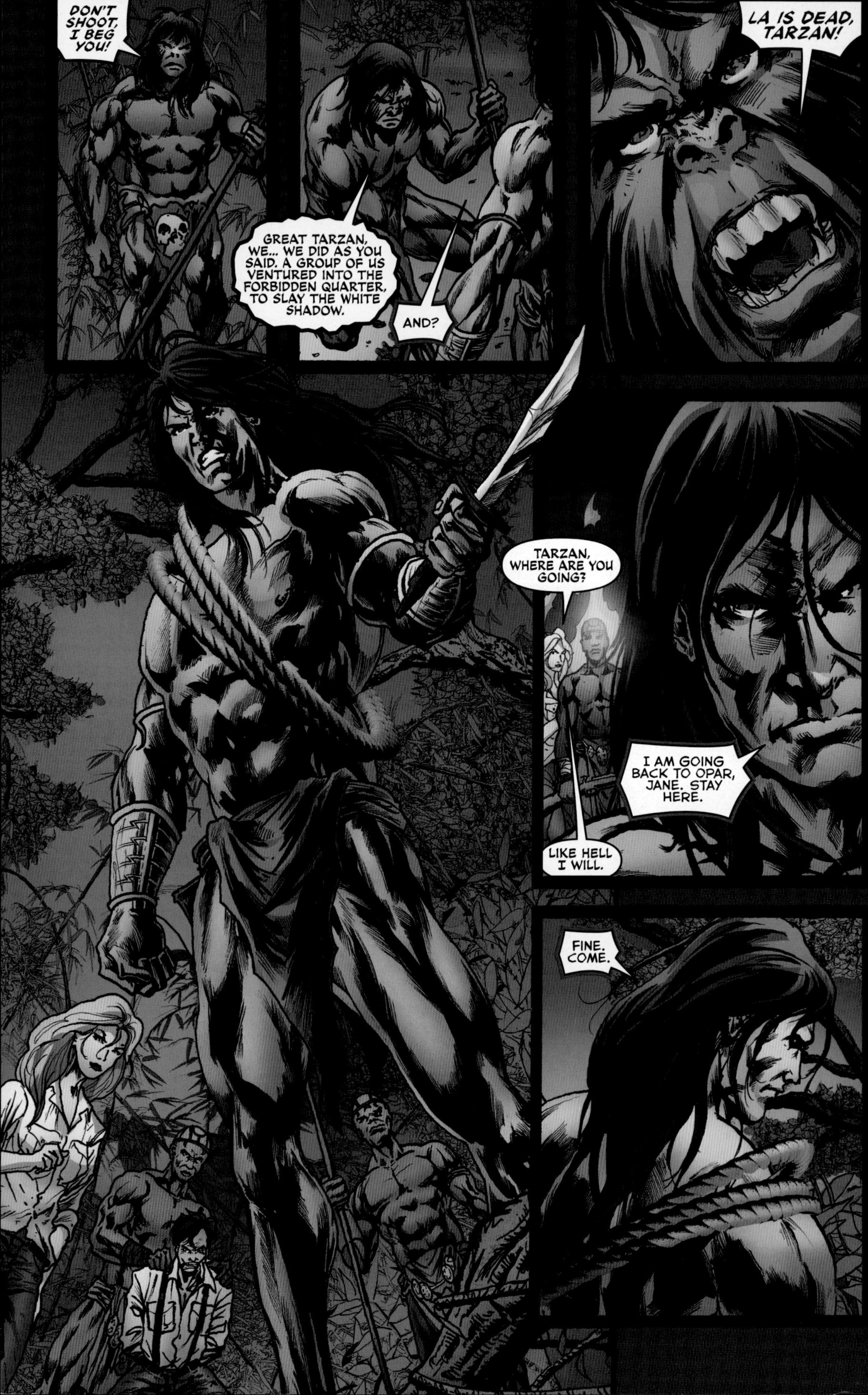
DON'T SHOOT, I BEG YOU!
GREAT TARZAN, WE... WE DID AS YOU SAID. A GROUP OF US VENTURED INTO THE FORBIDDEN QUARTER, TO SLAY THE WHITE SHADOW.
AND?
LA IS DEAD, TARZAN!
TARZAN, WHERE ARE YOU GOING?
I AM GOING BACK TO OPAR, JANE. STAY HERE.
LIKE HELL I WILL.
FINE. COME.

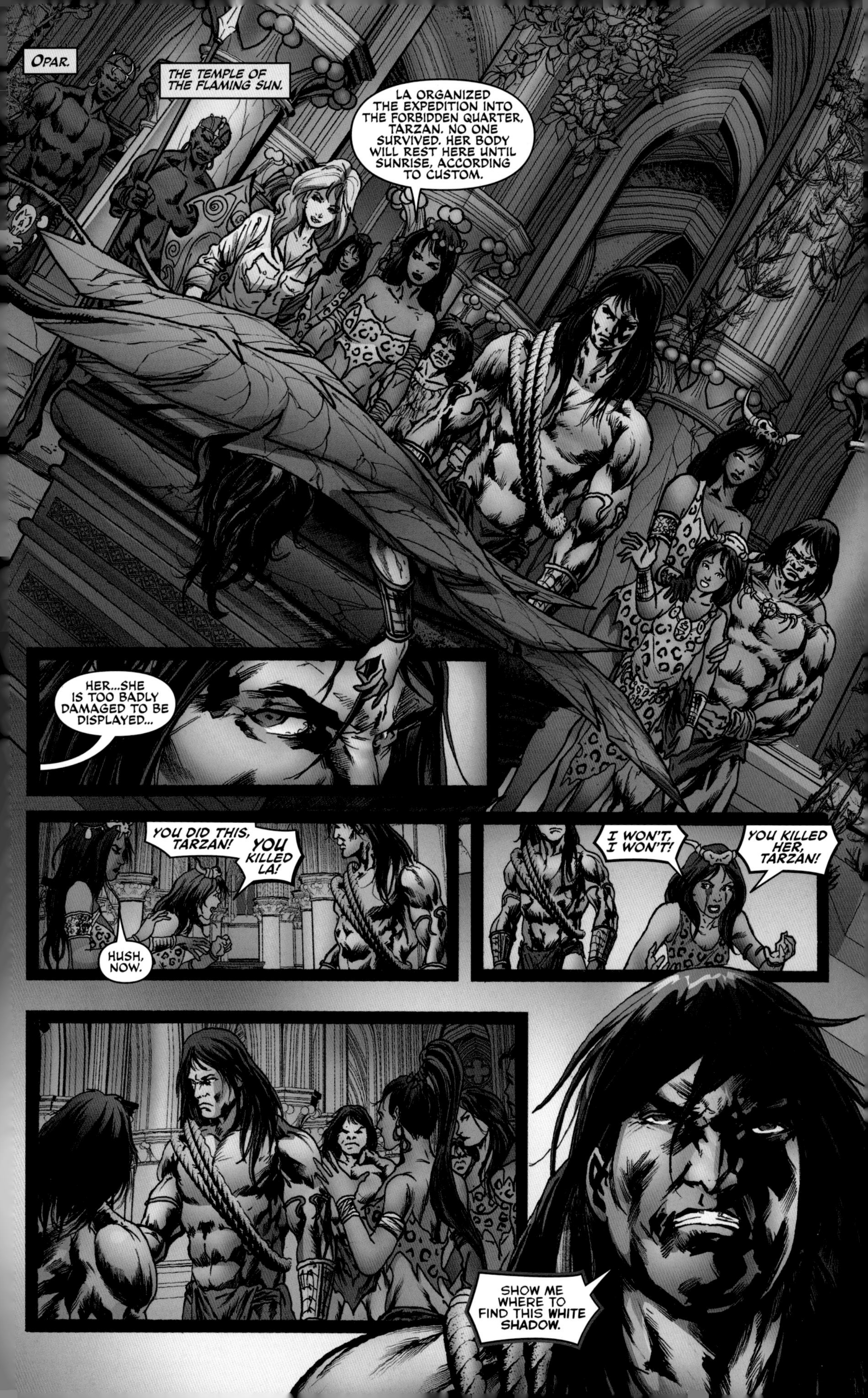

OPAR.
THE TEMPLE OF THE FLAMING SUN.
LA ORGANIZED THE EXPEDITION INTO THE FORBIDDEN QUARTER, TARZAN. NO ONE SURVIVED. HER BODY WILL REST HERE UNTIL SUNRISE, ACCORDING TO CUSTOM.
HER...SHE IS TOO BADLY DAMAGED TO BE DISPLAYED...
YOU DID THIS, TARZAN!
YOU KILLED LA!
HUSH, NOW.
I WON'T, I WON'T!
YOU KILLED HER, TARZAN!
SHOW ME WHERE TO FIND THIS WHITE SHADOW.

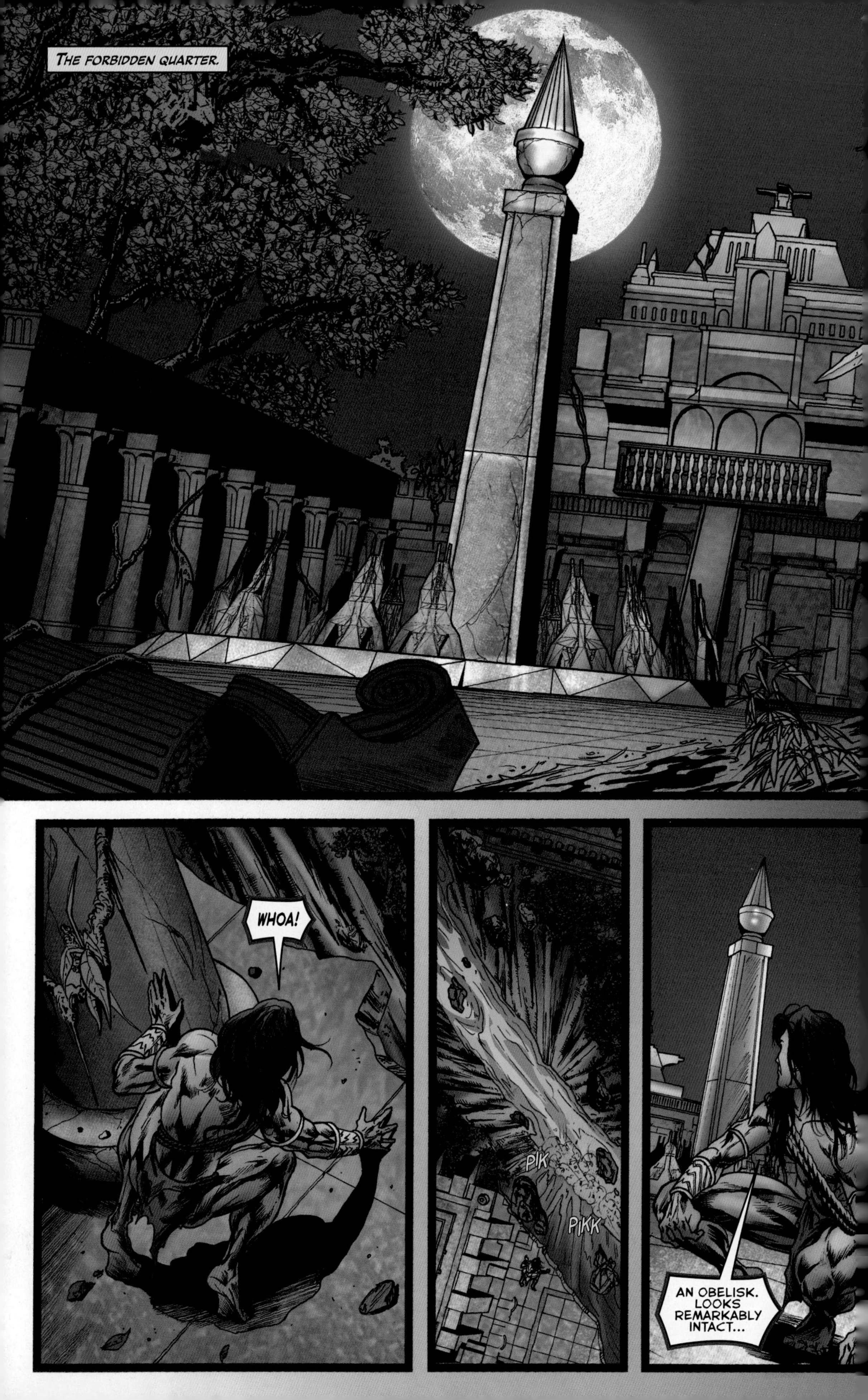
THE FORBIDDEN QUARTER.
WHOA!
PIK
PIKK
AN OBELISK. LOOKS REMARKABLY INTACT...

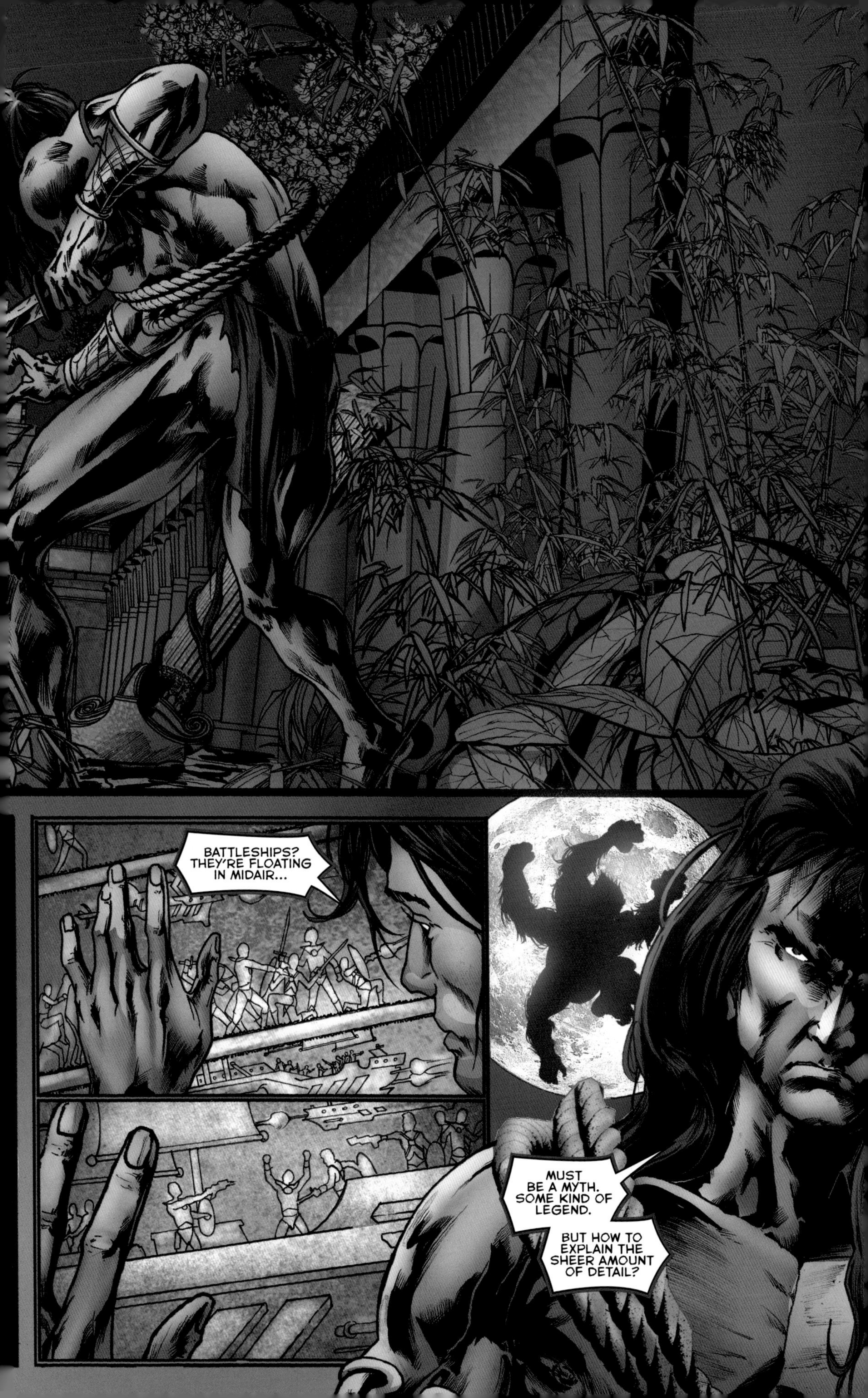
BATTLESHIPS? THEY'RE FLOATING IN MIDAIR...
MUST BE A MYTH. SOME KIND OF LEGEND.
BUT HOW TO EXPLAIN THE SHEER AMOUNT OF DETAIL?

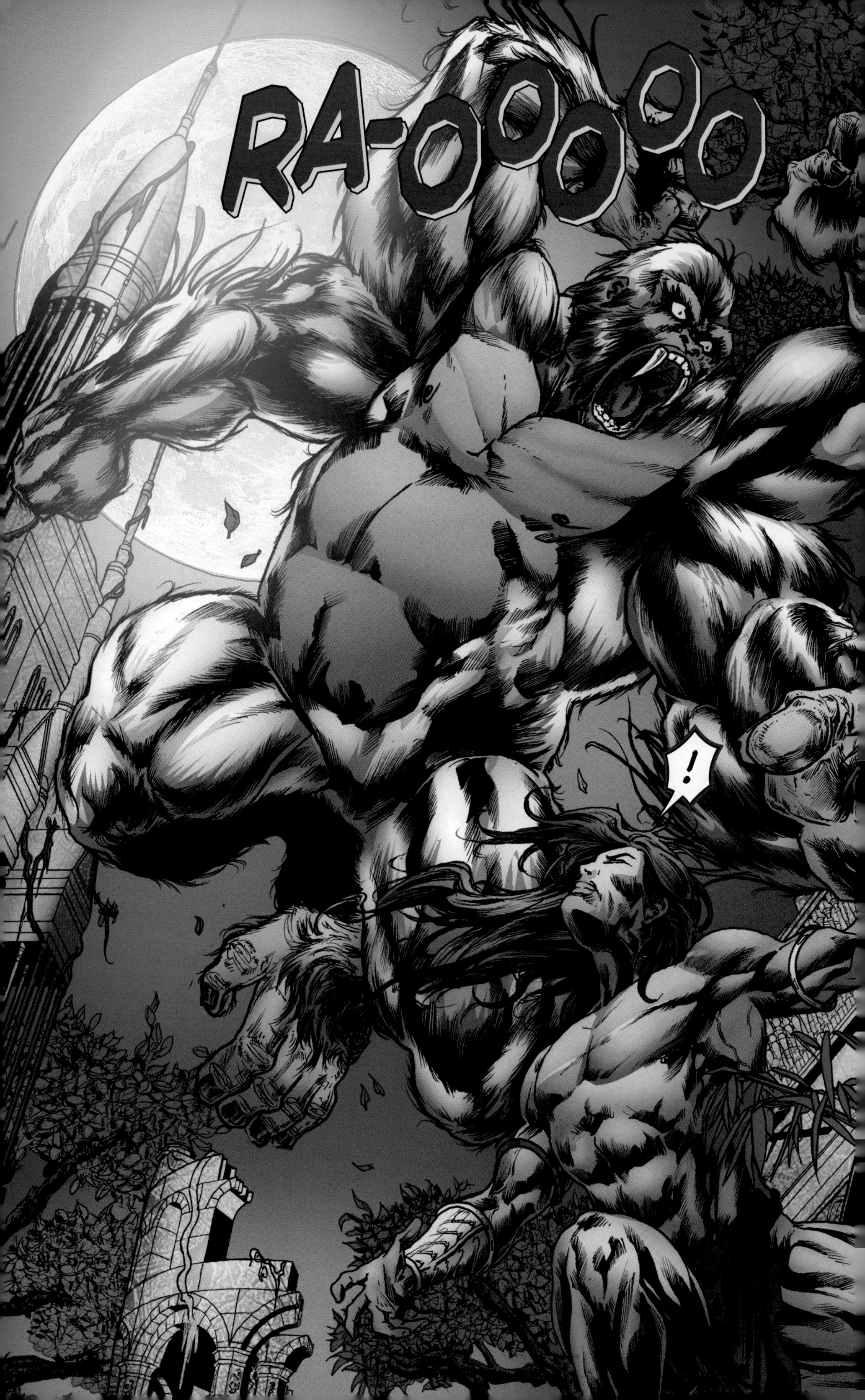
RA-OOOOO
!

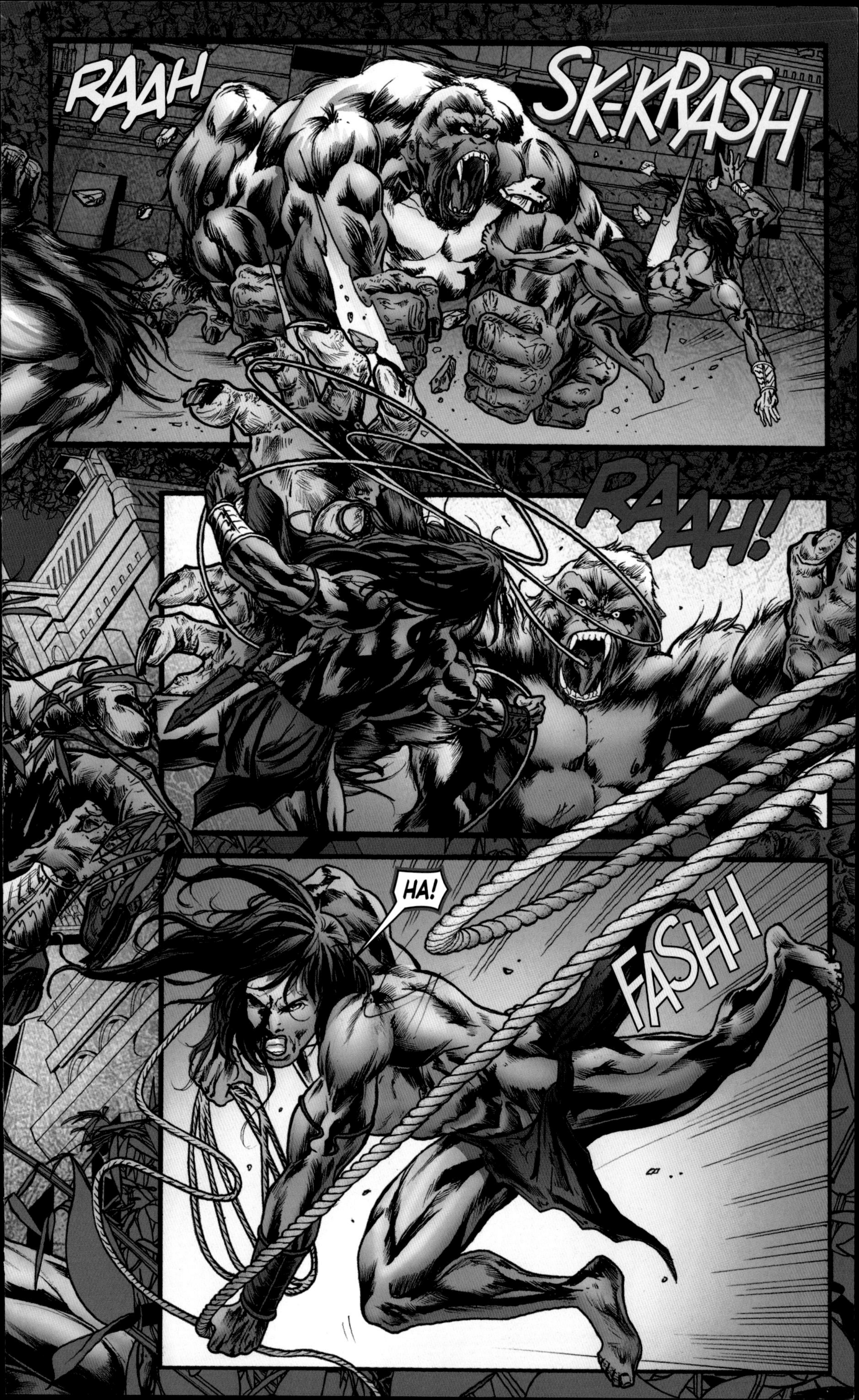
RAAH
SK-KRASH
RAAH!!
HA!
FASHH

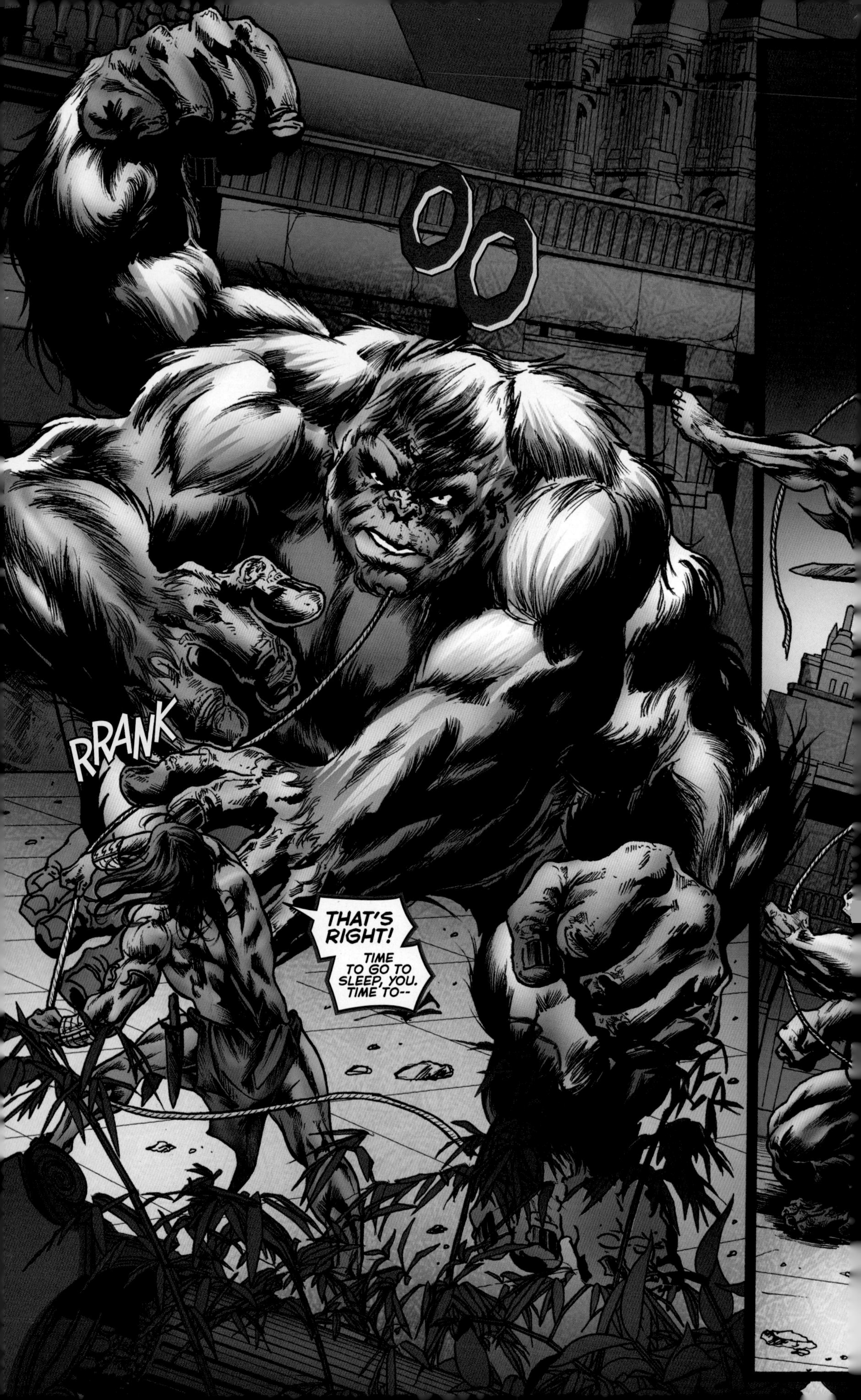
RRANK
THAT'S RIGHT!
TIME TO GO TO SLEEP, YOU. TIME TO--

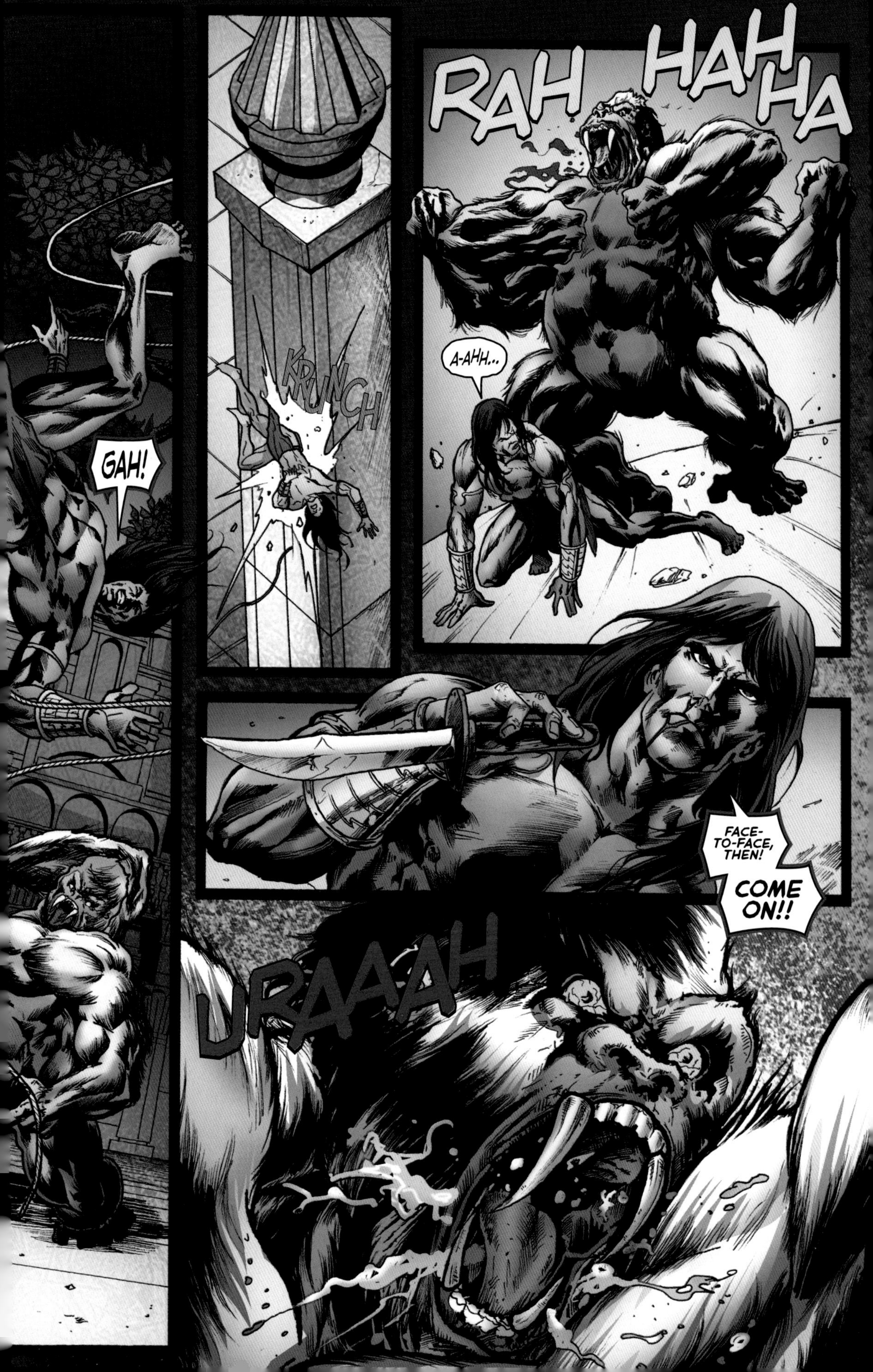
GAH!
KRUNCH
RAH HAH HAH HA
A-AHH...
FACE-TO-FACE, THEN!
COME ON!!
URAAAH

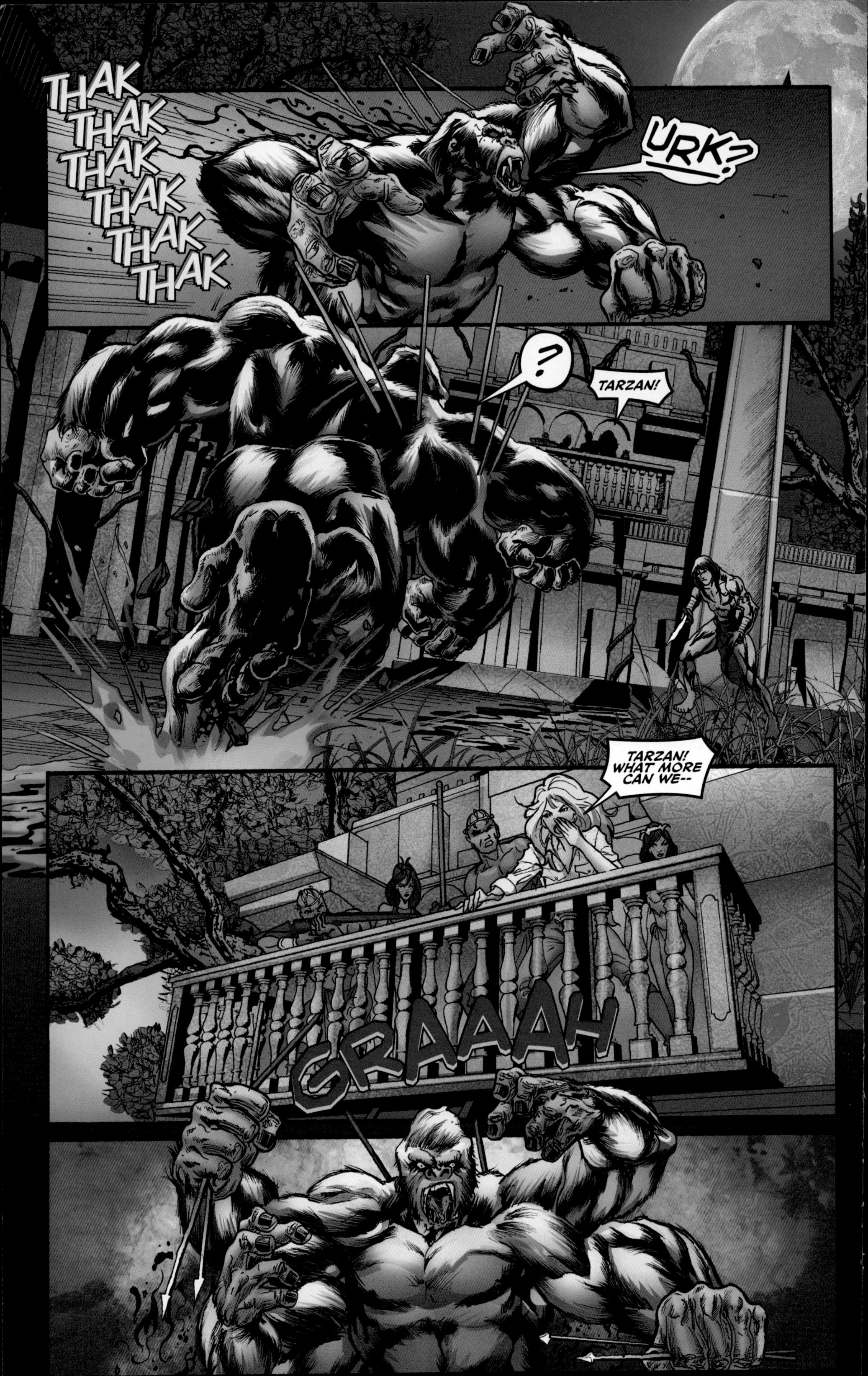

THAK THAK THAK THAK THAK THAK
URK?
?
TARZAN!
TARZAN! WHAT MORE CAN WE--
GRAAAH

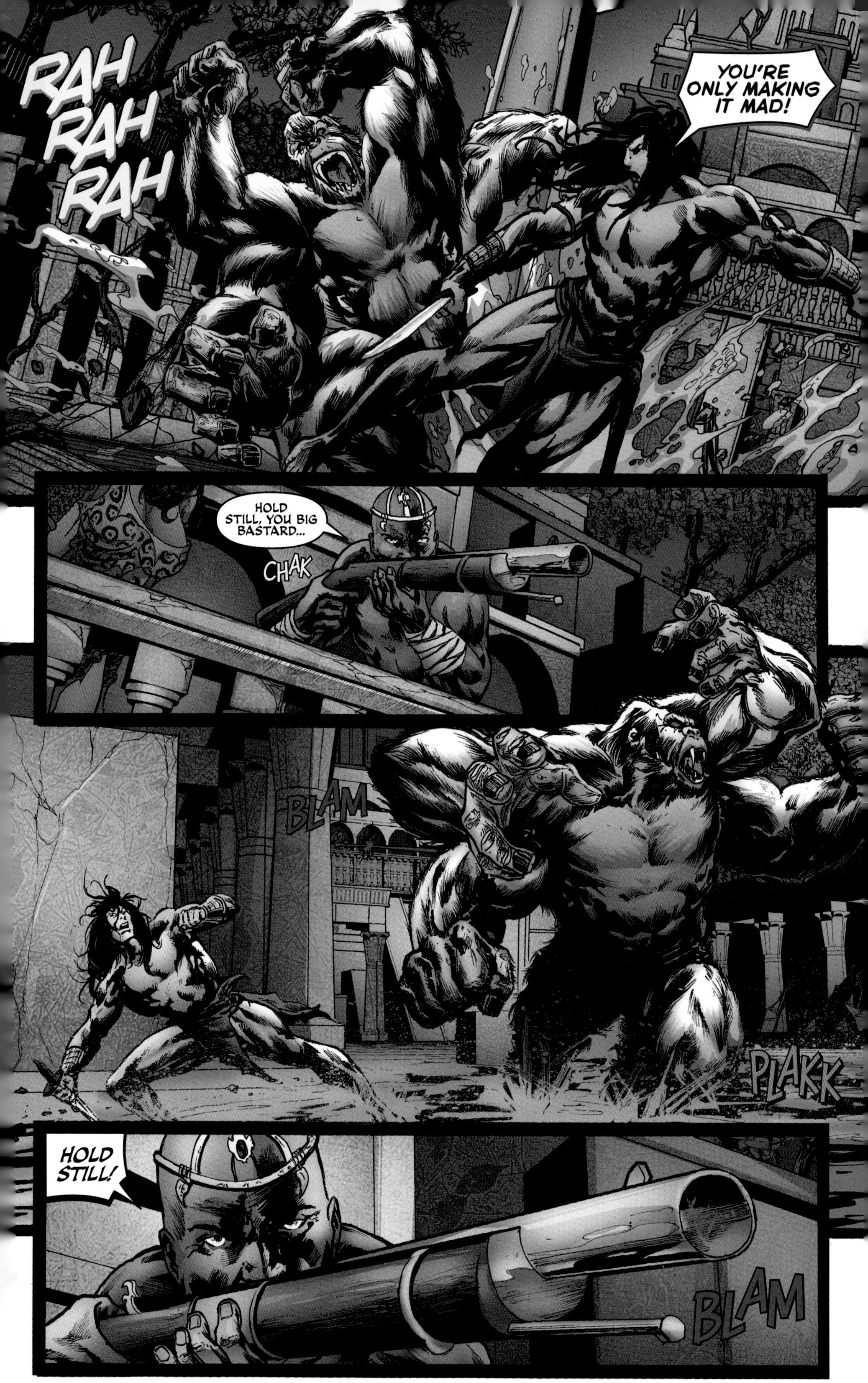
RAH
RAH
RAH
YOU'RE ONLY MAKING IT MAD!
HOLD STILL, YOU BIG BASTARD...
CHAK
BLAM
PLAKK
HOLD STILL!
BLAM

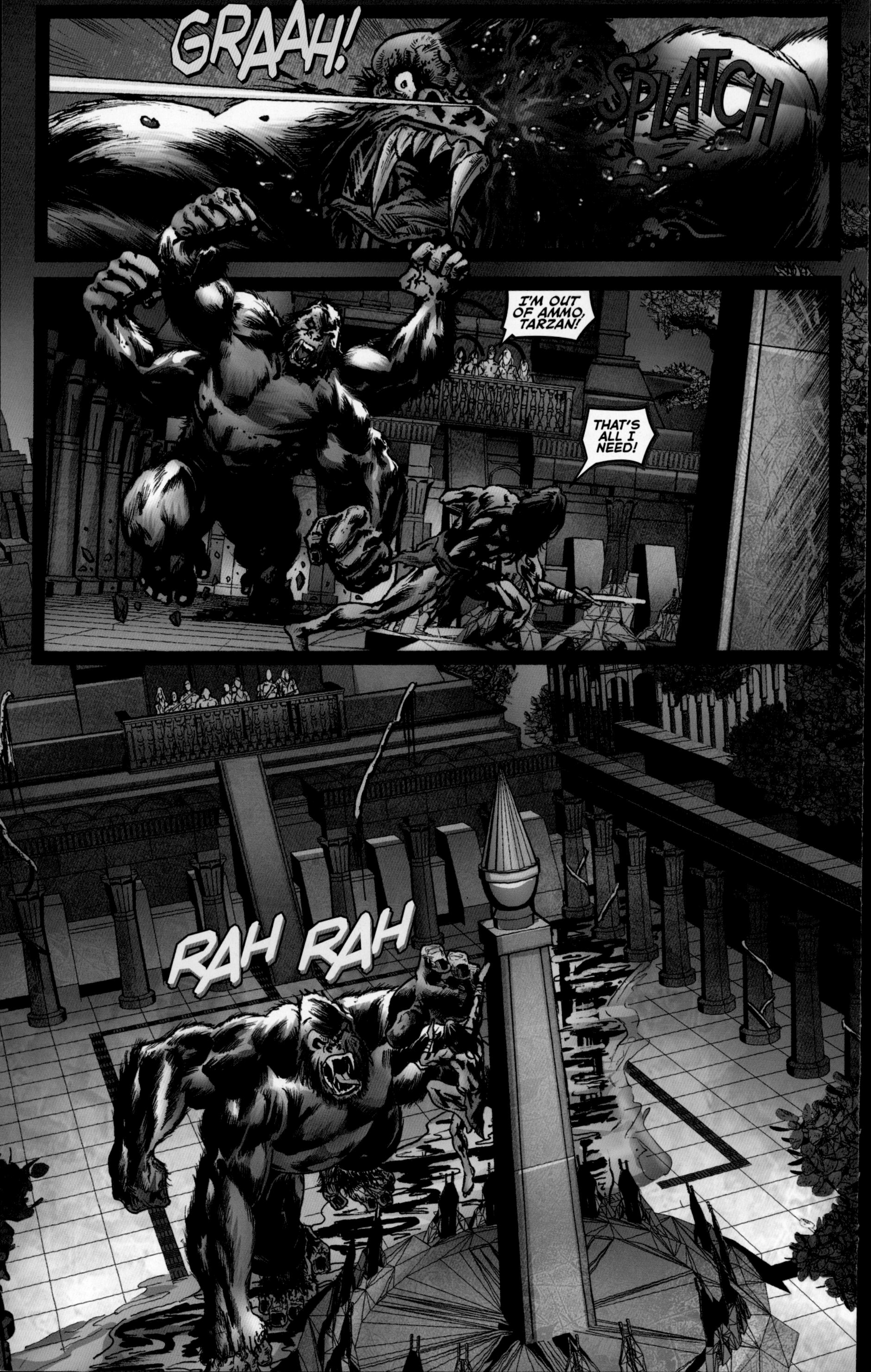
GRAAH!
SPLATCH
I'M OUT OF AMMO, TARZAN!
THAT'S ALL I NEED!
RAH RAH

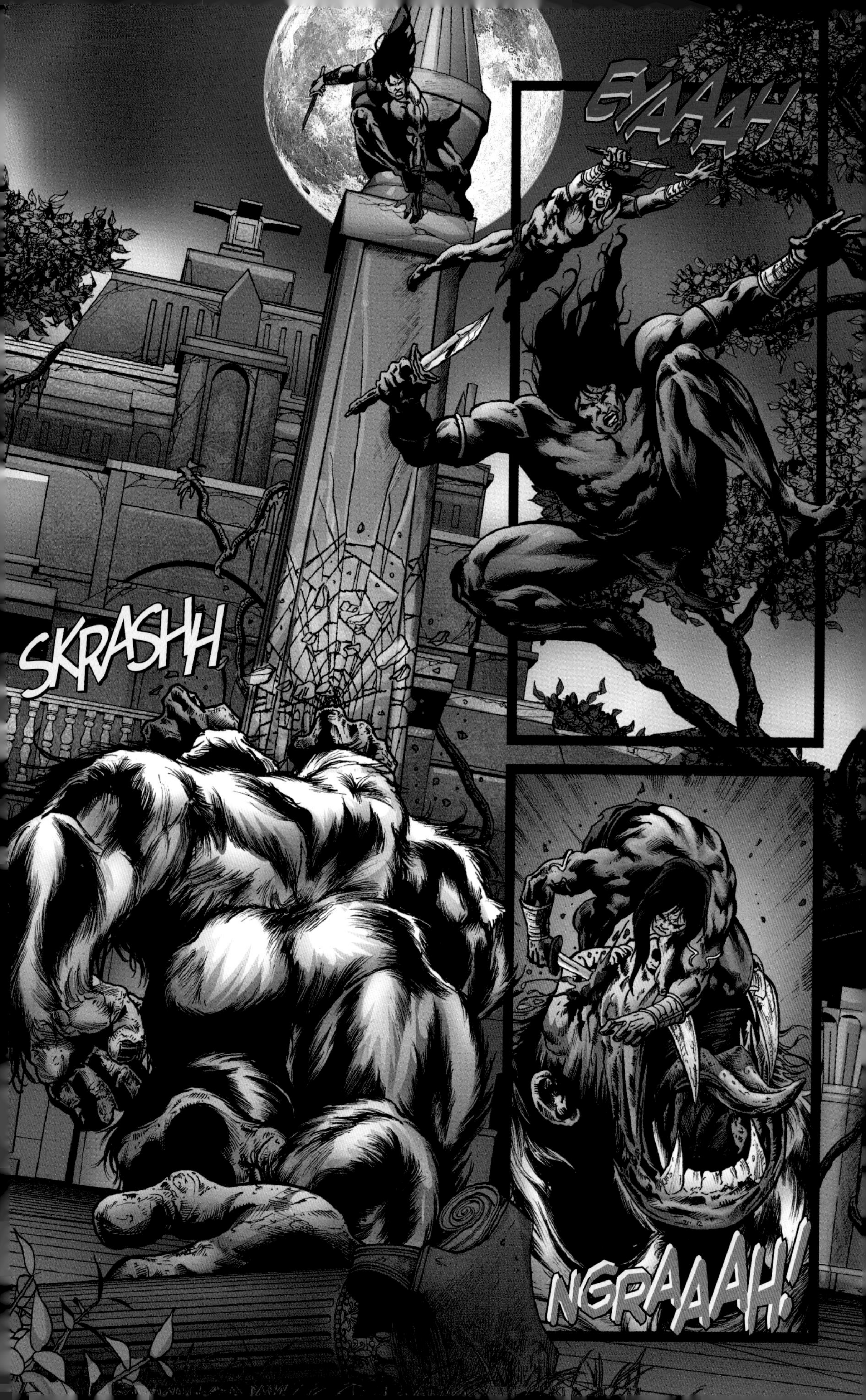
EYAAAH
SKRASHH
NGRAAAH!

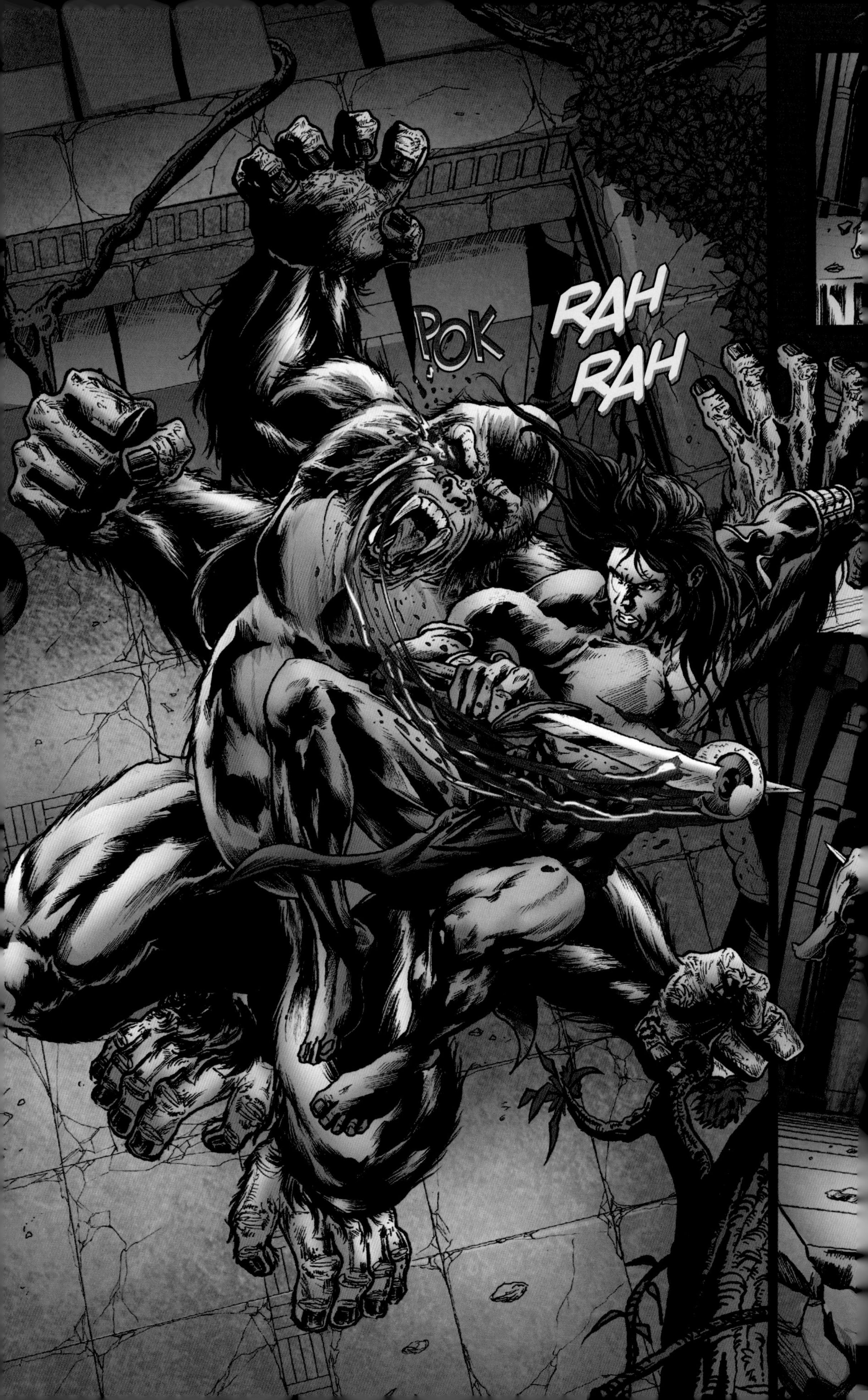
POK
RAH
RAH

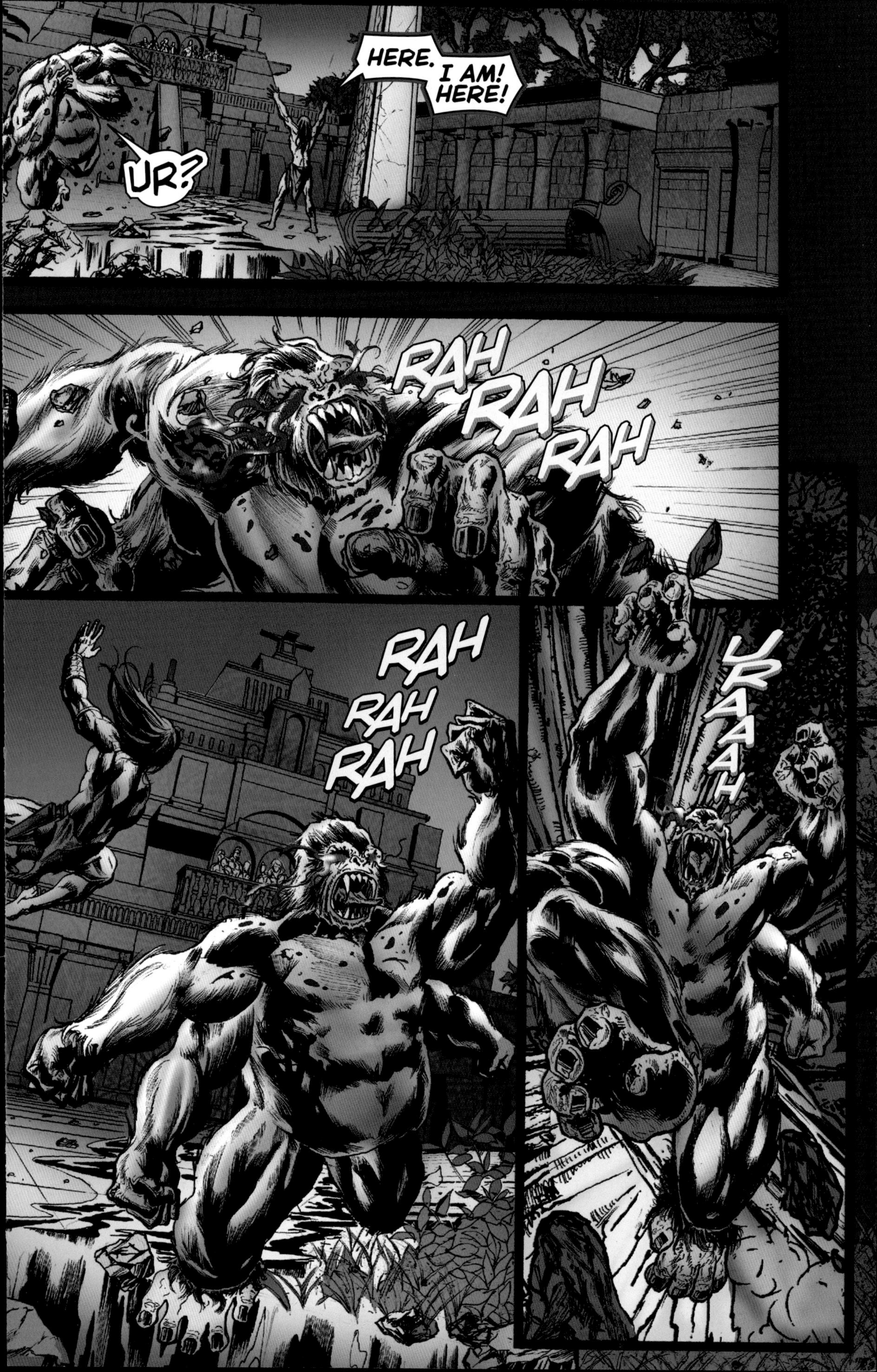
HERE. I AM! HERE!
UR?
RAH RAH RAH
RAH RAH RAH
URAAAH

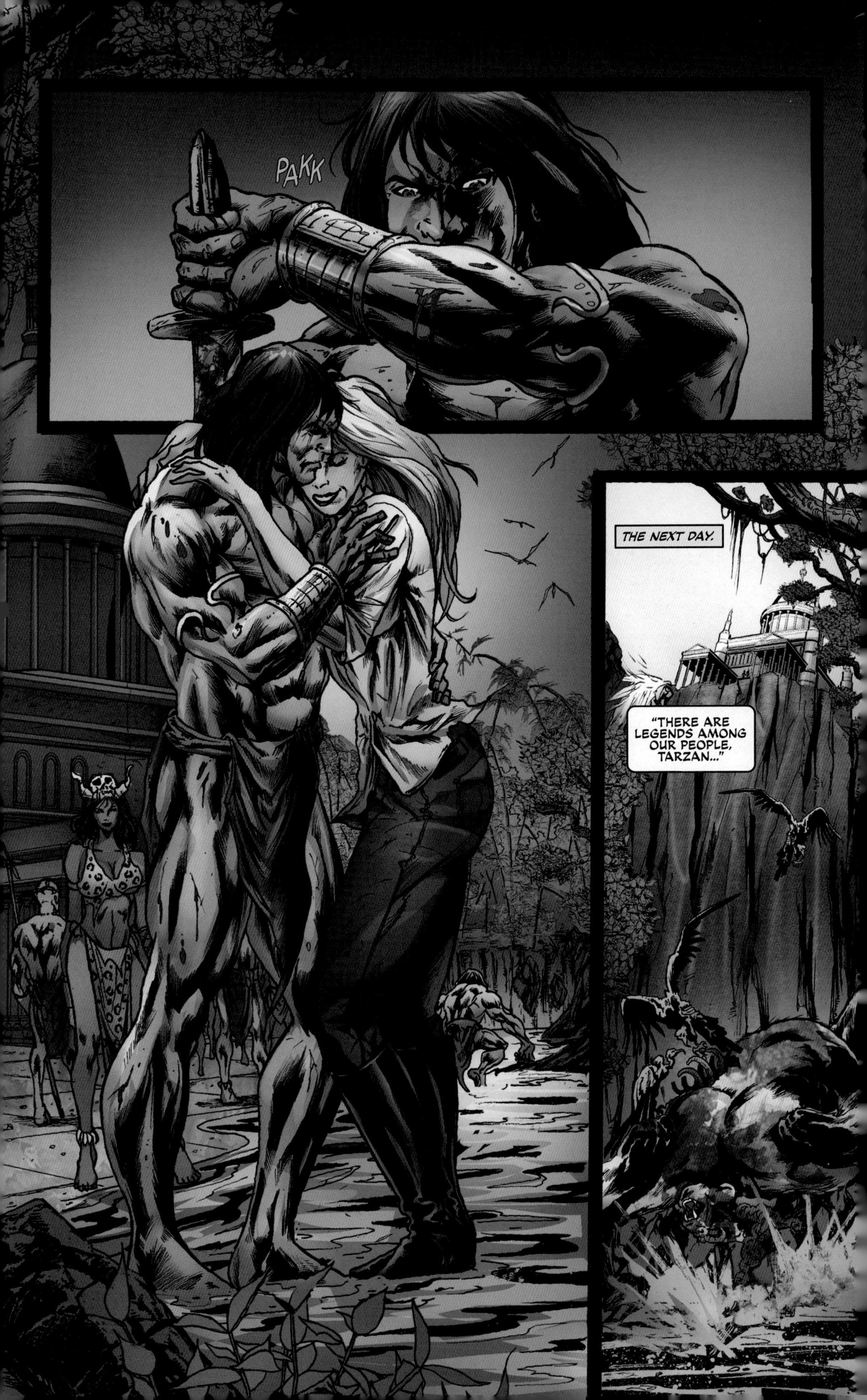
PAKK
THE NEXT DAY.
"THERE ARE LEGENDS AMONG OUR PEOPLE, TARZAN..."

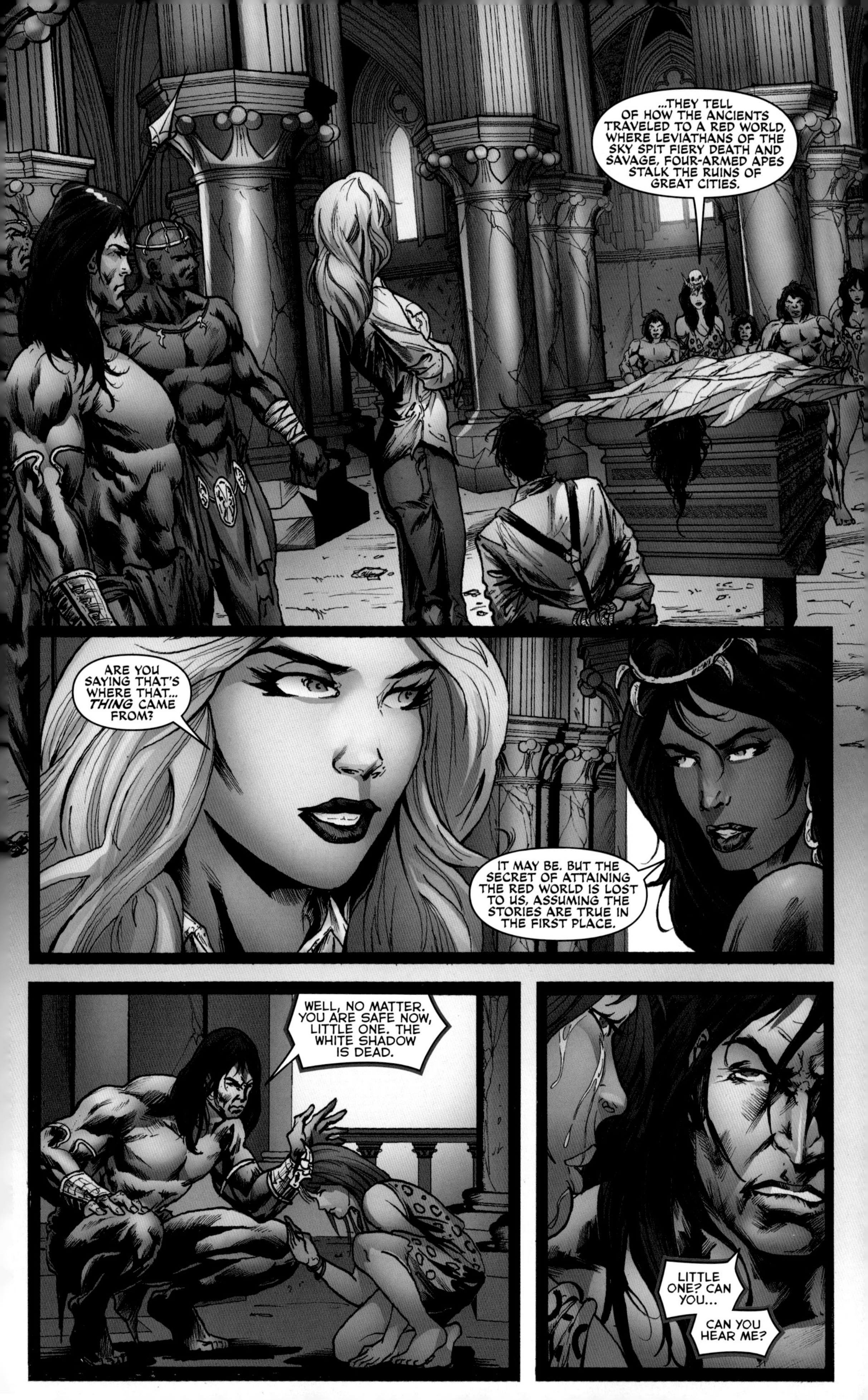
...THEY TELL OF HOW THE ANCIENTS TRAVELED TO A RED WORLD, WHERE LEVIATHANS OF THE SKY SPIT FIERY DEATH AND SAVAGE, FOUR-ARMED APES STALK THE RUINS OF GREAT CITIES.
ARE YOU SAYING THAT'S WHERE THAT... *THING* CAME FROM?
IT MAY BE. BUT THE SECRET OF ATTAINING THE RED WORLD IS LOST TO US, ASSUMING THE STORIES ARE TRUE IN THE FIRST PLACE.
WELL, NO MATTER. YOU ARE SAFE NOW, LITTLE ONE. THE WHITE SHADOW IS DEAD.
LITTLE ONE? CAN YOU...
CAN YOU HEAR ME?

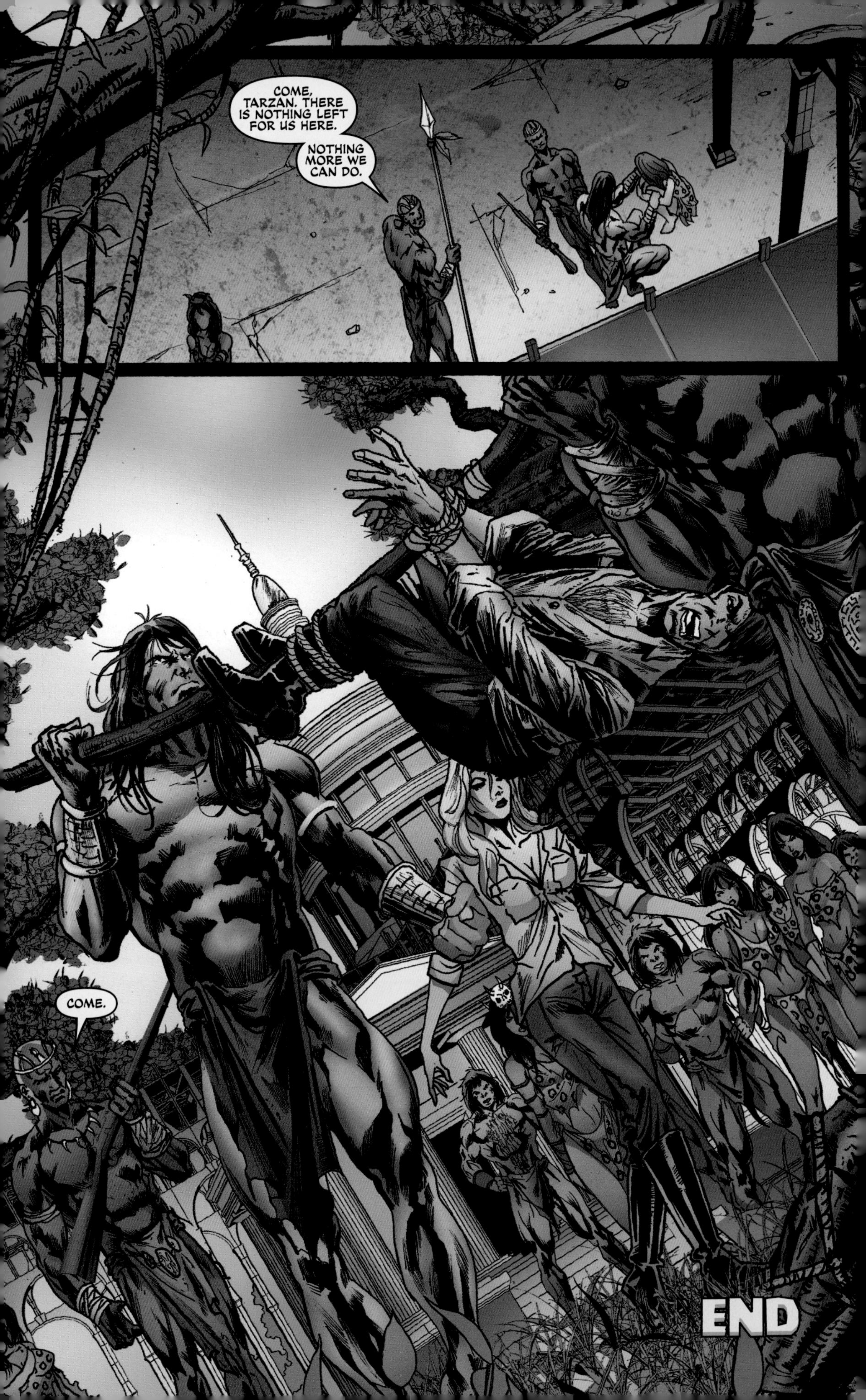
COME, TARZAN. THERE IS NOTHING LEFT FOR US HERE.
NOTHING MORE WE CAN DO.
COME.
END

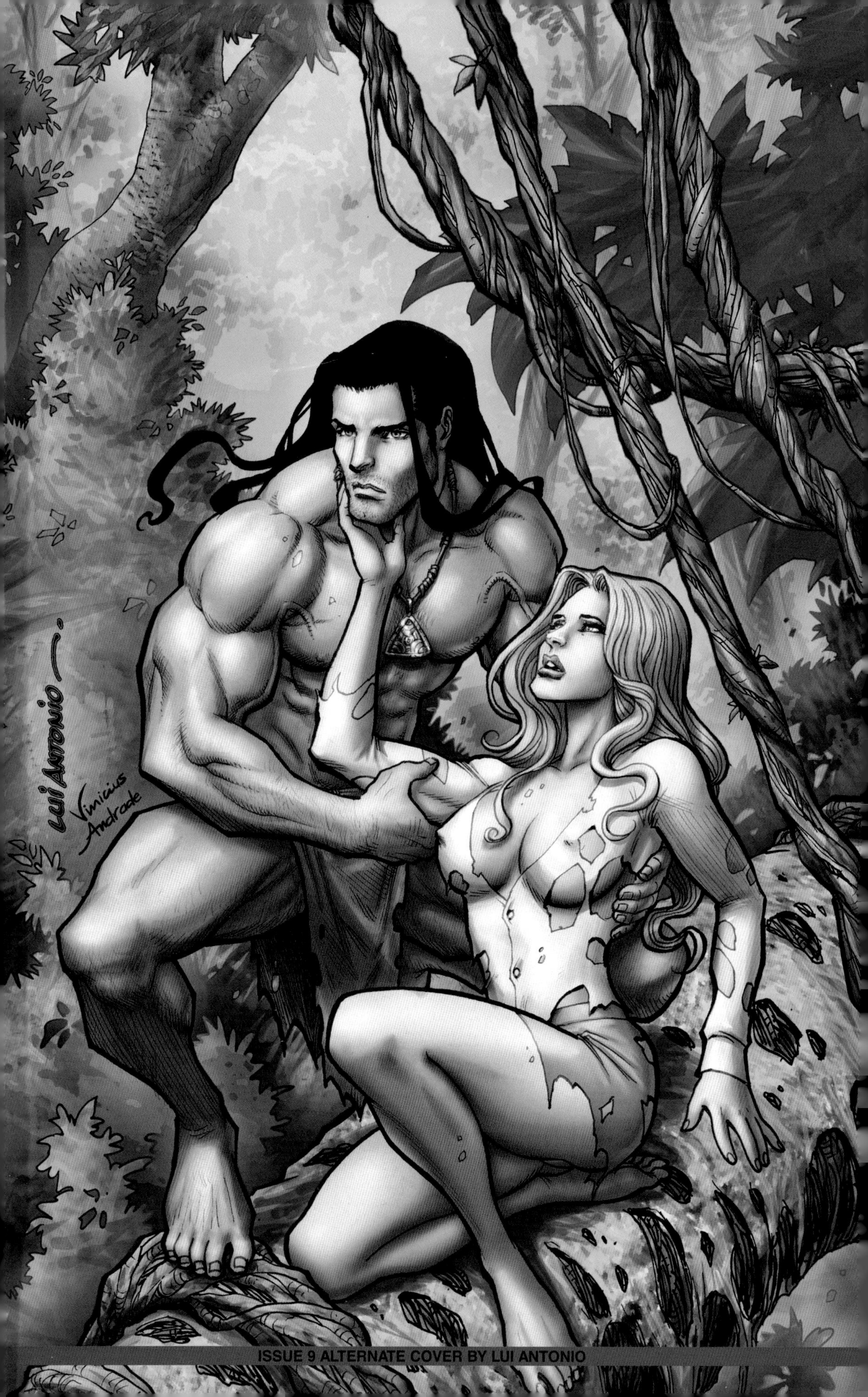
Lui Antonio
Vinicius Andrade
ISSUE 9 ALTERNATE COVER BY LUI ANTONIO

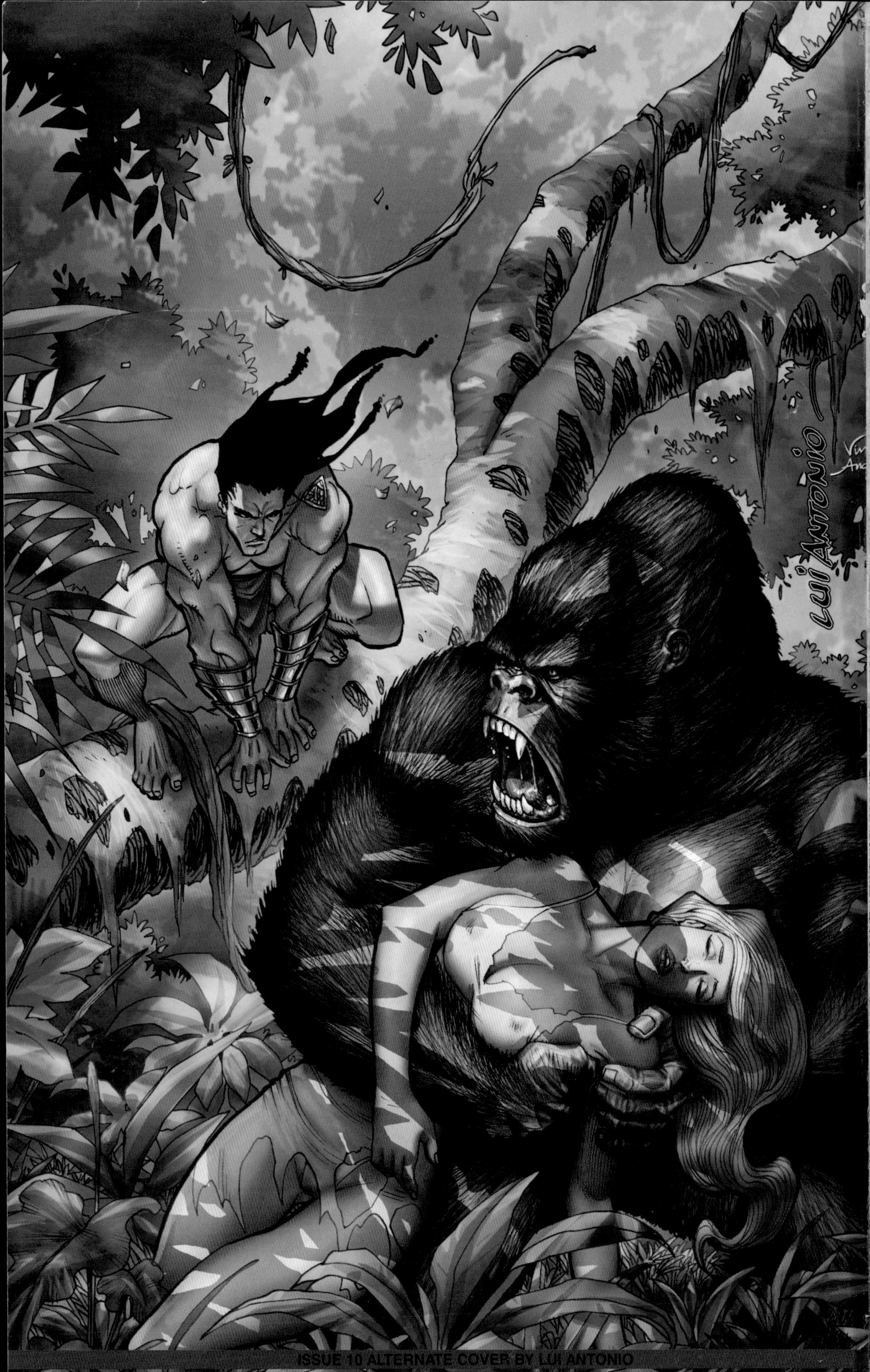
LUI ANTONIO

ISSUE 10 ALTERNATE COVER BY LUI ANTONIO